CHRISTIAN
MATURITY

CHRISTIAN MATURITY

E. Stanley Jones
The world's most-read religious writer

ABINGDON
Nashville

CHRISTIAN MATURITY

Scripture quotations unless otherwise noted are from the Revised Standard Version of the Bible and are copyright 1946 and 1952 by the Division of Christian Education of the National Council of the Churches of Christ in the U.S.A. and are used by permission.

The quotations on pp. 126, 158, 159, 162, 186, are from *The Meaning of Love*, ed. M. F. Ashley Montagu. Used by permission of Julian Press. Quotations on pp. 38, 40, 126, 127, 321, by Viktor Frankl, are from *The Doctor and the Soul*, tr. Richard and Clara Winston. Used by permission of Alfred A. Knopf. Quotations on pp. 16, 65, 127, 128, 129, 136, 137, by Anders Nygren, are from *Agape and Eros*. Copyright, 1953, The Westminster Press. Used by permission of the author and The Westminster Press.

The quotation on p. 140 is used courtesy *Time*; copyright Time, Inc., 1955. The quotations on pp. 159, 181, 233, by Smiley Blanton, are from *Love or Perish*. Used by permission of Simon and Schuster. The quotations on pp. 24, 339, by Karl Menninger, are from *Love Against Hate*. Used by permission of Harcourt, Brace & Co. The quotations on p. 342, by Kenneth Hildebrand, are from *Achieving Real Happiness*. Used by permission of Harper and Bros. The quotations on pp. 224, 309, by Franz Alexander, are from *Emotional Maturity*. Used by permission of the author.

MANUFACTURED BY THE PARTHENON PRESS AT
NASHVILLE, TENNESSEE, UNITED STATES OF AMERICA

INTRODUCTION

As a firsthand observer of individual and collective problems and possibilities in both East and West, over a long period of years, if I were called upon to put my finger on the most pressing need of our age, I would unhesitatingly say one thing—maturity. We are very immature people attempting to handle very mature problems. Our problems are outrunning our capacity to handle them. And more especially so since in the harnessing of nuclear energy, we find ourselves in possession of very mature power—the power of the atom. It has been suddenly dumped into our lap. The hiatus between the maturity of both our problems and our powers and the immaturity of our person is the most serious gap in human existence on our planet. Unless that gap can be filled we will suffer from frustrations which may prove fatal. For we have the awful power to ruin ourselves on a world scale.

A statement of this kind can be a spur or it can be paralyzing. It can produce the attitude often seen in India. When one is confronted with an insoluble problem, he turns over his hands in helplessness and says, *"Ham kya karen?"* ("What can I do?") Meaning, "I can do nothing." This problem of ours is now so vast that it becomes impersonal, and hence seemingly insoluble. But on the other hand, the whole thing can be a spur—it can be personalized in me. I can ask, and ask hopefully: "How can I be a mature person, handling, in my situation, my problems and my possibilities in a mature way?" If that is the attitude then we can proceed—proceed to find for ourselves the most necessary thing this business of human living demands—maturity. The quest is not a marginal one; it is central and fundamental—a *must*. A marriage counselor told me that the center of marriage problems is immaturity in either the husband or the wife, or in both.

But the quest for maturity is not a hopeless quest, for I'm persuaded that we are made in the inner structure of our beings for maturity. Everything within us "lifts up strong hands after prefection." In all life there is an urge for more life, abundant life. So when we long for maturity we are not longing against the grain of our beings, but with it. If we don't become mature we block the thing for which we are made. In that case we become self-sidetracked, self-stultified, and self-stunted. For we are made for maturity.

And moreover, I am convinced that there is an overruling Providence manifesting itself in the discovery of nuclear energy at this period of human history. We were crawling along in compartmentalized grooves—mental, emotional, national, racial, social—when suddenly we were shocked out of those grooves—shocked out by the discovery of the power of atomic energy. We have been shocked into rethinking everything. This Divine Shock-Treatment has broken up old grooves of mind and emotion and has sent the energies of mind and emotion and interest into new channels. And hopeful channels too—we have begun to think, not here and there but on a mass scale, in terms of the underprivileged, the dispossessed portions of humanity. The atomic age has hastened the social revolution, galvanized our dead concerns for the underprivileged and made us alive to human need. This has taken place partly through fear of Russia and partly through our Christian impulses. In any case we are aroused. God uses any instrument at hand to further the rise of man.

So we are caught between two pressures—one from within and one from without. The inner pressure goads us toward maturity, and the outer pressure demands the same maturity—to grow up to handle grown-up problems. This pincer movement of God is pressing us toward grown-upness. We can resist both pressures, but if we do so we will not be able to live with ourselves or others. We will be frustrated rather than fruitful.

Some of the pressure for maturity comes from a world pressure. But what of the demands for maturity which come from our immediate surroundings? And from within? A father goes into a temper tantrum to have his way in a household; a mother goes into the sulks because something hasn't gone her way; a member of a firm nurses self-pity because he hasn't been promoted, and, incidentally, thereby postpones the promotion; a youth retires into himself, introverted, because he lacks the courage to face life and its responsibilities; a member of a household retreats into illness as an escape from assuming duties and responsibilities: "If I were well I could do them, but I'm not well, so I don't have to do them"; many revert to the infantilism of letting the crowd make their decisions for them, absolving themselves of the responsibility; others show a childish egotism that parades and struts and bids for attention, though often in quite civilized and acceptable ways; some domineer over others as one child dominates another; some are aggressive toward others to cover latent inferiorities; many are grown-up in some respects, but have "pockets" of immaturities, and are still held in the grip of infantilism; some argue over marginal issues as children argue over nothingnesses; some build their lives religiously around marginal doctrines and ideas turn out to be immature examples of the Christian faith; some hold emotional attachments to childish things and never grow up; others hold leftover prejudices that cause them to have blind spots; some have childish fears of this, that, and the other; some manifest jealousies and envies that characterize childhood but can be upsetting to situations among physically grown-up people; others have such an immature religious faith that it leaves them immature personalities—caught and cramped in the molds of immature religion; and worst of all, many are caught on a low level of living and have ceased to grow and have ceased to aspire to grow—living in a daily grind instead of a daily growth. And most pathetic of all is the person who finds that life has lost its joy, its sparkle, its zest, its energy—life run down at the heels, life turned into mere existence, and existence into boredom.

If the demand for maturity is upon us and is inexorable, then the bigger question arises: According to what standard shall we be mature? What norm, what pattern? For if we move we must know the direction, lest we move in circles, or ravel a road with a dead end. There are many suggested standards and they differ and differ vitally. And it matters which one you take, for the results register in you—in your very makeup. You become like that at which you habitually gaze and to which you aspire.

Some psychologists suggest that you are mature when you are adjusted to your surroundings. But that may be a low level of adjustment, an adjustment to immaturity. The sixth-grade son of a psychologist was seated dejectedly on the front steps. There was no one to play with, because all his friends were doing their homework. "And why," asked his father, "aren't you doing yours?" The boy replied: "Well, Dad, I never bring any work home, for you see I've adjusted myself to inferior grades." You can adjust yourself to low levels and become permanently immature by the very immaturity of your level.

Some suggest a maturity which reflects standards worked out on a purely human basis without relationship to God, as if God didn't matter. This turns out to be a very immature maturity. It cannot stand up under the demands of human living—demands which stretch into time and eternity. The pattern is too small for beings who have "eternity set in their hearts." The Kinsey report on sex practices in American life depicts, according to its data, the sex standards of contemporary society and comes to the conclusion that that which is, is the normal. The implication is that these conditions should be accepted as such. This means a succumbing to the sordid Is, instead of rising to the sacred Ought-to-be.

The Christian faith steps amidst all this confusion and moral collapse and has something definite and something very important to say. For it specializes in maturity—its central aim is to produce mature character. Its greatest exponent puts it this way: "Him we proclaim, warning every man and teaching every man in all wisdom, that we may present every man mature in Christ. For this I toil, striving with all the energy which he mightily inspires within me" (Col. 1:28-29). And again he puts it even more definitely: "And his gifts were that some should be apostles, some prophets, some evangelists, some pastors and teachers . . . until we all attain . . . to mature manhood, to the measure of the stature of the fullness of Christ" (Eph. 4:11-13). The whole of the Christian resources, coming through apostles, prophets, evangelists, pastors, and teachers, converges on the production of one thing: mature manhood. And a mature manhood according to a very definite pattern: the measure of the stature of the fullness of Christ. Nothing could be clearer: the aim and purpose of the whole impact of the Christian faith is to produce maturity. And nothing is more gloriously breathtaking than the pattern of that maturity: the measure of the stature of the fullness of Christ.

With this clarity of purpose and with this definiteness of pattern, it is a mystery—and a tragedy—that Christian writers on maturity should turn, for the most part, to contemporaneous thought patterns, psychological and social, for their own faith. They seem to pick up a few crumbs that fall from the table of psychology. In this book we shall try not to fall into that tragic mistake. We shall turn to the Christian faith for its concept and pattern of maturity and from that standpoint we shall work down to all our problems of immaturity. This is a book on *Christian* maturity. For we know nothing higher, we can be content with nothing less. We shall use many of the real insights that modern psychology provides, but we shall not begin there. For we have a Viewpoint and a Starting Point—Christ! In His light we will see the meaning and life of maturity.

In order to get the Christian view of maturity we are concentrating on the Epistle of Christian Maturity—I John. This Epistle of I John was probably the last of the Epistles written and it is really the capstone of the Christian revelation. Here Christian maturity really becomes mature. Here we find the cream of the Christian revelation rising to the surface. Westcott says: "In the long series of spiritual records the Epistle of John holds the last place. It is probably the final interpretation of the whole series of the divine revelation; and under this aspect it proclaims and satisfies the highest hope of man."

The kind of maturity given in this Epistle is not verbal maturity, but vital maturity. It had been worked out through life—had become incarnate in a person. Jesus had said: "I have yet many things to say to you, but you cannot bear them now. When the Spirit of truth comes, he will guide you into all the truth . . . for he will take what is mine and declare it to you" (John 16:12-14). The word of love which Jesus spoke had had time, through the sixty years which had elapsed to become worked out as a fact in life—the fact was John. This Epistle is a transcript of his own maturity. He wrote what he was.

And the hopeful thing for all of us is that John didn't start out that way. He and his brother James started out as "sons of thunder"—very tempestuous and immature in their actions and reactions. When John's boat sailed into the serene harbor of this Epistle, it had sailed through storm-tossed seas—within and without—and his was a seasoned maturity.

And if the person who wrote this Epistle on maturity was important, the place at which he wrote it was also important. Ephesus was the meeting place of Greek philosophy, Hebrew morality, and Oriental mysticism. The setting was a universal setting. The Christian faith had outgrown many of its early problems. Neither the Law, nor circumcision, nor works is mentioned in the Epistle. All these had been worked through, and now the Christian faith was facing mature problems—facing world philosophies and world conditions. The setting was mature.

So the time, the person, and the setting were ready for the ripest unfolding of the meaning of maturity which our planet has seen or will ever see. This is It.

The Epistle is streamlined. There is no mention of places or persons, and yet it is not impersonal—it throbs with personal application. "The coloring is not local but moral and it offers a picture of Christian Society without parellel in the New Testament." Just as John, without mentioning the word "Gnosticism," writes with this system in view, so he, without mentioning the word "maturity," unfolds the meaning of Christian maturity in its most perfect form.

But while John writes out of a mature personal experience of God and life, so that there is a ring of firsthandedness about it, we are not making John the pattern for our maturity. He illustrates in his own person this maturity and shows that it works; but while John is good, he is not good enough. We turn to the center of our faith—Jesus—as the pattern and goal of our maturity. I once inquired of Adolf Harnack, the great German theologian and church historian, the Christian solution to a certain problem, and he answered: "Christianity does not provide solutions—it provides a goal and power to move on to that goal." A Goal and power to move on to that Goal! The Goal, the Pattern, is Jesus, and the power we get to move on to that Goal comes from the same Source.

If Jesus is the Goal and if He gives power to move on to that Goal, then we can look forward to the possibility of real maturity—and maturity *now*. For maturity is not an aging process—you may age into infantilism! Maturity is getting hold of a mature faith, responding to it in a mature way, disciplining yourself to its requirements and becoming mature, gradually or suddenly, by that response and that discipline. I say "gradually" or "suddenly," for I've seen people become mature persons overnight, washed from a thousand immaturities and with their feet firmly planted upon the road of a developing maturity. For instance, this letter came a few days ago:

I was breathing and walking around but not alive. The soul, the morale, the everything that spelled L-I-F-E was at a very low ebb. This week I am alive. I feel like my real self. I am taking an interest, a real interest in my personal appearance and my general well-being. Before this week, it was a matter of routine with a hidden desire to appear better, but I only seemed to think of doing the necessities. Now I am even meticulous about everything being just right. Before, I only thought about it; now I think about it and do something about it. To express it better; my soul is beginning to live within me and it is expressed outwardly. My true spiritual being has come into real existence. I am alive.

That is essential maturity in the process of becoming more mature. But this woman's basic attitudes are mature. She has opened her life to the Maturity that is in Jesus, and mature *life* has come into being.

If I write of maturity from an experience stretching across half a century, learned among all nations of the world, I know that maturity does not come by accumulated experiences. It comes through basis responses to grace. I am as mature as my basic responses to grace. And no more mature. And I've seen people respond to grace wholeheartedly and with abandon and become mature almost overnight, with mature attitudes, mature judgments, and mature reactions to life. If the above letter was written by one who signed herself "a Colored Woman," another comes from a leading manufacturer of the same Southland who had been a very immature Christian all his life, "giving," as he said, "my money to God but not myself." He made that inner surrender to God, and when he taught his Sunday-school class the next Sunday a young woman said at the close: "Mr B., you didn't get that out of a book." The immaturity of a secondhand faith had dropped away. He was no longer speaking in quotation marks. He spoke mature thoughts out of the heart of reality and showed mature attitudes. He was a mature person—overnight.

So maturity is not a matter of age but of attitudes. And these changed attitudes can be sudden and lasting. But they may also be gradual. In this book we will provide for both the sudden and the gradual. But in either case you become mature to the degree that you relate yourself to God, respond to His grace, and work it out in life. Receptivity to grace is the secret of maturity.

The key thought of this book will be found in two passages. "Now in putting everything in subjection to man, he left nothing outside his control. As it is, we do not yet see everything in subjection to him. But we see Jesus" (Heb. 2:8-9). Note: "not yet . . . everything . . . in subjection to him," but "we see Jesus." Here is the pledge and the power that everything will be in subjection to the one who, instead of looking at his failures, his sins, his immaturities, looks at Jesus—the answer to our sins and immaturities and the pledge of our maturity.

The other passage is this: "You have come to fulness of life in him" (Col. 2:10). These two passages are the basis of Christian maturity: here we see man, given the possibility of subjecting everything under his control, but not yet arriving at his full destiny, but we see Jesus as the pledge of that arriving, and that man will "come to fulness of life in him."

People can usually squeeze out of my books the substance of them in about two years, hence the two-year spacing of my books. One year is spent in immersing myself in the subject and another year in writing. But if my books can be exhausted in about two years, I have the consolation that I am introducing my readers to the Inexhaustible! If you ask my definition of maturity, I give you not a verbal but a vital definition: Jesus! He is Incarnate Maturity. The Word of Maturity become flesh. Being immersed in I John for a year has taught me more about Jesus than has anything else. For it has emphasized anew the central thing in Jesus—love. This will be a study and adventure in love. For we are mature as we are mature in love.

As with the rest of my devotional books, this book can be read a page a day for daily devotional reading. But since it has been brought together in weekly units, it can be used as a study book for groups and classes. And then, since the subject of maturity is treated as a whole, it can be read straight through as an ordinary book.

As I sit in the upper room of the Ashram in my beloved Sat Tal, in the Himalaya Mountains, where so many of my books have been written, wholly or in part, I wonder at my temerity in putting out another, the twentieth. How dare I continue to do it? But the Father said to me when I passed seventy: "I'm giving you the best ten years of your life—the next ten ahead." Two of them have passed and they have literally been the best two years of my life. Eight to go! But I've given advance notice that when I get to the end of this first ten years, I'm going to ask for an extension of another ten! The going I find to be good—very good indeed. Life is fun and getting funnier all the time! Practically all my question marks have now been straightened out into dancing exclamation points. And since this book has been included in "the best ten years" period, it may partake of some of that best-ness. At any rate the payoff is in the person—I've learned more about maturity in this last year than I have learned in a lifetime, for I have found out that to be mature is to be mature in love. This book, then, is an adventure in maturity in love.

E. STANLEY JONES

CONTENTS

CONTENTS

WE DEFINE MATURITY

We would define a mature person as one who is able to function happily, usefully, and at his maximum capacity in a given situation. This definition needs correction at the place of "his maximum capacity," for it is possible to lay hold of capacities not your own, and to make them your own, through grace. But we will let the definition stand for the time being.

If this definition of maturity is somewhere near being accurate, then it is obvious that many of us are not mature; for we do not function happily, usefully, and at our maximum powers in our situation. Why? The temptation will be strong, and very ancient—the most ancient of temptations—to lay the blame on someone else: "The woman whom thou gavest to be with me, she gave me fruit of the tree, and I ate." Adam blamed God for giving him the woman and he blamed the woman for giving him the fruit; God and the woman, and not Adam, were to blame. Such an attitude showed immaturity. To blame others and our surroundings shows our immaturity.

The first step in gaining maturity is to accept the responsibility for being what we are. I do not deny that our surroundings of people and place can and do influence us. But only that part of our environment to which we respond influences us. We do the responding. The choice is always ours. If you are a half-person with a half-life output, then it is because by a series of choices you have consented to be that half-person. But no one need be a half-person.

For both God and life will maturity. Life wills maturity. Within everything, from the lowest cell to the highest man, is an urge after completion, after fuller, more abundant life—everything reaches up after maturity. If therefore, we are not mature it is obvious that we are blocking the life urge within us. Somehow, some way we are choking those urges. And God, too, wills maturity. All His resources are behind those who will to be mature persons.

O God, my Father, I cannot bear being what I am—half-made, half-baked, a half-person. So today I put my feet upon the way that leads me out of immaturities into Thy wholeness, into Thy abundance. Amen.

AFFIRMATION FOR THE DAY: *My First step in maturity— I accept responsibility for what I am.*

1

GOD AND LIFE WILL OUR MATURITY

We stopped yesterday with the statement that both God and life will maturity. But they do more than passively will our maturity; they conspire in every possible way, short of breaking down our wills, to make us mature. Life makes us discontented and unhappy in our immaturities. Suppose we could settle down happy and contented in being a half-person, then that would be a tragic situation. But we cannot. That divine discontent is a part of our salvation. It is a goad that impels us into higher, fuller life. Life won't let us settle down—to nothingness.

And what kind of Father would God be if He did not disturb us toward maturity? No earthly parent could be content to have a child who refused to grow up. The parents' joy is in development, in growth, in going on toward maturity. God cannot be otherwise and still be God, our Father. So the disturbances we feel in our immaturities are not signs of His anger, but a manifestation of His love. He loves us too much to let us settle down in halfwayness.

But if God should stop at the point of making us discontent, then He would stop this side of being God, our Father. To be our Father, He must provide literally everything for our maturity. And He has! He has put at our disposal all the resources for our being what we ought to be—everything except coercion. There He draws the line, for if He coerced us into maturity—took us by the back of the neck and shook us into maturity then of course we couldn't be mature. The will to be mature must be at the center of our maturity.

If God and life and we ourselves will maturity, then there is nothing in heaven or earth that can stop us from being the mature persons we ought to be. We are destined to be mature, and that destiny is written in every cell of our bodies. We can slow down or block that destiny. The choice is always ours.

Father, hope begins to spring up within my breast, for if I am destined to be mature then I can and do accept that destiny and make it my own. Show me the restrictions in me and the resources in Thee. I put my feet on the Way. Amen.

AFFIRMATION FOR THE DAY: *Since I am destined to be mature, I accept that destiny as my own.*

A MATURE FAITH—FIRST NECESSITY

We have insisted that God must do more than vaguely will our maturity: He must provide the resources. Has He done so? I believe He has, perfectly and adequately and finally in Jesus.

If we are to be mature we must get hold of a mature faith—or better, it must get hold of us. For the immaturities of our faith will soon show themselves in immaturities in our actions and our attitudes. "The creed of today becomes the deed of tomorrow." Nothing can be more immature than the oft-repeated statement: "It doesn't matter what you believe just so you live right." For *belief* is literally *by-lief, by-life*—the thing you live by. And if your belief is wrong your life will be wrong.

Don't misunderstand me. I don't mean to say that if you have a correct belief you'll necessarily have a correct life. That doesn't follow. The creed, to be a creed, must be a vital rather than a verbal one. For the only thing we really believe in is the thing we believe in enough to act upon. Your deed is your creed. But it does matter what you hold as the basic assumptions of your life. If you have no Starting Point, you'll have no ending point.

Where do we start? From what Viewpoint do we view all life? We have taken the Epistle which was written last, the Epistle of I John as the basis of our quest for maturity. Was it mere chance, or was it providence, that made this Epistle the last one in the Canon of Scripture? The answer is that providence could not have been more providential than in putting this Epistle as the capstone of revelation. For it belongs there inherently. In substance it sums up the Christian revelation. The Gospel of John gives the facts; the Epistle of John give the fruits of those facts. Here in the Epistle of John is graphically depicted the most mature living ever seen upon our planet. This is the text—all else is commentary. Beyond the maturity in I John the human race will never progress. This is the norm.

O God, my Father, I am all eager to begin, for I feel that I am about to be introduced to Reality itself. Help me to be real as I do so. For I cannot be unreal facing the Real. Cleanse me from all unreality. In Jesus' name. Amen.

AFFIRMATION FOR THE DAY: *Since a mature faith is the first necessity, I am an open candidate for a mature faith.*

OUR FAITH CENTERED IN A PERSON

We said yesterday that the Epistle of I John depicts the greatest maturity seen upon our earth. Not that we would discount Paul. He has had a greater influence upon the world than has John and he was perhaps a greater man. But Paul laid foundations; John puts on a capstone. And God can use a lesser to complete the greater. He did so here. Paul's chief insistence is faith—and rightly so; John's chief insistence is love—and more rightly so. For "the greatest of these is love." Here maturity is maturity in love.

But John didn't begin with the word "maturity," or with "love"—he began with a Person: "That which was from the beginning . . . that which we have seen and heard we proclaim also to you" (1:1-3)—that Person Jesus. It was not mere chance that made John begin there. For he was facing an invasion into Christianity by a movement that attempted to take over Christianity, using its names and forms but rejecting its substance—the movement of Gnosticism. The name "Gnosticism" is not mentioned in the Epistle, but its presence is all-pervading, and John presents the Christian faith against that background.

Gnosticism, coming from the Greek *gnosis* ("to know") was an attempt at maturity by knowing God directly, bypassing Jesus, the Incarnate. You didn't need to go through Jesus to God; if you had the key, the gnosis, you could know immediately. Gnosticism supplied mysterious formulas and passwords which gave the soul access to the higher world and brought about perfect union with the Divine. But it rejected the material. "Gnosticism, on the other hand, cannot find words strong enough to express its abhorrence of the world we live in. It is not beautiful, but full of misery, filth and uncleanness." Spirit is good; matter is evil. "Man's spirit is a divine being imprisoned, contrary to its nature, in the body, a divine seed sown in hostile matter." The idea of the Incarnation, of the Word becoming flesh, was abhorrent to it. So Jesus was taken over, not as God becoming man, but as a revealer of the secrets of Gnosticism—another Jesus.

O God, our Father, guide us as we decide about the place upon which to fasten our loyalty and our love. For if we make the wrong choice here, all life will go wrong with it, and our maturity will turn into futility. Amen.

AFFIRMATION FOR THE DAY: *The real Jesus, and only the real Jesus, is the center of my quest.*

GOD-SALVATION OR SELF-SALVATION?

We are coming to grips with the most important question we can face: Does salvation, and hence maturity, come up from man through his striving, illuminated by the Divine; or does salvation, and hence maturity, come from above—from God—through the act of God and our receptivity of that act? Is it an attainment or an obtainment?

That question divides all religions into just two types—salvation as the work of man and salvation as the gift of God—self-salvation or God-salvation. There are no other types: all fall into one category or the other. They did so in ancient times, they do so in modern. The question which John faced in Gnosticism is alive today in many guises and many forms, but the same issue: Does man strive up through the Divine beckoning, or, Does God come down to redeem us through the Incarnate Jesus? Do we go to Him, or does God come to us?

The sharpness of this alternative cannot be blunted by saying, "It is both." By the nature of things it cannot be both, for the starting point is different—one begins with man and the other begins with God. Since the directions are different, the ending points will be different and the type of maturity produced will be different.

Since maturity cannot be found unless we have a faith that is mature, it is all-important to fasten our loyalty and our love upon the maturest faith that can be found. Where is that faith? John has no hesitancy in pointing straight to the heart of the matter: the center of that faith is a Person and that Person—Jesus: "That which was from the beginning, which we have heard, which we have seen with our eyes, which we have looked upon and touched with our hands, concerning the word of life—the life was made manifest" (1:1-2). Here, over against man's speculations about God, John pointed to God's authentic self-revelation: Jesus—the Word become flesh. Gnosticism was the word become idea.

O, Jesus, Thou art our alpha and our omega—the beginning and the end of all our maturities. We want to be mature according to thy pattern, for all else is immaturity. We know where we want to head in. Amen.

AFFIRMATION FOR THE DAY: *As Jesus is the center of my faith, He shall be the center of my loyalty and love.*

RELIGIONS—MAN'S SEARCH FOR GOD

"In Jesus the Word became flesh; in Gnosticism the word became idea." We must broaden and even universalize that statement by saying: In Jesus the Word became flesh; in all other systems of religion and philosophy the word became word. Jesus is Good News; all else is good views. All religions are man's attempt to climb to God; Jesus is God's descent to man. All religions are man's search for God; Jesus is God's search for man. Therefore there are many religions, but there is but one gospel. So Jesus did not bring a religion to set alongside of other religions—one a little better, more moral, more spiritual. He came to set the gospel over against human need, whether that need be in this religion, that religion, or in no religion. As the Son of man He confronts the sons of men with God's offer to man. He Himself is that offer. The gospel lies in His person—He is the Good News. He didn't *proclaim* the gospel so much as He *was* the gospel.

So over against the vagaries of Gnostic speculation, John set the vitalities of gospel sureties. And he planted those sureties right down amid the material—the Word become flesh—right down where we live. With all their vaunted knowledge, the Gnostics were immature in thinking that life could be compartmentalized—the life of the spirit good, the life of the flesh evil—and that life could be worked out on that basis. The question of good and evil is not a question of spirit and matter; it is a question of will. "There is nothing bad but a bad will." The seat of evil is in the will, not in matter. The attempt to place evil in matter was an immature attempt to blame evil on something other than personal responsibility—an immature evasion.

So the Christian faith meets us where we are—in the flesh—and offers us redemption *in* the flesh, not *from* the flesh—a workable offer. We are to be mature in the midst of material relations, not apart from them: that is maturity.

O Jesus, my Lord, I am grateful that Thou art not offering me immature fancies, but mature fact. I lean heavily upon Thy realism. For I cannot rest this side of the Real. I have the feeling that Thou art Reality itself. I thank Thee. Amen.

AFFIRMATION FOR THE DAY: *My attachment shall be a personal attachment to the personal Jesus with all my person.*

JESUS IS GOD INCARNATE

In order to be sure that we see that the Word really became flesh, John piles statement upon statement to make clear his meaning. Each statement gives an added intimacy: "which we have heard"—but hearing may be at such a distance that it can be almost hearsay; "which we have seen with our eyes"—that brings the speaker in range of the eye—nearer; "which we have looked upon"—not a fleeting glance, but a steady gaze; "and touched with our hands"—referring to Jesus' statement after His resurrection when He invites the disciples to touch Him, to handle Him, to thrust their hands in His side! In four statements involving three of the senses—hearing, seeing, touching—he nails down the fact that the Word actually did become flesh. For John saw its vast importance. So important was it that later he makes this question of Jesus' coming in the flesh the test of whether the Spirit of God is present: "By this you know the Spirit of God: every spirit which confesses that Jesus Christ has come in the flesh is of God, and every spirit which does not confess Jesus is not of God" (4:2-3). Everything hinged on Jesus as Incarnate, not Jesus as inspiration, not Jesus as moral teacher, not Jesus as philosopher. But Jesus as Incarnate God—that was the issue! And well might it be the issue, for if Jesus is Incarnate God, then everything pales into insignificance beside the importance of the fact. As a Hindu chairman said at the close of my address: "If what the speaker has said tonight isn't true, it doesn't matter, but if it is true then nothing else matters." He was right. If the Eternal God confronts us in Jesus, then that is the banner headline in the cosmic scroll. Every creature with a grain of intelligence would gasp in wonder.

So John, with an abrupt relevance, comes right to the heart of the whole matter: "The life was made manifest." God has spoken, not in words but in the Word. And in that speaking He reveals His heart. Jesus is the heart of God wrapped in flesh—and made manifest.

O Father, Thy unveiling in Jesus makes me see what lies back in eternity. And what I see makes me inwardly grateful to my fingertips. For I see that Thou art good and only good, purity and only purity, love and only love. Amen.

AFFIRMATION FOR THE DAY: *If Jesus is the life of God made manifest,*
I shall be the life of Jesus made manifest.

THE ETERNAL GOD BECOMES LIKE US

The center of the Christian faith is the Incarnation—God becoming flesh in man. Beside this central fact of the Divine Invasion of us, all else is comparatively irrelevant. Miracles? This is the central miracle—the Eternal God become like us that we may become like Him. Teaching? What greater teaching could there be than this teaching of God in act? For in it we see as in a flash the meaning of humility, of service, of self-giving goodness, of love, of everything. Morality? This is morality, not thundering the law, but washing our feet. Spirituality? This is spirituality, not aloof and lifted up on some Olympus, but walking in sandals. Doctrine? This is a doctrine that is a Deed. Ritual? Here ritual is not in form but in fact, the free flowing of love in adoration. Sermons? Here we do not merely hear one—we see one—every act, every word, every attitude a living sermon. Philosophy? Philosophy talks about *Life*. Science? His statement "You will know the truth, and the truth will make you free" is the essence of science. But deeper: He revealed the science of living. Religion? He never mentioned the word, but if you were to ask my definition of religion I would point to Him: He is religion. Law? Here law becomes love. Love? The highest definition of love. The love of the cross. Sacrifice? Not the sacrifice of giving animals, or fruits, or deeds to God to appease Him, but the very God Himself giving Himself in sacrifice for us on a cross. The triumph of the good? He didn't declare it; He demonstrated it—demonstrated it in the resurrection. Salvation? He didn't preach about it; He gave it to any open heart, however sinful, that would receive it. The meaning of God? He is the meaning of God. Knowledge? To know Him!

This Epistle, in its opening sentences, reveals the nature of God, of life, of redemption, of love, of everything. All else is unfolding commentary; this is unfolded fact. And what a fact!

O Jesus, Thou dost come to us out of the eternities as if Thou wert coming out of our lowly doors. And the touch of both are upon Thee—so high and so lowly, so terrible and so tender, so like God yet so like us. We are at Thy feet. Amen.

AFFIRMATION FOR THE DAY: *As Jesus is the opening of the meaning of God to me, I shall be the opening of the meaning of Jesus to others.*

JESUS IS THE WORD

In view of the tremendous meanings he saw in the face of Jesus Christ, John burst out in repetitions that sound at first like the repetitions of senility, but are soon seen as the repetitions born of a passionate desire to tell what he knew was untellable. Another interpreter, Paul, cried out that Jesus as "the inexpressible gift." He couldn't catch the Word in the web of his words, so he repeated many words in saying the Word.

Lao-tse, the Chinese philosopher, had said: "The word that can be uttered is not the Divine Word." He was right, if the Divine Word was to be uttered only. But in Jesus the Divine Word was not merely uttered, it was shown: Jesus is the Word—the Word of Eternity translated into the language of time.

In John's Gospel, Jesus is called the Word: "In the beginning was the Word, and the Word was with God, and the Word was God." Why is Jesus called "the Word"? Well, the word is the expression of the hidden thought. Without my words you cannot get my thoughts. The words are the thought become available; the words are the offspring of the thought, the son of the thought. To let us get the Thought, God puts Himself into a Word. Jesus is the Word. I look up through Jesus, the Word, and now I know what God, the Thought, is like. The Thought and the Word are one. "I and the Father are one." But the thought is greater than the word. For to express the thought you have to limit it in putting it into words. All expression is limitation. So the unexpressed God—the Father—is greater than the expressed God—the Son. "The Father is greater than I." So Jesus and the Father are one and yet the Father is greater than Jesus. But Jesus is not a third person standing between us and God—when you take hold of Him you take hold of the very Self of God. When you take hold of my words you take hold of my thought—the words mediate the thought. So Jesus is a mediator only in the sense that He mediates God to us. To know Jesus is to know God.

O Father, Thou hast shown us Thyself where we are—in flesh and blood. We thank Thee Father, for coming in at our lowly doors. We could not come to Thee—our sins forbade it; but Thou didst come to us—Thy love impelled Thee. Amen.

AFFIRMATION FOR THE DAY: *Today my creed and my deed and my thought and my word shall be one.*

THE WORD BECOME FLESH

We have seen that God could reveal Himself only partially through a Law, through nature, through a Book, through prophet and teacher; He could perfectly reveal Himself only through a Person—that Person Jesus. The Bible is not the revelation of God; it is the inspired record of the revelation, the revelation we see in the face of Jesus Christ. These words of the Bible take me by the hand and lead me beyond the words, to the Word—"the Word made flesh."

The whole of this Epistle revolves around the Person and work of Jesus, anticipating the controversy that would arise around the Person of Jesus. A controversy which is still going on. A letter received a few days ago protested against my "attempt to unite all the Christians around the alleged deity of Jesus Christ." The writer suggested that groups here and there can unite, but why try to unite all around one Person! Of course, if that person is just a person, why should we try to unite around one person? But suppose that person turns out to be the Person, the Absolute Person, the meeting place of the human and the Divine, then it is inevitable that we get together around Him, or perish. This is the Eternal God confronting us, and something does happen to us when we take Him or leave Him alone—something vital. Every man bears within himself the results of taking Him or leaving Him alone—and bears those results now.

The controversy raged then: The Ebionites said Jesus was a mere man; the Docetists said that Jesus was a phantom—He was a God who just seemed to be a man; the Cerinthianists, a third group, endeavored to combine these two opinions and supposed that the divine element, Christ, was united with the man Jesus at His baptism, but left Him before the cross. All three of these are alike in this: they were all attempts to obviate the difficulty of God dying on a cross. "God on a cross" scandalized that ancient world of philosophy wherein matter was evil, and God the ineffably aloof. All these attempts perished, embalmed in history as names; the Christian affirmation of "God on a cross" lives on. And how!

O God, our Father, the unfolding of Thy meaning and purpose through Jesus leaves me awed and atingle. "How can it be that I should gain an interest in the Savior's blood?" And yet 'tis so, 'tis so. And all my heart is aglow with gratitude. Amen.

AFFIRMATION FOR THE DAY: *Since Jesus is the Word become flesh, I shall be that same word become flesh again.*

A SO-CALLED INCARNATION SWEARS

We have said that the attempts to explain Jesus by explaining Him away, perished, or lived on as eddies in the great current of conviction about Jesus. The one conviction that has lived on, and with power, is the conviction that Jesus is God's authentic Self-disclosure. Wherever there has been a dimmed emphasis on Jesus, there has been decay; wherever there has been a rediscovery of and a renewed emphasis upon Jesus, there has been a revival. Fifty years ago when I came to India, the Brahmo Samaj, an electric movement of intellectuals who put Jesus as one among the many, was a movement very much alive. Today it is dying—a cut-flower movement, no roots.

Theosophy, which tried under Mrs. Besant to displace the historic Jesus with a modern reincarnation of Jesus, Krishnamurti, is on its way out. I talked with Krishnamurti and asked him if this business of his being a reincarnation of Jesus Christ is still being held to, and he replied: "Oh, I say, let that go and let's get on with the work." I said: "That's good. But do you put your foot on it and stop it?" He replied: "That would be very difficult. It would pain some of my best friends. Besides I don't know what I may become five years from now, my next birth. Suppose I should repudiate it and then become it?" I answered: "As I talk with you I find you a nice, lovable young man, but just about what the rest of us are. I want you to be like Jesus, but to be another Christ is a very tall order. Many have tried it and failed." And he replied: "Oh, d—— it all." A reincarnation swearing! And that is exactly what has happened. It has been damned by its own preposterousness—self-cursed.

The movements that have tried to dim Jesus, trying to explain Him away, and the movements which have tried to produce another Jesus, have both alike perished. One view holds the field with increasing power and deepening conviction: Jesus is God's final but unfolding Word about Himself—the same yesterday, today, and forever.

O living Jesus, the ages have not dimmed Thee, nor exhausted Thee. Thou hast survived the ages and hast helped the ages to survive. I thank Thee that in Thee I, too, am inexhaustible and become a power to help others to survive. Amen.

AFFIRMATION FOR THE DAY: *If I am identified with Jesus I am inexhaustible. I am identified.*

JESUS IN A COSMIC SETTING

John placed Jesus in a cosmic setting: "That which was from the beginning." Jesus has a cosmic setting and therefore a cosmic significance. It is obvious that he who has a beginning this side of the beginning will have an end this side of the end—he is bounded by time. But Jesus, the Timeless, holds all time in His hand—and all eternity. And that is the secret of the incarnation: "Jesus knowing that the Father had given all things into his hands, and that he had come from God and was going to God . . . began to wash the disciples' feet" (John 13:3-5). The consciousness of greatness was the secret of humility—all things had been given into His hands, so He used those hands to wash the disciples' feet. Knowing He was God, He could become man. Had He been man trying to become God. He would have considered being God something to be grasped at. But He "though . . . in the form of God, did not count equality with God a thing to be grasped, but emptied himself, taking the form of a servant, being born in the likeness of men" (Phil. 2:6-7).

Since He had a cosmic setting He could choose the setting of a stable. Since He held all power in heaven and on earth, He could become powerless in the hands of men and let them crucify Him. Since He had a name which was above every name. He could take the name of a criminal. He who had everything could choose to have nothing. He who was deathless could choose a tomb.

All of this, *provided* He is love. No other motive would or could make Him do what He did except one—love. Neither self-interest, nor wisdom, nor knowledge, nor pity, nor anything else could make Him become Incarnate—except love. "I wouldn't do that for a million," said a wealthy visitor as he watched a missionary nurse wash the sores of a leper. "Neither would I," replied the nurse. But she would do it for *love*.

The Incarnation is the incredible—except on one basis—love. If love is at the heart of God, then you can expect Him to do anything, anything that love would do. And love did this: He who was the Cosmic became the Carpenter.

O Jesus, Thou didst stoop to conquer. And Thou hast conquered me—conquered me to my depths. If Thou dost hold the world in Thy hands, Thou dost hold me too—Thy glad, willing, and eternal slave. I thank Thee. Amen.

AFFIRMATION FOR THE DAY: *Love will do anything for the loved one. I am identified with love, so I'm ready to do anything.*

NO "BUILD UP" IN JESUS

John found the Incarnation so humanly incredible that he had to insist that he wasn't spinning this out of a fevered imagination but recounting sober fact: "which we have heard, which we have seen with our eyes, which we have looked upon and touched with our hands . . . and we saw it . . . that which we have seen and heard." With seven nails of fact he nailed his thesis on the door of the temple of the world. No, not a "thesis," but a This; not an idea, but an Incarnation. Eternal God becomes mortal man! Nothing like that had ever happened and nothing like that could happen again. It was "once and for all" by its very nature. All talk of a reincarnation of Christ is piffle—and blasphemy.

A few days ago I sat in an Ashram where a group of people were consciously or unconsciously trying to groom their swami to be another incarnation of Christ. A portion of the Ashram was a photographic section, and the walls were filled with framed photographs and the floors overlaid with drying pictures of the swami which were to be sent into all parts of the world to the devotees. But it was a "build up"—the halo around his head was the result of an artists' skill, and the withering lips were touched with lipstick—a man being made into a God. Face-to-face he was a man like myself and nothing more. All the hopes built up around him were doomed hopes, doomed by death to death.

I do not have to "build up" Jesus by skill of art and words. His greatness is not painted on: "Raise the stone and thou shalt find me, cleave the wood and I am there." He is not built up; He is built into the nature of things, the manifestation of Reality. John puts it: "Concerning the world of life—the life was made manifest." All else was "life"—this was "*the* life." When you look at Him you know that everything you have seen so far has been existence, or life; this is "*the* life"—life itself. You are spoiled for lesser visions—this is It!

O Master of my heart, I look into thy face and I know I am looking into the face of the Eternal God—The Eternal God become approachable, understandable, lovable. And my heart grows quiet and still and deeply satisfied. Amen.

AFFIRMATION FOR THE DAY: *I have looked into His face at this hour; now I'm ready to look at the face of the world.*

13

SEVEN TO FOUR

After John has said seven times that they had heard, seen, looked upon, and handled Jesus the word of life, he goes on and says four times that they "testify," "proclaim" (vv 2, 3, 5). The seven times express what they had seen, heard, handled; the four times express what they could say about what they had seen. Is it about seven to four? Yes, that's about it. The revelation of the Word is bigger than the revelation of our words. Our words burst at the seams in trying to hold their weight of new, expansive meaning. Glover says that "the Holy Ghost disorganized Paul's grammar." No wonder! For Paul had seen Something that can't be put into words. He tried and said it was "the unutterable glory." When a lady told Henry Ward Beecher that she had found three errors in his grammar while he was preaching, he replied: "May God have mercy on grammar if it gets in my way while I am preaching." Words tumble over one another in trying to get to His feet and lay their tribute of gratitude.

But with some preaching it is seven times as much preaching to four times the seeing. Hence it is words, instead of the Word. And words grow stale, but the Word is eternally fresh.

And note the order: we "testify" and "proclaim"—the testimony was first. The proclaiming was the unfolding of the meaning of the testimony. The preaching that is not primarily testimony is not Christian preaching. Of the Disciples it was said: "When they had testified and preached . . . " (Acts 8:25 KJV)—same order. That which is to reach the heart must come from the heart, must be testimony. Said a young man standing before the altar, after making his surrender to Jesus: "I've got to set up a tent or something and tell this that I've found!" He was in the authentic tradition, the true apostolic succession. We have seen and must testify, for if we don't the stones will cry out! When we see Jesus the Word, the words flow.

O God, when we look in the face of Thy Son, the Word, then our words burst at the seams in trying to tell what we have seen. We often end in mute adoration. For we see in that face the meaning of everything in heaven and on earth. Amen.

AFFIRMATION FOR THE DAY: *I shall listen to Him and receive, and then give to others in a seven-to-four proportion.*

GETTING OUR STARTING POINT STRAIGHT

We have spent the first two weeks in getting straight our starting point in the quest for maturity. For if this starting point is wrong, the ending point will be wrong. The Starting Point of the Christian faith is Jesus. As I said in another book:

You cannot say God till you have first said Jesus, for Jesus puts character-content into God; you cannot say Christ until you have first said Jesus, for Jesus puts character-content into Christ—the Jews had thought of Christ as a conquering Messiah; you cannot say the Holy Spirit until you have first said Jesus, for Jesus puts character-content into the Holy Spirit—a less than New Testament content was in "the Spirit of the Lord" in Old Testament; you cannot say "the Kindom of God" until you first say Jesus, for Jesus puts character-content into the Kingdom of God—the Jews had the content of a Davidic kingdom in their conception of the Kingdom of God.

In this Epistle you do not get to God until the third verse. It is all Jesus in its initial presentation. The gospel is presented with Jesus foremost. But when you do get to God in this Epistle, He is presented with no question marks—it is with clarity and certainty: "God is light and in him is no darkness at all." But you cannot say that unless you are looking in the face of Jesus while you are saying it! Begin with God and you end with a question mark—a question mark about His character and intentions; begin with Jesus and you end with an exclamation point—as exclamation point about God's character and intentions!

You will be tempted in your quest for maturity to do what the Gnostics did—to bypass Jesus and turn to something that seems more intellectual, more modern, more in keeping with the times, more intellectually fashionable. And you will end where the Gnostics ended—in oblivion. Gnosticism has died—Jesus lives on. All the intellectual descendants of Gnosticism will also end in futility and oblivion. Everything not centered in Jesus is off the center—ec-centric.

O Jesus, my Center and my All, I thank Thee that when I have Thee I have all: God, eternal life, purity, power, the mastery of the art of living, maturity. Outside of Thee I have question marks, immaturity. Amen.

AFFIRMATION FOR THE DAY: *As I face life today I shall not bypass Jesus at any point, on any question.*

EGOCENTRIC OR GOD-CENTRIC?

Gnosticism, we have seen, bypassed Jesus and ended in oblivion. Verbally, the Gnostics did not bypass Jesus, for they kept Christian nomenclature and stuck in Christian ideas here and there; but vitally they did—Jesus was not at the center—the Gnostics were at the center. It was an egocentric philosophy.

That is the dividing line. Is our salvation and our maturity to be Jesus-centric or egocentric? Is it Savior-salvation or self-salvation?

The spiritual descendants of the Gnostics, under other names and forms, are many, both inside and outside the Christian church. To the Gnostic, Jesus was the giver of passwords and formulas to help him find his illumination of God, to climb the ladder of thirty-six steps to union with God. He is not a savior—He is a teacher and revealer of the Gnostic secrets and forerunner of the Gnostic way of salvation. As Nygren puts it in *Agape and Eros*: "The task of the Gnostic Saviour is that of Forerunner and Example for the self-salvation of the human spirit."

Jesus, instead of being the starting point, is called in to guide and illuminate the Gnostics' own basic presuppositions. Jesus is kept but made into the image of Gnosticism. Not the Savior but the self is at the center. Obviously, the ghost of Gnosticism is back again and is taking reincarnation in many modern movements.

When we turn from surrender to Christ and dependence on Him for salvation and maturity and turn to group dependence—this group has the answer and will save me; or to denomination dependence—my denomination has the truth and I can find salvation and maturity in this fold; or to slogans and formulas—if I repeat these slogans and go through these techniques I shall find salvation and maturity; or to this set of doctrines and beliefs—if I believe in these hard enough and single-pointedly enough I shall be saved—when we turn to any of these instead of the living Savior, we are in line with Gnosticism and its self-salvation.

O living Christ, when we turn from Thee, the foundation of living waters, we turn to broken cisterns that leave us thristy and confused. Forgive us. We turn to Thee again. May we find in Thee our Springs and never thirst again. Amen.

AFFIRMATION FOR THE DAY: *"All my springs are in you"*—*My springs of salvation, of adequacy, of life.*

16

THE CULTS OF SELF-DISCOVERY AND
SELF-CULTIVATION

To the spiritual descendants of Gnosticism we must add the cults of self-discovery and self-cultivation. Now I believe in self-discovery and self-cultivation but only as a by-product of Christ-discovery and Christ-cultivation. The first thing in life is not "Know thyself," as the Greeks supposed; for if you begin with yourself and your self-discovery, you'll end with yourself and the losing of your self in disintegration. As long as we held to Ptolemaic astronomy—making everything revolve around the earth as the center—we ended in confusion. Nothing came out right. But the moment we turned from the Ptolemaic to the Copernican astronomy wherein the earth revolved around the sun, and not everything around the earth, then everything began to fall into its place. All the sums began to add up to sense. As long as we are egocentric, even in religion, nothing will add up, except to confusion. But the moment you make God the center by surrender of yourself to Him, then and then only are you on the right center, and then and then only will your life sums begin to add up to sense.

From that center in God you can and will discover yourself. You discover yourself by losing the self in God—it comes back to you again, and you cultivate fellowship with and obedience to God. As a by-product of that fellowship the self is cultivated.

But when you make self-discovery and self-cultivation the center, then the result is an egocentric bypassing of Jesus. It is the same error as Gnosticism's. And it will perish as did Gnosticism by its own egocentricity. It will break itself upon the immutable law that he that saveth his life shall lose it.

If you bypass Jesus you bypass Life. "This is eternal life, that they know thee the only true God, and Jesus Christ whom thou hast sent." Not "Know thyself," but know Him, and in knowing Him you know yourself.

O Jesus, I turn from the vagaries of self-knowledge to the vitalities of Thy-knowlege. When I know Thee, then I know. And I know that I know. For everything within me witnesses to this Reality. I thank Thee. Amen.

AFFIRMATION FOR THE DAY: *I will not look at myself, except in Thee. In Thee everything is possible.*

THE EMPHASIS ON "THIS"

We have been emphasizing the point that when we turn to egocentric ways of salvation and cultivation, then we wander amid the mazes of a jigsaw puzzle that is made in its inner structure so that is will not come out right on the basis of egocentricity. The result is a vast futility. "But," someone answers, "at least, I am close to myself. And when you give me a slogan or a technique, I can at least begin. To begin with God is to begin with the far-off. I want the close-at-hand."

And that is just the point in beginning with Jesus. He is the near-at-hand. He is God-available, God-approachable, God-simplified, God-inviting-us, God-with-stretched-out-arms.

In the Epistle the word "this" is used twenty-nine times. The emphasis is not on "that" or "the other"—things far away—but on "this"—the near, the available, the now, the here. The "thisness" of God in Jesus is a surprise to everyone who really tries it. It hits you like a bolt out of the blue, or it wells up from within like the breaking forth of a sealed fountain, or the settling upon you of an infinite Quiet that tells you He is here. Peter, standing up after receiving the gift of the Holy Spirit, said to the multitudes: "This is that" (KJV)—that which had been prophecy was now fact—glorious, bubbling, self-authenticating fact. This is just the difference between the way of Christ and the other way: other ways are all "that"—something just beyond their fingertips, something hoped for but not possessed, something in the realm of idea. But Jesus is the word become flesh, not only in His flesh, but in your flesh and mine. The coming of the Word into flesh is the pledge of its coming into your flesh and mine, provided we take it by receptivity. God is no further away than yes—your "yes" to His "yes." So that no one is further than one word from God—"yes."

Everything else, then, is far off, beyond the horizon; this is breathtakingly and availably near. It is the only real thing that can be had for the asking.

O Jesus, Thou art God at the lintel of the doorstep of my being, with nothing between Thee and me except my opening the door from within. I am awed that salvation and maturity are so close at hand, awaiting my taking. Amen.

AFFIRMATION FOR THE DAY: *Thou art my maturity. I know maturity as I know Thee. I shall know Thee deeper today.*

18

MATURITY—ATTITUDES CAN BE SUDDEN

Salvation and maturity, we have asserted, are near at hand—at our doors in Jesus. "Yes," someone suggests, "I can see that salvation may be at hand, but I thought that maturity was a long slow growth." It is, in one sense; but in another, it is not. For the moment that you get into vital contact with Jesus, the most mature Fact of the universe, then you have maturity in its essence. The rest is simply unfolding what has been infolded.

"Mary," of whom I have written in *Growing Spiritually*, was accustomed to run to the telephone and listen in on a party line in a country district. Everybody did it. The morning after she was converted she automatically went to the telephone to listen in, but, pausing a moment before lifting the receiver, she found herself saying: "Why, I don't need to any more." And she didn't pick up the receiver. That was maturity—straight off.

For a month after "Mary" was converted a woman in the neighborhood snubbed her deliberately, turned her back on her on every occasion. "Mary" found herself saying: "Lord, what's wrong with me that she treats me this way? Something must be wrong with me. Show me and I'll correct it." That was maturity—looking for the cause in herself instead of blaming the other person. At the end of a month the woman suddenly flung her arms around "Mary." They were friends, and from that day to this neither has mentioned the matter. That, too, was maturity—they accepted each other as friends and silently buried the past.

When I arose from my knees after looking into the face of Jesus and reading forgiveness and reconciliation there, I felt as though I could put my arms around the world and share this with everybody. That, too, was maturity. Five minutes before, I was an immature egocentric. Five minutes later, the basis of my life was shifted and I was a person who cared. And "to care" is a sign, an authentic sign, of maturity.

Maturity is primarily a gift, then it is a growth—so it is a gift and a growth. The gift makes maturity possible now.

O Jesus, I thank Thee that the depth of my receptivity is the depth of my maturity. I don't grow into This—I go into it by open-armed receptivity. The Way is an open Way and I can put both feet on it now. I thank Thee. Amen.

AFFIRMATION FOR THE DAY: *I reverse all my immature attitudes and receive all Thy mature attitudes.*

MATURITY IN THE YOUNG

We must continue today to look at maturity as a possibility *now*. For many think of it as associated with long processes and long years, with gray hair and gray beards. That is to kill the whole idea and possibility now. Gray heads and gray beards may cover immature persons, while the very young can be quite mature spiritually.

We were in an Ashram in a mountain retreat in Japan at the Morning of the Open Heart. We were telling our needs. A Japanese professor, with the face of a real scholar and with a deep sensitivity, was telling us that he had been baptized only the past Christmas and that it was the prayer of his little daughter that led him to Christ. He said he was sowing some seeds in a garden, and the little girl prayed that the seeds he was sowing might grow into a beautiful flower. And immediately he transferred that prayer to himself—he wanted to grow into a good man. That prayer of the little girl was according to God's laws—seed into flower—and was answered. She didn't pray for a miracle against the laws of nature. That was maturity!

Here was a girl of sixteen who played the piano at one of our Ashrams, a beautiful and accomplished girl. But she had a disease and no one with that disease had been known to live beyond the age of twenty-two. In the face of this prospect she was poised and radiant. When someone insisted that she get people to pray for her healing she replied: "I believe I am healed, for I am living with God's laws for me. I am living on a diet and on this diet I am healthy." That was maturity—a maturity of a very beautiful kind. She was healed by obedience to God's laws for her. Such obedience was much more mature than is the action of many people who ask God to pass a miracle over them and heal them without their obeying His laws and cooperating with Him.

Maturity, then, is an attitude toward life instead of life spelled out by the years. Said a Negro: "If you count how old I am by the years, I'm twenty-five, but if you count by the fun I've had, I'm a hundred." It is the intensity of the years and not their extensity that measure maturity. We can be mature *now*.

O Jesus, Lord and Savior, I thank Thee that Thou art the Near, the Available-now. We do not have to wait for Thee, for Thou art waiting for us. We do not have to overcome Thy reluctance but have to lay hold on Thy highest willingness. Amen.

AFFIRMATION FOR THE DAY: *By the years I may be a toddler; by yearning receptivity I am full-grown.*

BY STEPS OR BY ELEVATOR?

We pause another day on the possibility of maturity as the gift of God. Take the disciples before the coming of the Holy Spirit. They were very immature—quarreling over first places, caving in under opposition, and behind closed doors for fear. Then came the Holy Spirit, and almost overnight they were mature, afraid of nothing and of no one, confronting a nation and calling it to repentance, standing up to Sanhedrins unabashed, reversing all the values of that ancient world, and causing greater changes in human history than have been made before or since—and they did it effortlessly. Why? Because they had come into contact with a mature Spirit—the Holy Spirit. He imparted His maturity immediately and effectively—and they stood up mature persons. So maturity can be obtained as well as attained—a gift as well as a process.

Paul, up to a moment, was an immature fanatic for a law, and in the next moment he was a mature servant of grace. In a few days after he was converted he had disciples. "His disciples" let him down in a basket over the wall of Damascus. He had maturity as a gift and was imparting it.

A letter was received a few days ago from a man who said: "This morning I was in the basement trying to climb to the first floor, when 'Mary' showed us a skyscraper and a penthouse at the top, and just when I felt I'd never have power to climb, Jesus showed me the elevator of the Holy Spirit. Now I'm going up the fast and easy way—not in *my* strength but in *His!*" There he learned a secret—the secret not of laboriously trying to climb the steps of skyscrapers, but of surrender to the elevator of the Spirit. Then you live by power and maturity not your own.

So maturity is not a clenched-teeth, doubled-up-fist affair, fighting to be mature. It is first and foremost a gift of grace. The measure of our receptivity is the measure of our maturity. That puts humble receptivity at the center of our maturity.

O Spirit Divine, Thou who art Maturity for Thou art Reality, help me to open to Thee every cell of my being and take Thy maturity. For in Thee I find all I need—and more. Give me life and give it to me more abundantly. Amen.

AFFIRMATION FOR THE DAY: *In receptive touch with the Spirit of Maturity, I am destined to become a mature person.*

GOD AT TOPMOST, OR THE LOWEST RUNG?

Last week we saw that we do not find God and maturity at the top rung of a long ladder up which we laboriously climb, for God is not to be found at the top rung of the ladder—He is on the bottom rung. We don't climb to Him—He has come down to us. That is the meaning of the Incarnation. The Incarnation is God on the bottom rung of the ladder to receive sinners. You don't have to be mature to find God. You have to be willing to be different, to be receptive—that is all.

And then, when through repentance and renunciation of our impossible ways of life and through self-surrender to Christ, we are adjusted to God—the ultimate Maturity became the ultimate Reality—then we are adjusted to ourselves and life, and to all intents and purposes we are mature persons. At last we are mature-persons-in-the-making, for the rest is unfoldment. I say "unfoldment," but of course there is a continuous surrender of things that do not fit into that central adjustment. However, when once there is a wholehearted and complete surrender to Christ, then real maturity has begun. Without that surrender we are tinkering with this business of being mature. We are like an engine puffing away, trying to be efficient when it is off the rails. Self-surrender puts you on the rails. When you are "on the rails," then you have made a mature adjustment. The rest is to keep on going on. And you do not go on alone. When you have made the adjustment to Him, then He and you work out life together—you supply willingness and He supplies power. Life has become a mutuality instead of a lonely climb toward a maturity that eludes. You appropriate maturity at every step of the way, for you are adjusted to the most mature Fact that this planet knows—Jesus. Maturity is caught—caught from Maturity.

So you do not become mature by clenching your teeth and steeling your will and saying: "Come now, I will be a mature person." That ties you all the tighter in knots. A mature person is relaxed and receptive.

O God, my Father, if I've been struggling to lift myself by my bootstraps instead of taking Thy proffered hand, forgive me. I know I surrender in order to ascend, I go down to go up. So I surrender—surrender at the center—myself. Amen.

AFFIRMATION FOR THE DAY: *Blessed are the renounced and receptive in spirit, for theirs is the kingdom of heaven.*

ALL SELF-CENTEREDNESS IS IMMATURITY

A tree is mature only when it is bearing fruit. Until then it is immature. A person is immature until he is outgoing and sharing. And how does a tree bear fruit? By struggling, trying, working iself up into a lather, by tense anxiety, by trying harder? No. It bears fruit by receptivity. Jesus said: "As the branch cannot bear fruit by itself, unless it abides in the vine, neither can you, unless you abide in me" (John 15:4). "As the branch cannot bear fruit by itself "—that verse is the death knell to all attempts at maturity by self-tinkering, striving for self-salvation. All these attempts leave you centered on yourself and when you are centered on yourself you are immature; however religious you may be and however psychological you may be. Something has to break the tyranny of self-preoccupation, and only a mighty flux of love from Christ can do that.

Down underneath a great deal of our religion and our patriotism is self-interest. In Calcutta a sadhu, a holy man, sat in the railway station reciting passages in a loud voice, with the Ramayana, a Hindu sacred book, unopened before him. The book was especially large and six inches thick. A member of the secret police, suspecting his loud protestation of religion and the thickness of the book, seized it and found in the center of its pages a box of contraband opium worth a large sum. At the center of the man's outward signs of religion was this illicit opium. At the center of a lot of our outward religious signs is an unsurrendered self, seeking its own ends through religious forms. Another member of the secret police in Calcutta saw a man carrying a plaster bust of Subash Chandra Bose, a national hero, through the station. But his hugging it too close as if it were heavy aroused suspicion, and the secret policeman seized the bust and found it was filled with illicit opium. Under a lot of our patriotism is a self-interest, using patriotism to its own ends. The inmost self must be offered on the altar and then, and then only, can we be redeemed.

O Jesus, Thou art redemption. Thou dost not give redemption—Thou art redemption. For to have Thee is to be redeemed from sin and immaturity—from everything that makes us little. So I open my being wide to Thee. Come—it's all yours. Amen.

AFFIRMATION FOR THE DAY: *Thou art the center of my preoccupation. I am in love with Thee, wholly and forever.*

RELEASE FROM EGOCENTRICITY

Yesterday we were speaking of release from self-centeredness as the first step to maturity.

In the Nurmanzil Psychiatric Center at Lucknow, the first of its kind in India, we undertook to define the purpose of psychiatry, under Christian auspices: "The purpose of psychiatry is to help people to be sufficiently foot-loose and free, emotionally and mentally, to make an intelligent surrender of themselves to God and then to provide useful insights and aids to human living." Note that the real purpose of the process is to get the patient to the point where he can get himself off his own hands into the hands of God. For as long as he is self-centered he is a sick, immature personality.

Karl Menninger, of the famous Menninger Clinic, says in his book *Love Against Hate:* "It will probably astonish many, therefore, when I say that the great problem in every well-conducted sanitarium is how to get the patients to do *anything!*" Especially for others, for they are not interested in others; they are interested solely in themselves—that's why they are there! Menninger tells of a patient who "would walk five or ten mils a day for exercise but would not lift a spadeful of dirt or make a single puppet: he would play tennis occasionally but he would never roll the tennis courts. He would play bridge until he had a blinding headache, but he would not set up a bridge table or manage a tournament for the pleasure of the other guests." Why? Because he wasn't interested in anything that concerned others. He was interested only in himself.

Gnosticism was a self-centered religious movement interested only in its own self-illumination. It died—self-strangled. Its religion couldn't save it, for it could not save the devotee from self-preoccupation. There the Christian faith is at its clearest and finest: for its first endeavor is to release you from self-preoccupation through surrender of the self to Christ.

O Jesus, Thou dost strike a dart at the very heart of our problems by Thy demand that we lose our lives to find them again. And Thou dost wound us there temporarily to make us whole forever. I would be whole, every whit. Amen.

AFFIRMATION FOR THE DAY: *I am lost in Thee, not by trying to be, but love impels me to be.*

IMMATURE PEOPLE OUT OF FELLOWSHIP

In view of what we have been saying it is no surprise to hear John say: "That which we have seen and heard we proclaim also to you, so that you may have fellowship with us; and our fellowship is with the Father and with his Son Jesus Christ" (I John 1:3). The purpose of his writing was "that you may have fellowship." This sounds commonplace, but it was far-reaching and most important.

The basis of our immaturity is a self-centeredness that keeps us from fellowship with God, ourselves, our brother, nature, and life itself. Every immature person is tied in on himself and cannot be outgoing, friendly, and loving—cannot have fellowship. So the first thing in the Christian purpose is to produce fellowship.

First of all with God. John seemed to say that the fellowship is "with us," but he hastens to add that "our fellowship is with the Father." The person who has no fellowship with God is an immature person. He feels, consciously or unconsciously, that he is cut off from the very root of his being. The prodigal son saw that he had sinned in three directions: "I have sinned against heaven"—the impersonal moral law: "and before you"—against the personal love of his father: and "I am no longer worthy to be called your son"—against himself, against his own sonship. The center of the three broken relationships was "before you"—against his father's love. So that was the first relationship to be restored—the father ran and kissed him. Restored to the father he was restored to the moral law and he was restored to himself.

In our moral and spiritual orphanage the first thing to do is to be restored to fellowship with God. To try to be restored to fellowship with the moral law through doing our duty, to try to be restored to fellowship with ourselves through psychological processes—these attempts leave the heart of the estrangement untouched—God. But when we are reconciled to God, we are automatically reconciled with the moral universe and we are reconciled with ourselves.

O God, we are homesick and heartsick for Thee and we don't know it. Make our sickness so acute that we will arise like the prodigal and go to our Father. But best of all, Thou dost come to us—come to us in Jesus. I thank Thee. Amen.

AFFIRMATION FOR THE DAY: *I cannot produce this fellowship by trying harder; I can only take it by trusting more.*

GOD COMES TO US

We saw yesterday that the first step, the very first step in maturity, is to be reconciled with God, our Father. As long as the feeling of inner estrangement from God is eating at the center of our being, we will never be mature.

And at this place there are just two types of religion: the one type tries to meet God in reconciliation and realization at the top rung of a long ladder; the other meets God at the lowest rung. In the one we go to God, climbing up by our good deeds, by our prayers, by our mortifying of ourselves, by our gaining of merit, by our obedience to rites and ceremonies, and by our faithfulness to law and duty—we can earn our maturity and our realization of God. Every way, except the Christian way, belongs to that category. It is man's search up for God.

The Christian way is quite different. We do not climb to Him and meet Him at the top rung; He comes down the ladder to us and meets us on the lowest rung—He receives us as sinners. "I came not to call the righteous, but sinners." That is new and that is revolutionary. It reverses all the values of all the religions, including the Jewish. For Judaism says: "God loves those and fellowships with those who keep His Law"—that means you meet Him at the top of the ladder. Hinduism says: "Practice austerities, renounce samsara (the world order), shut out everything but the realization of God, and you will find Him"—again at the top of the ladder. Islam says: "Pray five times a day, fast, obey Allah's commands, and you will get heaven and God at the end"—again at the top of the ladder. Unitarianism says: "Salvation by character"—again at the top of the ladder. Modern humanism says: "Serve your neighbor, do good to all, and it will be well with you"—again at the top of the ladder.

Only One dared reverse all this and they crucified Him for it—Jesus. He rendered vain all these attempts at self-salvation and said: "God isn't at the top of the ladder—He is at the bottom." Breathtaking.

O Jesus, what can I say? I am speechless before the wonder of This. I am in the dust. But there I find Thee—in the dust before me, ready to receive me and lift me to the highest heaven. O Gracious Condescension, I belong to Thee—forever. Amen.

AFFIRMATION FOR THE DAY: *Only empty hands can take this Gift—my uplifted hands are empty.*

PSYCHOLOGIST: "I WANT TO BE SAVED"

When we are reconciled to God and therefore in fellowship with Him, we feel we have cosmic backing for our way of life. The sum total of reality is behind us; the universe approves of us; a sense of cosmic security takes hold of us. A realization of maturity is ours, for we feel that we *belong*—the feeling of orphanage is over.

A wealthy man died and it was found that he had belonged to twenty-five clubs. He was reaching out through his wealth toward security, toward belonging, but it was all marginal belonging. Centrally he felt he didn't belong to anything significant, so he added the many in lieu of the One. He was an immature person picking up club after club as a child picks up toy after toy—none of it was It.

A very able man, a Ph.D., head of the personnel department of an educational institution, came into my room and, without preliminaries, said: "I want to be saved." When we arose from our knees a few minutes later his face was changed—he was released and radiant. And in the twinkling of an eye he was a mature person. For up until that moment his knowledge, his ability, his opportunities, all lacked a central cohesion—they were all around a central emptiness. When that central emptiness was filled with God, then everything took on meaning, purpose, goal. He was mature. The rest was unfoldment.

The Christian presentation of God meeting us at the lowest rung of the ladder opens the door to salvation and maturity to everybody. I link salvation and maturity; for no one is, or can be, mature unless he is saved—saved from a central emptiness, a central futility, a central lack of God. When you have God at the center of your being and are in fellowship with Him, then maturity is there; for you are in contact with Maturity—with God. The rest is a maturing of your essential maturity. You are a mature person.

God, offering fellowship to the estranged—estranged from God, themselves, and life—and that at the lowest rung of the ladder—that is grace!

O God, Thy down-reach is my hope. My up-reach is feeble and goes little higher than my head. Thy down-reach goes to the lowest of the low, the emptiest of the empty—it reaches me. I take hold of Thy grace and I am lifted—to Thee. Amen.

AFFIRMATION FOR THE DAY: *Thy down-reach is perfect; my up-reach shall be forever perfected.*

THE WORM OF EGOCENTRICITY

This idea of God's meeting us at the lowest rung of the ladder, and not the highest rung, scandalized the intellectuals of Christ's day, as it does in this. Celsus, the opponent of Christianity, saw this point in Christianity and attacked it:

He never tires of pointing out to Christians the absurdity, the contemptibleness, the revoltingness of their conception of God. Every other religion has some regard for itself, and admits only the respectable, cultivated, irreproachable people into its fellowship; but Christianity runs after the riffraff of the streets. As if it were positively a bad thing to have committed no sin, or as if God were a robber chief who gathered criminals around him! . . . "The Deity has dealings only with the pure," was . . . the inviolable axiom.

The answer to this was that at the heart of all this apparent moral and religious respectability the worm of egocentricity was eating. These people were attempting self-salvation and were proud of it. They were standing in the temple of God and saying: "God, I thank thee that I am not like other men." That was their central immaturity and of that it died.

On the other hand, those people who met the inviting God at the lowest rung of the ladder did not remain what they were. Here is what happened: " . . . the gospel which has come to you, as indeed in the whole world it is bearing fruit and growing—so among yourselves, from the day you heard and understood the grace of God in truth . . . Epaphras . . . has made known to us your love in the Spirit" (Col. 1:5-8). "From the [first] day," "bearing fruit and growing," and showing "love in the Spirit." You don't bear "fruit" until you are mature, and you don't show an outgoing "love in the Spirit" until you are mature. And they had this "from the [first] day."

What did it? Fellowship with God in Christ. Living in intimate contact with the most mature fact in the universe—God—they took on His maturity. The maturity was caught not taught. The lowest rung of the ladder had suddenly become the highest rung—through grace.

O Gracious Father, Thy lowliness is our exaltation. We meet Thee at the lowest rung and, lo! we are at the topmost. And yet our hearts at the very topmost are filled with an inexpressible humility. We are on our knees. Amen.

AFFIRMATION FOR THE DAY: *My origins no longer appall, for my destinations appeal.*

"THIS MAN RECEIVES SINNERS"

We have seen that the central fact in being a mature person is to get into fellowship with God. But we cannot get into fellowship with God—God must get into fellowship with us. He does—and does so at the lowest rung of the ladder. "This man receives sinners and eats with them"—that was scandalized religion's most bitter complaint. The complaint is now a compliment. For if He received sinners, they didn't remain sinners—they became saints, straight off. And if He ate with them, they were soon eating with Him—the Bread of Communion.

The elder brother in the parable represents the attempts at fellowship with the father at the highest rung of the ladder of goodness: "I never disobeyed your command; yet you never gave me a kid, that I might make merry with my friends. But when this son of yours came, who has devoured your living with harlots, you killed him the fatted calf!" He represented an attempt at fellowship through keeping the Law. It failed. The younger son met the father at the lowest rung of the ladder—the rung of grace. He succeeded. Everything was open to him—the father's arms, the feasting, the rejoicing, the reconciliation. When the parable ends, the one who tried to *earn* the fellowship with the father was on the outside sulking, and the one who took the fellowship through grace was on the inside rejoicing. God cannot be found at the top of the ladder, for He is not there. He is at the lowest rung receiving sinners. If you feel you are not a sinner then there is no place for you. But if you do, everything is open to you—especially the Father's heart.

But we could never have seen all of this except through Jesus. John's Epistle begins with Jesus and ends up with fellowship with God. It doesn't begin with God. For apart from Jesus we know little or nothing about God, and what we know is wrong. Jesus is God coming down the ladder in Incarnation and meeting us at the lowest rung. We meet Him there or we miss Him.

O Jesus, we know that Thou art the way to the Father, for Thou art the way of the Father to us. And we cannot be grateful enough that Thou hast met us at the lowest rung of the ladder, for we could not have met Thee anywhere else. Amen.

AFFIRMATION FOR THE DAY: *The Way is not in me, nor in others, nor in things—the Way is in Thee. Thou art the Way.*

CENTRAL THING IN MATURITY—FELLOWSHIP

We have been introduced to the central thing in maturity—fellowship. Those who are drawn in upon themselves, ingrown, are incapable of fellowship, and hence immature persons. When once you get in touch with the expansive God, you find yourself expanded. You are inwardly untied, become outgoing, become capable of love, of fellowship—you are a mature person-in-the-making.

The maturest society ever seen on or planet was the group of early Christians in the Acts of the Apostles. Their fellowship was so deep they had called it "the Fellowship"—the *Koinonia*. Out of that fellowship their maturity arose spontaneously and immediately. It was a double fellowship—with God and one another. It was "the Fellowship."

In John's Epistle the fellowship was with both God and man: " . . . so that you may have fellowship with us: and our fellowship is with the Father and with his Son Jesus Christ" (1:3). The mentioning of "fellowship with us" is important and purposive. For the Gnostics, the Knowers, were snobbish in their pretended knowing. They were the elite, the *illuminati*. They had no more care for the common people than if these were of a lower order—beasts. For this lower order of people lived in the material; the Gnostics lived in the spiritual—the esoteric group.

John sent a dart at the heart of all this spiritual snobbery when he quietly said: "That which we have seen and heard we proclaim also to you, so that you may have fellowship with us" (1:3). The esoteric was gone; everything was open to everybody. Through familiarity, the radical nature of that simple statement has been lost on us. As God's arms are open to everybody in everything, so our arms are open to everybody and everything. The barriers are down between God and man and between man and man. That simple statement has enough social and spiritual dynamite in it to blow our existing institutions and attitudes to pieces.

O Father, Thou dost quietly drop the seed of Thy truth into our hearts, and lo, we find that seed become revolution. If we are to have fellowship with Thee, how can we refuse to have fellowship with any man, anywhere? Amen.

AFFIRMATION FOR THE DAY: *As an outer expression of my fellowship with Thee, I shall fellowship with everybody I can.*

"SMARTER THAN I AM"

This statement of John's about having "fellowship with us" is like the seed of a pepul tree in India which falls into the crack of a temple, and if left alone will create a set of ruins at the base of a large and spreading tree. This statement is dynamic. For if fellowship is in the spiritual it has a way of going over into the social and economic—it has a way of going into all of life. The moment you try to confine it to one realm only, it ceases to be fellowship.

I asked a little girl of ten, daughter of missionaries in Malaya, whether she liked her school in which there were all races, and she replied: "Yes, I like it very much, for it gives me an opportunity to study along with Asiatic children and to know them." And then she added: "Some of them are very smart, smarter than I am." That child was mature in her attitudes—far more mature than many of the older generation who draw the line of fellowship with other races and narrow themselves in the process.

A Georgia boy, when asked if he favored the coming of Negro children into white schools, replied: "Yes, of course. That will give us an opportunity to give them the same privileges that we have had; then we can lift them." That boy was more mature in his attitudes than are those who see in other races problems rather than possibilities. The future belongs to that boy and what he represents.

We will wake up to the fact some day that if we refuse fellowship we lose fellowship. Vast sections of the world are shaping their attitudes toward America according to the attitudes that America takes toward the Negro. If we refuse full fellowship toward the Negro in our democracy, then vast portions of the earth will and do refuse full fellowship with us. And that is important—and expensive. We are spending millions of dollars throughout the world to gain good will, and it is all canceled in a moment by a refusal of educational fellowship. It is expensive in more ways than one.

O God our Father, we are learning the hard way, the way of experience, that to reap fellowship we must give fellowship. Help us then to give fellowship openhandedly and openheartedly, not because we want to reap it, but because we can't help it. Amen.

AFFIRMATION FOR THE DAY: *I shall shut no one out of my fellowship lest in so doing I shut Him out.*

SEGREGATING FROM NATIONAL LEADERSHIP

Yesterday we said that if we refuse fellowship we lose fellowship. We reap what we sow.

On Thanksgiving Day I was speaking over the radio in a Mississippi city on the subject "A Nation's Struggle with a Word—All." That word "all" has precipitated eight great crises in our national life, and now we are struggling with the question of whether we shall apply it to the Negro. We accept the word when we read in our Declaration of Independence: "All men are created equal." We accept it again when we repeat the Pledge of Allegiance to the flag: "with liberty and justice for all." We accept these statements in our national standards, but not as our national standard of conduct. And then I added: "But if we of the South—for I come from the South—segregate the Negro, we will segregate ourselves from national leadership. For you cannot elect to the presidency any man from the South who holds these views on segregation. The rest of the country won't stand for it. So in segregating the Negro we are simply segregating ourselves—from national leadership. The moral law is at work—we reap what we sow." The broadcast was not turned off! And if it had been we could not have turned off the voice of our consciences. It is speaking and in the end will conquer us. For we are bound in every man's bondage and we are free in every man's freedom. America will never be a free country until the Negro is given his full freedom. We are down with him and will rise when he rises—fully.

Gnosticism died, for one reason, because it was a snobbery—selfstrangled. Christianity lived on because at its heart it was not a snobbery, but a fellowship. That fellowship beckoned the underprivileged, and they came. And in their coming were transformed. And in their being transformed they transformed. They became the teachers and saviors of the world. The nobodies became the somebodies. We fellowship with their fellowship, for we know that in the end it will become "the Fellowship"—the New Order in which we fellowship across all barriers of race and class.

O Divine Redeemer, redeem us at the place of narrowed fellowships and make us as broad as Thy mind, as loving as Thy heart, and as sympathetic as Thy sympathy. For we cannot fellowship with Thee unless we fellowship with all. Amen.

AFFIRMATION FOR THE DAY: *If my fellowship is narrowed, I am narrowed. I am as great as my fellowship.*

FELLOWSHIP WITH OTHER CHRISTIANS

Those who are out of fellowship with God and man are immature, undeveloped human beings. The measure of our maturity can be and is measured by the breadth and depth of our capacity for fellowship. We are as mature as our fellowships. So if we cannot fellowship with other races, we reveal our immaturity. All segregation segregates into immaturity those who segregate. The payoff is in the person.

This statement holds good in regard to our capacity to fellowship with other Christians. If we can fellowship only with those who belong to our group, our denomination, our particular set of doctrinal beliefs, then in such measure we are immature. What, then, is the basis of our fellowship? One thing and one thing only: everyone who belongs to Christ belongs to everyone who belongs to Christ. The basis of our fellowship is not around this doctrine, that doctrine, the other doctrine; or around this group, that group, or the other group—it is around Christ and only around Christ.

When the disciples said to Jesus that they had seen a man casting out devils in His name and they had forbidden him, "because he was not following us," they were revealing their immaturity. They would probably have said in justification that they were trying to protect the movement from irregularities, but actually they were trying to protect their own prestige.

There are those who justify this exclusiveness toward other followers of Christ by the command

Therefore come out from them,
and be separate from them, says the Lord (II Cor. 6:17).

But this passage does not refer to fellow Christians, but to the non-Christian, pagan world around them, for a part of the passage says: "Do not be mismated with unbelievers . . . What accord has Christ with Belial? . . . What agreement has the temple of God with idols?" (vv 14-16). To justify divisiveness in the Christian fellowship by this passage is a sign of great spiritual and intellectual immaturity. If we shut out our brother we shut out Christ.

O Christ of the stretched-out arms, help me to open my arms and my heart to everyone who names Thy name. For if I do not fellowship with him, I refuse fellowship to one for whom Christ died. Amen.

AFFIRMATION FOR THE DAY: *When prejudice shuts out my brother, then penury sits in my bosom.*

RELIGIOUS SNOBBERY

If we smile at childish religious immaturity such as mentioned yesterday, as representing the uneducated fringe of Christianity, what are we to say to a clipping from a newspaper which states that thirteen hundred priests of the Church of England petitioned the Convocation of Canterbury not to recognize the Church of South India, since there are elements still left in the Church of South India not episcopally ordained according to the particular brand of episcopal ordination of the Anglican Church? The item further states: "Finally the petition asks the Convocation to defer consideration of any further schemes of re-union with non-episcopal bodies for 21 years." Why twenty-one years? I suppose, since twenty-one is the age when one is thought to come to physical maturity, it was unconsciously used to give these men time in which to grow up to maturity! For this is immaturity—pure and simple. As if fellowship with other Christians should be based on episcopacy rather than on Christ! The bishop of a particular type becomes the center of our loyalty—he decides whether we fellowship with other Christians or not. This is immaturity—pure and simple. It is episcopal-centered instead of Christ-centered, and therefore an immature, off-centered type of Christianity. The fellowships of these persons are narrowed to a particular type of episcopal ordination. The thing which has narrowed their fellowships has therefore narrowed them. The payoff is in the person.

I will fellowship with persons who hold these views on the basis that they belong to Christ and I belong to Christ. But I cannot fellowship with these attitudes and views. I fellowship in spite of them. Their belonging to Christ makes such people belong to maturity; their belonging to these attitudes and views makes them belong to immaturity. There I will have to wait the "21 years," hoping they will outgrow these immaturities.

Our capacity to fellowship across all race, all class, all denominations, determines our maturity. Lord increase our capacity!

Dear Father, I ask Thee to enlarge the borders of my heart so I can take in every man whether I agree with him or not—take him in in real love. And where I balk, wilt Thou fill me with Thy love so I can love with it. Amen.

AFFIRMATION FOR THE DAY: *I cannot include my Father, if I exclude my brother—so every brother to my heart!*

"WHY DOES HE ACT THIS WAY?"

We spend one more day on the subject of our capacity to fellowship as a measure of our maturity. Many have difficulty in fellowshiping with particular people. They make us draw in on ourselves. With them we find it difficult to be outgoing and friendly and generous. How do we overcome this inner withdrawal?

Perhaps in two ways: first, by saying to yourself, "He is a man for whom Christ died. Christ loves him, so must I." Say that over and over to yourself. Second, ask the question: "Why does he act this way? I will have to try to understand him." Then project yourself into his situation and see life from his standpoint.

That capacity to project yourself into another person's situation will be the measure of your maturity. When someone asked Daniel Willard, head of the Baltimore and Ohio Railroad, to state the chief characteristic necessary for a good executive, he replied: "The willingness and the power to project yourself into the other man's situation and to see things from his standpoint."

As I wrote the above at Sat Tal in India, a widow with six children, all under eight, trooped into my room without knocking and without permission, and interrupted my writing. And I had given orders that no one should disturb me. My first reaction was to shoo them out abruptly and get on with my writing. But I asked myself, "Why does she act this way?" The answer was obvious: need! She will get the modest monthly allowance she asked for. And I can go on with my writing on fellowship as a sign of maturity. Had I not asked that question: "Why does she act this way?" I would have saved my time and money, but my writing on maturity would have been halting and uncertain—and worse— just words.

If you find someone who sets up a barrier to fellowship, find out the reason; and if the reason is unreasonable, then dissolve it by your love. If that amount of love doesn't dissolve it, give more love and still more love.

O Father, Thou dost fellowship with me, not on the basis of my being worthy of that fellowship, but on the basis of being what Thou art. Help me to fellowship with everybody, everywhere, because of what I am—a lover of Thee. Amen.

AFFIRMATION FOR THE DAY: *If God fellowships with me in spite of what I am, I'll fellowship with everybody.*

JOY, A MARK OF MATURITY

We take another step in the interpretation of maturity in this Epistle: "And we are writing this that our joy may be complete" (I John 1:4).

Joy is a mark of maturity. The sad, morose type of person is immature. For that unhappiness is being caused, almost entirely, through inner conflicts and wrong attitudes toward life. When we get rid of inner conflicts and wrong attitudes toward life, we will almost automatically burst into joy. For we are made for joy—made for it in the inner structure of our beings. And when we are truly ourselves by being truly His, then we are joyous, constitutionally. Rendell Harris says: "Joy is the strength of the people of God; it is their chief characteristic." Where there is no joy there is no Christianity, and where there is Christianity there is joy. "So there was much joy in that city," was said of the Samaritan city, because "Philip . . . proclaimed to them the Christ." Christ and joy go together. Where He is, there is joy; and where He is not, there is sadness. "And he went away sadly"—everybody goes away from Christ sadly. For when you go away from Christ you go away from joy. He is joy—a fountain of joy. The Christian way is piety set to music. It is fun!

"Mary" says: "How little it takes to make us happy when we are Christians and how little it takes to make us unhappy when we are not." This is profoundly true, for the Christian is basically happy, and any little thing will set off that basic happiness into bubbling. But when you are not a Christian you are basically unhappy, and any little thing will bring out that basic unhappiness.

However, when everything is going Christ's way, then you have a glorious feeling, for His way and our way are the same—basically the same. But when "His way" and your way conflict, you do not have the glorious feeling—you have a gloomy feeling. Sin is sad. It cannot be otherwise, for it is "missing the mark."

O Jesus, to know Thee is to know joy. And it is joy that is not spasmodic, but continuous. For as long as Thou art within, joy is within, and any little thing sets it off. I am joyous at the thought of Thy joy. Amen.

AFFIRMATION FOR THE DAY: *All my deepest joys will be joys of creative sharing with others. Let me begin today.*

"JOY SURGING"

We continue our meditation on joy as a mark of maturity. A lady, wife of a missionary who had suffered much in China, wrote me these lines:

> Holding Your hand I walk the Way,
> You understand all I would say;
> Holding Your hand I need not pray.
> Lord, I belong here at Your side,
> Singing Your song, swinging Your stride,
> Joy surging with the strength of a tide.
> Beside us each tree shines against the blue,
> No need to see some distant view.
> The future must be here, now, with You.

Note: "Singing Your song, swinging Your stride, Joy surging with the strength of a tide." When you sing His song and swing His stride, then automatically joy surges with the strength of a tide. You don't seek happiness—it seeks you. But when you sing your own song and take your own stride, gloom automatically surges within you.

I have just been in Burma, now called the Union of Burma. But the "Union" is a name. Down underneath the word "Union" is a deep disunion. About four distinct rebel movements—each with its particular aim and its particular cause for rebellion—struggle with the government. We had an Ashram (a place of religous retreat) 325 miles from Rangoon, and a party of twenty-five going from Rangoon to Kalaw spent four days on the train to get there. Thirty-six bridges had been blown up between Rangoon and Kalaw: seven of them in one night when this group was on its way, one of them a half mile from the station where their train was standing. And no one would know which group of rebels had done it unless they left leaflets behind, a kind of calling card! The "Union" holds its position as dominant, but precariously. The joy of freedom is dimmed by disunion within. Many of us are like that. We are called "Christians" but harbor very unchristian rebel elements. When we become inwardly one by surrender, then we are free indeed. A deep joy is ours.

O Master, may I be mastered by Thee, wholly and completely—no pockets of rebellion left—all under Thy sway. Then I shall know the purest joy known to human breast, the joy of being Thine and the joy of inward oneness. Amen.

AFFIRMATION FOR THE DAY: *I am joyous in His joy, because unified in His unity. I am at one with Him, and hence myself.*

THE JOY OF CREATIVE SHARING

We have been looking at joy as a sign of maturity. For joy comes as a result of inner harmony. When there is no civil war within; when everything is under a single control, Christ; when everything is directed toward a single end, His will—then joy is a natural concomitant. You do not seek it—it is there inherently. And it is there permanently—does not come and go; for the conditions that produce it are there as a permanent part of us—those conditions are us. So we don't have joy—we are joy.

But here at this place in John's Epistle the joy is of a particular kind. It is the joy of creative sharing: "And we are writing this that our joy may be complete." It was a joy, not of what happened *to* him, but of what happened *through* him. If our joy is the result of what happens to us—success comes to us, people give us gifts, we are held high in the esteem of others, the market is going our way—then our joy is immature and precarious. It is immature and precarious because it is egocentric. And anything, including joy, if it is egocentric is off-center and will not and cannot abide.

Only that joy abides which is a creative joy. It creates joy in others and therefore brings joy to the creator in the rebound.

Viktor Frankl, in *The Doctor and the Soul*, tells of a young man, who through a long spell of unemployment, which drove him to despair and almost to suicide, had one good hour. He was sitting alone on a park bench and noticed on the next bench a weeping girl. When he went over and asked her what was the matter she told him her troubles and that she was firmly resolved to commit suicide. The young man summoned up all his powers of persuasion to talk the girl out of her intention and finally succeeded.

That was his "one good hour." Why? Because the joy of being creative came to him. Not what happened to him but *through* him made the difference.

If our joy is creatively outgoing to others it will always be incoming.

O God, I want to taste and know Thy joy—the joy of continuous creation. For Thou hast created me for creation. And I know I fulfill Thy will and my own self when I create. So make me this day the instrument of Thy creation. Amen.

AFFIRMATION FOR THE DAY: *Perhaps I cannot create in the big, but I can always create in the little acts of creative love.*

38

JOY SEEKS US

As John had seen the unfolding of the ages from his heavenly viewpoint, he must have found that he wrote more than he knew when he said: "And we are writing this that our joy may be complete." For the joy which people of all ages have received from this letter has rebounded into his bosom—good measure, pressed down and running over.

People retire to enjoy their wealth. Nothing is more elusive and fatuous. You cannot enjoy your wealth. Your wealth must be creative in creating and in augmenting the joy of others, or else it is ill-th, not weal-th. I was told that a certain residential resort holds more wealth and more misery than any other place on earth in a given space. Why? The people there came almost solely to *enjoy* their wealth—wonderful climate, wonderful scenery—but the unhappiness moved within.

On the other hand, you can be in the midst of very unfavorable circumstances and be full of joy. Dorothy (which wasn't her name) was. Her husband had married three times. The first wife turned to drink to escape his torments. The second wife turned to sex. And Dorothy, his third wife, turned to God. When she found God, then her husband lost all power to torment her. She slipped out from under his control when she went under God-control. It made her husband wild; he didn't know what to do with her. He said to a friend in a baffled way: "Dorothy and her friends are praying for me and I have to act like a hellion or they will get me." So he has gone to the Tropics to enjoy his wealth; no, ill-th. For he is a very sick man—within. Dorothy stays in the North, in America's worst climate, but she is radiantly happy; for she is teaching school, raising her children, sharing her joys with the defeated and beaten. She arose in one of our meetings and said: "I'm the woman who is living in heaven and in hell at the same time." But really there was no hell; it was all heaven—in spite of!

So joy is not to be sought; it seeks us when we are creative and outgoing. We become incorrigibly happy, for our happiness is not based on happenings.

O Father God, Thou art trying to share Thy joy with our small joyless hearts. Help us to open wide to Thy creative love, which would make us creative too. Then we will know the joy of being outgoing and helpful and loving. Amen.

AFFIRMATION FOR THE DAY: *My eyes and my heart will be wide open today to seek situations in which I can love.*

JOY MAKES US IMMUNE

This overflowing joy makes us immune to unconscious slights, to pinpricks, to the daily rubbing of events, to the intentional hurts, to the drabness of things, to disease. And when I use the word "immune," I mean "immune." Here is what Viktor Frankl, a doctor, says:

When blood serum was taken at a time of joyful excitement, the agglutination titer against typhus bacilli was found to be enormously higher than when blood was taken from the same subject in a saddened state. These researches throw light upon the lowered resistance to infection of an anxious hypochondriac. They also suggest why nurses at hospitals for contagious diseases, or even at leper stations, nurses who are filled with a sense of moral dedication, have escaped infection to such an extent that people hitherto have always spoken of their immunity as "miraculous."

We have in our Ashram in India a Greek woman who is an expert masseuse, filled with the love of God and people. She massages the patients who have contagious diseases, lepers included, and she is more than immune—she is life-giving. I tell her she gives a massage and a message at the same time. She rubs hope and life and love into withered souls and bodies. The Hindu pilgrims dying on the pilgrim route to the Himalayas have asked to hold her hand as they slipped across to the other world. And she held their hands, without regard to what contagious disease they may have had. She herself is the picture of heath. She is not only healthy, she is health-giving. She can look at a physical body and tell whether it belongs to God or to egoism. The results are apparent in the very body. She rubs God and self-surrender into the souls and bodies of people, and does it joyously and without tiring.

"Mary" does that too. She says: "People come to me with faces pale, with lips pale or purple—withered in body and soul—and as we talk about the love of God and His joy, I can almost see a blood transfusion take place. Blood comes back into their faces. They go away with joy."

O Jesus of the joyous heart, I bury my sadness in Thy joy. I leave my gloom at the foot of the cross. I drink deep of Thy resurrection victory and I am whole again. I thank Thee, thank Thee for this joy that passes understanding. Amen.

AFFIRMATION FOR THE DAY: *I belong not to the next day after the Crucifixion—the day of gloom—but to the third day, the day of glory.*

SELF-ACCEPTANCE—SIGN OF MATURITY

We pause to look to another sign of maturity in connection with this joy: the fact that John frankly says he is writing for a dual purpose. First, "That which we have seen and heard we proclaim also to you, so that you have fellowship with us" (1:3). We want to share what we have found with others—this is social. Second, "And we are writing this that our joy may be complete" (1:4). We want to share this joy with ourselves—this is personal.

This, in John, shows a very mature attitude—toward himself. He didn't try to be overly spiritual and say that he had no interest in himself—he was thinking only of others. That would mean that he was "screwing himself up so high that he would be of no use for anything beneath the sky." For self-acceptance is as necessary as other-acceptance. Those who, to impress their high spirituality, are always insisting that they don't think about themselves are unconsciously revealing their self-interest in talking about their self-denial. You have to accept yourself and provide for yourself in the scheme of redemption. The only question is, In what order? Are you first, Jesus second, and others third? Then that is egotistic immaturity. But here the order is right: Jesus first, others second, and you third. For the first two verses deal with Jesus: "That which was from the beginning." The third verse deals with others: "So that you may have fellowship with us." The fourth verse deals with John himself: "And we are writing this that our joy may be complete." The self is there, but last. Such an attitude made John a Christ-centric, other-centric, self-centric person, in that order. It made him mature. Reverse the order and you have immaturity. And you have no joy. For J-O-Y—Jesus first, others second, you third.

But "you" are in it, frankly so. You can safely talk about yourself after you have talked about Jesus and others—but not until. To try to act as though the self and its joy were not there is a species of self-rejection, and self-rejection is as bad as other-rejection. John showed the maturity of self-acceptance.

O Father, Thou dost accept me, so I accept myself. I cannot reject what Thou hast accepted. So I accept myself but only in Thee. There myself is safe and secure. And I can accept it and love it, because I love Thee more. Amen.

AFFIRMATION FOR THE DAY: *I accept and love myself in Him, for He accepts me and loves me.*

41

FIVE THINGS NECESSARY FOR MATURITY

We come on this last day of the week to sum up the five things in these first four verses which form the basic ground for our maturity. They are important.

Our Christian maturity is grounded: first, in the ultimate Reality, God, the Father; second, in the ultimate revelation of the Father in the Incarnation—in Jesus; third, in personal realization of the revelation—"that which we have seen"; fourth, in a desire to share this with everyone—"you may have fellowship with us"—no esoteric knowledge; fifth, in a desire "that our joy may be complete"—self-love safely follows the other two loves, love for God and others.

Here is a perfect ground for maturity. Take out any one item and you land in immaturity. Take out God from your attempt at maturity, and your maturity will be immaturity, for it will lack ultimate meanings. For if there is no God there is no goal, no goal no meaning, no meaning no value. Take out the revelation of God in Jesus and you have a vast question mark—God is the Great Enigma. If you take out personal realization of that revelation, then we have turned the Word made flesh into the Word made word—no personal experience. If you take out the desire to share this experience of God in Christ with others, you have an ingrown, festering type of human living—the esoteric knowledge become exhibitionist ignorance. If you take out the desire that our joy may be complete, you end with the one most concerned in all this—the self—out in the cold.

No, the five steps are all there and they are all necessary: God, Jesus, personal experience, sharing of that experience, and partaking of the joy of it personally. And they are all vital, none marginal. Is it any wonder that we have insisted on the fact of a *Christian* maturity—a maturity that is unique and that makes all other types look immature? For this maturity is grounded in ultimate Reality, with ultimate meanings and ultimate Resources behind it.

O Father, I thank Thee that my maturity has a mature basis—the sum total of Reality guarantees it. So I can let my full weight down. I am not following the precarious but the Permanent. I thank Thee, thank Thee. Amen.

AFFIRMATION FOR THE DAY: *The ground of my maturity is all laid. It is for me patiently to build on it day by day.*

WE DON'T BEGIN WITH GOD, BUT JESUS

We come now to another phase in John's unfolding of the life of Christian maturity. It is notable, both in his Gospel and in his Epistle, that John begins not with God but with Jesus—the Word. In the Gospel it is the "Word"; in the Epistle it is the "Word of Life." For he saw that the Word had become to him the "Word of Life," revealing the very nature of Life—the Life of God, of man, of his relationships, of nature, and the life that is to be. So he had to begin with Jesus. You cannot begin with your ideas of God, which are not God. Jesus is God's idea of Himself, presented in understandable form—human form. The Gospel begins with God: "God was in Christ reconciling the world to himself." But we can't begin with God, for if we do we will lose God in our maze of contradictory thought about Him.

A man belonging to a group with a Unitarian emphasis came to me and said: "Will you come to our convention and help us find God? We are drifting into a humanism." Here was a group specializing on God and losing Him, and here was I, specializing on Jesus and finding Him. That always happens. I was with a group, obviously sincere and dedicated, but in their services they read an essay on religion and then added what they desired from their own thinking. Hence they got their spiritual guidance from the thoughts of others—the essays they read—and from their own sharing of thoughts with one another. It was weak at the place of God's self-revelation in Jesus, and hence weak at the place of God. A little girl, in another situation, put her finger on this weakness when she said: "I don't want to go to this Sunday school where they talk about flowers and the stars and the moon. I want to go to the other Sunday school where they talk about Jesus."

So John, beginning with Jesus, could now come out with some unequivocal statements about God: "This is the message we have heard from him and proclaim to you, that God is light and in him is no darkness at all" (1:5).

O Jesus, since coming to Thee and through Thee, we can now come face to face with the Father. And what a face we see! We have seen His face in Thy face and we are satisfied and more than satisfied—we are at His feet forever. Amen.

AFFIRMATION FOR THE DAY: *God is light. I am in God. Therefore I shall be light in every situation.*

"NO DARKNESS AT ALL"

We saw yesterday that the mention of God was not made in the Epistle until the second and third verses, and not specifically until the fifth. The gospel was presented by Jesus—foremost and rightly. For in Jesus we see what God is like. So John bursts out with this: "God is light and in him is no darkness at all" (1:5).

That sounds commonplace to us now, but only because Jesus made that statement possible. You cannot say as you look up to God through nature that "God is light and in him is no darkness at all," for there are cruel spots in nature that throw a shadow of darkness upon God. In the Old Testament view of God there is the dark spot of vengefulness; in Vedantic Hinduism a spot of final impersonality; in popular Hinduism the spot of polytheism with contradictory ideas of God; in Islam the spot of God's autocracy; in Unitarianism the spot of haziness and uncertainty: in modern thought a spot of moral blur; in Buddhism a spot of doubt as to his existence. Everywhere spots of darkness, except in one place—the face of Jesus Christ. The God that I see there is light with "no darkness at all."

Jesus could say to His disciples: "you are already made clean by the word which I have spoken to you"; especially their view of God had been cleansed. And our view of God needs cleansing. In Malaya some people came at night and stole the Confucian idols from the temple. Why? To get the god's help in a thirty-six character lottery then going on! A man said to me: "If you will pray that I get the winning number in the Derby Race I will give you a share of the prize for your church." Some little girls were playing when a cloud came over the sun, and one said to the other: "That mean old God again, always spoiling our fun." The mother told the father what the little girl had said and then asked: "Where in the world did she get such an idea?" And then she added: "I made her say her prayers over ten times as punishment." Prayers as punishment! The mother was unconscious of her part in forming that idea of God! Turn your face away from Jesus and you turn toward the darkness—about God.

O Lord Jesus, Thy lips, Thy life, and Thy face have made God beautiful and tender and approachable. And now I come boldly and without question marks and I find God goes beyond my expectations. What a Father! And what a Son! Amen.

AFFIRMATION FOR THE DAY: *If I am to be light in every situation, then no darkness can be tolerated in me.*

FOUR THINGS ABOUT GOD

In this Epistle, John, looking at Jesus, says four things about God: God is Light (1:5); God is Law (2:3-5); God is Life (5:11); God is Love (4:8, 16). And we need these four things: light on the mystery of life; law for the guidance of life; life for the living of life; love for the redemption of life.

But the first thing we need is light. In Jesus we know where we are going—we know the Way. He said: "As long as I am in the world, I am the light of the world" (John 9:5). Jesus is light in every situation He is in. Take Him out of any situation and you stumble in half-lights, or worse—in darkness. Put Him in and He is light. Again and again in India, a Hindu official will say: "We have got to get the Christian spirit." One said: "We have to think out our problems from the Christian viewpoint." In every situation where Jesus was, He was the light of that situation. It is always so.

In Burma a woman was undercharged by the grocer, and she handed back some money. A woman standing nearby said to the grocer: "She must be a Christian." In India two women were asked by the Hindu doctor for the slips of paper given by the compounder. They replied that the compounder did not give them any. The compounder, on being called, asserted that he did give the slips. The Hindu doctor replied: "Go get those slips of paper. These women are Christian women, and don't you know that Christians never lie?" A little missionary boy awoke and found Hudson Taylor, who wore a long beard, in bed with him. He was frightened. He quickly asked Taylor: "Are you a Christian?" And when told that he was, the little boy replied: "Then it is all right." In every situation where Christ is, He is light.

The Christian spirit is the ultimate spirit. Where that spirit is, there is solution; where it is absent, there is confusion.

O Lord Jesus, we see Thee and we cannot rest this side of Thy blessed Maturity. In Thy face we have seen light and only light. And all else is darkness compared to Thy light. So in Thy light we see life. We walk the road of life with confidence. Amen.

AFFIRMATION FOR THE DAY: *I shall be light today because in every situation I will take the viewpoint of Jesus.*

GOD IS LIGHT ON FOUR THINGS

When you see God in the face of Jesus, then "God is light"—light on everything. When you lose Him you lose everything, and when you find Him you find everything.

God is light on these four things: (1) creation, (2) character, (3) conversion, (4) consummation. God is light on creation. He is light on the purpose of creation. Since God is love, it is the nature of love to create. For love wants beings with whom it can share that love. Parents create because they want children upon whom they can lavish their love and from whom they can receive love in return. God, the Heavenly Parent, is love, and therefore He wants children upon whom He can lavish His love and receive their love in return.

God is light on character. In Jesus we see the character of God. God couldn't do an un-Christlike thing and still be God. So Jesus is the key to the character of God and man. In Him we see what God is like and what we can be like. He sets the pattern of character for God and man. You can transfer to God every single quality of character in Jesus without lowering your idea of God. Lower your idea of God? You heighten it! For if God isn't like Jesus He isn't good. You ask me my definition of goodness; I do not add virtue to virtue—I point to Jesus. He is goodness. If God isn't like Jesus I'm not interested in God. If He is, then He can have my heart without qualification or reservation. Having seen the character of God in Jesus I now know here I must head in.

God is light on conversion. If God is light on character, when I look at my character and see His character in Jesus, then I know my character has to be changed. But how? In Jesus I see the door, the only door, through conversion. He said, "Except ye be converted. . . . ye shall not enter into the kingdom of heaven" (Matt. 18:3 KJV). There are just two classes of people—the converted and the unconverted—a division that really divides and the only division that really divides. And through Jesus He provides all the resources for conversion, a total conversion of the total person.

O God, Thou art light and only light. When we see Thee we see how to live and find in Thee resources to live by. Thy wonder overwhelms me. And yet lifts me to the highest heaven. Let me express my gratitude by my life every moment. Amen.

AFFIRMATION FOR THE DAY: *The really converted convert. I shall be a converting illustration that God is light on conversion.*

GOD IS LIGHT ON CONSUMMATION

We come now to the next thing upon which God is light. Upon the consummation. The world process is not moving with aimless feet. There is a goal for all created things and that goal has been revealed. It is nothing less than the coming of the kingdom of God on earth. The earth and everything in it has a destiny and that destiny is to be the scene of the kingdom of God. That gives meaning and dignity to everything and makes every act in every human being significant—it is for or against the New Order.

Without the light which God sheds upon the consummation, life is a dull, drab thing moving with leaden feet toward extinction. With it, we see the meaning of the statement of Paul: "For the creation waits with eager longing for the revealing of the sons of God; for the creation was subjected to futility, not of its own will but by the will of him who subjected it in hope; because the creation itself will be set free from its bondage to decay and obtain the glorious liberty of the children of God" (Rom. 8:19-21). So creation, too, is a part of redemption. But it cannot be redeemed until man is redeemed. For instance, an official of the Forestry Service said to me: "You cannot run the forests unless you apply Christian principles. For unless you do unto future generations as you would that they should do to you, your forests will never prosper. If you are selfish and exploit and cut down without replanting, then your forests will be ruined. And your fields will be ruined by floods from denuded hills." I look out upon mountainsides in these Himalayas where the people have cut off the leaves and branches of trees for their cattle, leaving stumps on denuded hillsides, entirely thoughtless of the future. Nature is stumped! So nature cries out in pain until the sons of God are revealed.

So God is light on creation, on character, on conversion, and on consummation. God is light when, and only when, you see that light in the face of Jesus.

O Father, we have seen in Thy Son everything we have wanted to know about Thee and Thy purposes. Now we are satisfied. We have seen. And yet forever unsatisfied. For we can never be fully satisfied till we wake in His likeness. Amen.

AFFIRMATION FOR THE DAY: *My harmony with nature shall come out of my harmony with nature's Creator.*

"SPIRIT IS GOOD, MATTER IS EVIL"

Yesterday's meditation brought us face to face with one of the most acute questions with which this Epistle deals—the question of the relation of matter and spirit.

The Gnostics had a simple answer. "Spirit is good, matter is evil." In order to save God to goodness, they propounded the idea that the world of matter was created by an inferior being, a demiurge, of doubtful character. For how could God, being good, create such an evil thing as matter? Concerning one of those who held this idea, it was said that "he was ashamed that he had a body." This, of course, created a lot of hypocrisy. For the Gnostic could say that the spirit was pure and unaffected by the body. Therefore, they could live in the lusts of the body without being affected by them.

The background of Hindu thought is similar. The world of matter is maya, or illusion. It is thrown out by the Creator as a magician throws out a world of illusion. You think it is real, but it isn't. So the thing to do is to get out of this world of illusion—the material—into the world of reality—the spiritual; to merge yourself into pure Spirit, into Brahman, the Impersonal Spirit. Redemption is redemption from samsara, the world order. On the way to that redemption you can be kindly to beings trapped in samsara, but the world order itself is subject to destruction. I listened to a very able Hindu swami expound on the subject of how the world of matter comes by projection from Brahma as a kind of *leela*, or sport, and how the devotee must turn his back on this world of matter and become a pilgrim of the Infinite. One of the pictures depicts three yellow-robed holy men turning their backs on the world and setting out to climb the mountains in search of the Infinite Spirit.

The sight of those three pilgrims with their backs toward the beholder, with only a bamboo staff in their hands, setting out to renounce the world, is indelibly fixed in my mind. How earnest and yet how erroneous!

O Father, Thy children, not seeing the face of Jesus, have misjudged Thee and Thy purposes. They have thought to find Thee where Thou art not—beyond the material. For Thou art on our dusty roads. There we will find Thee—in Jesus. Amen.

AFFIRMATION FOR THE DAY: *I cannot live beyond the material nor for the material; I will live through the material for something beyond.*

48

ONE DENIES, OTHER DEIFIES

We saw yesterday how both Gnosticism and Hinduism have coincided in their views of the material. Matter is evil or illusory. A sadhu said to me: "Please, sir, teach me how to get rid of my body. It is an enemy to my search for God."

If these systems make matter evil, then modern materialism, in both East and West, particularly the West, makes matter the only good. It is sought ardently as the only thing worthwhile. And a man's "worth" is counted in terms of his accumulation of material things. A new caste system is built up around accumulation. In one place I saw a sign up, "The Cadillac Club"—you could belong to it only if you owned a Cadillac. So the caste of the Cadillac is the highest caste in the kingdom of materialism. But the Cadillac is so common, particularly in Texas, that the next step is a club of the Two-Cadillac Owners. They are the super-Brahmins of materialism.

We can see how ridiculous this attitude may become, A Negro employee of a wealthy man was asked, after his employer's death, "How much did he leave?" And the Negro replied: "He left everything." You can't take it with you. A young man was telling his psychiatrist how he was contemplating suicide and that he had decided to take a tramcar to the edge of the city and, from there, a taxi to the place where he intended to destroy himself: "But I can't do that, for to take the taxi will be expensive." He smiled later at his hesitation to spend a few dollars more when he was about to leave everything material.

Someone has said: "Oh, Money, Money, Money, thou art health and life and peace; he that hath thee can rattle his pockets at the devil." Can he? Can he rattle his pockets at unhappiness, at sickness, at death? A Tamil proverb says: "Say *panum* (money) and a *penum* (corpse) will open its eyes."

But there must be an answer somewhere between saying that the material is nothing or that the material is everything. What is that answer? Has the revelation of God in Christ shed any light at this place?

We turn to Thee, Father, for light for the material, for we are embodied, not ghosts. We need guidance at the place where the shoe pinches—at the place of the material. And we believe that Jesus has that light, for He was the embodied. Amen.

AFFIRMATION FOR THE DAY: *The material can minister to me, but it shall not master me.*

49

"THE CHRISTIAN FAITH MOST MATERIALISTIC"

We turn now to see whether God is light in regard to the material. In the face of Jesus and from the lips of Jesus, we see that answer. And the answer is quite different from those of Gnosticism, Hinduism, and Buddhism, on one side, and modern materialism on the other.

First of all, the Christian answer is that God is creator. And when God looked upon the material universe, He saw that it was good—very good. Matter is the direct creation of God and has His stamp upon it. Moreover, the center of the Christian faith is the Incarnation, wherein the Divine Word becomes flesh—God becomes Man. If the material were evil, how could God become incarnate in it? "Lo, I came to do Thy will . . . a body Thou hast prepared me"—the will of God for the Divine Son of God was to be done in and through the body. The body was to be an instrument of redemption. Another fact: the kingdom of God is to come on earth:

> Thy kingdom come,
> Thy will be done
> On earth . . .

Therefore the earth, the world of material things, has a destiny. Its end is not to be an ash, but to be an instrument of God's plan.

The Christian faith is therefore the most materialistic of religions, as Bishop Temple has said—and rightly. It is the only religion that takes the material seriously. It works out its destiny amid material relations, and it is out to make a new earth as well as a new humanity. The spirit is not to be redeemed apart from the material, but through the material: and in the process the material is also to be redeemed.

The dividing place is not: spirit good and matter evil. The dividing place in moral values is at the place of the human will. Evil is to be found at one place and only one place—at the place of our moral choices. "There is nothing good but a good will; there is nothing bad but a bad will." We, as free human beings, are responsible and we are solely responsible. This is morally sound.

Dear Father, I thank Thee that when I inhabit a body I am not inhabiting an enemy, but an ally. My spirit and my body, made by Thee, are made for each other. Teach me the relationship and help me to work it out. Amen.

AFFIRMATION FOR THE DAY: *My body and my soul have one Master—Christ—and one objective—the Kingdom.*

"MATERIAL, AN ENEMY ALIEN"

We saw that God had created the material, and He created it for a purpose. It is not a magician's illusion which will be withdrawn at the will of the Divine Magician. It is not maya—illusion; it is matter—a reality. I do not say it is an ultimate reality, but it is real and a part of God's purpose and given to man as a part of his purpose; "And God blessed them, and God said to them, 'Be fruitful and multiply, and fill the earth and subdue it; and have dominion over . . . every living thing that moves upon the earth.' " Man was to work out his destiny in a material environment. It wasn't to master him; he was to master it. He was to take it up into his purposes and work out his destiny through it. In making the earth he was to make himself. God made the earth unfinished, an incomplete creation. He left certain things at loose ends. He created man and made him a creator to help God finish His creation. And in finishing creation, man would perfect himself. He would work on matter and matter would work on him. They would affect each other for good or ill.

If this is so, what is to be man's attitude toward the material? In Hinduism and in Gnosticism there is a repudiation of the material as an enemy alien. Paul puts the Gnostic position, and incidentally the Hindu position, in these words: "Why do you submit to regulations, 'Do not handle, Do not taste, Do not touch.' . . . These have indeed an appearance of wisdom in promoting rigor of devotion and self-abasement and severity to the body, but they are of no value in checking the indulgence of the flesh" (Col. 2:20-23). Here religion was presented as aloofness: Do not handle. Do not taste. Do not touch. But you cannot live and live aloof from the body and material things. If you try to, then the material which is put out at the door comes back by the window. The Muslims, fasting through the day during the month of Ramadan, feast at night. So night and day they are thinking of food! Out at the door, back by the window—and how! You must handle the material in God's way, or it will handle you.

O Father, help me to relate myself to the physical and help me to relate the physical to me. For we are made for each other. Teach us how to live together—on Thy basis and Thy plan. For if I miss Thy way I will miss my own. Amen.

AFFIRMATION FOR THE DAY: *My body and I will walk the ways of life together, in His Way, toward His ends.*

"RIGOR OF DEVOTION"

We have looked at the Gnostic and the Hindu way of dealing with the material—they try to reduce contacts. But to try to reduce contacts is to produce contacts—in thought. You are thinking all the time on how to reduce contacts—the material dominates your thought. Paul says that this method has an appearance of wisdom. It produces rigor of devotion, self-abasement, and severity to the body. But this wisdom is spiritual foolishness, for products of all three are wrong.

"Rigor of devotion" sounds spiritual and desirable, but its whole attitude is wrong. For it means that you try to climb to God by the ladder of devotion. It is your trying to merit God and His favor. It is based on your efforts rather than on God's gift. In Christianity we go to Him in devotion, because He has come to us in salvation. The devotion is an expression of our gratitude and of our longing to be in communion with Him.

A Hindu came to our Ashram at Sat Tal, India, and when he left he wrote me: "I expected to find you in great austerity of devotion, but instead I found you a God-intoxicated child of nature." Here in a nutshell we find the essential difference between the two systems of outlook and practice: Hinduism gains favors from God by the rigor of its devotions, wrings from heaven by its very rigor the boons heaven seems reluctant to give. Christianity tells us that God comes to us and offers us salvation as a gift. And when we take it we belong forever to the Giver. Our devotion becomes a fountain from within. And then we are God-intoxicated children of nature—natural, spontaneous, joyous. Instead of devotion's being an imposition (something imposed from without by duty) it is an exposition (something exposed from within by love).

Then, since you are natural, you increase your contacts with the material; for all those contacts are an expression of love and appreciation. It is all yours, for you are His.

O Father, since I belong to Thee, everything belongs to me. Nothing is alien to me if it is made by Thy hand. For the material is shot through and through with Thee. I love it, for I love Thee more than it. I love Thee wholly. Amen.

AFFIRMATION FOR THE DAY: *My spiritual life is supreme; my material life is subordinate. We get along well.*

"SELF-ABASEMENT"

We have seen how Gnosticism of yesterday and Hinduism of today insist on "rigor of devotion, self-abasement, and severity to the body." We have looked at "rigor of devotion"; we must now look at "self-abasement." That, too, sounds spiritual—has "an appearance of wisdom."

Christianity teaches not self-abasement, but self-surrender. Self-abasement means self–debasement. The self is the gift of God and was never intended to be debased. It is an insult to the Creator to treat His gifts with contempt. Self-hate is as bad as other-hate. Self-abasement is man's attempt to destroy the self in order to replace it by the Self. As if God should desire to sit enthroned on the ruins of the self, a self which He made! That kind of God would be a monster devouring His own offspring.

No, Christianity, in teaching self-surrender, leads us to self-realization. For in losing one's self in surrender, it is found—found a different and enhanced self. It is given back to us—heightened. It is cleansed from a thousand conflicts and contradictions by surrender, and then it is given back again unified. Yourself is never so much your own as when it is most His. Bound to Him it is free. Since it is His, it is yours. You can live with God; therefore you can live with yourself. But if you won't live with God, by refusal to surrender to Him, you can't live with yourself. I asked a group at the Ashram at Sat Tal if one can live with a self-centered person, and a Hindu replied: "For a few days." The veneer of outer politeness rubs thin, and the essential egotism shows through. But surrendered to Him you can live, and live forever, with yourself, and so can others. "I wouldn't want to live with myself forever," said a skeptic. No wonder! But if you love God supremely, you can love yourself subordinately. Love yourself—and like yourself and enjoy yourself. For it is a self accepted by Him and therefore accepted by you. The renounced self becomes, strangely enough, the realized self.

O Father God, I thank Thee that Thou hast not given me a self only to cancel it out. But out of gratitude I lovingly yield it back to the Giver. And now it is mine because wholly Thine. This freedom in Thee—it is bliss for evermore. Amen.

AFFIRMATION FOR THE DAY: *Myself, not canceled but consecrated, is now free—free to live and serve.*

EGO—WILLINGLY CRUCIFIED, OR UNWILLINGLY?

We are meditating on "self-abasement and severity to the body." Paul knew the secret of dealing with the self. It is in this passage: "I have been crucified with Christ; it is no longer I who live, but Christ who lives in me; and the life I now live in the flesh I live by faith in the Son of God, who loved me and gave himself for me" (Gal. 2:20).

Here the essential ego is not suppressed and hated and debased. It is offered up lovingly as Jesus offered Himself on the cross as a sacrifice—"who loved me and gave himself for me." The offering was out of love. Our offering of ourselves to be crucified with Him is out of the same love. We love him so much that we can withhold nothing from Him, not even the very self.

But if you don't willingly consent to be crucified with Christ, then you unwillingly crucify yourself through its own conflicts and contradictions. So it is crucifixion—willing or unwilling. The unwilling crucifixion has no resurrection in it—it is death and only death. But the willing crucifixion has a resurrection in it. We die with Him and rise with Him. I recently received a letter from a European turned Hindu ascetic. He signs himself "Sunya Bhai" (literally, "Brother of Emptiness"); he had emptied himself into nothingness. The Christian empties himself into fullness—the very fullness of God. But my brother above had reduced life to that of a vegetable and called it victory. He has lived alone in the Himalayas in meditation for many years—does nothing but meditate, and vegetate. You can see that he hates his ego and would destroy it, and that he has nearly succeeded. He has been in our Ashram for several weeks at a time, and, after saying scarcely a word during such a period, he will say good-by and add: "I've shared with you my silence"—and his emptiness.

But after being crucified with Christ, Paul was more alive than ever—alive to his fingertips: "Nevertheless I live"—and how! For Christ who is Life was now living within him, heightening all his powers, putting a plus to everything, setting him atingle with Life.

O Master of my heart, I give Thee the one and only thing I own, myself, and find that self mine again, no longer a conflict-self, but a concord-self. I can live with it, because I can live with Thee. I thank Thee, thank Thee. Amen.

AFFIRMATION FOR THE DAY: *Anyone nailed to the cross willingly, walks the earth free.*

"MADAM, ARE YOU RELIGIOUS?"

We are meditating on being crucified with Christ and yet living, and living to the full.

Look how contradictory Paul's statement seems: "crucified" . . . "live" . . . "yet not I" . . . "but Christ lives within me" . . . "the life I now live." He is talking death and life in the same breath—Christ and himself in the next breath. Life was now flowing into life so amazingly that he couldn't tell where he ended and Christ began, and where Christ ended and he began. They were interfused but not confused; they were separate and yet one!

In the marginal reading of John 1:4 is this: "That which has been made was life in him." That is an important statement and far-reaching. All created things, when surrendered to Him, become life in Him. They become life only when surrendered to Him. They pass from existence to life by surrender. Anything that is *in itself* is existence; anything that is *in Him* is life. Our money in itself is existence and perishes with all existing things, but our money in Him becomes life. It is alive and it creates life, opens opportunity for others, creates new hopes and new lives. Our influence in itself is existence—non-creative and ineffectual—but our influence in Him becomes creative, effectual, and makes alive everything it touches. Our words in themselves are existence—mere words—but in Him they are life. They are living and life-giving, winging their way to the needs of others. Our very faces in themselves are existence—deadpan existence—uninspiring and unilluminated; but in Him they are life—they glow with glory and shine with the Spirit. A redcap came up to "Mary," took off his hat, and held it on his arm for a while. Then he said: "Madam, excuse me, but are you religious?" And she replied: "Well, I love Jesus." And he replied, "I thought so." Her face was life in Him. Our very self, the ego, in itself is existence—no contagion, no creation: but in Him the self becomes life, creating life in place of dead hopes, courage out of fears, newborn souls out of mere existence.

O Lord Jesus, I pass from existence to life when I pass from unsurrender to surrender. I want to live fully so I pass fully, nothing left behind. Now I am no longer mere existence; I am life, life, life in Thee forevermore. Amen.

AFFIRMATION FOR THE DAY: *Nothing connected with me shall be mere existence. It shall be life, because of Him.*

"BECAME LIFE IN HIM"

We said yesterday that "that which has been made became life in Him"—existence turned to life when it was placed in Him by surrender. This means total existence. For by the Incarnation, Jesus redeemed the whole world process. He came into matter—the Word was made flesh; and now the world process is not to be deserted but to be dedicated. The whole material process becomes sacramental—you see God through it, you love God through it, and you serve God through it. Then your universe becomes life. It is vibrant with meaning and purpose and goal and destiny. This earth of ours is to be the scene of the coming of the kingdom of God—"May thy kingdom come . . . on earth." Events are not moving with goalless feet. They are moving toward His Kingdom—or they destroy themselves.

This hopefulness toward the material is important. For you cannot throw yourself behind schemes and movements for human advancement unless you really believe in life and really believe in life here amid material human conditions. As long as you look on the material process as illusion, or maya, you will have an inner hesitation to back schemes for human betterment. That inner hesitation will lay a dead hand on all your endeavor for a better world. Your inner philosophy works itself out as outer fact. For this reason, as long as India really believed that the world process was maya, or illusion, all reforms were haltingly backed. Only as this philosophy is quietly being laid aside do reforms really go on. It is no mere chance that there is no department of philosophy in the Madras University, for there are no students to take philosophy—they all want science. And yet Madras is the home of Indian Philosophy. Why this neglect? The students know instinctively that you can't make a new India out of a philosophy which says that the world process is maya, or illusion.

Only in an atmosphere of Christian faith and hopefulness in the world process can reforms flourish and be sustained.

O Father, Thou art the Creator and Thou wilt help us to be the recreators of the world process. We have pulled that world process down through our wrong attitudes. Help us to pull it up by regaining Thy attitudes. Help us to dedicate the material to Thee. Amen.

AFFIRMATION FOR THE DAY: *I shall go into everything today with a faith that everything can be changed, for God wills it.*

THE MORAL AND SPIRITUAL BECOME ONE

We come now to a further step in maturity—Christian maturity. We have seen that in the Incarnation the material and the spiritual were made a living whole. The words of Browning sum up this, words which could have been written only from a Christian background:

Let us not always say, "Spite of this flesh today
I strove, made head, gained ground upon the whole!"
As the bird wings and sings, let us cry, "All good things
Are ours, nor soul helps flesh more, now, than flesh helps soul!"

This is maturity of attitude regarding the material and the spiritual. The next step is inevitable—the putting together of the moral and the spiritual and making them one. The Gnostics, with all their supposed superior enlightenment, were really immature, in that they thought they could live in fellowship with God and be unaffected by the morality or immorality of their material relations. They affected to despise matter as evil and then took the attitude that living in contact with evil matter did not affect their pure spirituality. They could do as they liked on the material plane, and it did not disturb or affect their life in the spirit. This was immaturity of a very important kind, for it separated religion and morality—compartmentalized the spiritual and the moral. This made for very high pretensions with very low practice— supposed high spirituality and low sensuality. But in spite of all the rationalizing in defense of this position, it produced an inner conflict. A man who tries this becomes a debate with himself, trying to make the morally wrong into the spiritually right. No mature character can grow out of this soil: its fruit is immaturity and always immaturity.

So John points a dart at this whole attitude: "If we say we have fellowship with him while we walk in darkness, we lie and do not live according to the truth" (I John 1:6). Here John announced an important truth: Morality is rooted in the very nature of God and you cannot be in fellowship with Him without being moral.

O my Father, I see that I cannot walk in spiritual light and moral darkness at one and the same time. I must make my choice. I choose light—spiritual light and moral light as one and indivisible. I thank Thee for this. Amen.

AFFIRMATION FOR THE DAY: *May my religion and my morals be like the words and music of a song—intertwined, one.*

MORALITY ROOTED IN NATURE OF GOD

We noted yesterday that it is immature to think that we can live in two opposite worlds at once—a world of pure spirituality and a world of impure sensuality. Those who try it end in inner conflict and consequent debate.

In the Christian view, morality is rooted in the nature of God, not merely in the will of God. Many think that God arbitrarily decides certain things to be right and certain things to be wrong and issues commands accordingly. These commands are based on the arbitrary will of God, and hence are not to be questioned—they are to be obeyed.

Nothing is further from the Christian position. For in Jesus we see revealed a God who does everything which He commands us to do. He obeys His own laws of right and wrong. For those laws are the transcript of His own character. He commands them, for He does them—does them because they are inherently right. That bases morality not on the whim of God, but on the very character of God. It makes the universe of morality one and indivisible for God and man. And it makes it possible to love and obey a God who illustrates in His own character and life everything He expects us to do. He is not a cosmic fingerpost, pointing the direction to confused humanity; He is a Shepherd who "goes before" His sheep and "leads them." He initiates nothing that He doesn't illustrate. That kind of God can have my wholehearted allegiance and my wholehearted love.

When George Washington found that his troops at Trenton had no shelter except cold tents in winter, he refused to live in the house reserved for his headquarters, choosing instead to live in a tent also until his troops got better quarters. No wonder they loved and followed a man like that! I cannot be a moral follower of an immoral God. My universe must be one if I am to be one. I must act, knowing that the sum total of reality is behind my acting.

O God, my Father, I thank Thee that when I look into the face of Jesus I see there a consistent God. This gives me a universe that holds together—is one. I can act, for Thou art acting with me. We are working life out together. Amen.

AFFIRMATION FOR THE DAY: *Since morality is rooted in God, it shall be rooted in me—an integral part of me.*

"TRUE IN HIM AND IN YOU"

In this Epistle, John distills into a sentence important truths, none more important than this one: "Yet I am writing you a new commandment, which is true in him and in you" (2:8). The phrase "true in him and in you" reveals the very heart of the Christian revelation. For whatever is true for God is true for us, and whatever is true for us is true for God. If God is light, then God is also law. And His laws are good and are good for us. God couldn't will anything but our highest good and still be God. These laws are good for God and hence good for us.

> By all that God requires of me,
> I know what He Himself must be.

His very laws are light upon the nature of God. Through them I see His very intention for Himself and me. He shows that He believes that to act in a certain way is good for everybody, including Himself.

If this be true, then morality is important. When you violate the laws of morality, you violate the very nature of God and of the universe. And you violate your own nature. We have mentioned that the prodigal son saw this when returning from the far country. He said: "I have sinned against heaven," the impersonal moral universe; "and before you," against the personal love of his father; and "am no longer worthy to be called your son," against his own sonship, against himself. He saw with profound insight that morality was not merely a convention built up by mores and customs. It was not built up—it was built into the very nature of things. He saw that you could not break these laws without breaking the heart of God. Sin, then, is serious—serious to God, to the universe, and to you. And morality is serious—serious to God, to the universe, and to you. It matters how we act. It effects everything, everywhere.

O Gracious Father, I thank Thee that I see a universe which is not indifferent to my virtue and my vice—it takes sides. And I'm glad it does take sides, for I cannot be morally earnest in a morally indifferent universe. I thank Thee. Amen.

AFFIRMATION FOR THE DAY: *As my moral universe is committed, so am I. We work for the same ends.*

"RIGHT IS RIGHT, EVERYWHERE AND ETERNALLY"

This linking of religion and morality is important, both for religion and for morality. There can be no real religion without morality, and there can be no real morality without religion; for both are rooted in the ultimate fact of the universe—God.

That fact saves us from the shifting sands of relativism in morals. Right is right, and right everywhere and eternally; and the wrong is wrong, and wrong everywhere and eternally. For God, in whom our morality inheres, is not different from place to place and from time to time. This rooting of our morality in the nature of God, and not in the arbitrary will of God, gives us a stable moral universe.

William Graham Cole, in *Sex in Christianity and Psychoanolysis,* has this to say in reference to the Kinsey report on the sex morals of America:

The assumption is that a new set of norms is to be produced by a statistical analysis of the prevailing practices. It would seem that society ought to define its norms in terms of what is typical. All that is needed in the future for moral standards is an accurate Gallup poll, indeed a triumph of scientific civilization! "Here we have the modern sociological approach to the problem of norms reduced to its final absurdity."

An able doctor, reviewing the Kinsey report, asks the relevant question, Does the fact that most people have colds in the winter establish colds as "normative"? And Niebuhr regards the so-called scientific attitude toward sex as represented in the Kinsey reports and the reception accorded them, as a symptom of a disease far more serious than the sickness it seeks to cure.

It is a fact that if you lose God—the kind of God revealed in the face of Jesus Christ—you lose your moral universe with that loss of God. Everything, then, is relative. Nothing is stable or fixed, and with this looseness comes a looseness of morals, and with that a decaying civilization.

O God, our Father, we are grateful that Thou art, and that Thou art moral and that Thou dost act upon everything Thou dost require of us. We can and do love and respect a God like that. We thank Thee that Thou art the Great Illustration. Amen.

AFFIRMATION FOR THE DAY: *I shall not be guided in moral questions by custom, but by Christ.*

ONE STANDARD FOR GOD AND MAN

We are meditating on the statement in the Epistle, that the new commandment "is true in him and in you," that Christian morality, when it is truly Christian, is a transcript of the nature of God. But this can be said only of the Christian revelation of God.

The law of karma—the vast and majestic system of the law of sowing and reaping—built up within Hinduism is not rooted in the nature of the highest god, Brahman. This system of rewards and punishments is independent of Brahman, for he, or rather it, is lifted up above all qualities of being. Brahman is morally neuter. Morality has no divine sanctions, for Brahman is not moral, nor is it immoral—it is amoral. This gives no moral leadership to the universe. The universe is without a moral head. And therefore morality does not ultimately matter, for in Brahman it is transcended.

I asked a Hindu sadhu, or holy man, why he drank bhang, the Indian marijuana. He replied: "It makes me see God." "It makes you drunk," I replied. "No," he answered, "an ordinary man like you it makes drunk, but me—it makes me see God." God was not found on the moral plane, but on the plane of the magical. Morality didn't enter into it.

Pointing to some lewd frescoes on a temple, I said to a priest: "Do these frescoes help you in your moral and spiritual life?" He replied: "You have to be very strong if you come to this temple; otherwise, you will go out and do the same as these gods do." Morality was not rooted in the gods. "To the strong there is no blame," is a saying referring to the gods—they are outside of morality.

To the Christian, the same laws of morality apply to God and man alike and equally. God couldn't do an un-Christlike thing and still be God. The universe has a moral Head, and a moral Head after the pattern of the highest moral standard known— Christlikeness. There are no dual standards of conduct for God and man, for man or woman. The norm is Christ.

O Father God, how grateful I am that I am not confused by Thy word and by Thy example! For Thy words and Thy example are one. For whatever Thou dost command by Thy words, Thou dost commend by Thy acting. I thank Thee. Amen.

AFFIRMATION FOR THE DAY: *Since my universe, my God, my Christ, are all morally dependable, I, too, shall be morally dependable.*

THE STANDARD OF CHRISTLIKENESS

The Christian has the only mature conception of the moral universe—a moral universe that is valid for God and man according to the highest standard of morality, the standard of Christlikeness. Hence Christian moral character is the highest moral character known or conceivable. It is emerging as the standard of conduct for all men. A Hindu said to me, in relation to the attitude he was taking toward a Mohammedan: "I hope I was taking the Christian attitude toward him in this matter." A Hindu talking about his Christian attitude toward his Mohammedan friend! Mixed, but illuminating!

A Hindu governor said to a Hindu doctor working in a leper colony: "You are doing a real piece of Christian service here." Also mixed, but illuminating.

In a book entitled *This I Believe*, containing the testimony of one hundred leading men and women on their faith, Wallace Stegner says: "I cannot say that I am even a sound Christian, though the code of conduct to which I subscribe was preached more eloquently by Jesus Christ than by any other. About God I do not know; I don't think I can know." Here was a skeptical mind fastening itself upon one certain thing in a world of uncertainty—upon the morality preached by Jesus. But he was this side of the morality of Jesus when he said "was preached more eloquently . . . than by any other." The morality of Jesus was not merely preached more eloquently, but illustrated more perfectly than by any other. In Him the word of morality became flesh. He didn't *preach* morality—He *was* morality. In Him you didn't hear so much about goodness, as you saw goodness. The word of goodness took shoes and walked; so that now when I think of goodness, I do not add virtue to virtue, but I think of Jesus of Nazareth. His morality is not hard and forbidding—it is winsome and appealing; for His morality was rooted in love and permeated by love—it was love in action. Therefore it does not drive—it draws. Morality looks at us with tender eyes, touches us with warm redemptive hands, and hence shakes us like a passion.

O Jesus, we see in Thee the revelation of what God is like and what we can and must be like if we are to live. We know now where we must head in. We know that He is no longer a lawgiver. He Himself is our very Code. Amen.

AFFIRMATION FOR THE DAY: *Since morality is personalized in Jesus, it will be personalized in me.*

"COME TO TERMS, OR GET HURT"

Individuals and nations will of necessity remain morally immature until they come to see and accept the most absolutely mature morality, namely that which was practiced and preached by Jesus. For Jesus was not a moralist, imposing a moral code upon humanity. He was a revealer of the nature of reality. He revealed the nature of God and the nature of the laws underlying the universe. He lifted them up out of the heart of reality. He seldom used the imperative, almost never the subjunctive, almost entirely the indicative. He kept saying: "This is, and you must come to terms with it or get hurt."

If morality is something imposed upon man by the authority of God, then it produces rebellion. But if morality is something exposed from the heart of reality, then it produces repentance and reformation. It is inescapable. You become moral, not from pressures without but from pressures within—a free man's morality. Christian morality is the most beautiful thing upon our planet. When you see it—really see it—the quest is over. You either fight it, or you succumb to it. But this is it! And there is no other.

Since our standard of morality is no longer a code, but a Character—the character of Jesus Christ—then this becomes no longer a static, rigid set of rules—it becomes an unfolding standard. It is fixed, but it is unfolding. The more you see, the more you see there is to be seen. The Christian knows deep down that he never is; he is only becoming. The best of us are only Christians-in-the-making. For this Character is constantly unfolding before our astonished face. And it does not bludgeon us into goodness; it beckons us into goodness. Our hearts are set on fire with desire to be like that which we see in Jesus. For He is It! There never was and there never can be another. If we are good according to Him, we are good. If we are not good according to Him, we are not good. And the highest product of moral and spiritual living is a Christlike man. There is no higher.

O Jesus, how can I thank Thee enough. I am at Thy feet. I see Thee and I'm forever spoiled for anything other or anything less. Thou art my Savior and Thou art my Standard. Beyond Thee I cannot go, nor do I want to. Amen.

AFFIRMATION FOR THE DAY: *My standard of conduct is fixed; my choice of conduct is open.*

MATURITY IN MORALITY NECESSARY

We have seen that the Christian conception of maturity includes, especially, maturity in morality. It knows nothing of trying to bypass morality in its attempt to reach intellectual, emotional, and spiritual maturity. That which is not moral is not mature. If you leave out morality you let in inner conflict, and if there is inner conflict there is no maturity. The amoral attitude of much of modern psychology is a breeder of much immaturity, both in the psychologist and in his adherents. This is a moral universe where we get results or we get consequences. If you work with the moral universe you get results. It will back you, sustain you and further you, approve of you; you will have cosmic backing for your way of life. If you work against the moral universe you will get consequences. You will be up against an imponderable something you can't go past. You will be frustrated and in outer and inner conflict. Some people go through life getting results; others get consequences.

Morality must be built into the structure of maturity or else it is immaturity, however intellectual and spiritual it pretends to be. This kind of modern so-called maturity takes its place alongside of Gnostic maturity—an attempt to belong to the "illuminated" spiritually while living in disregard to basic moral laws. Just as Gnostic maturity perished by its moral immaturity, likewise much of modern psychological maturity will perish by its moral immaturities.

Christian maturity is mature in the highest morality—a morality based upon the character of Jesus Christ. Hence, being sound at the core, it will survive all so-called maturities based on moral immaturities. Gnosticism broke itself upon the moral universe, and all other systems based on the same fallacies will do the same. The moral universe will not approve of amoral or immoral maturity. Maturity that isn't moral maturity is immaturity pure and simple. The Christian conception of maturity is maturity pure and simple—the highest maturity conceivable.

O Jesus, Thou hast redeemed us and our standards of redemption. For as we see Thee, our thoughts, our emotions, our characters, rise. We cannot really see Thee without this happening. So our very conception of maturity becomes mature. Amen.

AFFIRMATION FOR THE DAY: *Morality shall be built into my maturity as a watermark is built into paper.*

FELLOWSHIP, THE STARTING POINT

After having made morality central in the Christian conception of maturity, we are ready for the next step, and a very important one: "But if we walk in the light, as he is in the light, we have fellowship with one another, and the blood of Jesus his Son cleanses us from all sin" (I John 1:7). Christian maturity is based on fellowship—fellowship with God, fellowship with "one another," and fellowship with one's own self. It is based on fellowship.

If morality were based on the commandments of God rather than on communion with God, it would be hard, legalistic, unattractive morality. But based as it is on fellowship with God, its special characteristic is love. Hence the maturity is moral, but it is a winsome morality. It loves the immoral without standing over them as a frowning Sinai, saying, "Thou shalt," and "Thou shalt not." Its morality is based on "Father, forgive them; for they know not what they do."

Some conceptions of morality can be egocentric: this is good for me; this isn't good for me. Such a conception is based on egocentric calculations. Therefore, it lives in a state of self-reference, is self-conscious and hence self-righteous, hence unattractive. But when morality is based on fellowship with God, it is theocentric; is living in a state of God-reference; is moral by contagion and not by command; is winsome, being based on love to God and love to man. Nygren says:

Now it is just in respect of this question that Christianity makes a revolutionary change; for Christianity consistently makes fellowship the starting-point for ethical discussion. . . . The meaning of this question [about where morality is based] must clearly vary according as the centre of gravity in the religious relationship is placed in man's ego or in the Divine: in the former case we get an egocentric, in the latter a theocentric religion.

Doing things because I am interested in myself produces a certain kind of character; doing things beause I am in fellowship with God and because of love to Him produces another kind of character.

O God, my Father, I thank Thee that Thou art the source and the fountain of all my desire for maturity. I have felt Thy love and I cannot stand now to be unloving. I have tasted Thy goodness and I cannot be less than good. Amen.

AFFIRMATION FOR THE DAY: *Since my morality is based on fellowship with God, it will be not legal but loving.*

"SUCH DIRT, DUST, AND DEBRIS!"

We are considering maturity based on fellowship. Without this maturity based on fellowship, there is simply no maturity at all. For maturity is a capacity for fellowship. The immature person has retreated in on himself, has withdrawn his relationships, and has become self-preoccupied, and hence by that very fact immature. Your capacity for fellowship gauges your maturity. You are mature to the degree, and only to the degree, that you can fellowship with God, with others, with yourself.

The center of the result of sin is estrangement—estrangement from God, from others, from yourself. Sin is not breaking a law; it is the breaking of a fellowship. The moment one sins there is a sense of orphanage, of estrangement, of being alone with one's guilt, of being out of harmony, of being underground. And on the other hand, the moment one is redeemed from sin there is a sense of fellowship with God, with one's fellows, and with one's self. This letter was received yesterday:

The Lord Jesus came and got into the car with me. He just moved right on into my heart. He took His broom and began to sweep. Such dirt, dust, and debris! There was resentment, impatience, ambitions, and all their clan. For the first time in my life I was clean. . . . All the people of my life came up before me and I loved them as I had never loved them before. I found myself saying, "It doesn't matter, it doesn't matter." Then there came wave after wave of pure joy into my heart and overflowing it until I felt drenched with it. . . . I am at one with myself, God, and my fellow man. . . . I feel like a man who has been suffering from a split personality suddenly become one man. For five months now this wonderful joy and love have lived with me constantly.

A self-centered, calculating, trying-hard type of attempted maturity could never produce that kind of spontaneous love for everybody—God, man, and himself—and especially himself. For you simply cannot love or fellowship with an egocentric self. It just cannot be done.

O God, our Father, we see that our maturity is based on fellowship and that fellowship is based on grace. So we turn to Thy grace. But to receive Thy grace we have to be humble and receptive, to be self-surrendered. I am. Amen.

AFFIRMATION FOR THE DAY: *Since I am not outside of God's fellowship, no one shall be outside of mine.*

"BUT"

We have seen that at the basis of Christian maturity is fellowship. The immature have withdrawn their fellowship, have retreated inside themselves, are walled-in persons. The problem is to get them out from behind those closed doors and to get them to be outgoing, giving and receiving fellowship and love. How is this to be done? The answer of John is simple: "But if we walk in the light, as he is in the light, we have fellowship with one another, and the blood of Jesus his Son cleanses us from all sin."

Some leading men were asked to name the saddest word, in their opinion, in the English language. One answered, "hopelessness"; another, "atheism"; another, "unloved"; another, "vacuum"; another, "but." That word "but" can be the saddest word—"I have this—but." On the other hand it can be the gladdest word, as here: "*But* if we walk in the light . . . we have fellowship." Here the word "but" is not linked with loss, but with gain; not with disintegration, but with integration. It is God's redemptive "but" interposed into our estrangement—our estrangement from God, man, ourselves, and nature. That word "but" takes us by the hand to lead us from darkness to light, from ourselves to God. The "but" becomes the most hopeful word in the language. You are immature—but! You are in inner conflict—but! You are ineffective—but! You are a completely dissatisfied person—but! You are a half-man—but! You are unredeemed—but!

And the condition is simple: "Walk in the light, as he is in the light." What does that mean? If it means anything it means this: To have fellowship with God, man, and yourself, you don't have to be good, or mature, or worthy, or acceptable, or lovable—you have only to "walk in the light, as he is in the light." You have only to take the next steps—the next steps of willing to be good, of willing to be mature, of willing to be worthy and acceptable and lovable. You have only to be willing; He does the rest. You supply the willingness and He supplies the power. That puts the latchstring where anybody, everybody can reach it.

O Jesus, my Lord, I thank Thee that Thou has made everything possible for the impossible. Maturity, then, is not a long struggle uphill; it is a gift before it is a growth. I cannot produce the growth, but I can take the gift. Amen.

AFFIRMATION FOR THE DAY: *My maturity is based on my receptivity, so today every pore of my being shall be open.*

WALKING IN THE LIGHT—FOUR STEPS

We say yesterday that the condition for fellowship is simple: "Walk in the light." To walk in the light means to take the first steps, and those first steps are four: reversal, sin- and self-surrender, faith, and obedience. First, reversal. You have been going in the wrong direction—turn around. You have been walking on not-the-Way. Now put your feet—both feet—upon the Way. Reversal is repentance. Second, sin- and self-surrender. You cannot carry any of the old darkness with you as you walk in this "light." And you don't need to clench your teeth, double up your fists, and fight with your sins. That is self-defeating. All you have to do is to be willing to surrender them. Mind you, just to be willing—He does the rest. You offer the willing heart; He offers the willing hand. But it is not enough to let the sin go. You must be willing to let the self behind the sin go. The sins are a symptom; the unsurrendered self is the disease. Until we have let that go we have really let nothing go. If the center of immaturity is making yourself God—trying to organize the universe around you as the center—then the center of maturity is to cease to be an egocentric person and to become a God-centric person. That can come only by self-surrender. The self is the one and only thing we own. We can decide who owns that one thing—God or the ego. The moment we say, "God owns it," then it is done. You, the essential you, is off your own hands into the hands of God.

Third, faith. Faith is simple receptivity. Since you have emptied your hands in the last step, you can take the gift—the gift of fellowship with God. It's free—to the receivers! It's all there—tune in! Faith is welcoming that which you believe in. You have believed in it—now welcome it. It's yours.

Fourth, obedience. Since you are His, He has the final say in your life. And His "say" is your "way." When you do His will, you do your own deepest will.

These are your four steps into light and freedom. And they are as simple as breathing, and as effective. Try it. It works.

O Jesus, I cannot walk in the light unless Thou dost take my hand. I give it to Thee. Hold it, for I cannot hold Thine. But one thing Thou hast—my complete willingness. So I'm beginning to walk in the light. We're off—together. Amen.

AFFIRMATION FOR THE DAY: *I reverse every wrong, surrender every ounce of me, believe with every part of me, and obey with everything I've got.*

HIS LIGHT, APPROACHABLE LIGHT

There is a consideration which is important: "as he is in the light." Just how is Jesus "in the light"? Is it a blinding light which you cannot approach? On the contrary, His light was the light so approachable that the worst were drawn to Him. It was a light that lighted the sinner out of darkness but didn't blind him in the process. It is true that Paul seemed the exception, for he was blinded by that flash of light on the road to Damascus. But his blindness was caused by what psychology calls conversion, the conversion of a spiritual symptom into a physical one. He was dumbfounded to find that in the persecution of the Christians he was persecuting the Lord: "Saul, Saul, why do you persecute me?" "Who are you, Lord?" "I am Jesus, whom you are persecuting." In that stunning moment Paul's whole life structure crashed; he had been deeply, darkly mistaken. All his values had been reversed in a moment. He was spiritually blind, and that spiritual blindness was transferred to the physical. When he saw the divine forgiveness through a human forgiveness in Ananias' revealing words "Brother Saul," he saw the way out—forgiveness and reconciliation! When he saw the way out spiritually, "something like scales fell from his eyes," and he was physically sound again. The spiritual and the physical were one.

But apart from the Saul-on-the-Damascus-Road episode, the light in which Jesus walks is not a light that blinds and blisters, but a light that blesses and only blesses. We are drawn to it and not driven by it. It is a "light" that reveals to the sinner, not only the sins of the past and the present, but the possibilities of the future. It was a "light" to which publicans and harlots and sinners in general were drawn. It was a "kindly light" amid their encircling gloom. The Bhagavad-Gita says that God incarnates Himself from the age to age "to establish righteousness, to save the righteous and punish the wicked." The "light" that was in Jesus was not to punish the wicked—they were already punished by their very wickedness—but to save them.

O Jesus, I thank Thee for Thy "light." It doesn't blind me into goodness, but beckons me. And I follow—follow with the consent of all my being. For this "light" fits me as physical light fits my eye. So I gladly respond. I thank Thee. Amen.

AFFIRMATION FOR THE DAY: *My religion approachable, my morality winsome, my feelings tender.*

THE END IS FELLOWSHIP

The verse we are considering says: "But if we walk in the light, as he is in the light, we have fellowship one with another." We would have expected the account to say: "But if we walk in the light, as he is in the light, we have forgiveness" for all the dark past. Forgiveness is there, but the emphasis is not on forgiveness; it is on the fellowship which is the result of that forgiveness. Forgiveness clears the way; it is a means, but not an end. The end is fellowship.

The fellowship with God in Christianity is unique. In all other faiths, barring none, fellowship with God is to be found, so they say, at the top of a long ladder. Step by step you purify yourself, and at the topmost rung you are worthy of fellowship with God. Since you merit it, you meet it. You fellowship with God on His level. In the Christian faith you do not meet God at the topmost rung of the ladder, but at the bottommost. We do not climb to Him; He comes down to us. We do not meet God at His level; He meets us at our level. "This man receives sinners!" was the scandalized cry of the religious leaders of His day. They felt that God loves the righteous and the righteous only. Here was Jesus saying that He "came not to call the righteous, but sinners." This reversed all the values of antiquity. And it reverses all the values of the present. It is breath-taking and precedent-smashing. How could it happen? Only on one basis: the fellowship is not based on our merit, but on His! We cannot claim any merit of our own, for we have none and we needn't have any. We can claim His worthiness as the basis for our fellowship—and only His worthiness. There is no other basis.

And note: "We have fellowship one with another." Who is this "one with another"? Is it with Christ, a divine fellowship; or is it with one another, a human fellowship? Or is it both? It is both! For the moment you come into fellowship with Christ you come into fellowship with others—automatically. They are two sides of one coin.

O Father, at one stroke Thou dost break down the barriers between Thee and me and between me and others. And the stroke is the stroke of love. Only love could do that. I marvel at it and I do more: I accept it with the deepest gratitude possible. Amen.

AFFIRMATION FOR THE DAY: *No barriers between God and me, between my brother and me, and between me and me.*

IMMATURITY—LITTLE CAPACITY FOR FELLOWSHIP

We pause another week to look at fellowship as an accompaniment of maturity. The immature are immature just because they have little capacity for fellowship, and the mature are mature just because they do have capacity for fellowship. When one is driven in on himself by fears, resentments, inhibitions, self-preoccupations, and guilt, then fellowship becomes impossible, and hence maturity becomes impossible. The shut-in are the shut-out from maturity, for maturity is outgoingness. You are loosed from self-centered preoccupation and are free to fellowship with God, your fellowman, yourself, and nature. You are free to fellowship.

Since the fellowship in Christianity is on a unique basis—God's taking the initiative and breaking down the barriers at a cross—so the quality of the fellowship is a unique quality. There is no fellowship in the Vedantic philosophy of Hinduism, for the ultimate god—Brahman—is an it. And you and I, being persons, cannot fellowship with an impersonal it. You can merge with Brahman, according to Vedanta, but you cannot fellowship with it. Since there is no fellowship with the highest Brahman, there can be no fellowship with man. "Please do not disturb my meditation," said an ex-High Court judge in India, as he sat, dressed in ashes, in his thatched hut on the banks of the Ganges at Hardwar. He impatiently waved me aside, for he was breaking every possible contact with the world of matter and men, and was trying to isolate himself, wrapped in meditation on the impersonal it. No fellowship possible. There, too, on the popular side of temple worship, no fellowship exists. Each worshiper goes on his own, unrelated to other worshipers; hence there is no fellowship, no congregational worship. The Zen Buddhists in Japan may sit together in one room, and yet they avoid being welded into a single group. They follow the dictum "It is better to sit back to back." On the contrary, it was said of the early Christian fellowship, "Now the company of those who believed were of one heart and soul."

Father, I thank Thee that the sweetest thing in life—fellowship—is the very center of Thy revelation in Jesus. In Him we have fellowship with Thee, with others, with ourselves, and with nature. We have fellowship, pure, unadulterated, and unlimited. Amen.

AFFIRMATION FOR THE DAY: *Since maturity is outgoingness, I will be outgoing in every situation to everybody.*

"THEY MIGHT BE WITH HIM"

We come now to look closer at the Christian fellowship. The Christian movement began as a fellowship: "And he appointed twelve to be with him." The first part of their calling was to "be with him"—a fellowship. The very first thing in our Christian life is not to do good or to be good—it is to be with Him. Out of being with Him everything comes. You come into contact with Goodness, Incarnate Goodness, and you begin to be good and begin to do good. The fellowship is the fountain from which everything flows: Without the fellowship it is like trying to have a stream without a spring, sunlight without the sun. Anything that breaks the fellowship, automatically dries up everything that flows from that fellowship. And that includes everything.

This being "with him" while He was here on earth deepened into the *koinonia* after He left them. This *koinonia*—literally, "fellowship" was the thing that emerged from Pentecost, the coming of the Holy Spirit. The Church was not born at Pentecost—the Church came later. (The Church was not mentioned in the same chapter of Acts.) But the *koinonia* was mentioned in the same chapter with the coming of the Holy Spirit. The Church was born out of this *koinonia*. The *koinonia* was the organism out of which the Church became the organization. What the soul is to the body, so the *koinonia* was to the Church. Without the *koinonia* the Church is soulless. But a body without a soul is a corpse. Without this inner fellowship, the *koinonia*, the Church is a mere body of doctrine and worship—it is dead. The Church is mature as an institution to the degree it can and does produce the *koinonia*.

Trueblood says: "Once the Church was a brave and revolutionary fellowship, changing the course of history by introducing discordant ideas; today it is a place where people go and sit on comfortable benches, waiting patiently until time to go home to their Sunday dinners." The *koinonia* turned the world upside down; we go home to turn our dinner plates right side up.

O Father, I thank Thee that we are made for Thy *koinonia* and we are restless and unhappy until we find it. This homesickness of the soul will yet drive us Home. In Thy fellowship we live; outside of Thy fellowship we perish and die. So I come. Amen.

AFFIRMATION FOR THE DAY: *I shall be the word of fellowship made flesh wherever I am today.*

THE NURSERY OF HUMAN NATURE

In the small group fellowships, the *koinonia*, we belong to what C. H. Cooley calls "the primary groups," the nursery of human nature. There, as one who belonged to such a group put it: "You discover it exerts a pressure on you in the right direction. You soon discover you can't let your friends down. Because they expect so much of you, you tend to live up to their expectations." There in that inner circle its members seek, in the words of George Fox, "to know each other in that which is eternal." Other contacts let us know one another in that which is temporal; the *koinonia* lets us know one another at our deepest depths and in that which is eternal. Whittier expressed it beautifully in poetry:

> Without spoken words, low breathings stole,
> Of a diviner life from Soul to soul
> Baptising into one tender thought the whole.

I spend three or four months each year in such a fellowship, called the Ashram—one in India, five in Japan, and six in America. I do not know how much I give to these Ashrams, but I know what they give to me. Without them I know when I speak of fellowship it is the word become word, but with them I know it is the word of fellowship become flesh. "Don't talk to us here in this college faculty," said an Indian college principal, "for we are sick of the idea of fellowship." Why? Because they had talked of having a fellowship—the word of fellowship remained word. But I'm never sick of the Ashram fellowship; for there we try, however imperfectly, to let the word of the Kingdom become flesh in a group. We try not *to find* an answer, but *to be* the answer in our corporate life. We endeavor to be the kind of society we would like to see universalized—the Kingdom in miniature. Here we live in a conspiracy of love to help one another to be at our spiritual best. It becomes a place where, as one put it, "we played we were in heaven and found we were."

O Spirit Divine, we pray Thee to mold us into a living fellowship, transcending all race and class and denomination. Give us the unity of the Spirit in the bonds of peace. For we live in fellowship—we perish without it. So help us to live in fellowship. Amen.

AFFIRMATION FOR THE DAY: *I will be in a conspiracy of love to make everyone come to his best.*

73

SOME DANGERS TO FELLOWSHIP

This fellowship is so precious that it has to be carefully cultivated; for while it is a tough-fibered tree and can stand almost any storms and pressures from without, nevertheless it is easily hurt from within. Little borers can eat out its heart and can ruin the tree and its fruit.

What are some of these inner dangers to the life of the fellowship? We could name these: (1) secret criticism, (2) lack of willingness to confess faults, (3) making the fellowship an end, (4) making it exclusive and self-superior, (5) attempts at dominating it, (6) not fulfilling: "In honour preferring one another" (KJV), (7) an expectation of perfection as a condition of fellowship.

These are important, so let us look at them one by one. First, *secret criticism*. On the walls of our Ashram at Sat Tal in the Himalayas in India is a motto:

> Fellowship is based on confidence;
> Secret criticism breaks that confidence;
> We will therefore renounce all secret criticism.

Each day at the Ashram we have what we call "The Family Meeting." In this family meeting we are given a chance each day to bring up any suggestions for a change, or anything that might be improved. And here the group votes on any change or rectification. We insist that if the members do not bring up things in the family meeting, they must not bring them up outside the meeting. So if nothing is brought up we take it for granted that there is nothing to bring up. Consequently, the fellowship can be relaxed. It is not enough to exhort the members to have no secret criticism, if at the same time they have no chance to bring up that criticism in order that the thing criticized may be corrected. This family meeting is an escape valve where pent-up steam can be blown off each day. There are no suppressed grievances. And moreover, the habit of constructive criticism can be formed.

O God, teach us how to live together in Thee. For we cannot live with Thee if we cannot live with one another. And we cannot live with ourselves unless we can live with Thee and one another. Thou hast given us the will to fellowship; teach us the way. Amen.

AFFIRMATION FOR THE DAY: *I will harbor no secret criticism which I do not bring up frankly and lovingly.*

WILLINGNESS TO CONFESS FAULTS—
A SIGN OF MATURITY

We are noting the seven things that must be cleansed away from a living fellowship if it is to remain sound. We have looked at one—secret criticism. We come now to the second—*an unwillingness to confess faults.*

In our Ashrams we start off the first day with what we call "The Morning of the Open Heart." We ask the group, "Why have you come? What do you want? What do you really need?" We remind them that we all have needs, for the best of us are only Christians-in-the-making. We suggest that if they act as though they have no needs, then we know they have the most, especially the need to acknowledge need. We remind them that they are not out of the fellowship if they don't speak, but that they, and we, will be poorer if they do not share their needs. Not all their needs, for God has a private office where He deals with some things. But a general sharing of faults is a catharsis. We further remind them that there is no special group of the "attained" working on the "unattained," but God working on us all; for we all belong to a fellowship of need.

I wouldn't have believed that people are willing and even anxious to share their needs, had I not seen it in operation. For they are eager to get up and out their inner festering problems. To get them up and out is halfway to the solution. Before the week is over, about 95 to 98 percent will be cleared up and cleared out and the persons made over again—really transformed. And the secret is simple—a willingness to confess faults. The moment we begin to confess faults, at that moment we melt into a fellowship. If fellowship begins by acknowledging faults, it is maintained in the same way.

It is a sign of immaturity to act as though one had no faults. It is a sign of maturity to confess them and to ask help in changing them. Only a person who is basically sure of himself can do that.

O Holy Spirit, help me to see myself in the light of Thy inner revealing, and when I see myself help me to acknowledge what I see before God and man. Thus shall I break the chrysalis of what I am and emerge what I want to be. Amen.

AFFIRMATION FOR THE DAY: *Faults are wrong, but they become doubly wrong if unconfessed.*

THE FELLOWSHIP NOT AN END
We come now to note another danger to fellowship: Third, *making the fellowship an end.* The fellowship is never an end—it is always a means. The kingdom of God is an end—it is the final order. All our fellowships are less than that Kingdom and are under its judgment and redemption. The attempt to make a fellowship into an end results in idolatry; for when a relative thing becomes an absolute thing, the result is idolatry. We look down on idolatry in non-Christian lands and practice it in Christian lands where we try to make the segment into the whole, the means into the end.

Fourth, *making the fellowship exclusive and self-superior.* This was the worm that ate at the heart of Gnosticism. The Gnostics, or Knowers, had possession of knowledge which the common herd did not possess. They were a species of Pharisaism which said: "I thank God I am not as other men." Paul struck a dart at this when he said: " 'Knowledge' puffs up, but love builds up." In that sentence is the essential difference between Christianity and Gnosticism: one built up the human race by its love and the other puffed up its devotees who blew themselves to pieces by their own puffing. The puffing perished, the loving lives on. The esoteric groups, claiming an inside and superior knowledge, strangle themselves by their own narrowness.

Fifth, *attempts at dominating the fellowship.* The moment any member tries to dominate the fellowship, at that moment the fellowship ceases to exist. For the fellowship, by its very nature, perishes when one member, or a group of members, attempts to dominate it. Someone has put it this way:

The relationship within the group places all on the same status. In the fellowship of the cell "leadership is simply brotherhood showing itself as initiative." . . . The role of the informal guide within the cell is that of Socrates—not to present polished and perfected pearls of his own, but rather to be a sort of intellectual midwife helping each in the group to give birth to his own "idea children."

The role of the person initiative is not to dominate the group but to develop it.

O Jesus, Thou who didst create strong men around Thee, help me to create around me in every situation today people who will be stronger for my strength. May my strength then be the strength of humility, for there is no other strength. Amen.

AFFIRMATION FOR THE DAY: *Strength is strength only if imparted to the weak. Unimparted it is unimportant.*

EXPECTATION OF PERFECTION, AN ILLUSION

We come now to the last two of the seven things which must be purged away from a fellowship if it is to remain a fellowship and not a hidden feud. Sixth, *not fulfilling: "In honour preferring one another"* (KJV). If we are afflicted with what Bishop Quayle, in his quaint way, called *"ichus publendi,"* or the itch for publicity, we will always be seeking the limelight. And he who is always seeking the limelight is not walking "in the light, as he is in the light." For He "made himself of no reputation" (Phil. 2:7 KJV). He hid Himself and succeeded in filling the world with His name and fame. Those who push themselves will have to, for no one else will push them.

Seventh, *an expectation of perfection as a condition of fellowship.* We must accept ourselves and others as we are— imperfect human beings. If we expect perfection in a group we are bound for disillusionment. For there is no such group. Jesus chose the Twelve, not because He found them to be perfect, but because they wanted to be different. That, and that alone, must be the condition of fellowship—a desire and a willingness to be different.

The last portion of the verse, "And the blood of Jesus his Son cleanses us from all sin," makes this fellowship possible. For there is a constant source of cleansing going through the fellowship, and that source is the blood of Jesus Christ. The Old Testament tells us that "the blood is the life." Then this should mean that the blood of Jesus Christ is the life of Jesus Christ, laid down sacrificially for us—that life cleanses us from all sin. And so at the heart of our gospel is a continuous cleansing element. This makes possible a fellowship, for within the fellowship is this redemptive principle and power at work, cleansing away the impediments to fellowship as they arise. It is like the lungs which take the impure blood and, by exposing it to the oxygen, send it back as pure blood. The poured-out life of Jesus, the Divine Oxygen, touches our impurities into purities. So fellowship is possible.

O Jesus, Thy blood, Thy life, has been, and continuously is, poured out for us. So we can be immersed in that cleansing fountain and find ourselves continuously pure with a purity not our own. And because of this purity we can fellowship one with another, a glorious fellowship. Amen.

AFFIRMATION FOR THE DAY: *I shall be the continuously cleansed instrument of a continuously cleansed fellowship.*

AN INNER CLEANSING TAKING PLACE

We ended last week in noting that there is possibility of Christian maturity in fellowship by two factors: walking "in the light, as he is in the light"—our part; and "the blood of Jesus his Son [cleansing] us from all sin"—His part. These two things taken together make for a relaxed fellowship, for it is not a fellowship of trying to have fellowship. If a group sits down and says, "Come now, let's have fellowship," the members immediately become self-conscious; and the moment they are self-conscious, fellowship vanishes. The self introduces itself and breaks the fellowship. Fellowship is a by-product of walking in the light, as He is in the light. He walked by the light of love and if we take the loving attitude toward everything and everybody, fellowship comes automatically. So the fellowship comes as a result of trysting instead of trying—trysting with Christ instead of trying on your own.

And all the time that this effortless fellowship is taking place, there is an inner cleansing taking place—the blood of Jesus Christ cleanses us from all sin. From personal sins? Yes. And from sins against the fellowship? Yes. From sin—all sin and all kinds of sin. Without that constant cleansing the fellowship would be impossible. Damascus is the oldest living city in the world. Why has it survived when others have perished? The reason is that the city is situated on a slope and there is a stream from the hills of Hermon constantly flowing through the city, through its gutters, gushing up in fountains. It is a perpetual cleansing —flushing out the whole city. Does that take place constantly in the person or group who is walking in the light, as He is in the light? Yes. We are being cleansed constantly from pride, self-seeking, unwillingness to cooperate, resentments, fears, and littleness. Any really Christian fellowship can survive its own mistakes and sins. The early Christian fellowship survived the dishonesty of Ananias and Sapphira, the racism of Peter, the contention of Paul and Barnabas over John Mark. The blood of Jesus Christ cleansed from all sin once for all.

O Jesus, Thou cleanser of the sins of the flesh and the sins of the disposition and the sins against fellowship, be Thou my cleansing this day. For without Thy cleansing I cannot live with myself or others. With it, I can live with everybody. Amen.

AFFIRMATION FOR THE DAY: *My sins of the flesh and disposition are both under His continual cleansing.*

FREEDOM FROM SIN-CONSCIOUSNESS

One of the greatest necessities for maturity is a freedom from sin-consciousness. As long as there is an undertone or overtone of sin-consciousness, there can never be real maturity of character and life. For sin—being an aberration, a departure from that for which we are inwardly made, a missing the mark—always results in a sense of frustration, of out-of-gearness. No person can be mature, with a gnawing sense of sin-consciousness within. It cancels him out, makes him a half-person. For sin is unnatural. It is life living itself against itself. The word "evil" is the word "live" spelled backward.

There are three great attempts to get rid of sin-consciousness. One is the way of the Gnostics. They denied that it existed—for the Gnostic. He lived "in the spirit" and was unaffected by his contacts with matter, which he looked on as evil. So he denied he had any sin. The second way is the way of the modern neoorthodoxy, which brings sin in and makes it a natural part of life, including the Christian life, and the Christian life especially. This passage in the Epistle, "If we say we have no sin, we deceive ourselves, and the truth is not in us" (I John 1:8), is the golden text of neoorthodoxy. But John was writing here, not about the real Christian, but about the pseudo-Christian, the Gnostic, who denied that he had any sin to be cleansed from. He waved sin out with a gesture. To take that reference to the Gnostic and make it universal is to "wrest the Scriptures" and make John contradict himself. For John plainly says: "The blood of Jesus his Son cleanses us from all sin" (1:7), and, "He is faithful and just, and will forgive our sins and cleanse us from all unrighteousness" (1:9). "All sin" and "all unrighteousness" means exactly what it says, or it means that John is involved in a hopeless contradiction. But John is clear-cut and consistent. We have all sinned and all are corrupted by sin—personal and inherited; in Jesus, however, sin is not waved out but wiped out—we are cleansed from "all sin."

O Jesus, we thank Thee that in Thee sin and evil have met their match, and that through Thee we can be freed from the consciousness and the power of sin. We can be free—really free. And we can rejoice in that freedom. Amen.

AFFIRMATION FOR THE DAY: *A guilt-ridden conscience has no place in a real Christian's life.*

ONLY GRACE MAKES US HUMBLE

We are considering whether the Christian faith provides for the cleansing from all sin and all unrighteousness. The question arises: Does not this expectancy and claim to be cleansed from all sin and all unrighteousness make for spiritual pride and hypocrisy? It can and often does, but it need not—need not if it remains truly Christian. It is a misconception to think that sin-consciousness makes one humble. It doesn't. It makes one feel humiliated, but not humble. Only grace makes us humble. The sense of what we have been and of being made over by grace sends us to our knees in the deepest humility known to the human spirit. This is not a word-humility—it is a fact-humility. You are broken up and broken down by grace.

It is not humility to say: "The only difference between the non-Christian and the Christian is that one is a sinner outside the church and the other is a sinner inside the church—they are both sinners." This is not Christian humility—it is Christ humiliation. This is a slur on the Redeemer. For of Him it is said: "You shall call his name Jesus, for he will save his people from their sins"—not *in* their sins, but *from* their sins. If He doesn't save us from sin, He doesn't save us from anything—He is not a Savior at all.

Then what about the sins we commit and the mistakes we make after we are His and are truly converted? Are we to wave them aside as irrelevant? No! But the remedy is here: "If we walk in the light, as he is in the light, we have fellowship one with another, and the blood of Jesus his Son cleanses us from all sin." Here is a cleansing for those who are walking in the light, as He is in the light, and are having fellowship with God and man—for real Christians. It is a once-and-for-all cleansing, and yet a continuous cleansing—the blood of Jesus *cleanses* from all sin. It is present continuous—"cleanses." It is as continuous as breathing and as cleansing as breathing—every breath of oxygen cleanses the impurities of the blood.

O Jesus, my Lord, Thou art my cleansing breath, purifying me every moment. Thy love covers not only a multitude of sins, but my sins and my sins continuously. So I'm at Thy feet continuously, in the deepest gratitude possible. Amen.

AFFIRMATION FOR THE DAY: *With the Cleansing Stream at hand, it is a sin to keep a fouled conscience within.*

A GUILT-RIDDEN PIETY

As we are discussing freedom from sin and sinning, we are met with the objection that Paul, in the seventh chapter of Romans, confesses:—I do not understand my own actions. For I do not do what I want, but I do the very thing I hate . . . So then it is no longer I that do it, but sin which dwells within me . . . Wretched man that I am! Who will deliver me from this body of death?" (7:15-24). Is this Christianity? Or is it Paul under the law in his pre-Christian state? If this had been Paul as a Christian, we would never have heard of him again. For what message would he have had? None! All this is pre-Christian and sub-Christian. The Christian answer to the question "Who will deliver me?" is emphatic and glorious: "Thanks be to God through Jesus Christ our Lord! . . . There is therefore now no condemnation for those who are in Christ Jesus. For the law of the Spirit of life in Christ Jesus has set me free from the law of sin and death" (Rom. 7:25-8:1-2). "Now no condemnation . . . has set me free from the law of sin and death"—that is authentic Christianity.

So this guilt-ridden piety of the modern neoorthodoxy is seventh-chapter Romans instead of eighth. It is sub-Christian. Of one modern exponent of this view, someone has said: "He reverses Paul when he said: 'Where sin abounded sin did much more abound.'" The emphasis is on sin and not on the Savior from sin.

In the mature Christian the emphasis is not: "See how perfect I am," but it is: "See what a perfect Savior I have." Such an emphasis puts your eyes on Him instead of on yourself, and that is healthy. This, then, is a realistic way to face sin: "I have sinned; I am still far from perfect; but I have a perfect Savior who saves me from sinning and cleanses me continuously from all sin and all unrighteousness. I therefore live free from condemnation—free in Him! I am God's happy child singing my way down the years. I do not groan under condemnation—I grow in grace!"

O Christ Jesus, my Lord, Thy nail-pierced hand has passed over my life, and I am clean—clean in Thee. And Thy continual cleansing keeps me clean. So I am redeemed, am being redeemed, and shall be forever redeemed. I thank Thee. Amen.

AFFIRMATION FOR THE DAY: *Where sin abounded in my life, grace shall much more abound today.*

SIX POSSIBLE WAYS TO FACE SIN

We are meditating upon the relationship of maturity and sin. John sends a dart straight to the heart of this whole problem of human living: "I am writing this to you so that you may not sin" (I John 2:1). Modern emphases would say: "I write this to you so that you may be healthy"—or "successful"—or "happy." But these are fruit—the root is freedom from sin. It is immature to deal with the symptoms instead of the disease. Unhealthiness, unsuccessfulness, and unhappiness are symptoms—the disease is sin. It lays a paralyzing hand on everything.

And John was an absolutist here. He did not say: "I write unto you that you may sin less," or "that you may not sin in such a base way." No, it is all clear-cut and absolute: "That you may not sin." It is immaturity to deal with anything else first and foremost.

There are these ways to try to solve the sin question: (1) Compartmentalize it in the material as the Gnostics did. Instead of laying the responsibility for sin on the human will, they laid it on the material: "Matter is evil; I live in the spirit; therefore I am not affected by evil matter"—an alibi. (2) Deny its existence, as the Vedanta philosophy of India does, and as modern cults do. (3) Say that sin is an integral part of human nature, thus making it inevitable and predestined, and therefore excusable. (4) Condemn it and resign yourself to it. (5) Expect that death will release you from it. (6) Acknowledge it as a foreign intrusion, confess our guilt in its acceptance as a part of our conduct and attitudes, and then have faith that the blood of Jesus cleanses us once and for all from sin and will keep on cleansing us. This last is the only realism, and therefore the only maturity. And this maturity is found especially in the fact that it lays the responsibility on the human will—not on this, that, and the other— and that is where the responsibility belongs. When you evade responsibility you are left with inherent doubt and uncertainty, and hence immaturity. Immature Gnostism perished; mature Christianity lives on, for it is dealing with sinful life in a mature way.

O Christ, my Redeemer from sin. I thank Thee that in Thy fountain I am cleansed and kept clean. In my self-salvation attempts I am caught in a thousand helpless dilemmas. I turn from myself to Thee—Thou art sufficient. Amen.

AFFIRMATION FOR THE DAY: *Only one way to deal with sin for me—renounce it and receive His grace.*

SAVED FROM PERFECTIONISM

But there is a lingering doubt: Doesn't this expectation of being cleansed from all sin produce a perfectionist mentality, and hence frustration, if it cannot be maintained? Normally it would. But there is this beautiful and penetrating passage following right on the heels of the other: "My little children, I am writing this to you so that you may not sin; but if any one does sin, we have an advocate with the Father, Jesus Christ the righteous" (I John 2:1). This saves the whole thing from perfectionism and hence discouragement.

The term "advocate," or literally "Paraclete" (one called alongside as a helper), is revealing. It is the same word that is used of the Holy Spirit, "the Comforter." If we sin we are not left in that sense of awful loneliness and estrangement which sin inevitably produces. "Jesus Christ the righteous" is there with you, not as a righteous judge to inflict punishment—for sin is its own punishment (you are punished by the very estrangement)—but to be your "advocate," one called alongside to speak in your behalf. And what does He speak to the Father? The same that He has always spoken, the language of love: "Father, forgive them; for they know not what they do." He doesn't condone the sin, or condemn the sinner. He says something deeper: "They know not what they do. They were blinded by immediate inducements or pressures and don't see the full consequences of what they are doing." And that is a fact—a stark fact in sin; we are momentarily "off our heads"—we "know not." Everybody who sins can say when he comes to himself: "I have played the fool." Whatever his lips may say, his inmost being, deep down, is saying just that.

All this saves us from a perfectionism that says with the Gnostic: "I am free from sin, unaffected by anything that may touch me from the world of sense." We are affected and vitally affected, and we know it *now*. Penitence saves us from perfectionism, for we know we are not and will never be perfect in character now. But the Christian faith saves us from consequent frustration by showing the way out: the "Advocate" is the Way!

O Jesus, Thou Divine Advocate, we thank Thee that when we sin we are not treated with stand-in-the-corner treatment. Thou art with us in our awful aloneness. And with us, not as adversary, but as Advocate. Amen.

AFFIRMATION FOR THE DAY: *I am no perfectionist, but one day I shall be perfect as my Heavenly Father is perfect.*

PERFECTION, NOT IN CHARACTER BUT IN LOVE

We finished yesterday by thinking about the way out of pefectionism, on the one hand, and frustration, on the other. We need not be impossible and impractical perfectionists, or futile frustrationists. Those who strive for impossible perfectionism and those who are torn with futile frustrations are both immature. The Christian position is the only mature position. It is free from perfectionism and from pessimism. It offers a perfection that is possible; namely, a perfection in love. Not a perfection in character. We are only Christians-in-the-making. But we can be perfect in love. And a maturity in love is possible and consistent with a great deal of imperfection in character. You can love God with all your heart, with all your mind, with all your soul, and with all your strength, and yet manifest that love imperfectly. For our actions are made up of intelligence and intentions. The intentions may be good, but the intelligence may be less perfect; therefore the action, which is the offspring of these imperfect parents, will be imperfect.

Those actions, which are imperfect, are constantly being cleansed by the blood, or the life, of Jesus Christ. He is the oxygen which we breathe, and that oxygen is constantly cleansing the impurities of the blood of daily human living. This constant cleansing saves us from frustration. When we fall, we fall on our knees. When we stumble, we stumble forwad—into His arms! He is there always! Never leaves us alone. He is the Advocate—the One-Called-Alongside-Of. And He is never closer than when we need Him most. "Those who are well have not need of a physician, but those who are sick." The mother loves the well child but gives special love and attention to the sick child, who needs it most. "I have not come to call the righteous, but sinners." And to call them to what? To call them to a life of perfect love to Him. And in contact with that perfect love of His, their love is perfected.

O Advocate with the Father, I could not get to the Father save through Thee. Thy merits are my merits—my only merits. Thy goodness is my goodness—my only goodness. Thy arms my refuge—my only refuge. Amen.

AFFIRMATION FOR THE DAY: *We are the imperfect masters of an imperfect world, both in the process of perfection.*

SELF-SALVATION, OR SALVATION THROUGH THE CROSS?

We come now to a question which is at the heart of our quest for maturity. It is raised in connection with this verse: "If any one does sin, we have an advocate with the Father, Jesus Christ the righteous; and he is the expiation for our sins, and not for ours only but also for the sins of the whole world" (I John 2:1-2). This verse raises the question of the cross. What relationship has the cross to maturity? Does the cross weaken character, with an offer of easy forgiveness, as some would say? Or is the cross the very center of maturity—no real maturity without it? That is perhaps the most vital question that can be raised in religion. It divides the religious world in two groups: those who depend on salvation by their own efforts and attainments—a self-salvation—and those who depend for salvation on what has been done for them at a cross—a God-salvation. Really there are no other issues in religion, except marginal ones—this is it!

The non-Christian world ranges itself on one side—the side of self-salvation—and largely around the idea of karma, the law of sowing and reaping. This law of karma underlies the systems of Hinduism and Buddhism, so its influence has spread from India to Japan and holds in its grip the whole of the East, except where Islam prevails. A holy man came out of his hut with a krait, the deadliest snake in India, caught with tongs, and he was about to drop it over the wall. I said: "Let me kill it. I am not afraid." "No," he said, "you may not be afraid, but the law of karma will get you whether you are afraid or not." An able and devoted American missionary, in his identification with India, became so identified that he became a Hindu and was inducted into caste Hinduism, not merely philosophical Hinduism, but into caste Hinduism. He couldn't eat with his own family until they, too, went through a process of purification. When I asked him why he had become a Hindu, he replied: "I prefer that my children be brought up under karma rather than redemption." That is the real issue.

O God, our Father, we are at the crossroads. We need guidance, real guidance, for the issue of salvation is at stake. We cannot afford to miss our step here, for time and eternity are bound up with it. Thou hast promised to guide the meek in judgment. Amen.

AFFIRMATION FOR THE DAY: *Since salvation for me is not an attainment, but an obtainment, I shall obtain today.*

KARMA AND THE CROSS

Karma says that there is no forgiveness—you reap what you sow, somewhere, somehow. The Hindu statement of it is: "Just as a calf will find its mother among a thousand cows, so your deeds will find you out among a thousand rebirths." An American who had become a Buddhist said: "My brother, who is a Roman Catholic priest, is praying for my soul, and the joke of it is that I have no soul. I'm just a coming together of past deeds, and when they are dissolved, I dissolve into Nirvana—*sunnyavadi*, or nothingness." And then he added: "I do not want a God offering to forgive my sins. I prefer to work them out myself." He implied that it was more mature to take the way of karma rather than redemption.

We must examine this matter carefully; a misstep here means a destiny misstep. The chairman of one of my meetings in India, a Hindu member of the Legislative Assembly, said to an audience: "Twenty-six years ago when I was a student in a Christian college I heard the speaker speak on a subject I've never forgotten. For weeks after that address, inside the classroom and outside, the students—and faculty—discussed that address. It was entitled "Karma and the Cross." He saw that that title brought to a head the religious choice of the whole of the East.

And this choice is at the basis of our religious life of the West. For this thought of self-salvation through positive thinking and affirmation is an atmosphere both inside and outside much of the church life of today. Now of course there is a truth underlying both "karma" and "New Thought." This is a world of moral law. You *do* reap what you sow. Christianity affirms that and affirms it strongly: "Do not be deceived; God is not mocked, for whatever a man sows, that he will also reap" (Gal. 6:7). If you work with the moral universe you get results—it will back you, sustain you, further you. But if you work against the moral universe you get consequences—you'll be up against it, frustrated. Some people go through life getting results; others get consequences.

O Father, I thank Thee for this moral universe. It is Thy preventive grace, preventing us from destroying ourselves. For our deeds do destroy us and they do build us up. We are, in many ways, the result of our doing. Help us to come to terms with Thy moral universe. Amen.

AFFIRMATION FOR THE DAY: *I shall get results today, for I shall work with God's moral universe.*

HIS RELIGION IS PRODUCING TENSION

We have seen that there is a truth in karma—the law of sowing and reaping. There is also a truth in salvation and health through affirmation, through being positive. Negative attitudes bring negative results. If you affirm disease—the negative of health—you'll probably have disease. Our lives, like the hands of a dyer, are colored by that with which we work. If the atmosphere of your mind is pessimistic, fearful, and negative, your body, mind, and spirit will be affected by it. You, as a person, will become negative.

Recently this letter came:

I ask you to pray with me for my husband who is tortured with anxiety over all kinds of things—his job, the children's noise and mistakes, doubt of my love, and unfounded fear of cancer and finances. If he could feel the living Presence as I have felt it, then he could have peace of mind, release from brutal war memories, unreasonable wrath, and healing of his ulcerous stomach. He is active in church work but has not made a surrender of his soul. He is, as they say, "hanging on for dear life," for fear he'll go to pieces if he doesn't.

Here is a man negative in his attitudes who has become negative in his very person, including his body, and his body especially. He is reaping physically what he has been sowing mentally and spiritually. And his religion is doing him little or no good—he is just "hanging on for dear life." It is struggle instead of surrender—it is resistance instead of receptivity.

So this positive attitude toward life will give you a shot in the arm. But it is only a shot in the arm, for at its best it is self-salvation. And anything that leaves you preoccupied with yourself, even an exhortation to forget yourself, leaves you in the quagmire of self-centeredness, even if it be a religious self-centeredness. That is the fatal defect of both karma and "New Thought"—they both leave you self-centered in their endeavor to improve, to release, and to realize yourself. You are still at the center of your world, hence off-center.

Father, Thou art my Center and my only Center. For if I try to organize life around me I'm making myself God. And I know I am not. Thou art God. Help me to look beyond myself to Thee. Then I shall lose myself and find it again—gloriously. Amen.

AFFIRMATION FOR THE DAY: *My feet, freed from the bog of self-salvation, are joyously walking the Way!*

DEEDS WITHOUT DESIRE FOR REWARD

We have seen that both "karma" and "New Thought" suffer from a fatal defect: they leave you preoccupied with yourself. Karma tries to get out of the tanglefoot of self-preoccupation by saying that you are to do good deeds without desire for reward—*nishphal karma*—karma without desire for fruit. This sounds wise and helpful, but actually it is self-defeating. For the very desire to have a desireless action is a desire for desireless action and leaves you struggling with yourself to be freed from yourself, hence more tied to yourself. It attempts to deliver you philosophically and leaves you concentrated on yourself in fact. The attempt to keep yourself from thinking of a certain thing brings that thing back into the focus of attention in the mind. If in riding a bicycle you try hard to miss a stone on the road by concentrating your attention on the stone, you will probably hit it. Whereas if you concentrate your attention on the road ahead, you'll probably easily miss the stone. So the emphasis on "action without desire for fruit" results in a self-conscious desire to be freed from desire for fruit. The fruit of the whole thing is a self-centered piety.

The same thing can be said of the movements which tell you that you have all the answers within you; just discover and develop your own divine potentialities, your own perfection. Here is a declaration of principles from a recent international gathering of such a movement: "We affirm the inseparable oneness of God and man, the realization of which comes through spiritual intuition, the implications of which are that man can reproduce the Divine perfection in his body, emotions, and in all his external affairs." Note that God and man are "inseparably" one; no matter what man is, has done, or will do, nothing will be able to break that oneness. It is not a moral and spiritual oneness—it is a oneness in essence, an inseparable oneness. If that means anything it is that since God and you are one in essence, then you are one in action—what you do God does. Then what kind of God is He if He does what we do? His character is gone.

O God, our Father, I cannot expect to find Thee in the morass of my doings. My vision of Thee is blurred when I try it. I can only see Thee, and see Thee perfectly, in the face of Jesus. There Thy face is not blurred. I thank Thee. Amen.

AFFIRMATION FOR THE DAY: *One with God in choice, more and more I shall become one with Him in character.*

INSEPARABLY ONE WITH GOD?

We were considering yesterday the position of those who find all the answers within themselves, asserting their own inseparable oneness with God. We stated that the character of God is lost in this viewpoint, for if we are inseparably one with God, then what we do God does. You cannot say you are metaphysically one and not morally one. You are one—in everything! But anyone who knows himself—and others—knows that when he acts, *he* acts and not *God*. For the outcome of that acting is the sum total of our moral mess. If all this mess we are in is the result of God's acting, then what kind of God is there? His character and His face are blackened. We have tried to make ourselves God and we have lost God in the process. For God is just ourselves writ large. But in the end our moral nature revolts against such a projection of ourselves. We simply cannot worship the God we project. He is too much like ourselves.

But this emphasis doesn't lead you to worship God. You are not to worship God, but to discover and realize God in yourself—you are to discover yourself as God. That doesn't take you outside of yourself as worship does: it leaves you concentrated on yourself to discover and to develop your own essential divinity.

There is no doubt that this gives you an initial shot in the arm—a lift, a sense of your worthwhileness. It is a reaction against the groveling worm-of-the-dust, self-depreciation, and even self-hate which are involved in much of the interpretation of Christianity of our churches.

But it has a fatal defect—it leaves you preoccupied with yourself. You are left with an endeavor to try by various slogans and practices to convince yourself that you are inseparably one with God. You are the center of your attention. That leaves you with a self-conscious piety—a piety that has to act a part, that must keep up its illusion of manifest divinity. That is playacting of a very serious kind.

O Father, we know when we play at being God, we play the fool. We know we are not God and were never intended to be. We know we are made to love Thee and become like Thee through that love, but never become Thee. That love releases us—from ourselves. Amen.

AFFIRMATION FOR THE DAY: *Myself, God's, is now my own.*

"AHAM BRAHM"

We are considering the self-preoccupation which results when we endeavor to make ourselves inseparably one with God. I was visiting a swami in his Ashram in India. He was supposed to be a *jiwan-mukta*—one who has attained salvation while alive, one who has realized that he is God—"*Aham Brahm*" ("I am God"). But that laid on him the burden of acting a part—the part of playing God. He showed himself at regular times so that his followers and devotees could take his *darsham*—literally, "take his presence." He sat in the meeting which I addressed in a be-pillowed kind of elongated chair, surrounded by flowers and burning incense. And he arose at a particular moment, about ten minutes after I had begun, interrupted the address, garlanded the speaker and the visitors, and returned to his reclining throne. This was staged for effect. And he received the adoration of his followers, who prostrated themselves before him with folded hands. He was the center of attention for himself and others. You didn't think of God—you thought of the swami! The whole thing was caught in the flypaper of attention on one's self, and this held for the swami and the devotees. It was all self-salvation, through self-realization by self-attention. And the nemesis was self-attention, and hence self-conscious attention. And it was all self-defeating.

Into that circle came a Greek woman who had renounced, not the world but herself, in complete self-surrender to Christ. This self-surrender released her from self-preoccupation and released her to give herself to others in pure disinterested service. She was a trained masseuse and treated everybody regardless of condition or race or religion, even lepers. She is now treating lepers with her own hands, massaging their sores. She rubs the love of God into everybody, giving a massage and a message at the same time. The swami, seeing the prodigality of her love and service given in self-forgetful humility, said to his followers; "This is the kind of love and service I would like to see produced here." But it simply could not be.

O God, our Father, we have our eyes on the wrong place when we have our eyes on ourselves. Help us to lift our eyes from ourselves to Thee. For in that lifting we will find our liberty—liberty from ourselves. So we look—to Thee! Amen.

AFFIRMATION FOR THE DAY: *Myself, off my own hands, is now in the hands of God to be used today.*

KNOW BY INTUITION, OR BY INCARNATION?

In the quotation given on Wednesday from the declaration of principles of a movement bent on the realization of its devotees as having "an inseparable oneness with God," it was stated that "the realization of which comes through spiritual intuition." You bypass the revelation of God in Jesus and look within to discover your own divinity—it is all discovered by "spiritual intuition." You are the means of the discovery of your own inseparable oneness with God. This is a modern version of Gnosticism. The Gnostics said they were the superior knowers—the Gnostics—from the Greek *gnosis*, to know. You know directly by turning in on yourself—you know by intuition. You do not have to turn to Jesus as the self-disclosure of God in understandable terms. You turn to yourself as the means of your own self-disclosure as God.

This outlook and method may be baptized here and there with Christian terminology to make it palatable to Christians, but it is fundamentally and basically unchristian. It urges that you see God through yourself by intuition and not through Jesus by interpretation. This is self-salvation through self-discovery. The Christian faith is God-salvation through self-surrender to Jesus Christ, who brings God to us. The self is surrendered, not discovered. The basis is changed from self to God. We are then God-centered persons, not self-centered persons. That leaves us on the right center—God.

The temptation of Eden was right here: If you eat of this tree of knowledge, "you will be like God." The temptation to make themselves "as God" through special knowledge. Adam fell for it and lost paradise—and himself. Jesus came to restore that paradise through knowledge of Himself, by self-surrender. And the moment we do it our paradise is back again. We have lost our lives through self-surrender and have found them again through God-realization. We come through Jesus and find God and ourselves—and everything!

O Jesus, Thou art the key—not we. Thou dost show us the Father and we discover not only the Father but ourselves as well. We are bowed in the deepest gratitude that human heart can know and express. We thank Thee. Amen.

AFFIRMATION FOR THE DAY: *Myself, realized and released, is free to freely give.*

"DRUNK WITH THE WINE OF WORDINESS"

We are considering whether we are saved by the cross—the self-giving of God; or by intuition—the discovery of ourselves. The quotation given on Wednesday ended with these words: "the implications of which are that man can reproduce the Divine perfection in his body, emotions, and in all his external affairs." Note that "man can reproduce the Divine perfection." It talks about God, but centers on man—as the center of this perfection and the producer of it. Man is deified. God doesn't come down, as in the Incarnation, but man goes up through an intuition. And this perfection is thoroughgoing—it includes his "body," his "emotions," and "all his external affairs."

This statement of course is "drunk with the wine of its own wordiness." It is the Word become words—and words only. It never becomes flesh. For where do we see the perfection in the body? If the body were perfect it would be deathless. When I saw the French "Mother" who mediated between Arabindo Ghose, the Hindu swami, and the outside world, she said to me: "He is trying something different. He is not only making his soul divine, he is making his body divine as well." But that "divine" body died like the rest. Mrs. Eddy said that death was an error of mortal mind and that there was no death; and when she died, someone remarked that "she was on third base and stole home on an error."

We gain physical perfection, not by asserting the perfection of the body, but by realizing that in Jesus our bodies are made perfect through His resurrection when we are identified by surrender to Him. His deathlessness becomes ours!

As to perfection of "emotions," you don't find it by asserting the perfection of the emotions, but by loving God "with all your heart"—the emotions—and in loving Him we find our emotions come back to us perfected as we perfectly love Him. As for "perfection in all our external affairs," that comes when the Kingdom comes and the Kingdom comes when we "receive" it by surrender. We make an external paradise through the internal Paraclete—the Holy Spirit within.

O Holy Spirit, Thou canst make me inwardly and outwardly adjusted to God, myself, and life. Thou canst do it by abiding within. So I open the depths for Thee to come in and rule the within. Then I shall be free—free indeed. Amen.

AFFIRMATION FOR THE DAY: *The Holy Spirit cleanses and controls my intuition and makes it safe.*

MAN TRIES TO RESTORE FELLOWSHIP

We have gone off to consider some of the ways—we must now return to the Way! We have been considering methods of self-salvation through self-assertions about the self. We now turn to the method of God-salvation through the Divine self-sacrifice—the cross.

Man, in feeling the estrangement between himself and God, has taken various ways to get back into fellowship with God. First, he has sacrificed to God to appease Him by offering his possessions—his cattle, his sheep, or his goats—in sacrifice. Sometimes it is the produce of his toil—his grain, his fruit, his money. Second and higher, he has offered to God in sacrifice his righteous deeds, his moral endeavors, his penances, and his piety; in short, his worthiness. Third, and this is the method we have just been considering, he offers to God his wordy assertion of his oneness with God, the claim that there is nothing between God and man except man's ignorance of his own divinity. This is man bridging the gulf between man and God, made by man's sin, by saying there is no sin and hence there is no gulf. These attempts heal everything by self-asserting words about man's Divine perfection.

But we cannot get to God, either by offering the sacrifice of the fruit of our work, or by the sacrifice of our works, or by the sacrifice of our words. We can't get to God by any of these ladders—God must come to us. The Word must become flesh. And that Divine Word must bear our sins in His own body on a tree. That happened.

We mentioned the truth in the law of karma, the truth that we reap what we sow. This is a universe that is not indifferent to your virtue or your vice. It takes sides. You are free to choose, but you are not free to choose the results or the consequences of your choices. They are in hands not your own. And you do not break these laws written into the nature of things; you break yourself on them. And these laws are color-blind, race-blind, and religion-blind. Break them and you get broken.

O Father, I know I have to come to terms with moral law. I cannot escape it, or disregard it, for its results or consequences are automatically registered in me. I am the payoff. Then give me sense to come to terms with it. Amen.

AFFIRMATION FOR THE DAY: *I shall not play the fool with God, with the moral universe, with myself. I shall be wise in obedience.*

THE TRUTH IN KARMA

We saw yesterday that there is an important and an all-embracing truth in karma. We cannot expect to evade the results or the consequences of our moral sowing. Our chickens come home to roost. Our deeds boomerang upon us. The result or the consequences register themselves in us automatically. The payoff is in the person. You don't break these laws, you break yourself upon them. Sin and its punishment are one and the same thing. You don't have to punish the eye for having sand in it, the body for having a cancer in it. Nor do you have to punish a boy for taking a skunk in bed with him! We said that the word "evil" is the word "live" spelled backward. It is an attempt to live life against itself. And it can't be done. Therefore, sin is not merely bad—it is stupid. It is trying to do something that simply cannot be done, an attempt to live life against reality.

But while there is a profound truth in karma, as usually interpreted, it is only a half-truth. For the usual interpretation is that the individual who does the sowing does all the reaping. According to the law of karma it would be unjust for anyone except the sower to get any of the reaping. But the facts indicate otherwise. The father who sows a good life passes on the results of his karma to his family, to his community, to his country, and faintly to the world. Everybody reaps what he sows. On the other hand, if he sows a bad life he passes on the consequences of his bad life to his family, to his country, and faintly to the world. He wishes that he alone could reap the consequences of his sowing and did not have to pass on to his children the shame of his deeds.

When Mahatma Gandhi sowed his life in sacrifice for the freedom of India, did he alone reap the results? No, the results of his karma were passed on to four hundred million people. They reaped freedom from this sowing. The fact that other people reap the results of our sowing opens the door to the vicarious. We can pass on to others through love the results of our sowing. This points us to the cross.

O God, we now stand face to face with the deepest possibility of the universe—the possibility that Thou, our God and Father, was offering Thyself in sacrifice in Jesus to redeem us. Help us to see this and to see it clearly. Amen.

AFFIRMATION FOR THE DAY: *Since the results of Thy karma are open to me, I'll live by them.*

WE COULD REAP WHAT HE SOWED

Yesterday we ended with the fact that other people reap what we sow, that we are all bound up in a bundle of life and anything that affects one affects all.

Then this supreme question is raised: Suppose there was one organically connected with the human race as Son of man and connected with God as Son of God; suppose He should sow Himself in sacrifice—could He pass on to the whole human race the results of that sowing, the results of His karma? If He were a man and only a man, then His death would be a martyrdom—as was Lincoln's or Gandhi's—influential, but only affecting the world faintly. But suppose He was God—God manifest in the flesh. Then, since He is Creator and since He is connected with every man in love, He could pass on to every man the results of that Divine self-sacrifice. We could reap what He sowed!

Would God do that? Well, if He is the God that I see in the face of Jesus Christ, He could not but do it. For the God that I see in the face of Jesus Christ is love—and only love. And it is the nature of love to insinuate itself into the sorrows and sins of the loved one and to make them its own. In a home where pure love meets sin in the loved one, a cross of pain is set up, inevitably, at the junction of that pure love and that sin. All love has the doom of bleeding upon it as long as there is sin in the loved one. That is inherent in every human heart if that heart has pure love in it. The psalmist raises this question:

> He who planted the ear, does he not hear?
> He who formed the eye, does he not see? (94:9).

And we may add: He that made love shall He not love? And He that put the deep principle that all love suffers when there is sin in the loved one, shall He not suffer when His love comes into contact with the sin in us, the loved ones? At the junction of that love and that sin would not a cross of pain be set up—inevitably?

O Father, we are looking into the very heart of the deepest thing in this universe of ours—Thy love. Help us to see it and really see it, for if we see it we see everything—everything in heaven and earth. In Jesus' name. Amen.

AFFIRMATION FOR THE DAY: *"The Cross is the ground plan of the universe."*

THE CROSS LIGHTS UP THE NATURE OF GOD

We ended yesterday with this question: If God is love and it is the nature of love to take on itself the burdens and sorrows and sins of the loved ones, would His love not crimson into suffering as that love meets sin in us, the loved ones? Would there not be an unseen cross upon the heart of God—He being what He is and we being what we are?

But God is a spirit and I am bounded by my flesh. How could I know that there is an unseen cross upon the heart of God? How could I know it, except He show me—show me by an outer cross that there is an inner cross upon His heart? Has that happened? Yes. The outer cross lifted up on a hilltop called Calvary is the outer cross through which I see the inner cross upon the heart of God. The cross lights up the nature of God as love. Through it I see that at the very center of the universe is redeeming love. No greater discovery could be made, or will be made, than that. That is the ultimate in discoveries.

And everything noble in human nature and human history points to the necessity of that fact of love in God. For if it isn't there, then the universe ends in a vast disappointment—God does not fulfill the prophecies of the noblest in nature and man.

Take this: A wildlife conservation officer drove past a grouse in the center of the road, and he was surprised that she did not move when he swerved around her. He came back and saw in the meantime that six other cars had swerved around her, and still she did not move. When he came near, six little chicks ran out from under her wings. One of her wings was broken and her head was bloody. But she was saving others; herself she could not save. He that put the impulse into the heart of that mother grouse to save her little family at cost to herself, shall He not save His family though His head be bloody and His heart be broken?

O Jesus, Thou art the One through whom I see into the heart of God. And what I see there sets my heart on fire. For I see love protecting us, shielding us, saving us, bleeding for us, amid the roar of human existence. Amen.

AFFIRMATION FOR THE DAY: *If the cross is in the very nature of God, it shall be in my very nature.*

NOBLEST IN NATURE POINTS TO NOBLEST IN GOD

We must pursue this fact, that the noblest in nature points to the noblest in God—the cross.

In Japan they have a saying when one has done something for another at cost to oneself: "You've broken your bones for me." Mrs. Nobu Jo, who had saved five thousand people from suicide when she put up a sign where suicides were taking place: "Don't! See Mrs. Nobu Jo first," held out her wrists to me and said: "I've literally broken my bones for others," and she said it with gay laughter. And she had, for in helping another she fell and broke her own wrists.

A certain father had to say to his son: "Son, since you will not cooperate in anything in the home, we will have to accept your refusal to cooperate. Since you won't work with us, pulling yourself apart from us in spirit and act, you will not sleep with us—you'll have to sleep alone in the attic." The boy went tearfully to the loneliness of the attic. After some time the father climbed the ladder and spent the night with his son, making the boy's isolation and shame his own. Would the son ever forget? Man would not cooperate with God, pulling himself apart from God in awful loneliness. Would God share that loneliness as He hung on a cross in such loneliness that He cried the cry that must be ours when we sin: "My God, my God, why hast thou forsaken me?" He would do so if He is the kind of God I see in Jesus.

It was the custom among the headhunters of Formosa to sacrifice several people each year to ensure the fertility of their crops and their families. A beloved Chinese teacher urged that they give up this custom. They couldn't, they said. Then would they agree to take one victim which the teacher would supply? They agreed. The victim was to be walking with a yellow sheet over his head in the early morning under a certain tree. When the people saw the provided victim, they hurled their spears into the hooded figure. They found, to their dismay, that it was their own beloved teacher. The custom of human sacrifice stopped. A monument marks the spot.

O Father God, the highest in man must be the deepest in Thee. For where else could this have come from except from Thee? We see in Thy Son the deepest in Thee—love. And what a love! We can never get over what we see. Amen.

AFFIRMATION FOR THE DAY: *The cross is in my blood and it will be in all my relationships.*

97

"YOU HAVEN'T HURT YOURSELF?"

We have been looking at the highest in man to see the deepest in God. A dramatic story is told of a young man who fell madly in love with a girl who hated the young man's mother. The girl laid down the hard condition that she would marry him only if he would bring the heart of his mother to her. His mad love for her got the better of him, so he killed his mother, took out her heart, wrapped it in a piece of paper, and ran with it to the girl. In his eagerness he tripped and fell, and the heart rolled out of the paper. The heart spoke and said: "Son, I hope you haven't hurt yourself?"

That story, of course, isn't true, and yet it is true. It came true on a cross when Jesus prayed: "Father, forgive them; for they know not what they do." That was God saying when they were murdering Him: "My sons, I hope you haven't hurt yourselves."

I quoted that prayer of Jesus to a skeptical Hindu, who didn't believe in God at all, and then I added: "I suppose that prayer is a high-water mark of morality in this universe." He took off his glasses, wiped an unbidden tear away, and said: "High-water mark! Man, that's the highest water mark conceivable." Nothing for God or man can ever go beyond that. It won't, it can't. This is It.

Coleridge once said: "Beyond that which is found in Jesus of Nazareth the human race will never progress." We may add: Beyond that which we see in the cross the human race will never progress. For the cross reveals the deepest in God—love! And there is nothing higher or deeper in this universe for God or man than love.

Since the maturest fact in the universe is love, and the maturest type of love is seen in Jesus, we come now to the very center of our quest for maturity. We must be mature in love if we are to be mature. Our maturity is maturity in love, or it is not maturity. And it must be maturity in the kind of love seen in Jesus or it is not mature love.

O Christ, my Lord, I am now about to turn my quest for maturity into a specific quest—the quest for maturity in love. If I take my eyes off Thee and put them on any other type of love, I'm astray. So help me here. Amen.

AFFIRMATION FOR THE DAY: *I have seen love's maturity at the cross—I am spoiled for anything less.*

LACK LOVE AND YOU LACK MATURITY

Last week we placed our finger on the center of our quest for maturity—maturity in love. We are as mature as we are mature in love, and no more mature. We may be mature in knowledge, but if we are not mature in love, we are immature human beings. We may be mature in religious practices and outlook, but if we are immature in love we are immature. Our maturity is maturity in love, or it is immaturity.

This is the central and consistent message of the New Testament. Its message is consistent from Jesus, through Paul, through Peter, through John. The finality of love as the highest characteristic of character is the same through all four of these. There is no wavering, no equivocation, no hesitation—love is central in God and must be central in man. There is nothing, absolutely nothing, that can take its place. Lack love and you lack maturity, no matter what else you may have beside. Nothing can atone for that lack.

Jesus, God's final Word to man, made love the final thing in character. When a scribe asked Jesus: "Which commandment is the first of all?" the ages and all heaven must have bent over to listen to His reply, for His answer would fix in the mind of all humanity the chief quality in character. A misstep here, and all the ages would go wrong with Him, and go wrong in the most important thing in living—the main emphasis in character. But Jesus did not go wrong. He unerringly picked out two commandments from among the thirty-six hundred which the Jewish law prescribed for conduct, and those two emphasize the same thing: "Thou shalt love" (KJV). Suppose He had picked out some good thing instead of the best thing; for instance: "Thou shalt be just," "Thou shalt be merciful," "Thou shalt be kind." Suppose He had chosen any good thing instead of this highest thing. Then the history of humanity would have been different, and humanity itself would have been impoverished. He sounded a clarion note, "Thou shalt love"; and all the ages, whether they have obeyed it or not, have echoed a deep "Amen."

O Jesus, how can we thank Thee enough for Thy insight and foresight; the ages were thirsting and dying for this word. And we are still thirsting and dying for this word. Teach it to us again. Without it we die. Amen.

AFFIRMATION FOR THE DAY: *Since the first obligation God lays on man is to love, I shall lay that same obligation on myself.*

FIRST COMMANDMENT—LOVE!

We have considered Jesus' emphasis on the primacy of love. We must look further and see not only the primacy of love, but the sweep of this love. It is not only primary, it embraces the total man, loving God totally and his neighbor and himself equally. Never was love so complete in its sweep and so deep in its depths as here defined in a few swift words: "You shall love the Lord your God with all your heart, and with all your soul, and with all your mind, and with all your strength" (Mark 12:30). Note that the total man was to love God totally: "with all your heart"—the affectional nature; "with all our soul"—the volitional, deciding nature; "with all your mind"—the intellectual nature; "with all your strength"—the physical nature. The whole man was to love God wholly—no part left out.

Note that Jesus put in "with all thy mind." It was not in the quotation from Deut. 6:4. That addition was important. It annexed the whole world of science, philosophy, and psychology in a single phrase. Had that phrase been left out, Christianity would have been on the edges of the modern world looking wistfully in, but not at home. Now it is at home in the world of science and investigation. When I was told by one of the atomic scientists at Oak Ridge, Tennessee, that more people go to church in Oak Ridge than any other place in America, I asked, "Why, are you frightened?" "No," he replied, "not frightened, but reverent. We are in the presence of a great mystery. It drives us to our knees." These people knew that love must control that energy or we perish, literally perish. The word of Jesus stood authoritative at the place of the greatest discovery of the mind of man—atomic energy. One of those scientists at Oak Ridge became a clergyman, having seen the necessity of the Christian faith, with its emphasis on love, as the controlling force in an age of atomic energy. "You shall love the Lord your God . . . with all your mind" is an up-to-the-minute imperative.

O Jesus, my Lord, as the ages advance, Thou art advancing beyond the ages. As the ages grow in need, Thou dost stand more and more adequate to meet the need. Thou inexaustible One, we are touching only the border of Thy garments. Amen.

AFFIRMATION FOR THE DAY: *My mind, controlled by love, shall think loving thoughts, and only loving thoughts.*

LOVING WITH THE STRENGTH OF ALL

We are studying the emphasis—the supreme emphasis—of Jesus on love. "With all your strength" may mean the physical strength, and I am certain it does. It involves our having the very best bodies we are capable of having if we are to love Him with all our strength. Otherwise we should be loving Him with our weakness. Some do. They punish their bodies to promote their souls. But body and soul according well must beat out music vaster than before. We must love Him with our physical strength.

But this loving Him with the "strength" may mean with the strength of the heart, the strength of the soul, the strength of the mind. Some love Him with the strength of the emotions and the weakness of the will. That makes the emotionalist in religion. Some love Him with the strength of the will and the weakness of the emotions. That makes the volitionalist in religion, the man of iron, but not very lovable. Some love Him with the strength of the mind and the weakness of the emotion. That makes the intellectualist in religion—no fire, no contagion. Some love Him with the strength of the emotion and the weakness of the mind. That makes the sentimentalist in religion. All of these types are immature.

The only mature person is the person who loves the Lord his God with the strength of the emotion, the strength of the will, the strength of the mind, and the strength of the body. The whole person wholly devoted to God. And this is psychologically as well as Christianly sound. For unless there is wholeness of devotion in the affections, in the will, in the mind, there will be inner division; and where there is inner division there is inner conflict; and where there is inner conflict there is breakdown and neurosis, or at the very least a cancellation of one's effectiveness. The important thing here is to note that the demand of Christ and the demands of human nature coincide. They demand the same thing—an individual and total love. That fact will loom larger and larger in our quest for maturity.

O God, our Father, we are grateful beyond words that Thou art demanding our total love, for in demanding a total love Thou art giving Thy total love. What more could we ask, or what more could we receive? We do receive. Amen.

AFFIRMATION FOR THE DAY: *I must go over my life with a fine-tooth comb for unbalanced loving.*

TWO SIDES OF ONE COIN

We are looking at the emphasis Jesus laid on love as the supreme thing in life. If God is the highest Being in the universe—and He is—then we must love Him with the highest thing in the universe, namely love. And that love must include the total person—emotion, will, mind, and strength. That absolute commandment expressed in that absolute form is as inevitable as the law of gravitation, and more so. For with it life holds together; without it life goes to pieces. And the whole of human history and the history of the individual are commentaries on that statement. This is not speculation, it is verified statement. If you don't love God totally you can't love yourself at all. For a divided self is a despised self. If you won't live with God in the harmony of love, you will have to live with yourself in the disharmony of hate. There is no alternative.

But if Jesus had stopped at the questioner's request for the greatest commandment and had left it at that, humanity would have been groping—groping in regard to our relationship with man. Life would have been left dangling, at loose ends—sound as to God, but uncertain as to man. So Jesus went on to complete the commandment to love: "You shall love your neighbor as yourself." Here, then, love to God was to be manifested in love to man. John adds: "For he who does not love his brother whom he has seen, cannot love God whom he has not seen" (I John 4:20).

Here are the two highest commandments ever given to man anywhere, at any time: Love God totally and love your neighbor as yourself. And Jesus added: "There is no other commandment greater than these" (Mark 12:31). He closed the discussion with absolute finality. And for the life of us we can't find it within ourselves to put up a question mark about this closed finality. It is as axiomatic as "two and two make four." To question it is to question our own sanity. It is self-verifying and inescapable. Take it or leave it—with results or consequences.

O Jesus, my Lord, how grateful I am for this finality. It hedges me in. If I try to escape from it, I escape from salvation. I do not want to escape except into Thy arms. So I come—all out for love, for Thy love. Amen.

AFFIRMATION FOR THE DAY: *The only way I can show my love to God is to show my love to man.*

TONING IT DOWN

We stated yesterday that the commandment to love God totally and our neighbor as ourselves is inescapable if we want to live and to live fully. But, as always when we are up against a demand, we try to find a loophole. The Jews tried. They didn't turn it down—they toned it down. They put it this way: "You shall not take vengeance or bear any grudge against the sons of your own people, but you shall love your neighbor as yourself" (Lev. 19:18). Here they defined the "neighbor" as "the sons of your own people"—the people of your race and religion. That toned it down.

So Jesus toned it up again. A lawyer, "desiring to justify himself," said to Jesus, "And who is my neighbor?" And then Jesus, in the parable of the Good Samaritan, defined the neighbor as a man of another race in need. And He added this sting to his statement: the hero was a despised Samaritan. The Jew did not come out of it playing the brother bountiful to a helpless Samaritan, but found himself as the recipient of the helpful ministrations of the despised Samaritan. So Jesus not only toned up the commandment, but in the deft strokes of the story He tuned down the pride and arrogance of the Jew. The story goes that in ancient days a man who made impenetrable armor met a man who made a sword so sharp it could penetrate anything. So they decided on a test. The first man, dressed in his armor, told the other man to strike him with his sword. This the latter did, striking his opponent on the helmet. After the blow: the man in the armor said: "There, I told you so; nothing happened." And the other man replied: "Shake yourself." The first man shook himself and fell in two pieces—the sword was so sharp he hadn't felt it."

Afterward when this lawyer shook himself he found himself falling in two pieces. His armor had been cut in two by the deft stroke of Jesus. The lawyer and the system he represented never recovered from that blow. The "neighbor" meant any man, anywhere.

O Jesus, Thou dost cut through my armored subterfuges with the sword of Thy Spirit. But Thy strokes save instead of severing. For Thou art love and only love. So I bare my soul to Thy strokes. For I want to be love and only love to everybody. Amen.

AFFIRMATION FOR THE DAY: *A restricted love is a canceled love.*

EGOISTIC AND ALTRUISTIC URGES

We have been studying the second greatest commandment: "You shall love your neighbor as yourself." A farm woman said: "I don't do anything bad or mean to my neighbors, but I just don't neighbor." She loved her own time and convenience and herself more than she loved her neighbors—she just didn't neighbor. And this commandment said: "You shall love your neighbor as yourself "—as positively as you love yourself.

The phrase "as yourself " is important. The love was not to be more, or less, but *as* yourself. This balanced the self-love and the other-love in exact proportion. There are three important urges in human nature—self, sex, and the herd or social urge. The self-urge is obviously self-regarding. The herd urge is obviously other-regarding. The sex urge is partly self-regarding and partly other-regarding. Then there are just two driving urges within us—the self-regarding and the other-regarding, the egoistic and the altruistic urges.

Which urge becomes predominant is important. If you organize life around the self-regarding urge, you become an egocentric person. You are at war with yourself, for the other-regarding urge within you is unfulfilled, and hence frustrated. Consequently, any individual who is self-centered is an unhappy person, at conflict with himself. On the other hand, suppose you organize your life entirely around the other-regarding urge. Then you become a herd-centric person. You are again at war with yourself, for the self-regarding urge is unfulfilled, and hence frustrated. Every other-regarding society or individual is unhappy because the unfulfilled self is unhappy.

Life organized around the self is individualism. Life organized around the herd is collectivism. Both of these are based on half-truths, and hence produce unsatisfied, because unfulfilled, human nature. Christianity steps in amid that dissatisfaction and offers something that will satisfy both: You shall love your neighbor (the other-regarding urge) as yourself (the self-regarding urge). Both balanced exactly.

O Christ, Thy words and my needs fit each other. For Thou art the author of my being and Thy words fit me as a hand fits the glove. I am not following the extraneous, but the intrinsic, when I follow Thee. Amen.

AFFIRMATION FOR THE DAY: *When I love, I am working with the grain of my being.*

"AS I HAVE LOVED YOU"

We note one more thing in regard to the commandment "You shall love your neighbor as yourself." James adds a touch to this: "If you really fulfill the royal law, according to the scripture, 'You shall love your neighbor as yourself,' you do well" (2:8). Why is the law of loving your neighbor as you love yourself called the "royal law"? The democratic law, yes—but the "royal law"? The reason for the use of "royal" seems to be that you belong to royalty if you obey that law. You can get along with yourself if you obey it and you can get along with others. You have mastered the art of living with yourself and others—you have mastered life.

If you don't love your neighbor as you love yourself, you can't get along with your neighbor, for the self that doesn't love the neighbor is a self that the neighbor doesn't like. Moreover, if you don't love your neighbor you can't get along with yourself, for the self that doesn't love others is an unlovely self. We don't have to love our neighbor, but if we don't, we can't live with ourselves and we can't live with our neighbor.

While this law is a "royal law," it had to be amended. A new content had to be put into the loving. For many do not love themselves wisely or well. Some hate themselves. Loving your neighbor as you love yourself may be an unsafe standard. Jesus, therefore, had to put a new content into this loving; He did so in these words: "This is my commandment, that you love one another as I have loved you" (John 15:12). The last phrase, "as I have loved you," raised the commandment from the Old Testament to the New, from law to grace. For He loved them, not as they loved themselves and one another, but with a different type and quality of love—a love that required a new word to express it—"agape." Around that word much of this book is written. But the word would have been barren had not Jesus filled it with the content of the purest and widest love which this planet has seen. "As I have loved you" becomes the standard of loving for God and man. Nothing higher.

O Lord Jesus, we look into Thy face and now we know the meaning of love. All other definitions of love fade into insignificance. We see it in Thee, or do not see it at all. For Thou art the word of love become flesh. Amen.

AFFIRMATION FOR THE DAY: *The love of Jesus shall be for me the love for Jesus and all others.*

PERFECT STANDARD AND PERFECT CONTENT

"Love one another as I have loved you" is the high-water mark of human conduct in the ethical history of mankind. What philosophers, moralists, and religious thinkers have reached after through the ages, Jesus distilled in a sentence. They could not utter that sentence, because the sentence isn't a verbal sentence—it is a vital sentence. The content of the most beautiful life that has ever been lived has gone into it. No one else could utter it, for it couldn't be uttered—it had to be lived. That sentence is vascular. Cut it and it will bleed—will bleed with the lifeblood of the Son of God. Thirty-three years of unstained living and loving have gone into it. And more—the cross has gone into it. And more still—the Resurrection has gone into it. It is suffering love, but it is also a triumphant love. That love won out, in the end. And it *will* win out—in the end. It is the purest and most potent power in the universe—the love of Christ.

The same thing is distilled into a sentence by Paul: "Treat one another with the same spirit as you experience in Christ Jesus" (Phil. 2:5 Moffatt). Treat one another as Christ treats you. This is far beyond the Golden Rule: "Whatever you wish that men would do to you, do so to them." For we often want people to do to us what is not the highest and best for us. So Jesus had to put a new content into His own Golden Rule. When He uttered the Golden Rule it was the highest standard ever reached. But it wasn't a perfect standard. Jesus perfected it by putting the content of His life and love into it. And now, as amended, it is the Absolutely Perfect Standard, with the Absolutely Perfect Content, illustrated by the Absolutely Perfect Life. Among standards, this is It! Beyond it the human race will never progress. For Christ is God's perfect and final self-disclosure. To look for another Christ is to use a candle at midday to look for the sun.

So we have the highest Life emphasizing the highest thing—love—and making it central in life and conduct. That fixes morality as love in action. Nothing higher.

O Christ, how can I be grateful enough that Thou didst not miss Thy step at this delicate place? For if Thou hadst gone astray we would have all gone astray with Thee. But Thou didst make love first. So must I. Amen.

AFFIRMATION FOR THE DAY: *I see the Perfect Character, with the Perfect Content. Now to head in.*

A CONSISTENT LINE?

We have seen that Jesus made love central in His own life, and He insisted that we do the same. Was this emphasis lost when it went through the early Church? Did Jesus pass on the torch of love as supreme, to Paul, to Peter, to John? And did they hold it aloft? Yes, they did—and gloriously.

Now Paul was a fighter. Before he was Christianized he loved God so much, in his own way, that he was ready to kill people to make them love Him. Then came the amazing change. He was conquered by the love of Christ, conquered in outlook, in thought, in act, in character. When he wrote to the Corinthians, what would his highest emphasis be? He was writing to a people of whom it was said in a world known for its profligacy: "He lives like a Corinthian." Some of that corruption had seeped into the Church. Did Paul lower his standards to suit his audience? No. He lifted the standard higher than it was ever lifted, save in His own Master:

> If I speak in the tongues of men and of angels, but have not love, I am a noisy gong or a clanging cymbal. And if I have prophetic powers, and understand all mysteries and all knowledge, and if I have all faith, so as to remove mountains, but have not love, I am nothing. If I give away all I have, and if I deliver my body to be burned, but have not love, I gain nothing (I Cor. 13:1-3).

Here he puts love above eloquence of speech, in this world or the next—"tongues of men and of angels"; above insights into the future—"prophetic powers," and the understanding "of all mysteries" of God and man, and "all knowledge" about things as they are, scientific and philosophical; above "faith" of such a high order that it could "remove mountains"; above a charity that is prepared to "give away" all it has; and above a self-sacrifice that gives its very "body to be burned." These five things are the very highest things that religion and ethics have valued: power of speech, understanding all knowledge, effective faith, a reckless charity, and self-sacrifice. Yet Paul pronounced them nothing without love.

O Father, I thank Thee for these words of Thy servant Paul, for He could not have uttered them without Thy very Spirit thinking and speaking through him. And He held the torch of love aloft. I am grateful. In Jesus' name. Amen.

AFFIRMATION FOR THE DAY: *I draw a canceling line through every act which has no love in it—it is nothing.*

MATURE ENOUGH TO REJECT

In lifting love high above eloquence, above knowledge, above a mountain-moving faith, and above an all-out sacrificing spirit, Paul has lifted it high indeed; nevertheless, it is not a mere word he is lifting up. It is a word with a very real content. "Love is patient and kind; love is not jealous or boastful; it is not arrogant or rude. Love does not insist on its own way; it is not irritable or resentful; it does not rejoice at wrong, but rejoices in the right. Love bears all things, believes all things, hopes all things, endures all things" (I Cor. 13:4-7). Of the fifteen qualities mentioned, seven are positive and eight are negative. Love has to say no more often than yes. For its one positive is itself. Love is the positive that comprehends all right positives.

Just being positive is not enough. You may be positive with the wrong positive, and with the wrong spirit behind that positive. You have to be negative to many things to be positive to the highest things. You have to be negative to eight things to be positive to the seven. Then you are positive with a clarified positive. No one can say yes who hasn't said no.

Look at the positives: patient and kind, rejoices in the right, bears, believes, hopes, endures all things. But they could not stand out unless they had a background of rejection behind them: not jealous or boastful, not arrogant or rude; does not insist on its own way; not irritable or resentful; does not rejoice at wrong. The very negatives imply a positive. So maturity demands that we be mature enough to reject in order to accept. No man is capable of accepting who is not capable of rejecting. Negativism is bad if it stops at negativism. But positivism is also bad if it stops at positivism. Back of that positivism must be a positive negativism that has said a positive no, in order to say a positive yes.

So Paul could wade through his negatives because his eyes were upon that positive of positives—love. When he said love, he said it—with emphasis!

My Lord and my God, I thank Thee that Thou didst breathe into Thy servant Paul the insight to keep his sight clear. For he sees with Thy eyes and loves with Thy love. And hence we are intent on listening. Amen.

AFFIRMATION FOR THE DAY: *I am positive in the loving, therefore negative to the unloving thing.*

EVERYTHING WILL PASS AWAY EXCEPT LOVE

We pause to look again at the greatest analysis of love ever given—I Cor. 13. Paul says that prophecy will pass away, tongues will cease, and knowledge also will pass away. What a death blow to many of our modern quests! To be told that our insights into events, our foretelling the wave of the future, our search for impressive speech, and our very knowledge—scientific and what not—is only temporary and will pass away as fuller knowledge dawns—well, that is to pull the rug out from under most of our modern endeavors! They all "end."

Is that too sweeping? No. Suppose a nuclear scientist should stand before God, his Judge, and should preent his degrees and his knowledge of the atom as credentials, and suppose God should ask him one question, "Did you have love behind that knowledge?" And if the scientist's tongue should hesitate or stammer, would he not stand self-condemned? Of what earthly or heavenly use would be knowledge of atomic energy if there were no love behind it to control it and direct it toward the good of man?

Of what use is knowledge of the secrets of nature in bringing forth improved crop yields, if at the back of that knowledge is the intent to capture those secrets and use them for one's personal ends alone—in the purpose of greed? Will not the hunger-bitten peoples of the world witness before God that those who possessed such secrets prostituted them to their own greed and refused them to the needs of the masses? And will not the possessors of that knowledge stand speechless? Of what use is knowledge without love behind that knowledge?

Yes, bare knowledge will pass away. What remains? Three things: "So faith, hope, love abide" (I Cor. 13:13). But beyond the good things—faith and hope—stands the greatest thing: "But the greatest of these is love." We are almost breathless to see Paul's conclusion; for had he missed his step here, he would have been out of step with his Master. But, thank God, he didn't! He takes the torch which Jesus handed on and holds it high: Love!

Dear God, we are grateful for this conclusion. We see how consistently our faith is holding to a single line—the line of the supremacy of love. Now we, too, can sound that note with no hesitation or fear. We thank Thee. Amen.

AFFIRMATION FOR THE DAY: *"Love never ends"; therefore I cannot fail if I love.*

"LOVE OF GOD SHED ABROAD"

When Paul came out with love as the greatest thing in the world, was it a chance note struck in an exalted moment, but isolated and alone? Or was his faith in love grounded in the nature of things, in the very nature of the universe, in the nature of man, in the very nature of God, and hence in the very nature of the revelation of God in Christ? Love was central in the whole of the outlook and teaching of Paul.

When he enumerates the fruits of the Spirit, we hold our breath to see which will come first. Will it be power? Or peace, Or joy? No, the first fruit of the Spirit was "love." The list is wonderful: "Love, joy, peace, patience, kindness, goodness, faithfulness, gentleness, self-control" (Gal. 5:22-23). Now suppose that any other than love of that list of beautiful qualities of character had been put first. It would have been a second best in the first place. Love is there because it belongs there. There is no other place for it except first place.

This observation fits in with what Paul says of the Holy Spirit: ". . . because God's love has been poured into our hearts through the Holy Spirit which has been given to us" (Rom. 5:5). This is important, for Jesus said when the Holy Spirit came upon them they would "receive power" (Acts 1:8). Wasn't "power," then, the characteristic thing that came when the Holy Spirit came? But with unerring insight, Paul saw that the "power" which came with the coming of the Holy Spirit was the power of love. It was the power to love everybody and everything, even enemies. Had the Holy Spirit poured anything other than love into the hearts of those ready to receive Him, no matter how good that thing might have been, it would have changed the nature of our faith and would have sent us off on a tangent after this, that, or the other second best. Here the Holy Spirit gives the highest gift that can be given by God or man—the gift of love. God's love is poured into our faculties and powers and drives, and converts those faculties, powers, and drives into love. Thus redeems them.

O Holy Spirit, we need love above all our needs. And we need Thy particular brand of love—God's love. We need it, not sprinkled here and there upon us, but poured into every nook and cranny of our beings. Pour on. Amen.

AFFIRMATION FOR THE DAY: *I do not have to love—I have to let love love me into loving.*

"PUT"

We have been studying the fact that Paul continues the emphasis of Jesus and makes love supreme. This comes out in unstudied ways. Love comes out on top every time Paul begins a discussion, since that is where it belongs. It comes out from its own inherent superiority.

Take Paul's discussion, in Col. 3:5-14, built around the word "put." He begins by telling us what to "put" to death. First, "Put to death therefore what is earthly in you: immorality, impurity, passion, evil desire, and covetousness, which is idolatry" (3:5). Here he names the sins of the flesh as things to be put to death. Along with these sex sins he names covetousness—a desire for things, which is just as bad as a desire for the body of another. He calls it idolatry—the idolatry of the golden calf, an idolatry just as prevalent in the West as the idolatry of graven images is prevalent in the East, and just as deadly.

Second, "But now put them all away: anger, wrath, malice, slander, and foul talk from your mouth" (3:8). The second "put" is the putting away of the sins of the disposition—anger, wrath, malice, slander, and foul talk. These are the sins of the disposition, in contrast to the sins of the flesh in the first putting away. Many moral and religious people who are not guilty of sex immorality are guilty of ugly tempers and bad dispositions.

Third, "Do not lie to one another seeing that you have put off the old nature with its practices" (3:9). Here he goes deeper in demanding that we not only put off the sins of the flesh and the sins of the disposition, we must "put off the old nature." Don't just try to lop off the deeds, the branches, says Paul; go back to the old nature, the trunk and the root.

Fourth, "And have put on the new nature which is being renewed in knowledge after the image of its creator" (3:10). He now begins three positives after naming three negatives. And the first positive is, "Put on the new nature." The old nature must be replaced by the new nature, not merely the old deeds with the new deeds.

O God, help me this day to take these steps—to put off the sins of the flesh and disposition, and the old nature behind those sins, and help me to put on the new nature which will be behind the new deeds. I must do this if I'm to live. Amen.

AFFIRMATION FOR THE DAY: *"There is much rubbish; we are not able to work on the wall"*—*I'm getting rid of rubbish, for I'm building.*

"ABOVE ALL PUT ON LOVE"

We continue to meditate upon the "puts" of Paul in Col. 3:5-14. We noted the "put" of "having put on the new nature, which is being renewed in knowledge after the image of its creator." The new nature is constantly "being renewed"—the newness becomes more new each day, and after a very definite pattern, which is the image of God, our Creator. Here we don't discover our innate divinity—an absurdity—but we become more and more like our Father, day by day—an attainable goal.

Fifth, "Put on then, as God's chosen ones, holy and beloved, compassion, kindness, lowliness, meekness, and patience, forbearing one another and, if one has a complaint against another, forgiving each other; as the Lord has forgiven you, so you also must forgive" (3:12-13). Here is a "put" which adds to the basic new nature these basic new virtues—compassion, kindness, lowliness, patience, forbearing, forgiveness. They are the gentler virtues, so rare and so beautiful—like a lily out of a muck heap.

But now we come to the "put" at which we have been aiming: "And above all of these put on love, which binds everything together in perfect harmony" (3:14). Here love is to be put on "above all these." In other words, love is the garment that shows before the world. It is the thing the world sees when it sees you. Your whole impact on your surroundings is to be a love impact. When others see you they think of love. So love is to be the first and last impression.

But love is not a mere impression—it is something deeper; for love is that "which binds everything together in perfect harmony." Without love the new life and the new virtues lack cohesion and they lack harmony. They are likely to get out of proportion, so that without love your virtues turn to vices.

And moreover, love makes all the other virtues blend "in perfect harmony." It is a color which can be worn with any color. Love is always "proper." It can be worn with overalls and evening dress. It is a harmony that brings harmony to all disharmonies. Love is it!

Father, we have come to see that without love we set everything in us awry, within and without. We cannot do without love any more than the lungs can do without air. Then help me to wear love in all my contacts. Amen.

AFFIRMATION FOR THE DAY: *Love shall harmonize all my thoughts, emotions, and will—harmonize everything.*

"LOVE THAT ISSUES FROM A PURE HEART"

We are studying the fact that Paul was in the line of succession of Jesus, who made love to God and love to man supreme, and made it after the pattern of His kind of love—"as I have loved you."

We have looked at certain passages which have been as clear as a bell in sounding the supremacy of love. Here is another:

As I urged you when I was going to Macedonia, remain at Ephesus that you may charge certain persons not to teach any different doctrine, nor to occupy themselves with myths and endless genealogies which promote speculations rather than the divine training that is in faith; whereas the aim of our charge is love that issues from a pure heart and a good conscience and sincere faith (I Tim. 1:3-5).

Note that Timothy was to remain at Ephesus, since the church there had gone off the track. They had a marvelous beginning when the Holy Spirit came upon them. They had been "twelve men" (Acts 19:7). But they were noncontagious. The other "twelve" were turning the world upside down, for they were working in the power of the Spirit. This group of "twelve" were turning nothing upside down. Their spiritual pulse was low, for the Holy Spirit had not come within them to raise their spiritual temperature to contagion point. But after Paul prayed for these men the Holy Spirit came upon them, and then something happened within them, around them. A revival ensued in which people who practiced magic arts came and publicly burned books worth fifty thousand pieces of silver. "So the word of the Lord grew and prevailed mightily." It was a great beginning. Why did Paul have to urge Timothy to stay at Ephesus to set the church aright? What had happened? The story of what had happened is related in Rev. 2:1-7; here John transmits this message to the church at Ephesus: "I know your works, your toil and your patient endurance, and how you cannot bear evil men. . . . I know you are enduring patiently and bearing up for my name's sake, and you have not grown weary. But I have this against you, that you have abandoned the love you had at first." They had fallen away in love.

O Christ, when we fall from love we fall in the central thing in our faith. Kindle my love with Thy love. Blow with the breath of Thy Spirit upon the embers of my heart and set me aflame with love. For Thy Name's sake. Amen.

AFFIRMATION FOR THE DAY: *I fall down as I fall down in love; I rise as I rise in love.*

"ABANDONED THE LOVE"

We were thinking yesterday upon what had happened to the church at Ephesus that caused Paul to urge Timothy to stay and set them right. The explanation is found in Rev. 2:1-7, wherein the Lord Jesus charged the Ephesians, through John, with having "abandoned the love you had at first." And then He adds: "Remember then from what you have fallen, repent and do the works you did at first. If not, I will come to you and remove your lampstand from its place, unless you repent. Yet this you have, you hate the works of the Nicolaitans, which I also hate." Above He had noted that "you cannot bear evil men." They began to "hate" more than "love." They could "not bear evil men," but in the despising of the evil they forgot to love the evildoers. Love faded out. And the Lord Jesus said that they were "fallen." But they were a church full of "toil," "patient endurance," a church that could not "bear evil men," a church that had not "grown weary." By all the standards of a modern church it was a topnotch church. In the eyes of Jesus it was a "fallen" church, because fallen in the only thing that matters—love. By that standard, then, three quarters of the churches of Christendom are "fallen"—correct in doctrine, beautiful in ritual, rich in culture, eloquent in preaching, but with a dimmed love.

And Jesus asked that church to "repent"—repent of its lovelessness. This is an altar call that should bring three quarters of Christendom to its knees. For nothing, absolutely nothing, can atone for this lovelessness. Without it our services are sounding brass and tinkling cymbal.

And more serious still, Jesus insists that if this lack of love is not repented of, then He will come and "remove your lampstand from its place." And what was the lampstand? A candelabrum? An adjunct to a service? No, it was the church itself: "The seven lampstands are the seven churches" (Rev. 1:20). And how does He remove the lampstands, the churches? By simply removing them from the "effective list." There they "have the name of being alive, and . . . are dead."

O Jesus, Thy relentless but loving eyes see where we are ailing—the central ailing. Help us not to wince or pull away or excuse or plead, but to face reality and repent and ask another chance—another chance to love—everybody. Amen.

AFFIRMATION FOR THE DAY: *The loving heart cannot fall, cannot fail, cannot be fruitless.*

"THE DIVINE TRAINING"

We have been studying the message of Jesus to the church at Ephesus. He ends the exhortation with the offer: "To him who conquers I will grant to eat of the tree of life, which is in the paradise of God" (Rev. 2:7). What does this imply? This: To love is to eat of the tree of life; not to love is not to eat of the tree of life. To love is to live; not to love is not to live. When the church at Ephesus shut itself off from love, it shut itself off from the tree of life. It fed itself on the husks of correct doctrine, works, a negative attitude toward evildoers, a hating of special groups—Nicolaitans. But the Ephesians were shut out from the tree of life which is in the paradise of God—shut themselves out.

We now turn back to Paul's appeal to this church, made through Timothy, who was to stay on at Ephesus and try to get the members to loving again. He says: "Charge certain persons" not "to occupy themselves" with anything except "the divine training that is in faith; whereas the aim of our charge is love that issues from a pure heart and a good conscience and sincere faith" (I Tim. 1:3-5). Here he says that "the divine training" is a training in love—a "love that issues"—issues out to everybody and everything.

This statement is important, for it says that the aim of the whole Christian discipline is to produce people who love and who love actively, with love issuing from the depths of the personality to the loveless, to enemies, to everybody.

And that "divine training" is not a training by imposing this law, that law, this restraint, that restraint. It is a training by love—"The love of Christ controls us." You do a thing, or you do not do a thing, because you love Him. It is "a divine training" from within out, and not from without in. One who is thus trained is natural and spontaneous, not compelled but impelled. Loving is the easiest thing he does—and the most profound.

O Lord Jesus, train me with this "divine training." What a Trainer Thou art for Thou dost train me by example and by leading the way. And more: Thou dost come within, and all I have to do is to yield to Thy love. Thou dost love me into loving. Amen.

AFFIRMATION FOR THE DAY: *I shall be a trained person—trained to appreciate, to encourage, to love.*

THE AIM—LOVE OUT OF A PURE HEART

We must pause another day on "the aim"—the fact that the Christian aim is "love that issues from a pure heart and a good conscience and sincere faith."

The personality is composed of three things: intelligence, feeling, will. It is interesting and important to note that Paul says love issues from the total personality: "out of a pure heart," the affectional or feeling urge; out of "a good conscience," the volitional or willing urge; out of "a sincere faith," the mind, or intellectual urge.

It is also interesting to note that the Hindus divide the three ways of salvation as the *Gyana Marg*—the way of knowledge, the mind; the *Bhakti Marg*—the way of affection, or devotion; the *Karma Marg*—the way of the will, of works. Now note that the Hindus designate love as one of the ways—but only one of the ways—the *Bhakti Marg*. But in the Christian way, love is not one of the ways set alongside of other ways—love is the way of each of these other ways. The love issues "from a pure heart"—the emotions; from "a good conscience"—the will; from "a sincere faith"—the mind. Love is the attitude and the atmosphere of all our feeling, all our willing, and all our thinking. It is not one virtue set alongside of our other virtues—it is the virtue of all our virtues. For without love the feelings feel wrongly, the will wills wrongly, and the mind thinks wrongly. But with love everything within us is harmonious, because love "binds everything together in perfect harmony." With love as the center and the spring of all our feeling, the center and spring of all our acting, the center and spring of all our thinking, each of us is a harmonized person.

But if any part lacks love we are disrupted persons. If we have an intellectual love and an emotional hate, or an emotional love and a volitional hate, we are a house divided against itself that cannot stand. Only as we feel lovingly, act lovingly, and think lovingly are we a completely harmonized person. As one instrument off-tune will upset a whole orchestra on-tune, so one portion of our nature off-tune without love, will make the total life a discord.

O Jesus, I want to know the art of loving. I want to think love and only love; feel love and only love; act love and only love. I want to become love and love alone. For only as I do, do I live. I want to be alive with love. Amen.

AFFIRMATION FOR THE DAY: *Not love in a pure heart, but love out of a pure heart—that is my aim.*

"THE LOVE IS THE VICTORY"

We have seen how sound is Paul's reasoning as he keeps the line of succession clean regarding Jesus' emphasis on love. Paul says: "Let love be genuine; . . . love one another with brotherly affection" (Rom. 12:9-10). And then he tells how far that love is to extend, not to the inside circle of brothers, but to enemies. "If your enemy is hungry, feed him; if he is thirsty, give him drink; for by so doing you will heap burning coals upon his head. Do not be overcome by evil, but overcome evil with good" (Rom. 12:20-21). Here was love unlimited, extending from the brotherhood to active enemies. This love overcomes hate by love. It has no other weapons. It throws away all other weapons. If it cannot conquer by love it goes down in defeat, depending on nothing else. But in going down in defeat it holds its banner aloft—victorious even in defeat. The victory of the stoners of Stephen was a marginal victory; the central victory was the prayer of love: "Lord, do not hold this sin against them." Their victory of hate died; his victory of love was deathless.

The writer of the Epistle to the Hebrews does not emphasize love except when he exhorts his readers: "Let us consider how to stir up one another to love" (10:24). When he wanted to get them to consider the supreme value, he put his finger on love. It was unescapable amid the clamoring interests pressing for attention. Love won out.

James, with his intense interest in pragmatic values, picks out one law as the "royal law"—the law that governs all laws: "You shall love your neighbor as yourslf" (2:8). He failed to put in the more royal law: "You shall love the Lord your God with all your heart . . . "; hence his epistle lacks height as well as depth. It is more horizontal than vertical. It is not "an epistle of straw," as Luther said, for there is much grain here. But failing to include love to God as the supreme impulse, thereby creating faith as the working force, he put in works toward man as the working force. His social passion is needed, but it lacked the reinforcement and motive of a supreme love to God.

O Father, I know I cannot love others unless my love to Thee is supreme and unalloyed. So breathe Thy love into my heart till it glows with passion for Thee. Then, and then only, will it burn with a passion for others. Amen.

AFFIRMATION FOR THE DAY: *I cannot be defeated if I love; if I don't love I'm already defeated.*

BROTHERLY AFFECTION BUT NOT LOVE

Does Peter, in his Epistles, keep up this supreme emphasis on love? He should do so, remembering the supreme emphasis that Jesus placed on love in the healing restoration after Peter's denial: "Simon, son of John, do you love me more than these?" . . . "Simon, son of John, do you love me?" . . . "Do you love me?" (John 21:15, 17). Simon has transferred his love for Christ to himself and so fears for his own safety. Now that love was being reclaimed and transferred back to Christ. Conversion is a conversion of our loves. Sin is our loves gone astray. So when Peter said three times that he loved Him, thus undoing the three-times denial, he was back again, "converted," as Jesus said he would be.

When Peter came to writing his Epistles would he keep that emphasis? When he puts together the virtues, which does he pick out for final emphasis? Here is the order:

For this very reason make every effort to supplement your faith with virtue, and virtue with knowledge, and knowledge with self-control, and self-control with steadfastness, and steadfastness with godliness, and godliness with brotherly affection, and brotherly affection with love. For if these things are yours and abound, they keep you from being ineffective or unfruitful in the knowledge of our Lord Jesus Christ (II Pet. 1:5-8).

When he comes to putting the capstone on all the moral and spiritual qualities—faith, virtue, knowledge, self-control, steadfastness, godliness, brotherly affection—he names "love" as that capstone. And love of a particular kind—a love that was beyond "brotherly affection." One could have "brotherly affection" and not have this "love."

We are now at the very heart of our discussion on maturity in love. Peter has introduced us to it. For the Christian faith does not introduce to love in general, but love in particular—Christian love.

The English language is poverty-stricken at this point, in that it has one word to describe love. This means that a dozen different kinds of love are comprehended under that word "love." Hence the confusion. The Greek language was richer—it had two words for love—" "eros" and "agape."

O Father God, as we thread our way through eros and agape, give us insight to see the difference—and deeper, to act upon that difference. For we may be loving with the wrong kind of love. Help us. Amen.

AFFIRMATION FOR THE DAY: *No cheap substitute for love—love shall be the real thing!*

TASTE OF LOVE IN FRUITS OF SPIRIT

We have seen that the dominant note from Jesus—through Stephen, Paul, James, and Peter—is love. Had it been a chance note struck here or there, the result would have been different. As it is, love is the note that binds all the other notes into harmony, until the whole becomes a symphony of love.

All the fruits of the Spirit have the taste of love in them: joy is the joy of love; peace is love grown quiet; long-suffering is love stretched out; kindness is love with hands outstretched; goodness is love relating itself to the moral law; faithfulness is love holding steady amid everything; gentleness is love expressing itself in relationships; self-control is love in charge within.

In all other faiths, love is tacked in here and there. Perhaps the high-water mark of Judaism is in this verse:

> He has showed you, O man, what is good;
>   and what does the Lord require of you
> But to do justice, and to love kindness,
>   And to walk humbly with your God? (Mic. 6:8).

But here "to love kindness" is a marginal note about one of the virtues—kindness. It is not the dominant note of the whole.

In Hinduism there is the beautiful suggestion: "We are to be like the sandlewood tree which when smitten by the axe pours its perfume upon the axe that smites it." Beautiful, but marginal, a chance note sounded among many more dominant notes. For instance, the dominant note in Hinduism is absorption into Brahman, not love for Brahman; for there is no love in Brahman to respond to the human love.

In Buddhism the word is "compassion," not "love." For the attitude is compassion for those caught in the round of weary rebirths. But compassion or pity for trapped people falls far short of love toward God and man and life.

In the gospel, love is not something put in and then canceled out by other emphases. It is the whole motif.

Father, I thank Thee that Thou hast struck one note as the supreme note, the note of love, wherever men have exposed themselves to Thee in Christ. For in Him we see love and only love and an overflowing love to everybody. Amen.

AFFIRMATION FOR THE DAY: *As love is the consistent motif of the gospel, it shall be the consistent motif of my life.*

LOVE—THE ALPHA AND THE OMEGA

We have seen that love is the alpha and the omega of the Christian faith. But it was John, the disciple of love, who put the capstone on this whole structure. For the dominant note in I John is just what we would expect—the note of love. Writing with the background of Gnosticism, John would have been expected to use the word "know"—gnosis—more often than any other. But John was not caught in the temptation to let one's opponent set the dominant note in the discussion. He did use the word "know" thirty-six times, but he used the word "love" forty-three times. To know was good, to love was best.

The other emphases in the Epistle are these: the word "life" is used thirteen times; "commandment" fifteen times and interestingly enough the word "this" is used twenty-nine times.

That last is important: if "love" is used forty-three times, the word "this" fixes that love, not as an abstract conception—it fixed it in history, in the concrete, in personal embodiment in Jesus and in God. The Word of love became flesh in Jesus. There love looks out at us with tender eyes and touches us with warm, redemptive hands.

Had the Epistle been a mere discussion of love it would have left us cold. It was not a discussion of love, but a demonstration of love. The incarnation was an incarnation of love. And that incarnation revealed something which lay back in the nature of things, in God. Jesus showed us that by revealing love in Himself, He was revealing love as the very heart of Reality. It was not a chance note—it was the dominant note in the music of the spheres.

The "thisness" of the discussion and description of love makes love take shoes and walk, and walk where we walk—along the dusty roads of life. You cannot get into a single situation where "this" does not apply. For "this" scattered twenty-nine times is saying that "this" is that which lies back in Reality.

O Father God, I thank Thee that I have my finger on the pulse-beat of the heart of the universe. For when I feel the pulse-beat of love I feel Thy heartbeat. *This is It.* Everything within me cries out that This is It. Amen.

AFFIRMATION FOR THE DAY: *Today I shall strive to make love "this" in every act—not "that," or "the other."*

"THIS," AND NOT "THAT"

We noted yesterday that in the Epistle of John the word "this" was used twenty-nine times. In all other faiths the word "that" is the word used. The words point beyond themselves to "that"—never to a "this." In the Vedanta philosophy the acme of "that" is reached when in describing God the word used is *"Neti," "Neti"*—"not that," "not that." God is even beyond the "that"—He, or rather It, is beyond description. Even words cannot point to It.

But in Jesus "that" becomes "this." For Jesus is the personal approach from the Unseen in which the unfathomable "That" becomes the incarnate "This."

In the Bhagavad-Gita, Krishna is supposed to be the incarnation of God. But it is a philosophical treatise with no grounding in history. The historic Krishna is anything but an incarnation of God—he is an incarnation of youthful pranks. So the Gita has no illustration of what it means by incarnation. It is a philosophy, not a Fact; a series of words instead of the Word made flesh, a book instead of a Babe.

The "thisness" of love in this Epistle makes it not a dissertation but a deed, not a recital but a revelation. This forever sets it apart as forever different, sole, unique.

So when John describes love he describes "This," not that, or the other. No wonder philosophy has fallen on evil days. We mentioned the fact that in Madras, the home of philosophy, the Madras University offers no courses in philosophy because no students are prepared to enroll in philosophy. They are turning to science. Why? Well, philosophy is something imposed on life, rather than something exposed out of life. Science, on the other hand, is something exposed out of life—it is a revelation of the facts and laws underlying nature. Hence its power. It is true that there are limitations of science, but that lack will not be supplied by philosophy—it will be supplied by a revelation of the laws underlying the world of spirit. In other words, it will be supplied by Incarnation and only by Incarnation.

Because the gospel is "This," and not "that" and "the other," it holds the future. And what a future—a future of love!

O Lord Jesus, Thou art set down down in the midst of life, revealing the meaning of life, redeeming life, and opening the gates of life. Now we are no longer fumbling amid theories about life; we have hold of the hand of This Revelation of life. Amen.

AFFIRMATION FOR THE DAY: *Love in the abstract bores us; love embodied in a person blesses us.*

"GOD IS LOVE"—HIGH-WATER MARK

When the final unfolding of love took place in the whole of the gradual revelation of God, it took place in these words:

Beloved, let us love one another; for love is of God, and he who loves is born of God and knows God. He who does not love does not know God; for God is love. In this the love of God was made manifest among us, that God sent his only Son into the world, so that we might live through him. In this is love, not that we loved God but that he loved us and sent his Son to be the expiation for our sins. Beloved, if God so loved us, we also ought to love one another. No man hath ever seen God; if we love one another, God abides in us and his love is perfected in us. . . . So we know and believe the love God has for us. God is love, and he who abides in love abides in God, and God abides in him. In this is love perfected with us, that we may have confidence for the day of judgment, because as he is so are we in this world. There is no fear in love but perfect love casts out fear. For fear has to do with punishment, and he who fears is not perfected in love. We love, because he first loved us (I John 4:7-12; 16-19).

In these ten verses love is mentioned twenty-two times. That in itself is striking, but the more striking thing is the content of the word "love" and its source. The content is here: "In this the love of God was made manifest among us; that God sent his only Son . . . to be the expiation for our sins." The content of love is to be found in Jesus—"made manifest among us." Jesus is love in character and attitude and action. And the culmination and supreme revelation of that love is the cross—"to be the expiation for our sins."

And the source of that love is God: "God is love."

From childhood we have repeated the phrase "God is love," until it has become as indistinct as a slick coin—slick from incessant circulation. But when John wrote those words it was the first time in human history that the words had been uttered. Men had speculated and asserted many things about God, but it was only here that at long last the phrase finally came out: "God is love." That was the last word of revelation. Nothing more could be said.

O Father, we thank Thee that at long, long last we have seen the ultimate truth about Thee. Thou art love. Our hearts pillow themselves upon that glorious, wondrous fact. We shall be exploring it forever. Amen.

AFFIRMATION FOR THE DAY: *Love shall first, last, and always be my word and my weapon.*

"HEAVEN BROKE OUT IN APPLAUSE"

"God is love," we have said, is the high-water mark of revelation. I can imagine that all heaven bent over as John neared the writing of that sentence and as he finally wrote it heaven broke out in rapturous applause, saying: "They've got it. At long last they've discovered it. They see that God is love!" And a sigh of deep satisfaction and infinite joy settled upon the redeemed portion of the universe. Man had arrived at maturity in his conception about God. God not only is the author of loving acts, He is love by His very nature. And therefore when He expresses Himself, He must, by His very nature, express Himself in terms of love and nothing but love. He cannot act except as He acts in love. To act in terms other than love would be for Him to be denatured.

Why was man so long in reaching this conclusion? The answer is simple: Man could not say this until he had looked into the face of Jesus. There he saw in the face of Jesus, as the revelation of God: "God is love."

Why didn't Jesus say it? Why did it have to wait to be said by John? Well, Jesus did say it—said it in the only way He could say it: by deed, by death, by life. The Word of Love had to become flesh before it could become word.

It took the most loving of the apostles, at the very last period of his long life, to put the finishing touch on the whole process of revelation. And then he could not have done it except as the Spirit of God wrote it through him. The most momentous hour of the long march of man upward toward God had come. The supreme revelation had dawned. From henceforth the whole development of man would be a development with his verse as a starting point. And his development would be a development in love. All else would be marginal—love would be central. Not that man would not stray from love and fight against love—he would; but the point is that if he did stray from it, or fight against it, he would break himself. The issue was now clear: Love or perish.

O God, my Father, we now see into Thy heart, and seeing, we are set on fire to be like Thee, to be love, and only love, in all we do and say and are. For we cannot live against Thee and not get hurt. Amen.

AFFIRMATION FOR THE DAY: *If love is the greatest thing in the world, then every little act done in love is great.*

"THEY HAD NO JESUS"

We wonder why India, in her long and patient quest for God, did not arrive at: God is Love. For never has the mind of man sought to grasp the meaning of God as it has in India. The philosophies of India are the high-water mark of man's philosophical search for God. Here the mind of man strained itself to the utmost to reach God by searching and speculating. Why did they miss it?

The answer is simple: they had no Jesus. They had Rama, Krishna, Shankara, Ramanuja, Buddha, and all the rest, but no Jesus. That lack was the vital lack. For Jesus was the Word of Love become flesh. The rest were the Word become word. And that is the difference.

The speculating mind of man reached its highest in the Vedanta philosophy of Shankara in the Advaita. In this philosophy the highest concept of God is in Brahman, who is *sat*, *chit*, and *ananda*. *Sat*—truth, or reality; *chit*—intelligence; *ananda*—bliss. Truth, intelligence, bliss, but no love. Why is love left out of the ultimate conception of God? Because had there been love in Brahman, it would have related it to man and that would have brought Brahman into relationships. And to be related would be less than perfect. So love, involving relationships with the object of love, is left out of God. And it if is left out of God then it is also left out of the seekers after God. They, too, must be the unrelated. They must sit in contemplation with attention fastened upon the tip of the nose, affirming themselves into identity with the unrelated Brahman. So good and evil are transcended. And the point is that love, too, is transcended.

But if love is transcended, then life is transcended, for love is life. That philosophy, if carried to its ultimate conclusion, unfits men to live. But the conception that God is love means that the highest man must be the man of love. That sets religion amid human relationships and sets it there with the highest characteristic in human relationships—the characteristic of love—nothing higher.

O God, our Father, since Thou art love, all Thy impacts upon me are impacts of love, and nothing but love. Then make all my impacts upon the life around me to be the impacts of love and nothing but love. In Jesus' name. Amen.

AFFIRMATION FOR THE DAY: *Since "love never fails," I will not fail, except as I fail in love.*

GOD IN DIFFERING SYSTEMS

The differing systems of thought and devotion have arrived at the following ideas concerning God: Egyptian—God is immortality; Hebrew—God is righteous law; Japanese—God is loyalty; Chinese—God is poise; Hindu—God is truth, intelligence, bliss; Buddhist—God is a question mark; Greek—God is eros; Mohammedanism—God is authority; modern secularism—God is irrelevant; modern science—God is natural law; Christian—God is love.

And not abstract love, but love as seen in the teaching, the life, the death, the resurrection of Jesus. It is love anchored to and interpreted by the fact of Jesus. As someone has said: "The victory must go to those ideas which are guaranteed by the facts." The idea of love in the gospel is guaranteed by the fact of Jesus.

And the fact of love as seen in Jesus was of such a type and kind that a new word had to be created to express and hold this new and revolutionary meaning. The new wine of love had to be put into a new wineskin. The old was inadequate. So the word "agape" was chosen to express this amazing newness. I say "chosen," for the word was in use here and there in Greek literature, but as a verb "agapen," not as a noun "agape." The Christians took over the word and used it as noun, adjective, verb—as everything. They poured the love of Jesus into that word until it meant everything that God intended in the revelation of Himself in Jesus. So the final word of that revelation was: *God is agape.*

Plato came nearest to this idea when in essence he said: God is eros. But the choice of a word was the choice of a world. For there is a world of difference between those two words. They both express love, but love with an entirely different content.

In Japan my interpreter, who rarely hesitated for a word, was embarrassed when I said: "Every day I awake saying to Jesus: 'I love you.'" The interpreter used the ordinary word for "love" in Japanese, and the audience burst out laughing. It was the word for sex love.

O Gracious God, Thou art redeeming us and our language. For our language has fallen as we have fallen. Redeem us and our words. And in all Thy redeeming, redeem our concept and practice of love. In Jesus' name. Amen.

AFFIRMATION FOR THE DAY: *Love, the highest, is the highest in the Highest, God—let it be the highest in me.*

DEFINITION OF LOVE

We come now to examine what we mean by love. Ashley Montagu, in his book *The Meaning of Love*, starts out with the dictionary definition of love as "a feeling of deep regard, fondness, devotion; deep affection, usually accompanied by yearning or desire for; affection between persons of opposite sex, more or less founded on or combined with desire or passion." In this definition, of course, we see the content of contemporaneous society poured into a word. As such it is sub-Christian.

Someone has said, "If you want to see the depravity of man, look into the dictionary"; for words associated with man become depraved by that association. The foregoing definition was created out of a "Christian" civilization. And yet it very faintly reflects, or does not reflect at all, the meaning of love as found in the distinctly Christian term "agape."

Freud, going further in his unconscious or conscious revolt against Christianity, defines love as sex love, or as almost entirely sex love.

I saw written on the wall of a compartment of an Indian train: "I loved a woman—a nurse—in this compartment between [a certain city] and [another]." Here a man had unconsciously defined love as the sex act, and the sex act on the low level of adultery.

Obviously, our words need to be redeemed. In English the word "love" is a medley of meanings, ranging from the highest to the lowest. So we cannot use the phrase "maturity in love" until we have fixed the content of "love." For if we go wrong as to the meaning of love, we will go wrong as to the meaning of maturity.

For this reason we cannot take our idea of maturity from psychology alone. Psychology is modern psychology, and modern psychology needs to be Christianized. As Viktor Frankl, a psychiatrist, has said: "We will apply psychologism to itself by examining its own psychogenesis—that is, the motives that underlie it. What is its hidden basic attitude, its secret tendency? Our reply is: a tendency toward devaluation."

O Christ, we turn to Thee for a breath of the fresh air of Thy spirit. For we suffocate in the smog that overhangs our civilization. We would have the freshness of Thee and Thy love blow across our conceptions, across us. Amen.

AFFIRMATION FOR THE DAY: *Lovelessness devaluates, love enhances.*

"BENT UPON DEBUNKING"

We have said that we cannot accept without question or reservation the content that psychologism puts into words, especially words like "love" and "maturity." As Viktor Frankl further says:

It [psychologism] . . . is forever bitterly bent upon debunking, is constantly hunting down extrinsic—that is, neurotic or culturo-pathological-motivations. . . . Everywhere, psychologism sees nothing but masks, insists that only neurotic motives lie behind these masks. Art, it asserts, is "in the final analysis nothing but" flight from life and flight from love. . . . Can there never be anything immediate, genuine, original? . . . Psychologism, then, is the favorite recourse of those with a tendency toward devaluation.

We must turn to our Christian sources—to Christ—to find the content of our words "maturity" and "love." "That you love one another, even as I have loved you," puts the Christian content into these words.

We must now seek to find the Christian content of the word "love." We can do this best by using the Greek words "eros" and "agape." In English they would both be translated "love," but the content would be decidedly different. The Greeks, especially Plato, adopted the word "eros" to express their idea of love for God and man; and the Christians adopted the word "agape." But the meaning the Christians put into agape did not reflect its Greek source. They adopted the word because it was the most suitable term, but the content became distinctly Christian. When filled with Christian meaning it became the most revolutionary idea ever presented to the mind of man. As Anders Nygren puts it: "The Christian idea of love . . . involves a revolution in ethical outlook without parallel in the history of ethics, a revolution rightly described by Nietzsche as a complete 'transvaluation of all ancient values.'" And yet that most revolutionary and original concept is "scarcely mentioned in the traditional histories of ethics." We must recover that lost emphasis and let agape again grip and control us.

O Lord Jesus, when we come in contact with Thy love we feel we are in contact with the most tremendous thing that life—human and divine—holds. So we expose ourselves to it. We would absorb it until it absorbs us. Amen.

AFFIRMATION FOR THE DAY: *Let me continue that basic "revolution of transvaluing all values"—continue it by love.*

LOVE OCCUPIES THE CENTRAL PLACE

We mentioned yesterday that "love" has had little theological treatment through the ages. Faith, atonement, eternal life, resurrection—all these have had plentiful treatment. But as Nygren says: "It is plain that the idea of love occupies a—not to say the—central place in Christianity, both from a religious and an ethical point of view. Yet we have only to glance at the treatment the subject has received from theologians in recent times, to see that it is among the most neglected."

We are now being pressed into a rediscovery of agape by the very pressures of modern demands—demands which call for love. When an outstanding psychiatrist like Karl Menninger writes a book entitled *Love Against Hate*, tracing all our personality conflicts to a lack of love; and when another psychiatrist, Smiley Blanton, writes a book entitled *Love or Perish*—it means that the Christian is driven to rediscover his own unique contribution to human living in terms of agape. To rediscover original agape means to uncover the answer—the answer to empty, disrupted modern living. For the world is sick—literally and metaphorically sick—for love. With it we can go anywhere, without it we perish.

In ancient times two men commented about God: Plato—"God is eros"; John—"God is agape." Just the difference of two words, and yet there was the difference of two worlds. For two worlds of different meanings went into those words. And this difference runs straight through all our ethics and all our religions. It divides—and divides them decisively. All systems range themselves unconsciously on one side or the other, according as they embody eros or agape. Says Nygren: "There is quite concrete proof of the existence both of an attitude to life of which the hallmark is eros, and equally concrete proof of the existence of another attitude to life of which the hallmark is agape." When we think of eros we think of Plato; when we think of agape we think of Jesus and Paul and John. In regard to love we are more Greek than Christian.

O Jesus, our Lord, be our Lord here. For if we come under some other dominance in regard to love we miss the way—fatally. We must not miss the meaning of love, for if we do, we miss the meaning of life. Amen.

AFFIRMATION FOR THE DAY: *In this—"We are more Greek than Christian"—my weight is on the Christian.*

EROS AND AGAPE CONTRASTED

The New Testament decisively refuses to use the word "eros" and consistently uses the word "agape." Why? What is the difference?

The difference was probably never put more concisely than in these parallels of contrast given by Nygren. One is the raising of the human to the Divine—the contention of egocentric religion, of eros; the other, the gracious condescension of the Divine to man—the contention of theocentric religion, of agape:

Eros is acquisitive desire and longing.	Agape is sacrificial giving.
Eros is an upward movement.	Agape comes down.
Eros is man's way to God.	Agape is God's way to man.
Eros is man's effort: it assumes that man's salvation is his own work.	Agape is God's grace: salvation is the work of divine love.
Eros is egocentric love, a form of self-assertion of the highest, noblest, sublimest kind.	Agape is unselfish love, it "seeketh not its own," it gives itself away.
Eros seeks to gain its life, a life divine, immortalized.	Agape lives the life of God, therefore dares to "lose it."
Eros is the will to get and possess which depends on want and need.	Agape is freedom in giving, which depends on wealth and plenty.
Eros is primarily *man's* love; God is the object of eros. Even when it is attributed to God, eros is patterned on human love.	Agape is primarily *God's* love; God *is* agape. Even when it is attributed to man, agape is patterned on divine love.
Eros is determined by the quality, the beauty and worth, of its object; it is not spontaneous, but "evoked," "motivated."	Agape is sovereign in relation to its object, and is directed to both "the evil and the good"; it is spontaneous, "overflowing," "unmotivated."
Eros *recognizes* value in its object—and loves it.	Agape loves—and *creates value in its* object.

Here the issues are drawn. All systems and all life line themselves up on one side or the other.

O Father God, Thou art striving to get across Thy love, Thy agape, to us. We pervert it and make it into something else—make it into our own image. Take our love and change it from eros to agape. In Jesus' name. Amen.

AFFIRMATION FOR THE DAY: *My sub-Christian eros loves I expose to conversion into Christian agape.*

TWO-THIRDS OF CHURCH LIFE, EROS

We now see the issues between eros and agape. Eros is the love that loves for what it can get out of it. It turns everything—even God—into means to our ends. We love people for what they give us in return. If there is no return, the love ceases. We love them because we see in them something that brings satisfaction to us—their beauty, their physical attractiveness. They meet a need in us; therefore we would like to acquire them.

God, too, comes under the acquisitive urge. We make God a means to our ends. He saves us from trouble, heals us of our sicknesses, gives us success in life, provides us a heaven hereafter; therefore we serve Him. We use God—we are the center and God is pulled into the sphere of our interests. All this may be very religious, but it is pure egocentricity.

We expect to get something out of our loving God. We go to church, we pray, we pay to church and charitable causes, we are faithful in our duties; therefore, we feel that God is under obligation to us—to shield us from harm and danger, ward off our sicknesses, provide us with plenty of material goods, and give us a home in heaven.

When I asked a group how much of our church life is built around the above motives, the group replied, "Two-thirds." If that be true, then two-thirds of our church life is built around eros. Therefore our church life is sub-Christian.

We even try to make the agape of God into eros for us. We say to ourselves: "If I love God, then God will love me. And I will have the most precious thing in the world—the love of God—for me." "The most precious thing in the world," but it always ends up for "me." It is egocentric. We do not love God for God; we love God for "me."

The "peace of mind" and "happiness" cults are rooted in eros. If I serve God, repeat certain slogans, obey certain rules, I'll have "peace of mind" and "happiness." It all comes back to me. I'm the center of the universe. Everything serves me.

O God, Thou art God—not I. Then help me to organize my life around Thee, not around me. For I am not the center of the universe—Thou art. Then by Thy agape convert my eros into Thy agape. In Jesus' name. Amen.

AFFIRMATION FOR THE DAY: *My greatest danger is not in being anti-Christian, but sub-Christian.*

"KNOWLEDGE" PUFFS UP—LOVE BUILDS UP

There is another phase of our eros type of religion. It not only tries to make everything, even God, means to our ends, it tries to get to God by our means. It is self-salvation.

God, in the eros attitude, is to be found at the end of a long climb up the ladder of salvation. God is to be found at the topmost rung of the ladder. We meet Him on His level. We have, by a process of self-purification and self-discipline, climbed the ladder of worthiness. We attain God by our efforts. We step from the topmost rung into union with God because we have attained such a state, and the next step is union with God. Man has attained his own salvation.

The Gnostics had thirty-six steps in the ladder up which they climbed into union with God. But Gnosticism was egocentric, not God-centric. Paul puts the difference in these words: "Gnosis puffs up, but agape builds up." The Greek spirit and the Christian spirit meet and part in that sentence of Paul's. One created an egocentric piety that was destined by the very nature of things to be puffed up; the other created a God-centric piety destined by the nature of things to be built up. They came out at two different places—poles apart. The Gnostic despised the common herd who did not have this special gnosis that he had. He was superior, belonged to the *illuminati*.

In the Christian conception we do not find God at the topmost rung of the ladder, but at the bottommost. For we do not get to God—God comes to us. He comes to us in Incarnation and meets us on our level. He meets us where we are and takes us where He is. He meets us on the level of our sin, not on the level of our attained righteousness. "I came not to call the righteous, but sinners," is the absolutely new thing in the gospel. That verse shatters all our attempts to climb to God. He has come to us on our level, the level of our deepest need—our sin. This idea is breathtaking and precedent-shattering. It is new, so new that it could be called nothing else except the Good News—the gospel.

O Father, we are breathless before the wonder of Thy agape—the agape that came to us when we couldn't come to Thee, that love that would not let us go. How can I close my heart to Thee? I cannot, I will not. I open it wide to all of Thee. Amen.

AFFIRMATION FOR THE DAY: *I shall illustrate not Gnosis, but Good News.*

"GOD LOVES THE RIGHTEOUS"—JUDAISM

All other religions teach us that we find God at the top of a ladder, which we climb by laws, by rules, by self-purification, by disciplines, by slogans. Only the Christian faith teaches that God finds us where we are—at the lowest rung of the ladder—as sinners. There we are saved "by grace."

The Jewish faith teaches us that God loves the righteous and loves them because they are righteous. It is like the attitudes shown by a mother who says to her child: "Mother won't love you if you are naughty." So the child tries to earn the mother's love by being "good." But the love manifested by both the mother and the child are in that case pure eros. The mother's love is based on the quality of goodness, and, in turn, the child is good in order to earn her love.

In the parable of the prodigal son, the elder son represented the attitude of the law and the younger son represented the gospel attitude. By all the rules of the law the elder brother had right on his side: "I never disobeyed your command; yet you never gave me a kid, that I might make merry with my friends"—I earned your love and yet you never gave it. "But when this son of yours [not "my brother"!] came who has devoured your living with harlots, you killed for him the fatted calf!"—it is unfair and irreligious. And according to the law the elder brother was right. God loves the righteous and metes out to them special treatment. And if He didn't the righteous would have a right to complain. That was the righteousness of the law. And it was eros—I gave you this, you give me that!

That father showed agape—pure agape. He met the son where he was—at the bottom rung of the ladder, at the place of his sin and degradation. And then the father proceeded to create by his agape what wasn't there: forgiveness and reconciliation, a sense of self-respect—the ring, robe, and shoes; the restored fellowship— they ate and drank; the wiped-out sadness—they began to be merry. Above all, the restored sonship. The eros of the elder brother could never have produced that—only agape could and did.

O Father, in that father we see Thee, our Father, and what we see sends us to our knees in deepest gratitude and penitence. And yet it raises us to the highest heaven—the heaven of restored fellowship and love. Help us to live our gratitude. Amen.

AFFIRMATION FOR THE DAY: *Since God is found at the lowest rung of the ladder, there is hope for everybody.*

GREEK PHILOSOPHY, HINDUISM,
AND BUDDHISM—EROS

We saw yesterday that the Jewish faith rested on eros—if we keep the law, God will love us.

The Greeks had the same attitude. We have seen that they felt that "the Deity has dealings only with the pure." To have relations with the impure would render God impure. He had to keep Himself aloof to keep Himself God. God was found at the top rung of the ladder of purity.

But the Greeks and the Hebrews made the same mistake as the Pharisee who invited Jesus to dine and then was shocked when a woman of the street, a prostitute, came up behind Him and stood weeping, and as the teardrops fell upon His feet, she began hastily to wipe the tears with the hair of her head. The Pharisee said: "If this man were a prophet, he would have known . . . who this is who is touching him, for she is a sinner." Note the tense—"she *is* a sinner." He was wrong there—"She *was* a sinner." In that moment, while the Pharisee was criticizing, agape was redeeming her. A prostitute had become a person—a person redeemed, made new, accepted by God and herself. Eros could never have produced that; only agape could.

Hinduism and Buddhism are based upon eros. While I was staying with Mahatma Gandhi in his Sabarmati Ashram for ten days, a sadhu (an ascetic) came to the Mahatma and asked him how to find God. After receiving Gandhi's reply, the sadhu came to me and asked the same question. Before I replied I asked him what the Mahatma had said. And this was the reply: "To find God you must have as much patience as a man who sits by the seashore and with a straw empties the ocean." That was the method of finding God at the topmost rung of the ladder of patience and self-purification—it was eros. My reply? I told him that I came to Jesus bankrupt with nothing to offer except my bankruptcy. And to my astonishment He took me, forgave me, and sent my happy soul singing its way down the years. It was agape. I couldn't have come in on any other basis.

O God, our Redeemer, we could not be redeemed by the blood of animals, nor by our works, nor by the righteousness of our deeds. We could be redeemed by agape—and only by Agape. Read the gratitude of my heart and my love response. Amen.

AFFIRMATION FOR THE DAY: *Agape was my hope, is my hope, and ever shall be my hope.*

"A LITTLE LESS THAN DIVINE".

The idea of "the inseparable oneness" of man and God—meeting God at the topmost rung of the ladder—has often been bolstered by this passage of scripture: Jesus answered them, "Is it not written in your law, I said, you are gods? If he called them gods to whom the word of God came . . . , do you say of him whom the Father consecrated and sent into the world, You are blaspheming, because I said, I am the Son of God?" (John 10:34-36). If this passage means that we are all "gods," therefore divine, then it flies in the face of the whole of the remaining scriptures, which teach and teach clearly, and without equivocation, that there is one God and one God only and that other "gods" are no gods. Then what does this passage mean? It is from the Psalms and the quotation makes it clear:

> I say, "You are gods
> sons of the Most High, all of you" (82:6).

The meaning attached to the word "gods" is that you are "sons of the Most High." That fits in with the rest of the teaching of Scripture, that we are "sons of the Most High," made in His image and are being remade into the image of God as seen in the face of Jesus Christ. This does not lay on us an impossible burden of living up to divinity, puts us on our level but makes it possible for us to rise through grace to an ever-increasing likeness of the Divine.

The Christian position is clear: God is creator, and we are creatures, made in His image, a little less than divine; that image has been, not canceled, but marred, by sin; but through God's coming to us in Incarnation, Jesus dying on the cross for our redemption, we are now being remade into that image of God as seen in the face of Jesus Christ. That process of redemption moves from one degree of glory to another until we are changed into His likeness. "This comes from the Lord who is the Spirit" (II Cor. 3:18) working within us. It "comes from the Lord" as the gift of grace. The process is self-surrender to the Divine leading, in order to be made in the image of the Divine Lord, Jesus. But that leaves Jesus as Lord, not us as Lord.

O Jesus, Thou art Lord. I feel this. I know this—I am grateful for this. This leaves me with no burden of divinity to sustain—too heavy a burden for me to bear. But it does leave me with the most glorious of goals—to be like Thee. Amen.

AFFIRMATION FOR THE DAY: *I am free of the burden of being Lord;*
Now I am free to be love.

"WE LOVE, BECAUSE HE FIRST LOVED"

There is another phase of this assertion of "the inseparable oneness of God and man." It leaves both God and man incapable of exercising agape. For if man exercises agape it is not toward someone other than himself; it is agape toward himself. And agape going around on the circle of one's self is not agape—it is eros. For agape is self-giving love. Eros is self-centered love.

Plato said definitely that God is eros. That eros inspires eros in us and we strive by eros to be one with the Divine. But Plato was confronted with this dilemma: eros is based on want and need; if God is eros, then God is in want and need—therefore imperfect and therefore not God. Plato got around this dilemma by saying that God had need to contemplate His own perfection. But this comes near arguing in a circle. In the end, God is in need.

But in agape the case is different. God is agape. He is self-giving love. But that self-giving love would want to create creatures upon whom He could lavish His agape. This saves His love from being eros—an acquisitive, self-centered love.

But if we are "inseparably one with God," when we love God we love ourselves, for we are one. Then that love cannot be anything but eros.

The relationship of man, made in the image of his Creator, and being remade into that image, gives room and motive for agape to operate, both on the side of God and the side of man. God is agape. And that overflowing, spontaneous, unmotivated agape creates agape in us toward God and toward others and toward ourselves—toward everything.

"We love, because he first loved us"—His agape creates and inspires agape in us. The source of this agape is in God, hence pure. If the source of our love is in us, it is bound to be eros—and acquisitive, self-centered love—hence impure. But is we love with eros, it is bound to produce eros in return. If we want something out of our love for God and others, then God and others will want something out of us—tit for tat.

O Father, Thou dost love me with the purest agape. I feel Thy love is unadulterated agape, wanting nothing but giving everything. Thou dost love me, not out of Thy want and need, but out of Thy fullness. Thy agape overwhelms me. Amen.

AFFIRMATION FOR THE DAY: *Today, identified with agape, I shall give, not out of want and need, but out of fullness.*

FOUR POINTS ABOUT AGAPE

To be sure, before we go on, that we have the meaning of agape clear, we must turn again to Nygren for his for points on agape:

(1) *Agape is spontaneous and "unmotivated."* . . . When it is said that God loves man, this is not a judgment on what man is like, but on what God is like . . . But in Christ there is revealed a Divine love which breaks all bounds, refusing to be controlled by the value of its object, and being determined only by its own intrinsic nature. . . . But Jesus is not concerned with love in this ordinary sense, but with the spontaneous, unmotivated love that is Agape; and for this there is fundamentally no place within the framework of legal order. To go back once more to the words of Jesus in Matt. ix-17, we may say that *Agape is the new wine which inevitably bursts the old wineskins.* . . .

(2) *Agape is "indifferent to value."* . . . If God, the Holy One, loves the sinner, it cannot be because of his sin, but in spite of his sin. But when God's love is shown to the righteous and godly, there is always the risk of our thinking that God loves the man on account of his righteousness and godliness. . . . It is only when all thought of the worthiness of the object is abandoned that we can understand what Agape is. . . .

(3) *Agape is creative.* . . . Agape is creative love. God does not love that which is already in itself worthy of love, but on the contrary, that which in itself has no worth acquires worth just by becoming the object of God's love. . . . Agape does not recognize value, but creates it. Agape loves, and imparts value by loving. . . . When He says, "Thy sins are forgiven thee," this is not merely formal attestation of the presence of a value which justifies the overlooking of faults; it is the bestowal of a gift. Something really new is introduced, something new is taking place.

Before taking up the fourth point tomorrow, we must emphasize the new and revolutionary character of the kind of thing which Jesus introduced in agape. It was so new and revolutionary that it turned the whole world of values upside down—"turned the world upside down."

O Jesus, Thou art so quiet and yet so revolutionary. Thy mind and spirit are pressing upon ours and, by love, are forcing a change upon us. Thou art purifying our loves, changing our eros into agape. We are grateful. Amen.

AFFIRMATION FOR THE DAY: *I belong to the Revolution of Love—reversing all values, changing all attitudes.*

"AGAPE IS GOD'S WAY TO MAN"

We continue Nygren's four points in the expounding of agape:

(4) *Agape is the initiator of fellowship with God.* . . . If we consider the implications of Agape, it becomes very plain that all the other ways by which man seeks to enter into fellowship with God are futile. . . . Repentance and amendment are no more able than righteousness to move God to love. . . . There is thus no way for man to come to God, but only a way for God to come to man: the way of Divine forgiveness, Divine love. *Agape is God's way to man.*

All of these points are important, but the last is the most important—the all-important. I have traveled the earth, in almost every country, for nearly half a century. I have been interested in one thing and in one thing only: seeing how men found God, or didn't find God. I have lived in that portion of the globe where the search for God through eros, self-salvation, has been most intense. The Indian people are a God-thirsty people—perhaps the most God-thirsty people that have ever existed. I have seen them trying to climb the ladder of eros by penances, by austerities, by self-immolation, by the suppression of their desires and passions, by meditation, by renunciation, by pilgrimages, by fastings and by prayer—by everything that eros could devise, everything except agape. The result? India is still a God-thirsty land, for the finding side is meager. As I have sat in my round-table conferences year after year and have listened to the testimony of the representatives—the best of the representatives—of the various faiths as to what their faiths have brought them in experience, the result has been the revelation of a thirst instead of a finding. It isn't because God doesn't love them—He does love them—but their love for Him *was* and *is* through eros—self-salvation. Only when people came through agape, through Jesus, did the note of finding begin to be sounded with clarion joy. For they were not finding God—they were allowing God to find them.

O Father God, Thy love, Thy agape—like the hound of heaven—is seeking me, seeking me. I cannot escape Thy love, nor would I. For one touch of Thy agape, and I am on fire to give back to Thee—and to everybody—what was so freely given to me. Amen.

AFFIRMATION FOR THE DAY: *I am no longer athirst, except to share; no longer longing, except to give.*

AGAPE REACHES TWO

When Paul says, "Love never fails," he is thinking of agape love and not eros love. Eros love *does* fail and fails very often. For at the center of eros love are the seeds of its own failure—it is self-seeking love. If you love people for what you get out of them, then they give you back in kind—they love you for what they get out of you. That is self-defeating. Each suspects the motives of the other, and in that suspicion real love dies.

I was on a private plane in company with two men, one a wealthy businessman, owner and pilot of the plane, and the other a test pilot. Both of them had stories behind them—and what stories! The wealthy businessman had been an alcoholic. On one continuous binge of thirty days he had consumed approximately three pints of liquor a day—114 pints in all. He was really a sick man—sick in soul, mind, and body. His nerves were beating like a trip hammer. Someone prayed for his healing, said a prayer and walked off. As this alcoholic stood there alone—quite alone—he was suddenly healed—healed in soul, mind, and body. His nerves ceased to pound: he was so natural he felt unnatural. He was so elated with God that somewhere in there he took off the braces which he wore on account of arthritis in his back. He has never been able to find those braces, literally doesn't know what has happened to them. And the alcohol, too, dropped away—it was gone without effort. He hasn't tasted it since, nor wanted it. He is now on fire with the love of God. He goes around in his private plane and holds evangelistic meetings. Everything is changed within and around him.

Now to have told that man that he must climb to God by eros, and at the topmost rung of the ladder of worthiness he would find God, would have been so laughable as to be tragic. Eros would have failed—completely. Only agape could reach that man, for agape found him at the bottommost rung of the ladder, found him as a sinner and left him a saint. Eros fails, agape never fails.

O God, Thy agape finds me at the bottom of my need and lifts me to the highest heaven of needs all met, plus. The wonder of it fills me with awe and gratitude. And yet fills me with a passion to share it. Amen.

AFFIRMATION FOR THE DAY: *If my "love" has been failing, perhaps it is tainted with eros, and lacking agape.*

"WHAT IS THE CATCH?"

Yesterday we wrote of two men in a plane. The other man, too, had been an alcoholic but had quit about ten years before. However, when alcohol left he had nothing to put in its place—nothing but hate. Before, alcoholism had been his defense—he tried to escape. Now hate became his defense—he would not escape, but he would fight and hate. And he did. He feared everybody and hated everybody and got the same in return. But he was such a good test pilot that he kept his job.

When he went up with this ex-alcoholic, the businessman, to test him for instrument flying, each was afraid of the other. But sensing something new and strange in his companion, the test pilot asked to have a talk with him. Next day they sat for six straight hours and talked about—Christ! The test pilot kept saying to himself: "What is the catch behind all this? Why should he spend time on me?" When the businessman got out some books, the other man said to himself with sinking heart: "Now this is the reason he's spent all this time on me—to sell me some books." The test pilot continued his story: "But when he gave them to me, I was puzzled and moved. And then he said: 'If I would give you a machine gun with which you could mow down your enemies would you take it?' 'Take it?' I replied, 'I'd jump at it, if I could get rid of my enemies.' 'Well,' he said, 'it's the machine gun of love. A sure way to get rid of enemies.' Well, I opened my heart to it all. Let love take me over. And do you know, I have mowed down my enemies. They are all gone. They are now my friends. Love did it. My attitude changed and so did theirs." And then he added thoughtfully: "Do you know, there was simply no way out of the dilemma I was in—no way except the way of God meeting me where I was—at the bottom rung of the ladder." The man's very face has changed—everything has changed.

Both of those men in that plane were incapable of being redeemed by eros—only agape could meet their need. Eros fails, but "agape never fails." God is agape.

O Father, even if agape seems to fail it cannot fail, for when we give agape and the other refuses it, we are the richer for having given it. So in either case we win. Then, Father, help me to believe in and to act upon agape. Amen.

AFFIRMATION FOR THE DAY: *Eros has a hook in it—a hook of self-interest; agape wants nothing—except to give itself.*

"WHERE THE FURROW HAD BEEN"

The way of love is the way to live—the way of not loving is not the way to live.

This comes from a news dispatch:

No one can be sure exactly how many men, women and children have been shot, stabbed or beaten to death since the village of San Simón (pop. 900) and El Guarda (pop. 600) declared war on each other, but the death toll is greater than the present population of either village. . . . The war started in 1891, when San Simón purchased 350 acres of government land that El Guarda was squatting on. Outraged, the El Guardians hastily plowed a big furrow around "their" property, challenged the San Simonites to cross. The men of San Simón accepted the challenge. On bloody raids they smashed and burned, attacked El Guardians. . . .

So it has been through the years; last year alone the feud took 40 lives. Recently, however, Mexico State Governor Salvador Sánches Colin proposed a solution: the state will pay San Simón 50,000 pesos for the 350 acres and cede the land to El Guarda. With a sigh, the elders of both villages agreed.

The San Simonites lined up on their side of the border and the El Guardians on the other. Solemnly, the Governor marched between them to the end of the line, then waved a signal. A band played the national anthem and enemies rushed forward to embrace enemies. "*Viva San Simón,*" shouted the people of El Guarda. "*Viva El Guarda,*" responded the people of San Simón, and they hugged and kissed, and trampled smooth the earth where the furrow had been.

Agape was created when the government said it would take the cost on itself to settle the dispute. That changed the atmosphere from legality to love, and when the atmosphere was changed, attitude and actions were changed. Eros would have failed where agape succeeded. And the giving of agape did something for the government—from a police state vainly trying to keep the peace, it became a reconciling state and was loved as such. Agape never fails.

O God, Thy agape works by whomsoever applied. For it is the basic power in the universe. Teach us the might of agape and the weakness of everything else. For agape opens closed doors and closed hearts. Agape wins. Amen.

AFFIRMATION FOR THE DAY: *If I have been working with eros, thinking it love, then I shift gears into agape.*

EROS AND AGAPE—TWO WAYS OF LIFE

We are looking at the two approaches to God—the eros approach and the agape approach.

The eros approach is self-salvation, trying to reach God by its own efforts and its own merits. Its key word is struggle. Agape is God-salvation—God comes to us and offers us salvation by grace. Its key word is surrender.

The eros approach is always wistful and uncertain, an attitude which it mistakes for humility. It never has a sense of arriving—it is always on the way. Agape is joyous and certain, with a deep sense of real humility, based on gratitude for grace. It knows it has arrived, for the arrival is God's reaching us on the lowest rung of the ladder.

The eros approach is tense and striving and therefore exhausting. Agape, on the other hand, is relaxed and receptive and therefore exhilarating.

The eros approach is a guilt-conscious piety based on self-condemnation with a sense of half-failure. Agape knows that condemnation has been lifted by grace, so it is free, abounding, and joyous.

The eros approach makes religion a demand upon the will, a constant whipping up of the will. Agape means the surrender of the will to God; hence the will is given back, purified and released.

Eros means suppression—the flesh must be put under in behalf of the spirit. Agape means expression—the flesh as well as the spirit are surrendered to God and then both are given back and can now be expressed, on a higher level.

Eros religion exhausts itself upon the problems of life. Agape lays hold by faith on the inexhaustible resources of God; hence the more it gives, the more it has.

Eros love looks for a return and is disappointed if it doesn't come. Agape love asks for nothing except the privilege of giving itself and gets everything in return.

O Father God, take my eros and turn it into agape. For eros leaves me frustrated and empty. And I want to be fruitful and full. But I see this can come only through grace, Thy grace, which is pure agape. Evermore give me this bread. Amen.

AFFIRMATION FOR THE DAY: *My faith today shall not be eros and exhausting, but agape and exhilarating.*

CONTRASTS OF EROS AND AGAPE CONTINUED

We go on with the contrasts between the eros approach and the agape approach.

Eros never produces witnesses. It produces the exhorting, struggling, tense type of religion. But the note of witness is absent. It cannot witness since to witness would be a witness to its own attainments or lack of them. Agape, on the other hand, can witness, for it is witnessing to the grace of Another. It is laying its tribute of gratitude at the feet of Another. It is Other-conscious, and hence its witness has the note of the Other in it.

Eros says: "We cannot speak of our attainments." It would be indelicate. Agape says: "We cannot help but speak of what we have seen and heard," and felt and known.

Eros is force-pump religion. Agape is an artesian-well religion. One drinks of the water of its own pumping and thirsts again. The other drinks of the water which Jesus gives to him—a gift—and that water becomes a well within, springing up into everlasting life.

Eros tries to gain purity of mind and spirit by lopping off here and lopping off there. Agape lumps it and lays the whole at the feet of Jesus in a glad, full surrender—a surrender which includes the self and all its attitudes and doings. It is not piecemeal—it is an attitude of allness in response to the allness of the divine agape.

Eros is gloomy, lacks spontaneous joy. Agape is piety set to music. It dances its way down the joyous years.

Eros doesn't know how to sing, for it hasn't much to sing about. Agape sings full-hearted and full-throated, for it has everything to sing about.

Eros is so preoccupied with itself and its attainments that it has little time to think of serving. Agape has "a heart leisured from itself" and is free to serve. Its song: "Freely have I received, so freely do I give."

Eros lives on question marks and problems. Agape has its question marks straightened out into exclamation points, and all its problems are possibilities. Agape is life.

O Jesus, how grateful I am that Thou hast uncovered to me the meaning and possibility of agape. For I see in agape the key to God, to myself, to the universe. I'm all out for agape, for I'm all out for Thee. Amen.

AFFIRMATION FOR THE DAY: *Eros closes my lips; agape opens them—in witness.*

THE WAY OF EROS—ILLUSTRATED

Before we leave these contrasts between eros and agape we must mention, with emphasis, what we have hinted at before, namely the self-conscious nature of eros religion.

To illustrate: I was in an Ashram in India where the guru was the center of everything. He showed himself four times a year to his followers. It all added to the mystery—and the adulation. A French woman was the go-between. When I was finally able to see her, after some delay, the stage was set for effect: the semidarkness, the burning incense, the specially draped chair, her long flowing robes, her color brightened a bit with rouge. She swept into the room without greeting me personally and took her seat on the draped chair, as if an oracle was to speak. I was told before she came in that she was in a trance, hence the delay. I asked her what had happened during the trance. And she replied: "I left my body and entered into the souls of some of the disciples to set them at rights within." The New Testment idea is that the Holy Spirit, God enters within us to set us at rights within. She was taking the place of the Holy Spirit.

The she said: "The guru is striving to do something that has never been attempted before—he is not only making his soul divine, he is making his body divine as well." The whole object of his concentrated meditation was to make his spirit and his body divine. It was a concentration on himself. He was the center of his endeavor and he was the center of gaping adulation when he showed the results to his followers, four times a year. He received and accepted divine honors. And Eastern and Western followers call themselves, "Disciples of _____." He was the center. That is the inevitable result of eros—man-conceived, man-centered. Note the contrast when the people at Lystra wanted to offer sacrifices to Paul and Barnabas: "But when the apostles . . . heard of it, they tore their garments. . . . crying: 'Men, why are you doing this? We also are men, of like nature with you'" (Acts 14:15). God was the center.

O Father, deliver us from our self-centered endeavors. For Thou art God, not we. Save us from our ego antics. And let us see the meaning of Thy agape. And seeing, we are forever cured of our egocentricity. We thank Thee. Amen.

AFFIRMATION FOR THE DAY: *My body shall be made like His resurrection body by the resurrection touch.*

"WE HAVE A LONG WAY TO GO"

We would add this word to yesterday's meditation. An American missionary, when he got his eyes off of Jesus and became tangled in marital upset, with a consequent divorce, became a disciple of the guru mentioned yesterday. And I mean just that—a disciple. He was advertised to speak as "a disciple of _____." I wrote him a letter: "My dear brother, what a comedown! You who were a disciple of Jesus, the Lord of lords, have now become a disciple of a dead guru. Come back, the door is still open." No reply. But his wife wrote this significant sentence to someone in America: "We are still seeking, but we still have a long way to go."

"We still have a long way to go"—that is the difference between eros and agape. The way of eros is a long, long climb upward with a question mark at the end. Agape begins with bent knees, a penitent, surrendered heart, empty hands which take the Gift. And immediately agape is on the way. Not on a way of human contriving, but the Way—God's Way to us. That Way extends from God down to us; and if we are in a hole, a pit of our own sinning, then that Way extends right down beneath our feet. All we have to do is to turn around and we are in the arms of agape. And agape and we walk the Way together. We supply willingness and agape supplies power. The point is that we are on the Way.

We, too, "have a long way to go," but not a long way to get to the Way. We are on the Way, the Way that extended clear down beneath our feet. All else is development. That development will be endless—the human forever approaching the Divine in character and life and likeness, but never becoming the Divine. In that eternal growth will be our eternal joy—the joy of adventure, the joy of discovery, the joy of finding. "A long way to go," said not with a sigh of longing, but with a shout of laughter. The going is good. You know that you have not arrived at the end of the Way, but you do know that you are on the Way. And gratitude, deep down, possesses us.

O Jesus, Thou art the Way—the Way come to us. And that Way extends clear to the mouth of hell. And all we have to do is to turn round and begin walking. What grace, what abounding grace! Will we ever get over the spell of it? Amen.

AFFIRMATION FOR THE DAY: *I am no further from the Way than one word—yes. I'm in a state of yes-ness.*

"LOOKS AT THE CALENDAR FOR MATURITY"

The implications of what we are saying about agape are tremendous in regard to maturity. Eros looks at the calendar for maturity. Agape looks at the Christ for maturity. One looks at it as a long-drawn-out process. Sin and evil and imperfection are to be worn down by attrition through the years. The other looks at the most mature fact that has ever struck our planet—the fact of Christ—surrenders to Him, begins a life of obedience to Him, starts to walk with Him, and finds to his utter astonishment that the soul has become mature—almost unconsciously mature, overnight. Maturity was not sought for. Had it been it would have been a self-conscious maturity, which, of course, would be immaturity. Maturity came as a by-product of a great love within—came from agape.

I have seen people become mature in their attitudes almost suddenly. One moment they were introverted, self-preoccupied, and unhappy; the next moment they were self-released, cleansed from a thousand canceling conflicts, with doubts dissolved. They were integrated and whole—and mature.

The case of Zacchaeus shows an amazing maturity which happened in a few moments. One moment he was a self-centered, grasping type of personality; the next moment he was mature in his outlook and spirit: "Lord, the half of my goods I give to the poor; and if I have defrauded any one of anything, I restore it fourfold" (Luke 19:8). Here is a basically mature attitude toward himself and money—two areas where a lot of immaturity is found. Conversion is the greatest influence for maturity that we have. And the calendar didn't do it—Christ did. The very young, when gripped by agape, can be mature; and the very old, gripped by eros, can be immature.

Here was the biggest grouch in Trenton, so it was said, and here is what he said over the long-distance telephone to a friend: "Everybody is different in Trenton today since that meeting in the high school last night with _____. Of course, it may be that only *I* am different, but everybody seems different." He was mature overnight.

O Jesus my Lord, one touch of Thee and my old immaturities vanish and my new maturities begin. For Thy impact is the impact of the Perfect upon the imperfect. An I do not look to my perfection, but to Thine. That releases me. Amen.

AFFIRMATION FOR THE DAY: *My maturity depends upon the depth of my response, not the length of my years.*

"WE DON'T DO THIS ANYMORE"

We ended yesterday on the hopeful note that maturity is not necessarily associated with long years and long striving. It may be, but it may not be. It all depends upon the amount and the completeness of the receptivity and obedience. "Mary," the young farm woman who put down the party-line telepone and was completely cured of curious snooping in less than a day, was also tested at the same point but on a higher level later on.

A woman who was skeptical of the possibility of sudden conversion came to "Mary" and said she wanted to find God. After "Mary" had talked at length with her, they were about to pray and make the surrender, when the seeking woman said, "Before we kneel perhaps you'd like to see the list of my sins written out." And she handed "Mary" the paper. Handing it back to her, "Mary" replied: "I'm only God's secretary and I don't read His private mail." Then they had prayer and the woman was converted. Afterwards she showed the paper to "Mary." And it was blank. The woman wanted to see if conversion had cured "Mary" of a snooping curiosity as to her neighbor's sins! And it had! Maturity straight off! Not full maturity, but the right attitudes were there. They needed only to be developed.

Another incident concerning "Mary." She was seeking the Holy Spirit and in a communion service He came—came as gently as the dew, but came with a blessed infilling. She was so overjoyed that she wanted to get to the chapel to pray, with the deepest thanksgiving. So eager was she to get to the chapel nearby, that she began pushing through the crowd. As she pushed others aside, the Spirit said to her: "Mary, we don't do that anymore now, do we?" And she became gentle and considerate. "We don't do that anymore now"—note the "We." When she put down the telephone receiver the words she said to herself were." The "I" had turned to a "We." That was agape. For agape had produced agape. And "love is never rude." All this was effortless, for it was agape.

O Father, how can I thank Thee enough for this gentle power of agape that makes me free from a thousand little self-assertions and self-displays. And because it holds me from within, it is so natural and unstrained. I thank Thee. Amen.

AFFIRMATION FOR THE DAY: *"We don't do this anymore"—that shall be my delicate spring of action today.*

EROS FAILS AND FADES

We come to tie up the essential differences between the eros and the agape outlooks on life.

Eros is self-conscious. It has to be, for it is self-salvation, therefore self-centered, however much it may clothe that self-centeredness in religious nomenclature.

Agape is God-conscious. It has to be, for it is God-salvation. Salvation originates in God, comes to us at the lowest rung of the ladder in God's Incarnation. It is the gift of God. "We love, because he first loved us." The center is God—in its origin, its application, its sustenance, and its goal.

Eros has little room for gratitude. It gives itself because of what it gets. It has the atmosphere of the bargain counter—I give this, you give that. There can be little or no place for bubbling gratitude—it is rather a bargaining "gimme."

Agape has little room for anything but gratitude. For God gave Himself a hundred percent for nothing. He loved us, not because we were good, bad, or indifferent; He loved us—full stop. Anyone who comes in contact with that overwhelming agape must respond in bubbling gratitude if he responds at all.

Eros can never let its full weight down. For it has to hold its universe together by its tense striving.

Agape does let its full weight down. For its universe is held together by agape. It rests in that fact. It can trust that which is so trustworthy.

Eros has to bolster up its goodness, for its whole outlook rests on maintaining that goodness. While I was speaking on the cross, to a select circle of devotees of religious eros, the leader of that group, the guru, had to, in the words of an observer, be duly displaying his spirituality—unconsciously, of course.

Agape has nothing to bolster up. It rests on bedrock Reality—God is love. It gazes at Jesus, and spirituality asserts itself unconsciously.

Eros fades and fails. Agape never fails. For if it remains agape, that is the victory.

O God, Thou who art pure agape, make me agape. For where there are areas in me not yet agape, they are festering areas. They are alien. They belong to something other than me, the real me. Then cleanse the lost remnant. Amen.

AFFIRMATION FOR THE DAY: *My victory is agape, so in success or failure I still succeed.*

IS THERE NO REWARD IN AGAPE?

As we draw the contrasts between agape and eros, questions are arising in your mind.

First, if agape is one hundred percent for nothing, wanting no reward, then doesn't the person acting on agape get anything out of it? Is there no reward? Yes, there is a reward, an indirect one, but the highest kind of reward.

Jesus said: "But I say to you, Love your enemies and pray for those who persecute you, so that you may be sons of your Father who is in heaven; for he makes his sun rise on the evil and the good, and sends rain on the just and on the unjust." (Matt. 5:44-45). Note: "So that you may be sons of your Father." The reward is in the quality of being—"so that you may be." The payoff is in the person. There can be no higher reward than that. If you give agape then you become agape, become agape in your inmost being. But agape is the highest quality of being for God or man, and hence the payoff is the highest reward there is. But if it had been sought for reward it would not be agape—it would be eros—for eros by its very nature is acquisitive desire.

But Jesus says that eros doesn't get a reward. "For if you love those who love you, what reward have you? Do not even the tax collectors do the same? And if you salute only your brethren, what more are you doing than others? Do not even the Gentiles do the same?" (Matt. 5:46-47). Here He says that the attempt to live by eros is self-defeating. Eros, being acquisitive desire, wants reward, but the reward slips through the fingers: "What reward have you?" Why does no reward come? Because the other person senses the desire for reward in your act and therefore can't give it. The springs of response are dried up. You cannot give love, except grudgingly, to anyone who loves you because of what they get out of you. It is self-defeating. The reward goes glimmering. But you shower your love on someone who loves you one hundred percent for nothing. The one hundred percent for nothing is self-rewarding. And yet it seeks no reward, for if it did it would not be agape. Agape is salvation.

O God, my Father, I thank Thee, thank Thee for what Thou art. Thou art agape and I, too, must be agape. But I cannot be agape unless I surrender all my eros to Thee for cleansing. I do. Take me over and make me over. In Jesus' name. Amen.

AFFIRMATION FOR THE DAY: *Since my reward is a quality of being, success is an inside job.*

"WE BECOME WHAT WE GIVE OUT"

We have been looking at one objection arising in regard to agape and eros. This must be added: We become what we give out. If you give out eros you become eros. You become the kind of person who wants something out of everything he does. And that pattern becomes fixed in the minds of the people who know you and expect that from you. I received a letter from a man who is prominent in Christian circles. I never get a letter from him unless he wants something, wants something for himself, however covered or indirect it may be. So when I received a letter from him recently, I said to myself in opening it. "Well, what does he want now?" As I read the letter to the end I said a quiet hallelujah to myself: "He doesn't want a thing. It's a beautiful letter." But I turned to the postscript, added in handwriting on the side of the letter, and there was the inevitable request! And what a request! More forceful for the smoothing of the way in the body of the letter. And the fact is that he got no reward, as Jesus said; for he dropped still lower, if possible, in my estimation.

If you give out agape you become agape and you tend to create agape around you. If you give out criticism you become critical in your very nature and you tend to create an atmosphere of criticism around you. If you give out hate you become hateful and tend to create an atmosphere of hate around you. If you give out heaven you become heavenly. If you give out hell you become hellish. If you give out heaven part of the time and hell part of the time, then you'll be in heaven part of the time and in hell part of the time. So give out agape love, and only agape love, and you will become agape love—the highest thing in the universe.

This payoff in the person is God's daily judgment day. The reward is not at the end of life—it is being given now as life goes on. And given in the most decisive manner possible—you get what you want. And further: you become what you want. The universe gives back your inmost desire—gives it back in you. It becomes you. It is therefore inescapable, for you cannot escape yourself. You have to live with what you want.

O Father, the thought of the above appalls me and yet inspires me. For I have seen agape in Thee and I know I can become that. So I let agape take possession, not only of my acts but of the total me. May I think agape, act agape, be agape. Amen.

AFFIRMATION FOR THE DAY: *Since I want only agape, I can easily live with what I want.*

IS DESIRE WIPED OUT?

We look at another objection to the attitude of agape.

Second, if agape is "unmotivated" love, does that mean that desire is wiped out? Does that mean a question? A passivism? No, for agape is desire—a desire to give and keep on giving. It is not "acquisitive" desire. It has no motive, save the motive of its own nature—the nature which is agape—self-giving love.

So this is far removed both from the Buddhist ideal of desirelessness and from the Hindu ideal of work without desire for fruit, or reward. For both are impossible. The Buddhist ideal of desirelessness is impossible, for the desire for desirelessness is desire. The Hindu ideal of work without desire for fruit or reward is impossible and self-defeating, for back of the idea of work without desire for fruit is the motive that if you do this you will have a reward. The reward will be release from rebirth—moksha, salvation. This ideal of work without fruit or reward is infected with eros. I do this because it will be of benefit to me—will bring me salvation.

Only agape fulfills the urge underlying both of these ideals. Our trouble is in desire, but not in desire itself, as Buddha suggested. It is in wrong desire. Desire is an inherent part of us and therefore ineradicable. To rid ourselves of all desire is to reduce our life to that of the vegetable and call it victory. We would be depersonalized. The only way to get rid of desire is to replace it with a higher desire. The only way to get rid of eros is to replace it by agape. Eros is the desire to get for yourself, and agape is the desire to give yourself. To give yourself is right desire, for God has it. So if I have what God has, then desire is redeemed, and with it I am redeemed. And interestingly enough, by thus losing myself through agape, I find myself again. The man filled with agape is the most self-realized person in the world. He wants nothing, except to give himself, and to his astonishment he finds himself—and salvation. Desire is harnessed to the good of others—and our own. Agape is the way to self-realization.

O Lord Jesus, Thou didst act upon this way of agape. Thou didst ask nothing of life except to give life. And now life has come back to Thee. Thou art upon the throne of the universe and the throne of our hearts. And we love to be conquered—by agape. Amen.

AFFIRMATION FOR THE DAY: *My vagrant desires have become one desire—the desire for agape. I'm free!*

CAN EROS BE CHANGED INTO AGAPE?

Another question arises regarding agape and eros.

Third, can eros be changed into agape? Here I must differ with Nygren, to whom I am indebted in this section, for he seems to feel that eros and agape are head-on opposites and cannot meet except in combat. It is true that eros is one basis of life, and agape another. One is based on self, and the other is based on God. But I have the conviction that eros is unconverted agape—it is agape gone astray. It is agape entwined around self and absorbed by self and used by self for its own purposes. It is true that this absorption of agape by the self changes the very nature of agape. It has degenerated into eros.

But can eros be converted into agape? Why not? But only by self-surrender. For self-surrender involves the surrender of the loves of the self. When self-surrender takes place, then the loves which inhere in the self can be disentangled from the self and fastened on God, who is agape. And then the eros becomes agape, transferred from self to God.

The fact is that conversion is the conversion of our loves. We have been loving the wrong things, for the wrong reasons, for the wrong ends. In other words, love has been perverted—perverted from agape to eros. All evil is perversion of the good. Then what is conversion? Conversion is conversion from perversion. Now we begin to love the right things for the right reasons and for the right ends. And we love them with the right kind of love—with agape.

But can eros be converted into agape? Is it not so deeply entangled that to disentangle it would be to kill the tree upon which it is entwined? If eros is taken out, will the personality, without the drive of self-interest, wither and die? No, for self-centeredness is perversion. We were never intended to be the center of the universe. God is the center. So when we are centered in God we are right-centered. Therefore, what has been perverted can be converted. When we see and feel agape we can no longer be content with eros. We put out our candle, for the sun is up.

O blessed Lord, I have seen Thy face, and in that face I have seen agape. How can I ever be content again with my shabby eros. From the unreal lead me to the real, from darkness lead me to the light, from my eros lead me to Thy agape. Amen.

AFFIRMATION FOR THE DAY: *Today all my eros is a subject of conversion—into agape.*

IS AGAPE TOO HIGH?

We come now to a question which goes to the very heart of our discussion.

Fourth, isn't agape too high and impossible? Isn't it an attempt to climb Everests of attainment which are not possible for ordinary human beings? Isn't it against nature? Isn't it trying to give human nature a bent that it won't take? Isn't agape for saints and exceptional people, but not for the garden run of human beings? Is agape practical? Can it take shoes and walk? Isn't it idealism and not realism?

We cannot take seriously something that is basically impossible. We can salute it as an ideal but cannot follow it as the real. It must be basically possible, to the extent that everything else becomes impossible, if we are to follow agape all out.

We are certain that according to the Christian revelation God is agape. Jesus Christ incarnated agape. He also made agape the first and second commandments. Paul, Peter, and John made agape supreme; the cross, which is the center of that revelation, is a revelation of agape; the first fruit of the Spirit of love. There is nothing more certain than that agape love is at the center of the Christian faith. If love turns out not to be central in life, then Christianity turns out marginal.

The question then arises, Is love central in us? In the very make up of our being? Are we made by love for love, and can we live without it? Is the demand for love not merely written in the Scriptures, but is that same demand written in us? Do the texts of Scripture and the textures of our lives speak the same thing? And is that same thing a demand—an insistent demand—for love? If so, we are on solid ground in this business of human living. If Christianity and the inmost basic demands of human nature are at cross-purposes, demanding opposite things, then we are in trouble—deep trouble, life trouble. But if they turn out to be the same, then we can be all-out Christians.

O Father, we need guidance. For if we miss our step here, all life goes wrong with it. So take us by the hand and guide us through the maze of alternate ways and help us to come out at Thy mind. Amen.

AFFIRMATION FOR THE DAY: *If agape is in the makeup of my being, then agape will be in my decisions.*

IS LOVE THE BASIC URGE?

We have raised the question of whether love is basic in human nature as well as in the Christian revelation.

On reading Karl Menninger's book *Love Against Hate*, I was impressed to find psychiatry coming out with love as the basic need of human nature, for without it life is disrupted emotionally, mentally, spiritually, and physically. And this thought occurred to me: If love is so necessary to good human living, is it possible that love is the deepest and most fundamental urge in man? Is it basic in human nature? Is it an urge that is deeper than all urges? Are we made fundamentally to love and be loved?

I struggled with that thought, for I had been building my thinking for many years on the idea that self, sex, and the herd, or social instinct, were the rock-bottom instincts or urges in human nature. Is there something deeper than self, sex, and the herd, and more basic? I hesitated to come to that conclusion, as I could not remember that I had seen it specifically stated, in my rather wide reading in psychology, that the love urge is the basic urge. There had been hints in that direction, signs that pointed to it, but no one, as far as I could remember, had come out flat-footed and said that love is the basic urge in human personality. So I hesitatingly took this suggestion to Dr. M. Boss, president of the International Psychiatric Association and professor of psychotherapy at the University of Zurich. He was spending six months in the Nurmanzil Psychiatric Center of Lucknow, a center which I, though not a psychiatrist, had founded. His reply was interesting and important: "Yes, self, sex, and the herd are the branches; love is the root." Here was psychiatry, and top psychiatry at that, coming out at the place that love, which is basic in Christianity, is also basic in human nature. This means that the study of human nature and the study of the Christian revelation come out at the same place—love.

O God, our Father, we are on the verge of the important, perhaps the all-important, for if love is basic in Thy nature it ought to be basic in us. Show us Thy intent in making us and help us to follow. Amen.

AFFIRMATION FOR THE DAY: *If agape is the root of my being, then agape shall be the fruit of all I do.*

TO LOVE AND BE LOVED—BASIC URGE

We pursue the thought that the urge to love and be loved is the basic urge in human nature. We can readily see that this is so. For if the self has no love as its basic outlook and drive, it is a disrupted self. Every loveless self is an unhappy, unfulfilled self. And this does not work here and there; it works everywhere—in all nations, in all ages, in all sexes, and in all situations. And it works with an almost mathematical precision. Without love the self withers; with love the self blooms. Then love is the *sine qua non* for the self.

And the same for sex. If love is not at the basis of sex, then sex degenerates into lust, and lust into disgust. The prostitute, female or male, undertakes to use sex without love. And the result? One invariable result: unhappiness and frustration. Where love is the basis of sex, however, in a lifelong committal of one man to one woman, in a mutual self-giving, sex ends not in frustration but in fruitfulness—fruitfulness in the total person. Who decreed the result in each case? The nature of things. No one imposed that result as punishment or reward—it was inherent. It was not imposed but exposed—exposed out of the nature of reality.

Take the herd urge or instinct. If there is no love in the herd urge, what happens? When we are driven together by the herd urge, but without love in that urge and consequently in that relationship, what happens? Social relationships can be hell. To be together without love in that togetherness is to be together in hell. The stage is set for clash, for intrigue, for confusion, for unhappiness. But when the social urge has love as its basis and love in its application, then that coming together can be and is heaven. There is nothing so beautiful and absolutely blessed in heaven or on earth as a social group, small or large, in which love is the basic and dominant bond. There is something deeper than self, sex, and the herd—love.

O God, who art love, how could this be otherwise? For Thou art striving to bring us to Thy self—to love. And when we do, we live. When we turn the shoulder to Thee and Thy love, we embrace unhappiness. Amen.

AFFIRMATION FOR THE DAY: *If the urge to love and be loved is my basic urge, I shall begin with loving.*

MADE IN THE IMAGE OF LOVE?

We continue this week to study the fact that the love urge is the basic urge in human nature. The urge to love and be loved is at the basis of all other urges.

From the Christian standpoint this ought to be so. For Christianity teaches us that God made us in His own image. According to that same Christian faith, God is love. Not that He loves, but that He is basically love and would violate His own nature if he acted in any way contrary to love. When He made man in His own image would He not make man in the image of love? Would He not stamp love as the deepest thing in human nature? He, being love, would have to make love basic in any beings He would create. It could not be otherwise.

And the kind of love He would stamp within us would be His own kind of love, agape. He could not stamp any other kind. He being agape could not make us in the image of eros. So He has stamped agape within us as our basic urge. If that be true there is no more important truth about human nature. It will set the wave of the future in our dealing with human nature. To deal with anything else as basic in human nature is to deal with the marginal, and hence dooms that dealing to a marginal movement. And to try to be mature without making agape the basis of that maturity is to make one immature in his dealing with maturity.

But is it true? Isn't that too rosy a view of human nature? Do the facts bear it out? For instance, what is a baby's basic manifest urge? Is it not to grasp and to get, to think of nothing but himself? Apparently, yes. But look a little closer. The baby that will not give back love in response to his mother's love, will not answer a smile with a smile, is an unhappy baby. Grasping and squalling to fulfill his own desires, and giving back no love, he is violating the law of his being; hence he is unhappy.

Father God, we must not violate the law of our beings; we must fulfill it. Help us to love this day in every situation. Then we shall walk in heaven, and we shall spread heaven, and we shall be heaven. Amen.

AFFIRMATION FOR THE DAY: *I am stamped in the inmost of my being with the stamp of love.*

UNLOVED BABIES WITHER

Yesterday we said that though a baby seems to be a bundle of self-centered demands, nevertheless when the baby refuses to return love when given love, then he is a frustrated, unhappy child. For he is violating the law of his own being, which is made for love—to love and be loved.

This statement has been given striking confirmation, in recent medical findings at one of the country's large hospitals. Ninety-one babies were given the best scientific feeding, sanitation, and surroundings—everything to meet their physical needs, except one thing—love. The nurses were too busy to give them love—professional attention, but no love. Result? Many of the babies sickened and died. Dr. Rene Spitz reported that thirty percent of the infants who had no love suffered a breakdown ending with death from minor ailments in the first year. Twenty-two percent were so damaged mentally as to be classed as idiots. A similar condition was noted in several of the larger hospitals, which prompted authorities to call for "love volunteers," women who would come in and give several hours a day to loving babies: taking them up and fondling them, becoming interested in them—really loving them. Dr. Randolph A. Wyman, medical superintendent at Bellevue Hospital in New York City, reports: "We could no more do without [these love volunteers] than we could do without penicillin." And then he adds these significant words: "A 'vitamin' without which babies weaken or lapse into idiocy, and older children tend to fade or turn delinquent—love." Here science and the Christian faith are putting their fingers on the same necessity—love.

The psychiatrists' offices are filled with people who, in childhood or later life, have not been given love or have not responded to love. In either case the results are deadly.

When some of the leading men of America were asked to name the saddest word in the English language, Karl Menninger, famous psychiatrist of Topeka, Kansas, said: "Unloved." But I think another could and should be added: "Unloving." If you are either "unloved" or "unloving," you are upset and disrupted.

O Lord Jesus, help me this day to love with love unlimited. For in doing so, I will only be responding to Thy love, unlimited. I cannot keep in touch with Thee without love and I would keep in touch with Thee. Amen.

AFFIRMATION FOR THE DAY: *Since love is implicit in me, I shall make it explicit to others.*

"UNLOVED" AND "UNLOVING"—SADDEST WORDS

We ended yesterday with Menninger's statement that the saddest word in the English language is "unloved." But perhaps "unloving" is a sadder word still, for if you are loving then you will be loved. You can even overcome the fact that you were "unloved." The greater loss, then, is to be "unloving." It is true that it is difficult to love if you have been unloved, but it is not impossible. For basically we are all loved by God and loved by agape. To get into responsive touch with that agape of God is to be awakened to love. We begin to love, not that man first loved us, but that God first loved us. So the "unloved" person can become the loving person when awakened by the love of God.

But back to the need for love in infants:

One of the latest studies along this line is that of Rene A. Spitz, who observed and filmed the death of thirty-four foundlings of a foundling home. These infants had all their needs cared for except that of motherly love. Its lack was sufficient to make them sicken and die. The whole process of the withering of their vitality was filmed by Dr. Spitz. After three months of separation from their parents, the babies lost sleep, and became shrunken, whimpering and trembling. After an additional two months, most of them began to look like idiots. Twenty-seven foundlings died in their first year of life; seven in the second. Twenty-one other children lived longer but were so altered that thereafter they could be classified only as idiots.

These films, taken in a Latin American foundling home, show that the same basic urge for love is found in all races, in all places, at all times. Of course, this account raises a question. If as much time and attention had been expended in loving the babies as in filming them, there wouldn't have been any babies to be filmed in their misery and death.

That raises a further question, Where do we get the impulse to love? Can science give us that spark? Must religion provide it?

O God, nothing but Thy grace, Thy agape, can help us to love the unlovely. Thy agape covers the lovely and the unlovely. For to Thy love nothing is unlovely. Help me then to love with Thy love, and everyone will be lovely. Amen.

AFFIRMATION FOR THE DAY: *Love is kindled by love, so I shall hold my heart up against love today.*

"THE HUNGER FOR LOVE"

We have seen how deeply love is needed in infants. Is it true of others beyond the infant stage? Must we discuss the need for love as an infantile demand which we outgrow? No, it is basic to human life from childhood to old age.

Ashley Montagu puts it in these words:

As adults they tend to become difficult people who cannot get along with anyone. They are recognized as "cold fish," "selfish," "egotistical" and uncompromisingly ruthless in their human relationships. They seem to behave as if they neither cared for other people, nor what other people think about them. But this is only appearance, for in reality more than anything else in the world they want to care for other people and have other people care for them. These are the people who are suffering from "primary affect hunger," as David Levy has called it, the hunger for love.

One such person tragically remarked: "I know it is all there, but it is as if a wall of concrete surrounded my heart, and desperately hard as I try to express it, the warmth won't come out."

Then Montagu, approaching this whole matter from a purely humanistic point of view, concludes: "The greatest of all needs of the human being is the need for love, the experiencing of the feeling conveyed by 'others' that one is wanted, needed, liked, appreciated, valued, and deeply involved with the 'other' or 'others.' " And then he adds this significant statement:

It is primary nature, and it should also be sound nature for human beings to love one another. As it is, primary nature remains striving to love and be loved while secondary nature often puts calculated restraints upon such striving and erects barriers deliberately designed to prevent its expression—all this because the true meaning of love has not been understood. To inhibit or prevent the expression of love is to do violence to the needs, to the structure, and to the functioning of the organism.

Here the humanistic approach is coming out at exactly the place that religion comes out—at the place of love.

O Holy Spirit, who art the spirit of love, shed abroad in my heart the spirit of love. With it I live; without it I perish. We all perish. Do for us what we cannot do for ourselves. Amen.

AFFIRMATION FOR THE DAY: *I shall not do violence to my being by being unloving today.*

"THE DEMANDS OF HUMAN NATURE"

Yesterday we observed that as humanistic science studies the demands of human nature it comes out at the place where the Christian faith comes out—at the basic need of love in human nature. Montagu closes his discussion with these words: "The most important thing to realize about the nature of human nature is that the most significant ingredient in its structure is love." No more important thing can be said about human nature. If it be true then all this drives us straight into the arms of Christ, as the purest embodiment of love this planet has seen.

I asked Dr. Boss, the Swiss psychiatrist mentioned earlier, what had led him back to the Christian faith, and he replied: "When I first began my psychiatry I had a battle to put Christian faith and psychiatry together. But the demands of human nature brought me back to Christianity." Note: "The demands of human nature" drove him to His feet.

Smiley Blanton, an American psychiatrist, has written a book with an arresting title, arresting from the viewpoint of our discussion: *Love or Perish.* He says:

For more than forty years I have sat in my office and listened while people of all ages and classes told me of their hopes and fears, their likes and dislikes, and of what they considered good or bad about themselves and the world around them. . . . As I look back over the long, full years, one truth emerges clearly in my mind—the universal need for love. Whether they think they do or not, all people want love. Their spoken words may tell of other things, but the psychiatrist must listen to their unconscious voice as well. . . . There he sees that people sit on the threshold of their personalities, as Robert Louis Stevenson put it, and call on the world to come and love them. They cannot survive without love: they must have it or they will perish. . . . Modern psychiatry teaches us that we fall ill, emotionally and physically, if we do not use love in this way to guide and control our behavior. When we cannot give and receive love freely, we become easy prey to the dread emotions of fear and resentment, of anxiety and guilt.

God, our Father, if we do not choose Thee by intelligent choice, we are being driven to Thee by the very demands of our nature. Starvation is driving us to the fullness of Thy love. We are grateful that anything drives us. Amen.

AFFIRMATION FOR THE DAY: *Love is the expression of my primary nature, hate of my second nature.*

THE SELF-URGE DECIDES

We have been saying that the Christian faith, as well as the psychiatric and the humanistic approaches, all converge upon the fact that love is the basic urge and the basic need in life. If so, the question arises: Why don't we live by love? Why is there so much hate and resentment among human beings? When we give vent to our natures, why doesn't love come out? When we do give vent, don't selfishness and hate come out more often than not?

This brings us to the crux of our problem. The answer seems to be that the self-urge can decide in which direction the deeper and more basic urges can go. Love is that deepest urge, but self is the deciding urge. The freedom of the personality lies in the self-urge. The self is free to choose. It can direct the love urge. It can entwine this love urge around itself. In that case self-love becomes dominant—the personality becomes self-centered. In that case agape becomes eros and is prostituted to lower ends. Perversion takes place. An unhappy, self-centered person results.

Or the self can direct the agape urge toward sex. The self becomes a sex-dominated being. Love degenerates and becomes love of physical emotion. But that is self-defeating, for those who are most sex-obsessed get the least out of it. It is a descending spiral. Said a woman to me: "This man and I set up relations apart from marriage and we lived together for seven years. At first we thought we were happy. But gradually we became dreadfully unhappy and miserable. Now we are completely disillusioned."

But where the self directs the agape toward the God-intended relationship of one man and one woman, joined together by God in a lifelong partnership, there joy reigns and the personalities of each are heightened, as heaven bends over and kisses the whole into beauty and blessedness. Nothing more beautiful. It is the self that decides. But if instead of intelligent decision, sex passion rules, then the personality is a chaos of conflicting emotions. Unhappiness rules.

O God, may we this day stand off from ourselves and see ourselves as Thou hast made us—free, but not free to choose the results or consequences of our choices. Then give us sense, and sense to act upon sense. In Jesus' name. Amen.

AFFIRMATION FOR THE DAY: *Since the self decides, the self must be safely His.*

THE HERD-CENTERED

We have been trying to answer this question: If love is the basic urge in human nature, why are we in such a mess, individually and collectively? The answer is that the self-urge has within it the power of choice and directs the love urge toward wrong ends. We have looked at the self-urge directing the basic love urge toward itself and producing the disrupted, self-centered person. Also, the self directing the love urge toward sex and producing a sex-centered person. We must now look at the self directing the love urge toward the herd, toward society.

Here is a girl of ten wearing five petticoats to school in the mild weather of September. Why? Because that strange power called the herd has decreed that girls' dresses should stick out almost like the hoop skirt of former generations, until one has to step off the sidewalk when two of the high-school age come swaying along like rolling ships. The next stage will probably be the clinging skirt. Then the girls will all abandon the sweeping skirt for the clinging. And the racketeers who appeal to this herd urge will rake in the shekels. And papa and mama will keep their nose to the grindstone, generation after generation.

Are the older generation any better? Worse, for they with all their experience should have developed some intelligence of choice. Instead, an otherwise intelligent woman, a chain-smoker—a religious woman, but a bundle of conflicts—said to this same girl of ten, "I'll teach you how to smoke, if your mother is willing." The suggestion was passed on to the mother, then to the grandfather, who suggested, not that the granddaughter should be spanked, but that the woman who made the proposal needed conversion—needed it as Nicodemus needed it when he came to Jesus by night, afraid of the opinion of the herd. A neighbor proposed that the woman be prosecuted "for contributing to the delinquency of a minor." But what made this otherwise intelligent woman act like that? The herd. "Everybody does it," and herd-centered persons come to heel—and propagate their slavery!

O God, our Father, we are a strange combination. The angel and the animal struggle within us. Sense and nonsense battle to control us. Help me this day to throw the switch in the direction of intelligent choice. In Jesus' name. Amen.

AFFIRMATION FOR THE DAY: *The self, not the herd, shall make the decisions of the self.*

"PRIMARY NATURE" AND "SECOND NATURE"

.Though love is the basic urge in us, why do we do unlovely things and land in unlovely messes? We find the answer in the fact that freedom lies in the self. And that self can throw the switch, turning love toward the self and producing a self-centered person; toward sex and producing a sex-centered person; toward the herd and producing a herd-centered person. "The choice is always ours."

But, the question still arises, why do we make such senseless choices and land ourselves in such senseless miseries? Can freedom of choice account for it all? Is there something within us, innate or acquired which leans toward evil?

In a quotation by Montagu there is this suggestion:

It is primary, and it also should be sound nature, for human beings to love one another. As it is, primary nature remains striving to love and be loved, while second nature often puts calculated restraints upon such striving and erects barriers deliberately designed to prevent its expression. All this because the true meaning of love has not been understood.

Here he makes a distinction between "primary nature" and "second nature." Primary nature wants to love; second nature often wants to block it because it hasn't "understood."

Have we, as a human race, built up, through the ages of contact with and choice of evil, a second nature? And does this second nature have a bent toward evil? Is there then a conflict within us between primary nature which is agape love, and second nature which is perverted love? Religion answers by calling this second nature "original sin." Note that it doesn't say "original nature," but "original sin." Sin is not nature—it is an alien introduction into nature. God made us in His own image, hence good. But we, by our freedom of choice, have built up a second nature. That second nature is really not "nature"—it is an acquired, unnatural imposition on nature. It is the unnatural becoming seemingly natural.

O Father, open our eyes and let us see—see Thy purposes and Thy plans in us and for us. For if we miss Thy purposes and Thy plan, we miss ourselves, We live not only against Thee but against ourselves. Love us from both. Amen.

AFFIRMATION FOR THE DAY: *I will manifest, not an alien second nature, but my primary nature.*

"SECOND NATURE" IN PAUL'S EPISTLES

We are considering the question of "primary nature" and "second nature." Paul puts this conflict between primary nature and second nature in these words: "For I delight in the law of God, in my inmost self, but I see in my members another law at war with the law of my mind and making me captive to the law of sin which dwells in my members. . . . So then, I of myself serve the law of God with my mind, but with my flesh I serve the law of sin" (Rom. 7:22-25). Here the apostle speaks of "my inmost self" and "I of myself" as being primary nature. But there is a second nature introduced which he calls "the flesh," or "the law of sin." Note, however, that it is not the "inmost self," nor "I myself"—it is an alien imposition on the self. The inmost self remains agape, but eros has taken over the driving urges of self, sex, and the herd. A divided soul results.

Paul puts it again in these words: "For the desires of the flesh are against the Spirit, and the desires of the Spirit are against the flesh; for these are opposed to each other, to prevent you from doing what you would" (Gal. 5:17). Note that he doesn't say this "flesh" is you, for these are opposed to each other, to prevent you from doing what "you would." The "you" is on one side and "the flesh" is on the other. Then "the flesh" is not "you." It is an alien imposition on the "you." The "you" is committed to agape—the law of God written within us. But the self, throwing its choices toward "the flesh"—the unnatural, built-up nature—turns the agape into eros. The loves or desires are perverted. A perverted person results.

Now the further question arises, Can this second nature be eliminated? The answer is that if it is second nature, and not primary nature, it can be eliminated. If it is primary nature, then of course it cannot be eliminated, for primary nature is us—the essential self. The self cannot be eliminated and should not, for it is God's creation. But this second nature is not God's creation; it is our creation and hence can be eliminated.

O Father, we thank Thee that we are on the threshold of something big. We are in sight of being free from this false, built-up second nature and being free to express our primary nature. Help us to take our freedom. Amen.

AFFIRMATION FOR THE DAY: *What has come in can go out. The second nature has come in—it shall go out—by grace.*

CAN "SECOND NATURE" BE WIPED OUT?

We are considering whether we can be free from this "second nature" and then become single-natured, hence a unified person? The answer is a flat-footed yes! Paul, after describing the two natures in the seventh chapter of Romans, proclaims his freedom in the eighth chapter: "For the law of the Spirit of life in Christ Jesus has set me free from the law of sin and death" (v. 2). The "law of sin" in his "flesh" has been canceled and he is under a new law: "the law of the Spirit of life in Christ Jesus."

What had been built up—the second nature—had been torn down. The primary nature remained intact, but that primary nature is now controlled by "the law of the Spirit of life in Christ Jesus." The primary nature is created by God; the second nature is created by man. In redemption the original abides and the imported goes.

In our confusion, we get these mixed up and try to eliminate primary nature along with second nature. We try to eliminate the self, the sex, and the herd urges. But they are an integral part of us and cannot by any known process be eliminated. The attempt to do so is futile—and disastrous. And yet it is tried—tried often in the name of Christianity. For instance, the hymn, each stanza of which ends thus: "All of self, and none of Thee"; "Some of self, and some of Thee"; "None of self, and all of Thee." This ends with the self eliminated. It is well intentioned but seriously misleading. The attempt to eliminate the self leads to hypocrisy—and worse, to inner confusion and conflict. For the self refuses to budge. And rightly. It is God-created and what God creates He doesn't cancel. Instead of trying to eliminate ourselves we must accept ourselves and love ourselves. "You shall love your neighbor *as yourself.*"

You must accept yourself. But the snag is this: You cannot accept yourself as you now are. If you did you would accept a self you could not respect. This would mean that you would be adjusted to a half-self.

O God, teach me how to accept myself. And the kind of self I must accept. I know I cannot accept the kind of self I am. I can only accept myself in Thee. And that means surrender to Thee. I do. In Jesus' name. Amen.

AFFIRMATION FOR THE DAY: *I renounce this false self and reverence the real self.*

ACCEPT YOURSELF IN GOD

We are discussing the subject of accepting yourself and loving yourself. When psychiatry urges you to accept yourself, both truth and fallacy are involved. It is true that you must not be rejecting and hating yourself. To live in a state of self-rejection and self-hate is as bad as living in other-rejection and other-hate. But there is a sense in which you cannot accept yourself—cannot accept yourself *as you are*. If you did you would settle down to accepting a half-self instead of a whole self. You would be adjusted on a very low level. And to be adjusted on a very low level is a very high tragedy. The end in view must not be adjustment, but adjustment to the Highest. And that highest is Christ.

Then the Christian position, as I see it, is this: Accept yourself in God. In yourself you do not accept yourself, for that would mean the acceptance of a low type of self. It would mean a moral and spiritual stalemate. But when you surrender yourself to God then you can accept yourself *there*. First of all, because God accepts you, and if He accepts you then you must accept what He accepts. And second, because you accept a self that is in the process of being made. You don't have to wait for a perfect self before you can accept yourself. You accept yourself as you are in God, for you accept a self that is being made into something other than what you are and more than what you are. You accept a being-redeemed self, and therefore a growing self. Such a self is acceptable.

And you can love yourself. But you do not love yourself in your self. You love yourself *in God*. God loves yourself and we should not hate what God loves. But we cannot love all-out what we do not approve. You can approve of yourself in God, however, since you are under the process of being redeemed. You are being changed from one type of person to another. You can love that type of person—love it in spite of marginal faults and marginal lapses, for the central person is lovable—he is consenting to redemption.

O God, our Father, how I do thank Thee that I am not bottled up to myself. I can get myself off my own hands into Thy hands by self-surrender, my open door. That door is always open. So I take it now. Amen.

AFFIRMATION FOR THE DAY: *I love myself because I love Someone more than myself.*

SEX BELONGS TO "PRIMARY NATURE"

We come now to another urge within human nature—the sex urge. It belongs to primary nature—God-created and God-approved. It was after making male and female that God looked at that which He had created and called it "very good." But the self can turn agape into eros at the place of sex, and simple natural desires can become "the flesh"—the seat of degradation and decay. But in striving to get rid of "the flesh," which is "second nature," many strive to get rid of sex, which is primary nature. It can't be done.

I have seen it attempted in India. I have seen sadhus, holy men, who spent most of their time suppressing their sex passions, using physical mutilation in the suppression. But the point is that they spent most of their time and energy in the process. It occupied their attention. Evidently sex was uppermost in their minds! The attempt to run away from sex was a dead failure. It was self-defeating.

The only way to get rid of sex as eros is to surrender it to God. Then it comes back as agape. You can love sex—love it in God. Then you can accept your sex—accept it with gratitude and without fear. For sex controlled by agape sets up a home on the basis of a lifelong partnership. When each member wants nothing except to give to the other, which is agape, both receive back an abundance of love, pressed down and running over.

But suppose there is no life partner to whom you can give agape, are you up against it and frustrated and unhappy? Not necessarily. For you can still marry yourself to humanity and give it agape in terms of a dedication to a human need. Rufus Moseley was married to humanity and gave agape to everybody, everywhere. And was he happily married? More happily married to humanity than 999 out of 1,000 are happily married in the ordinary way. So happily married that when he did fall in love in his late seventies, and I asked if he was going to be married, he replied: "No, we love each other too much to get married!"

O Father, we thank Thee for the strange, beautiful tenderness of agape love between man and woman. We thank Thee that it adds a plus to everything we are and do. And we thank Thee that we can love sex in Thee. Amen.

AFFIRMATION FOR THE DAY: *I shall love love and hate lust.*

POSSIBLE ATTITUDES TOWARD THE HERD

We come now to the next urge in primary nature—the herd or social urge.

Concerning the herd urge, these attitudes are possible: (1) Try to eliminate it. Turn your back on society and walk away from it—become a hermit. (2) Stay in society and succumb to it; merge yourself into the herd and become anonymous. (3) Stay in society but be on the defensive against it—fight it. (4) Stay in society and encase yourself; be inwardly aloof, so that society doesn't affect you. (5) Surrender the herd to God; stay in society—love it and serve it.

The first four are not the answer. To renounce the herd and live apart from it is impossible—and disastrous. The sadhus of India, who renounce the world, attempting to cut all ties, bind themselves to the world more so than any other group. The nemesis is this: they have to depend on the herd for their physical sustenance, so they are compelled to beg their food from society. No one is more dependent on society than a beggar, religious or secular. So the attempt to renounce the world has made him rely on the world more than ever. To stay in society and succumb to it, echoing its attitudes, is deadly to personality. You become no longer a person but a thing. To be in society and fight its dominance is to produce an unlovely character—always "agin" any proposal that comes up—the porcupine type of personality. To stay in society inwardly aloof and encased against it, is to produce the unsocial person.

All of these ways are self-defeating except the last way: the way of surrender of the herd to God. That breaks the dominance of the herd, inwardly emancipating you, and then you are free to love the herd and serve it with a leisured heart. And you can love the herd because you love something more than the herd—God. You then love the herd in God. This second nature—"the world"—is dethroned; and primary nature, the social being, is emancipated. Then you can love the world with agape; wanting nothing, you can give everything.

Gracious Lord, I make Thee Lord. Many false lords bid for my allegiance. I have one sole allegiance to Thee. All else bends the knee. And now I am emancipated, free—free to love everybody and everything with agape. Amen.

AFFIRMATION FOR THE DAY: *"Delivering you from the people . . . to whom I send you"*—this is my freedom.

THE FALSE WORLD PASSES AWAY

We have seen that "primary nature" is here to stay, an integral part of us. But "second nature" is man-made and an unnatural imposition on life. It can be cleansed away and a new freedom found from unnatural bondages.

This is what John means when he says: "Do not love the world or the things in the world. . . . For all that is in the world, the lust of the flesh and the lust of the eyes and the pride of life, is not of the Father but is of the world" (I John 2:15-16). The "world" is life organized apart from God—it is second nature built up by man. Of it is said: "And the world passes away" (v. 17). But "he who does the will of God abides for ever"—that is life organized around the will of God—that life abides, for it is primary nature.

I never saw the "world"—the real world, God's world—until I had renounced the dominance of this false "world" and accepted a world organized around God. I never saw the sky, the trees—everything—as I did the morning after I was converted. Every bush was aflame with God. The village fountain "was bubbling out of paradise"—everything had a heavenly origin and a heavenly flavor. I saw everything with agape.

The three things John mentions here: "the lust of the flesh," sexuality; "the lust of the eyes," acquisitiveness; "the pride of life," egocentricity—all are perversions of agape. The basic urge to love has been turned toward the flesh and has produced sexuality; toward the lust of the eyes and has produced an acquisitive, grasping type; toward the ego and has produced the proud, egocentric type. Love has been turned into "lust"—agape into eros. Second nature takes the place of primary nature and rules over primary nature. The person is topsy-turvy.

Eros is agape unconverted, gone astray. Conversion is conversion from perversion. Conversion replaces eros with agape. Redemption is therefore a redemption of our loves. It redeems from the unnatural to the natural—the supernaturally natural. It makes us "whole" again.

O Father, I would be made "whole." For I cannot live half slave and half free. I would be one person, with a single goal, a single love, and a single drive. Only Thy agape can draw me together into wholeness. Amen.

AFFIRMATION FOR THE DAY: *All my loves redeemed by agape, I am free to love with agape.*

IS AGAPE REALISTIC?

We turn now to the question of whether life controlled and motivated by agape is realistic. Can it be done? Or is it impossible idealism?

Whenever I've read or heard the highest and the second highest commandments: "You shall love the Lord your God with all your heart, and with all your soul, and with all your mind"; and "you shall love your neighbor as yourself," I've found a tiny question mark arising within. It has been this: How can you command love? You can command a person not to do this, and to do that—a deed. But to command love is commanding the impossible. Love is an attitude of the inmost spirit and you can hardly produce an attitude by a command. You can't hold the stick of a commandment over a person's head and say to him, "Now love, or else." You love or you don't love—from within. And a commandment can't produce it.

But in view of what we have been saying, all this is reversed, and the question marks straighten out into exclamation points. For if the basic urge in human nature is to love and be loved, then it is not an imposition on human nature when we are commanded to love. To command us to love is simply to command us to do what our natures demand. So what He commands, our nature commends. In other words, he commands what our nature demands. His commandment to love is no unnatural imposition on nature; it is a natural exposition of nature. The commandment and the deepest need of our nature fit like the hand and the glove. They are made for each other, since He who made human nature for love made the commandment to love. And the two are one.

Nothing, absolutely nothing, is more important for the Christian faith than just that. Suppose a study of the needs of human nature had brought us to a conclusion at variance to the Christian commandment. This would mean that the basic needs of human nature are demanding one thing and the Christian commandment another. But since both are saying the same thing, and since that same thing is not marginal, but centrally important, then that is news, good news!

O God, we are tracing Thy designs in the Scriptures and in us, and we are grateful that we find the same intention in both. Thou art leading us to agape, for Thou art agape. Where else couldst Thou lead us? Amen.

AFFIRMATION FOR THE DAY: *My inner demands and God's outer commands are one.*

"HIS COMMANDMENTS ARE NOT BURDENSOME"

In the light of the conclusions we have reached, we can now understand the statement of John: "For this is the love of God, that we keep his commandments. And his commandments are not burdensome" (I John 5:3). "His commandments are not burdensome." Why? Because He lets us off lightly, laying nothing of consequence upon us? On the contrary, He lays on us the heaviest burden a human being could be called on to carry. And the burden is this: Love God with all your heart, all your mind, all your soul, all your strength, and love your neighbor as yourself. Could anything be more inexorable, more demanding, more imperious than just this double demand to love? And note that it's *all* your heart, *all* your mind, *all* your soul, and *all* your strength. *Not* a demand for a portion of your heart, a portion of your mind, a portion of your soul, a portion of your strength—the demand is for *all*. And the love toward your neighbor is to be equal to the love for the most precious thing you have—yourself.

Nothing could be conceived by God or man more sweeping and imperious and more demanding than this. And yet John quietly and decisively says: "His commandments are not burdensome." Anyone who has tried it, as John himself tried it, gives a full-hearted, "Amen." It works out exactly as John says: "His commandments are not burdensome." Why? Because the thing that God commanded is our highest good and our deepest need. So when I fulfill His commandments I fulfill myself. If I revolt against His commandments I revolt against myself. If I won't live with God I can't live with myself. If I do live with God in full-hearted obedience to His commandment to love, I can live with myself joyously and freely. Then the highest in God is the deepest in nature. The highest Good is good for us. The Good is not only good, it is good for us. The bad is not only bad, it is bad for us. Then God's highest will is our highest interest. So when God wills us to love He wills according to the grain of our primary nature. Not to love is to go against the grain of our primary nature as well as to go against the will of God.

O Blessed Lord Jesus, Thy revelation of God is also a revelation of us. When we have seen His image in Thee we have seen His image stamped in us. Defaced to be sure by our sins and folly, but still there, ready to respond to Thy love. Amen.

AFFIRMATION FOR THE DAY: *His burden is the same burden that wings are to a bird.*

"ONLY LOVE CAN CURE IT"

Before we draw our final and tighter conclusions, we must turn back and reinforce our premises in order to gather up that last doubting soul. Is love the deepest and most basic urge or instinct in human nature?

Here is what a psychiatrist at a mental institution in Peoria, Illinois, says: "No matter what a psychiatrist knows he cannot cure a patient with knowledge. Someone has to love that patient, for the lack of love produced the neurosis. And only love can cure it." His observation is significant, for psychiatry had thought for a long time that knowledge could cure the patient. "To know thyself" was synonymous with "To cure thyself." They were one. Now that is changed. Knowledge is moonlight; only love is sunlight.

Here was a child brought up in a home where everything was provided for his development—sanitation, scientific feeding—everything except love. The parents didn't know how to give that. The child, in spite of medical and parental care, withered and faded. He became pale and anemic. The doctor and the parents were at their wit's end, when the Negro maid stepped in and said: "You give me a chance with that child, but on one condition, that you take your hands off and leave him to me and don't interfere." They agreed hesitatingly. The child soon began to blossom and bloom. The mother, puzzled, peeped through the glass panel of the kitchen door to see what was happening. The baby, smiling and laughing, was on the kitchen floor, sucking on a piece of charcoal; the maid was down beside him singing to him—and loving him! Sucking on that piece of charcoal upset the ideas of the mother regarding sanitation, but the idea of the maid regarding love set up the baby. The parents had learned ignorance and the maid had ignorant knowledge. Someone has said that the unpardonable sin of science is knowledge without love. It is. But the unpardonable sin of parents, of teachers, of employers, of everybody, is knowledge without love. It is the sin for which there is no forgiveness.

O Father, Thou art gently driving us into love by the sheer pressure of the facts. We are glad to be driven, for we are being driven into salvation—ours and others'. So we are grateful for that love that will not let us go. Amen.

AFFIRMATION FOR THE DAY: *His burden is as burdensome as is love to the heart.*

"SIGN OF A NORMAL MIND"

We are gathering up scattered strands of evidence that the basic urge in human nature is the urge to love and be loved.

The feeling of having "no one to care" is the reason that men in prison—hardened criminals—try to tame and make pets of mice and rats that come into their cells. These men want companionship, something to love. And criminals are not changed by punishment—they are changed only if someone loves them and cares about them. That, and that alone, is redemptive.

Julian Huxley, the humanist, says: "Love is an indispensable. Mother love is indispensable for children's happy and healthy growth, both physical and spiritual."

Robert Bridges, the poet, says: "Love is the fire in whose devouring flames all earthly ills are consumed."

Walter C. Alvarez, formerly of the Mayo Clinic, puts it this way: "One of the sure signs of a normal mind is the ability of a person to love someone, and to love disinterestedly, affectionately and generously." Note: "to love disinterestedly"—that is agape. If there is no agape the person is not normal, but abnormal.

Here is Bertrand Russell, the humanist philosopher, lecturing at Columbia University:

Science can offer man greater well-being than he has ever known provided three conditions are met: War must be abolished, ultimate power must be evenly distributed, and the growth of population must be limited. But how are these to be fulfilled? The root of the matter is a simple and old-fashioned thing, a thing so simple I am almost ashamed to mention it, for fear of the derisive smile with which wise cynics will greet my words. The thing I mean—please forgive me for mentioning it—is love, Christian love, or compassion. If you feel this you have a motive for existence, a guide in action, a reason for courage, an imperative necessity for intellectual honesty.

Note the hesitancy of Bertrand Russell and the apology, for this was a reversal of all his attitudes and values. But as a scientific philosopher he found love inescapable and inevitable.

Gracious Father, Thou art throwing Thy net of love wide and Thou art drawing the hearts and minds of men to the shore of Thy purposes. We are glad to be drawn, for we feel we are being drawn to Thee and to ourselves. Amen.

AFFIRMATION FOR THE DAY: *Today I shall love one hundred percent for nothing.*

"SECOND NATURE" IS PAGAN

We come now to a conclusion which has gradually been forcing itself upon us. And the conclusion is this: The Christian way is the natural way. All else is unnatural and doomed to break itself upon the system of things, the nature of Reality.

Those who have followed my writings and my addresses across the years will be familiar with that conclusion. It is a startling conclusion, for I've maintained it against the popular trend in modern theological circles to adopt the neoorthodox position stated by Niebuhr, that "the soul is naturally pagan." Man's basic and fundamental nature is to organize life around itself—it is fundamentally and basically selfish. Therefore, all that he does and thinks and loves is tainted with this basic and fundamentally sinful egocentricity. Therefore, Christianity is an unnatural intrusion into human nature. Human nature is against it. It is alien.

I am persuaded that there is a confusion here between "primary nature" and "second nature." I agree that this second nature, built up by habits and attitudes through the sinful centuries, is primarily egoistic and aggressive. As such it is sin. But primary nature, which is deeper down and more fundamental than this man-produced second nature, is made to love and be loved. That is our real nature; second nature is unnatural.

When this second nature is surrendered to God, then it is cleansed away and we return to the truly natural—the primary nature. The primary nature controlled by God begins to control the life and motives and attitudes. We are controlled by agape. As such we are natural—supernaturally natural.

The emphasis that "the soul is naturally pagan" has made Christianity an alien intrusion into life—as such, an unnatural demand. This has put two strikes against Christianity before it begins. It sets Christianity against all these tendencies in modern science and discoveries in human nature which are driving toward the Christian position. It takes Christianity out of the stream of life and puts it on the protesting edges.

O Father God, I am glad I see Thy footprints everywhere. I am glad I see Thee supremely in the pages of Scripture and in the face of Jesus Christ, but I'm also glad to find Thee in nature and in human nature. Amen.

AFFIRMATION FOR THE DAY: *My faith is not an eddy in the current of life—it is the current itself.*

THE CHRISTIAN WAY THE NATURAL WAY

We have been saying that God is love and that the basic urge in human nature is the love urge—the urge to love and be loved. If this is true, we are driven inevitably to the conclusion that the Christian way is the natural way.

I came to that conclusion years ago and the years have but confirmed it. And this discussion on love has put the capstone on the whole conviction. If I repeat in the next day or so what I've been saying through the years, I repeat it with a deeper content, brought on by a deeper conviction.

I know that the Christian theological slant has been the other way, contending that sin is natural and Christianity is supernatural but not natural. Certain passages are brought up to prove that sin is natural: "The natural man receiveth not the things of the Spirit of God" (I Cor. 2:14 KJV). But the Revised Standard Version puts it: "The unspiritual man does not receive the gifts of the Spirit of God." So it is not a question between the natural and unnatural, but between the spiritual and the unspiritual. Another passage: "But Jesus did not trust himself to them, because he knew all men . . . for he himself knew what was in man" (John 2:24-25). But this passage is neutral. We do not say that sin is not in man—it is, and it has corrupted and depraved man. Sin is in man, but we deny it is natural. If it were natural why should it deprave and corrupt man? If it were natural, then under sin we should blossom and bloom because we are fulfilling our own nature. But I know, and everybody else knows, exactly what happens when we sin. We are orphaned, estranged, out of gear, alienated; life is driven underground. Everything within us cries out: "This is not the way to live." On the other hand, I know exactly what happens when I take the Christian attitude and do the Christian thing: I am universalized, at home in the universe, free: the sum total of reality is behind me. I have cosmic backing for my way of life, and everything within me cries out: "This is your homeland, the way you are made to live." This is the universal experience.

O Father, I am made for Thee and I am restless until I rest in Thee. Since Augustine uttered those words we have repeated them after him, silently or vocally. And the ages to come will repeat the same. For it is as true as truth. I accept it. Amen.

AFFIRMATION FOR THE DAY: *I am at home in God; outside of God I am an orphan, estranged.*

"TOUCH OF CHRIST UPON ALL CREATION?"

We are insisting that the Christian way is the natural way and that every other way of life is unnatural and doomed to perish.

I grant you that a "second nature" has been built up in us by our contact with racial sin and our own choices. But that second nature is not natural. When paper is manufactured, the watermark in the paper is not stamped on the paper; it is wrought into the texture of the paper, a part of the paper. Whatever is written on the paper afterwards is not a natural part of the paper. It is something imposed on the nature of the paper. When God made you and me and the universe, He stamped within the nature of things His own urge—the love urge. The urge to love and be loved is written into our natures, not *on* our natures, but *into* our natures. Whatever we may write on that primary nature is our writing, not God's. By our full choice in writing we build up a body of ideas, attitudes, and emotions; we build up a second nature—an unnatural nature imposed on the natural nature, the primary nature.

Does this fit in with Scripture? Yes. The New Testament teaches that God created all things through Christ: "He was in the beginning with God; all things were made through him, and without him was not anything made that was made" (John 1:2-3). "For in him [Christ] all things were created. . . . All things were created through him and for him" (Col. 1:16): ". . . through whom [Christ] also he created the world" (Heb. 1:2). What do these strange passages which say that God created the world through Christ mean? Do they mean that the touch of Christ is upon all creation? That everything is made in its inner structure to work in the Christian way? That when it works in the Christian way it works well, harmoniously, at its best? And that when it works some other way it works it own ruin? I believe that everything in creation answers a deep Amen of approval to those questions. More and more, all life, all experience, is corroborating that fact. And the most exciting thing in my life is to watch the unfolding of this drama of corroboration. This *is* exciting!

O Lord Jesus, as we follow Thee through the mazes of human living we find this jigsaw puzzle coming out to sense, Glorious Sense. And it fills us with a divine excitement, for it means that we are on the Way! Am I grateful? Read my gratitude. Amen.

AFFIRMATION FOR THE DAY: *If I am made to work in His Way, I will not try to unmake His making.*

"NOTHING IS NATURALLY ON OUR SIDE"

We continue to explore the Christian way as the natural way. In his interesting *Screwtape Letters*, C. S. Lewis records the letters of a senior devil to a junior devil, which advise how to get hold of men. The senior devil makes this important observation: "Nothing is naturally on our side. We labor under a heavy handicap. For everything has to be twisted to be of any use to us." That is profoundly true. Love has to be turned into lust; love of the self has to be perverted into selfish self-love; giving has to be turned into self-display. All evil is twisted good. Evil is an attempt to live life against itself. And it can't be done. So evil is not only bad—it's stupid. It is living against the grain of the universe and against the grain of our own natures.

Is the Christian way, then, the hard way? No, the other way is the hard way! A man came to Sam Jones, the evangelist, and said: "Mr. Jones, I know only one verse of Scripture and I know that one is true: 'The way of the transgressor is hard.' " It is. It's hard to be a liar, for you have to live with yourself without self-respect. It's hard to be impure because you can't respect the person you see in the looking glass. It's hard to be a self-centered person, for you don't like the self you are loving.

In a religious journal I read this from a prominent churchman: "The more difficult path you contemplate is likely to be God's will, the easier one, your own ideas." This is true in a sense, but only in a sense. It is true only in the beginning. My way seems easy in the beginning, but it turns out to be hard. God's way seems hard in the beginning, but it turns out to be easy. In the book of Revelation is this verse: "It was sweet as honey in my mouth, but when I had eaten it my stomach was made bitter" (10:10). The morsel of my desire against God's desire tastes sweet on the tongue of "second nature," but it turns bitter in the stomach of "primary nature." Primary nature can't assimilate it—it is bitter to the interests of primary nature. The good seems bitter to the taste of second nature, but it is sweet to primary nature—it can be assimilated. The good is good for me.

Father, teach me the difference between the temporary sweet and the permanent bitter, between the temporary bitter and the permanent sweet. And give me the sense to act upon that difference, for I get my values twisted and I get twisted with them. Amen.

AFFIRMATION FOR THE DAY: *Nothing will be taken into me which cannot be totally assimilated in my total nature.*

"DOES NOT LOVE REMAIN IN DEATH?"

We are thinking on the Christian way as the natural way to live. We must rid ourselves of the idea that the will of God lies along the line of the disagreeable. It always lies along the line of the agreeable to us, the "primary nature." God's will is always the best thing for us at that particular moment, under those particular circumstances. God couldn't be love and yet will anything less or other than our highest interest. In our limited and often twisted vision we may think it against our interest, but it simply cannot be.

Jesus said: "My meat is to do the will of him that sent me" (John 4:34 KJV). The will of God was His meat—His food. His nature assimilated it, for His nature and that food were made for each other. My poison is to do my own will against the will of God.

Is that the moralistic conclusion of a preacher? Or is it the conclusion, scientifically corroborated, of the psychologist and the scientist? We have mentioned Menninger's book *Love Against Hate*—that title tells the story. Love builds, hate blasts. It's all on the table—of science. The title of Smiley Blanton's book *Love or Perish* is as pointed as it can be made, and these two titles represent the distilled experience of long-time psychiatrists. These titles express what the Christian revelation revealed two thousand years ago: "He who does not love remains in death" (I John 3:14). Psychology could accept every word of that, with every word underscored. And it would not be merely future death in some other world, but death here and now—"remains in death." For where there is love there is life; where there is no love there is death.

A German doctor was fighting the Christian demand for self-surrender. She sent back the New Testament I gave her with these words written on the wrapper: "I hate you. Where are you?" Two voices were speaking: the voice of second nature, "I hate you and the demand you represent for self-surrender"; the voice of primary nature, "Where are you? I need and want what you are offering in Christ."

O Jesus, if there is surface rebellion against Thee, there is depth thirst for Thee. My primary nature is in death without Thee. So listen to the cry of the deepest me, the real me, for I cry for Thee as thirst cries for water. Amen.

AFFIRMATION FOR THE DAY: *All departure from love will bring immediate death to something in me.*

"HIS BURDEN IS LIGHT"

Schopenhauer, the philosopher, was "opposed to love for," he said, "it only brings trouble." Did his revolt against love bring him freedom from trouble? On the contrary, it brought him a life trouble. As he sat on a park bench a policeman, thinking him to be a tramp, said to him: "What are you doing here? Who are you?" The sad-faced philosopher looked up and replied: "I wish I knew." He was lost—lost amid his knowledge, lost without love.

But in a way, Schopenhauer was right; love does bring trouble, that is, the wrong kind of love—eros, an acquisitive love. Agape, however, is the banisher of trouble, for if you have agape you are happy amid troubles. For "love feels no loads." I saw a man struggling through a railway station in Japan with a huge carton labeled "The Universe." Some people are struggling with the weight of the universe on their shoulders. Well, Jesus puts the universe into your heart. To love, there are no burdens. "My yoke is easy, and my burden is light," said Jesus. Why? Does He put nothing on you if you come to Him? On the contrary, He puts everything on you if you follow Him. He puts the world and its troubles into your heart. Says Friedrich von Hügel, the Roman Catholic layman: "A Christian is one who cares"—a good definition of a Christian. The more you are in touch with Jesus the more you will care—care for everybody, everywhere. And that caring will make you take upon yourself burdens for everybody. I have mentioned "Sister Lila," a Greek, a woman filled with the love of God. She came to our Ashram at Sat Tal, India. She was going from our Ashram to a leper asylum, where she intended to apply her methods of massage, for she was a trained and expert masseuse, to lepers. This meant that she would massage the sores of lepers with her bare hands. Her love took upon itself the burdens of others—she really cared, not in words but in loving deeds. Did her love get her into trouble? Yes, in a way. But her very love turned the troubles into opportunity. For her, everything was opportunity to manifest the love of God. And was she gay? Yes, gay with God!

O Father God, put on me the burdens of love, but be sure to give me the love at the same time, for burdens without love are intolerable. With love I can "bear all things" and bear them rejoicingly and gaily. In Jesus' name. Amen.

AFFIRMATION FOR THE DAY: *I live in a state of yes-ness to God and of no-ness to everything alien to that.*

"TO KEEP IT FROM FUNCTIONING NATURALLY"

We return to the passage upon which we are meditating: "And his commandments are not burdensome." We have seen that His commandments are not burdensome, since what He commands is what we are made in our inner structure to do. It is not burdensome for a car to run—that is what it's made to do. It is not burdensome for a canary to sing. It loves to sing. As one Indian professor put it: "It's not burdensome to be told to eat." A commandment to lovers telling them to love would not be burdensome—it would be bliss.

And yet we find many who look on Christianity as a burden—an imposition. As Solomon Richter put it: "Christianity is a set of scruples imposed on the ordinary framework of humanity to keep it from functioning naturally and normally." That fits in with a passage from Hosea wherein God complains:

> Were I to write for [them] my laws,
> [they] would but think them foreigners' saws (8:12) Moffatt).

God's laws were looked on as foreign saws, or sayings, something alien or foreign to his people. But God's laws and our primary nature are not aliens, they are allies. When we fulfill them we fulfill ourselves. As for Richter's statement that Christianity is a set of scruples imposed on human nature to keep it from functioning naturally and normally, it is the very opposite. The real Christian is the most natural person in the world. He has natural joys, natural gaiety, natural laughter, natural culture, natural grace—he is a man reduced to simple naturalness. When one is not living the Christian way all his pleasures have to be induced—induced by entertainment from without, by liquor, by stimulation of various kinds. They have to *try* to have a good time. I don't try to have a good time—I just have one, naturally and normally. A simple, bubbling gaiety from within, what Rufus Moseley called "the Divine frisky." As you get cleaned up and cleaned out within, you develop a hair-trigger laugh—one with which you can laugh at yourself if you cannot laugh at anything else.

O Divine Lord, how can I cease to be grateful for this fountain within. Thy agape makes me bubble with a joy unspeakable and full of glory. I find this well of thanksgiving springing up to everlasting life. I am grateful. Amen.

AFFIRMATION FOR THE DAY: *A natural joy, a natural peace—a naturalness which will be supernatural.*

"THIS IS MY HOMELAND"

We are insisting that "his commandments are not burdensome," because what He commands our "primary nature" commends. We are made for His commandments as the eye is made for light, as the heart is made for love, as the conscience is made for truth. When we find Him we find ourselves. Bound to Him we walk the earth free. Low at His feet, we stand straight before everything else. We bow to Him, but if we do then we don't bow to anything else.

All coming to Jesus has the feel of a homecoming upon it. The parable of the prodigal son has the sure touch of reality upon it: When "he came to himself," he immediately said, "I will arise and go to my father." When he found himself he found his home, and vice versa, when he found his home he found himself.

As I was describing to a group the amazing agape of "Mary," a dour Scotch minister from Canada said afterward: "When you were describing the love that 'Mary' had for everybody and everything I said to myself: 'This is my homeland.' " Why did this Scotchman think of the homeland of his soul when love incarnate was being described? Because love is the homeland of the soul. Love is its native air. In an atmosphere of love you breathe freely, fully, deeply. This is the air for which you are made. But in a loveless atmosphere you feel choked, stifled. I sat at a table where love was absent. I said to the group: "I'm sorry I cannot stay. My digestion will go back on me if I do." For hate does stop digestion, drying up the gastric juices. Love makes the gastric juices flow. "You must take good will to the table with you," said a doctor, "if you want to digest your food." During an experiment observers watched the process of digestion through an opening in a man's stomach. They found that when the man observed was in a good humor, on good terms with everybody, digestion was normal, the stomach blushed a rosy red, the gastric juices poured down like sweat on one's face. But the moment he became angry the color of the stomach changed, the gastric juices stopped, and digestion was at an end.

O Christ, Thou hast wrought love and the necessity for love into the very fiber of everything, within us and without. We are made by love for love. And when we find love we find everything, for love glorifies all. Amen.

AFFIRMATION FOR THE DAY: *Since I am made for love I shall fulfill my destiny.*

"LOVE'S ETERNAL GOAL IS LIFE"

We are looking at the fact that love is our native air—our homeland. Without it we suffer from a nostalgia which affects body, mind, and spirit. As Smiley Blanton says: "Love's greatest glory lies in the fact that it alone provides the strength, protection and encouragement without which full growth is impossible." Again he says:

Love, in our psychic life, is the great combining force *that seeks to join all parts together*. It is the organizing element in our emotional structure. It is the power that reaches out to build and construct. Love is the immortal flow of energy that *nourishes, extends and preserves*. Its eternal goal is life.

Side by side with it there exists the antagonistic force of aggression. This is the dark instinct that strives constantly *to pull the parts asunder*. It is the power that conquers and dissolves. It bores inward, seeking to separate and destroy. Aggression's goal is death.

As Dante puts it: "It is love that spins the universe." It is lovelessness that puts the brakes on everything, inside and out.

Carlyle says: "Love is ever the beginning of knowledge, as fire is of light." That is why Gnosticism failed—it tried to have knowledge without love. And Christianity succeeded because it first had love, therefore had knowledge. You cannot understand a person until you love that person.

Longfellow puts it in these lovely lines:

> Ah, how skillful grows the hand
> That obeyeth Love's command!
> It is the heart, and not the brain,
> That to the highest doth attain,
> And he who followeth Love's behest
> Far excelleth all the rest!

So the psychologist, the poet, and the preacher can stand side by side and preach the same thing in differing language—love and live, be loveless and perish.

O Blessed Redeemer, redeem me from all lovelessness of thought, motive, and act. And may I begin to practice love on everything and everybody I meet today. If I do I know I shall walk in heaven and have heaven within. Amen.

AFFIRMATION FOR THE DAY: *Love is my freedom and my freedom is love.*

"ROOTED AND GROUNDED IN LOVE"

Paul speaks of being "rooted and grounded in love" (Eph. 3:17). The roots of love are in us and when we put those roots into the world ground—in God—then we are rooted and grounded in love. The roots and the soil fit each other as the stomach and the food fit each other. If we put our roots of love into the soil of God's love, we bear fruit and the first fruit is "love."

But suppose we put the roots of our love into the soil of self-love, then we bear bitter fruit—the fruit of unhappiness and frustration. If we put the roots of our love into sex, as an end in itself, then love will turn to lust and the fruit will be disgust. If we put the roots of our love in the soil of "the world," life organized without God, then we eat the Dead Sea fruit of disappointment that turns to ashes in our mouths.

But when the roots of our love are grounded in God's love, that soil nourishes us with everything required for growth and maturity. You don't have to *try* to be mature; you just *are* mature. You are natural, unstrained, receptive.

As I was about to plant some fruit trees in Sat Tal, India, an agricultural expert said to me: "Put a layer of manure at the bottom of the pit, then a layer of earth, then another layer of manure and another layer of earth, and so on clear to the top. Thus the roots will always be reaching for a deeper level of richness and will send the tree higher as the roots go deeper." When planted in the soil of God we are constantly reaching new levels of richness. The more we get the more we know there is to get. Our maturity is only relative maturity, for the more mature we become the more maturity there is to be had. So we never come to a static maturity—it is always a growing maturity. And the maturity is effortless and unstrained. We live by passive receptivity—a passive receptivity which is an active passivity. He gives, we receive, and then we give: He gives, we receive, and then we give—the glorious circle of love from Him, to me, to others.

O Father, I am rooted and grounded in love, in Thee. I need not be anxious about my fruits if my roots are in Thee. The fruits will take care of themselves. Help me to have all my roots in Thee and then there will be no mixed fruit. Amen.

AFFIRMATION FOR THE DAY: *Rooted and grounded in love, all my fruit shall be the fruit of love.*

PEACE RETURNS TO YOU

We have seen that the highest in God—love—is the deepest in us. And when we act on love we act naturally and normally. For the Norm—God—is love and when we love we act normally. Everything else is abnormal. But the question remains: always to act on love may be beautiful, but will it work? In a hard world of this kind will it not prove to be sentimentality? Is it impossible idealism or is it realism?

I am persuaded that in every situation to act on love is realism—the only realism. To act on anything but love is to inject in any situation a disruptive tendency which will sooner or later tie that situation in knots. For I am convinced that, inherently, everything is made to work in love's way and in no other way. If we try to work life in any way other than love we work our own ruin.

I do not say that the other person will always respond to love, that love will always succeed in gaining its object. It can fail in gaining its object. The apostle says: "Love never fails." Is that true? But note that it doesn't say, "Love never fails to gain its object." It does say, "Love never fails." Even though you don't succeed in a situation when acting on love nevertheless you have not failed, for you yourself are the better for acting on love. Jesus said: "As you enter the house, salute it. And if the house is worthy, let your peace come upon it; but if it is not worthy, let your peace return to you" (Matt. 10:12-13). You give peace to the people of the house. If they receive it, well and good; but if they don't receive it, then let your peace return to you. You are more peaceful for having given the peace. So in either case you win. If they take it, good; if they don't take it, still good. Heads you win, tails you also win. The payoff is in the person. The loving person always wins for he becomes more loving in giving out love, even if the other person doesn't receive his love. "Love never fails," for it never fails to enrich the giver of love. It just can't fail. The unloving act can't succeed for the same reason.

O Father, Thou hast shut us up to love. There is no way out except love. Help us not to be driven to love by necessity but to choose love by intelligence. Give us a mind to love as Thou dost love. In Jesus' name. Amen.

AFFIRMATION FOR THE DAY: *Since love is the victory, I cannot fail if I love.*

GIVE OUT LOVE AND ONLY LOVE

We ended yesterday with the statement: "The unloving act can't succeed for the same reason." For if you should succeed in getting your way by an unloving attitude or deed you wouldn't succeed, since the unloving attitude or deed registers itself in you, becomes you. Your very being is lowered by the unloving attitude or deed—the payoff is the person. So your very outer success is an inner failure. If "love never fails," unlove never succeeds. Can't, by its very nature.

Here is a letter from one who was always intent on transforming everybody. And she failed. Then she found a secret. She writes to "Mary":

The last morning I knew I was His and wasn't trying to do anything, or change anybody, and seemingly out of nowhere there you were with your precious words about love and Jesus. You didn't know it, but you came forth with Everything just at the right moment. The amazing thing is that I had been so concerned as to how I could transform everyone else, and then suddenly, as I looked at them through the eyes of Jesus, they all looked wonderful, looked transformed. And how right you were about every man being a lonely island, needing love! When one finds Jesus He does the transforming from the inside out. We are not capable of transforming anyone. But to love them and help them find Him is the answer. Thank you for showing me that.

Here was a simple remedy: She, who had been trying to transform everybody, was herself transformed by the love of Jesus within. Then as she looked on people with His eyes and His love they were transformed. They looked different. The miracle had been performed—within her. So love transforms everything it touches and everything it sees. So love is the touch that transforms all it touches, not into gold as did the touch of Midas, but into love, more precious than gold.

Then give out love and only love. For you are born of the qualities you give out. And in the giving out of love you transform the other person—and yourself. A double cure.

O Incarnate Love, help me to love this day with Thy love. Then all ugliness will be turned into beauty, and all littleness turned into greatness, and all pettiness turned into significance. I would love with Thy love. Amen.

AFFIRMATION FOR THE DAY: *I shall not try to transform people—I shall love them.*

LOVE CONQUERS

If what we said yesterday seems intangible and vague, let us look at a hard situation, neither intangible nor vague and yet transformed by love. I once stayed with a theological professor in Nanking, China; after the Communists had put him out of China, I saw him again in Singapore—still working for and loving Chinese. His love was put to the test—a real one. When the Communist portion of Chiang Kai-shek's army took over Nanking, they began to loot. They broke into the mission compound and began to loot this missionary's home. He said to himself: "I'm not much of a Christian, but I'm going to try out Christian love, the Sermon on the Mount." So when a soldier struck him on one side of the chest with the butt of his gun, the missionary turned the other side and said: "This too, please." The soldier dropped his gun in astonishment. Then my friend found local people trying to get his big brass bed down the stairway from the second story. They couldn't, for it was stuck. He said to them: "Let me help you get it down." They blushed to the roots of their hair and fled out of the house. Others brought to him canned things and asked what was in them. So he got a can opener and opened the cans for them. Others came with cans and he opened them.

At last the Communists determined to take him off and shoot him. As he was being led away he put his arm through the arm of the ringleader and said to him: "You are my friend; I expect you to protect me." And they marched along arm in arm—to his execution! The crowd which followed began to see the anomaly of a man going to his execution arm in arm with his executioner, so they stopped and said: "Ah, let him go." Then they added: "Let's have three cheers for America." And they actually had a "Hip-hip-hurrah" for America. And let him go! The missionary said he was more astonished than they at the outcome, amazed that love really worked and worked on Communists and the people of the city alike. Love never fails.

O Lord Jesus, Ruler by love, let me be ruled by love, so that I, too, can rule every situation by love. And then the ruling will not seem to be ruling—it will seem a fellowship of service. In Thy name. Amen.

AFFIRMATION FOR THE DAY: *If love never fails, then I can fail only as I fail in love.*

"I AM NOT AFRAID OF HATE"

We are looking at the question of whether it is practical to live by love, whether it will work. This incident is to the point:

A friend of mine, an elderly Quaker lady, entered her Paris hotel room to find a burglar rifling her bureau drawers, where she had considerable jewelry and money. He had a gun which he brandished. She talked to him quietly, told him to go right ahead and help himself to anything she had, as obviously he needed it more than she did, if he had to be stealing it. She even told him some places to look where there were valuables he had overlooked. Suddenly the man let out a low cry . . . and ran from the room taking nothing. The next day she received a letter from him in which he said: "I am not afraid of hate. But you showed love and kindness. It disarmed me."

Incidentally, during and after World War I nearly one thousand Quaker relief workers went unarmed into hostile countries. None met a violent death, nor were any of their relief goods plundered by robbers or by the needy people.

It was said of Kagawa that he "has so much security on the inside that he can afford to go without any on the outside." While he was alone in his room in the Shinkawa slums, he was awakened one night by a half-drunk gangster, with sword uplifted. Kagawa got to his knees and bowed his head in prayer as he awaited the blow. Instead the man said: "Kagawa, do you love me?" And Kagawa answered, "I do." Soon the man said, "Here's a present," and he left Kagawa his sword.

The Canadian counterpart of that: a Canadian named Michael was awakened one night by a professional robber. Unafraid, he began to talk with the robber and gave him some coffee and a sandwich. The robber shook hands when he left and, instead of taking anything, left his gun with Michael.

O God, our Father, teach us the power of overcoming evil with good, hate by love, and the world by a cross. Strip from my soul all arms, save the arms of love, and help me to go out to conquer by love. Amen.

AFFIRMATION FOR THE DAY: *Armed with love I am invincible in every situation, everywhere.*

LOVE DISARMS

We see the might, the sheer might of love. A certain miner, who provided well for his family, buying groceries and clothes from his paycheck, would then go and drink up the rest over the weekend. He was strong and a dangerous fighter when full of liquor. But this man was converted. A man whom he had beaten in a fight met him and said, "You're a Christian, are you? Well, I'm told if one hits you on one cheek you're to turn the other." And he struck the miner and knocked him down. When he got up he was hit on the other cheek and again knocked down. His opponent swore at him and knocked him down four times. When the miner didn't strike back the aggressor burst into tears. He was disarmed by love. This miner was a radiant Christian and, testifying about his experience of the joy of Christ, he said: "If they should put me in a big barrel and put on the lid, I'd shout, 'Glory to God,' through the bunghole." His son became a minister.

A pastor sat giving a young alcoholic a good scolding which was richly deserved. The young man sat with his head down and did not say a word. He knew he deserved everything that was being said. He had no defense. And yet he was really unmoved by the pastor, until his mother came over to him and planted a kiss upon his bloated lips. That changed him. He could not withstand this silent, suffering love. What a moral lecture could not do—love did.

A woman stopped an alcoholic in his car and said that she wanted to talk with him. "What do you want to do, scold me?" "No," replied the woman, "I want to love you." And her love pulled him out of his alcoholism. An article in the newspaper tells of the comparative failure of psychiatry to redeem alcoholics. Why? its method is largely based on knowledge—on knowledge instead of love. And nothing can succeed without love.

Everything, however well contrived, fails without love.

O God, my Gracious Father, I want to think love, feel love, act love, and be love. Then I shall be, in some faint way, like Thee. Kindle all my feeble loves into flame; make me afire with love. Amen.

AFFIRMATION FOR THE DAY: *One loving heart sets other hearts aflame.*

"LOVE NEVER FAILS"

We are looking at the question of whether love—agape love—is a practicable way to live.

The four greatest characters in the New Testament are Jesus, Stephen, Paul, and John. And they all died with love as the last word on their lips: "Father, forgive them"; "Lord, do not hold this sin against them"; "All deserted me. May it not be charged against them"; "We ought to lay down our lives for the brethren." Love produced the four greatest characters that ever lived. And we must include Peter, who in dying said: "Crucify me feet up and head down—I'm not worthy to die like my Lord." All agape.

A. A. Hunter, writing in *Fellowship*, tells this story. An American missionary, Merlin Bishop, politely but firmly refused to hand over the keys of an abandoned American university entrusted to his care in China to the Japanese officer demanding them. The Japanese officer said Bishop would be shot unless he did. Three men were elected and lined up, with their rifles aimed at the missionary. He smiled and waited. "The officer seemed uncertain, the men uneasy. Then one at a time they relaxed, lowered their rifles, and sheepish grins replaced their looks of grim determination." But one of the soldiers was apparently disgusted with this outcome, for he charged the missionary with a fixed bayonet on the end of his rifle. At the last instant the missionary dodged, grabbed the soldier and the butt of his rifle, pulling the man toward him. "Our glances locked and held for seconds that seemed ages long. Then I smiled down at him, and it was like a spring thaw melting the ice on a frozen river. The hatred vanished, and after a sheepish momment, he smiled back!" Then Bishop gave the soldiers tea before they left on their return journey. Love conquered. I have personally faced hostile crowds in India waving black flags—faced them with friendliness and love—and was given one of the black flags to take home as a souvenir!

O Blessed, Blessed God, teach me Thy weapons of forgiving love. For I see that Thy way works and nothing else will. But I cling to the old, afraid of the new. Teach me to launch out on love and take it as my only attitude. Amen.

AFFIRMATION FOR THE DAY: *I forgive everything beforehand as Jesus forgave me beforehand.*

A WIDE RANGE OF APPLICATION

Even animals can sense and feel the power of love and its absence. They tell us that a dog whose master has stomach ulcers may also develop ulcers.

A G. I. came home after a long absence abroad and as he walked into his yard he ran to his huge German police dog, threw his arms around him, and cried, "Hello, old pal," and the dog responded with affectionate joy. When the soldier got into the house his parents told him that this was not the same dog they had when he went away, that this one was vicious and would make friends with no one. When the G. I. came out of the house again he was wary and obviously frightened. The dog bristled and growled at him. The dog understood love and he also understood suspicion.

Writing from her place of exile in North Siberia, a Christian woman says, "There is a Godless Society here. One of its members is especially attracted to me. She said, 'I cannot understand what sort of person you are. So many people insult and abuse you, but you love them all.' " This woman herself was converted, as a result was thrown behind prison bars, but is joyous—in prison!

A Hindu businessman, visiting at our Ashram in India, said that he saw the meaning of Christianity in a moment when he was a boy. He and some other boys threw tomatoes at a missionary preaching in a bazaar. Instead of getting angry, the missionary wiped the mess from his face, went to the sweetshop, and bought the boys some sweets. Through the years that incident influenced this businessman and gave him a lifelong interest in Christianity.

Kagawa, my friend of Japan, was attacked at the close of a service by ten hooligans with long bamboo sticks. He stood with no change of expression as the blows fell and the blood streamed. When they stopped, Kagawa led the congregation in a closing prayer. He then invited the hooligans into his study to talk to them. They apologized profusely. Love never fails.

Dear Lord of love, Thou dost love me into loving. So I open my depths to Thy love and respond with all my ransomed being. For I know I live as I love, and others live as I love. In Thy name. Amen.

AFFIRMATION FOR THE DAY: *I have loved too little and for the wrong reasons—now I love all out for the right reason.*

ALL LIVING CREATURES RESPOND TO LOVE

We have noted that animals respond to love. They answer love with love, and hate with hate. Do flowers respond to love and do they wither without it? Henry Ward Beecher once said: "Flowers are the sweetest things that God ever made and forgot to put a soul into." He may be right—there is no soul in a flower, but the experiments in East and West point to something in a flower that responds to love. The experiments of Bose in India and experiments in America have pointed to the conclusion that plants which are loved grow better than those which are not loved. And this is not imagination—it is investigation.

We speak of some people as having "green thumbs"—everything grows under their touch. Why? They love what they cultivate. Someone asked a lady why her African violets were more beautiful than those of any other person, and she replied: "I love them and express my love to them." And the flowers respond. No soul in them? We cannot tell. But something does respond to love. "Mary" once said: "They say that at the heart of a flower is pollen. I call it love." Was she right? More right than wrong.

"Mary," when given a chance to choose a puppy from a litter, chose the most unpromising looking one of all, saying: "No one will want this one. I'll take it and love it and make it as good as the rest." And she has loved it into beauty. Why do the little rabbits put up their lips to be kissed when she comes near them? Chance? No, they know she really loves them. And why did another dog of hers put up his paw to shake hands with me when I arrived in this home where love ruled? When the first dog was killed by a car, "Mary" wrote: "I am so glad I had a chance to fill his life with love and happiness." And in putting love into that unwanted dog and making it beautiful, "Mary" herself became more beautiful within—and without. Love is the universal language understood by all peoples, all animals, all flowers—everything!

O Father, I thank Thee that Thou hast wrought love into Thy whole creation. How couldst Thou, who art love, do otherwise? Help me to speak this universal language to everything and everybody today. Amen.

AFFIRMATION FOR THE DAY: *Love is the key that unlocks all doors, all situations, all hearts.*

LOVE APPLIED ON A MASS SCALE

We have seen that this method of agape works with individuals. Could it be applied on a mass scale to influence and change the masses?

The early Christians disarmed themselves of everything save the arms of love. They conquered by their suffering love. They matched their capacity to suffer against the capacity of a cruel Roman government to torture them—and they conquered by love. Telemachus, a monk of Asia Minor, traveled a thousand miles to Rome to see if he could do anything to stop the cruel gladiatorial shows in which men fought to their death to provide entertainment for the bloodthirsty multitudes. He ran from his seat in the amphitheater and called upon the combatants to stop killing each other. The spectators, furious because of the interruption of the show, rushed in and beat him to death with sticks and stones. But his love conquered, for Honorius, the emperor, issued a rescript forbidding all gladiatorial shows. They were never held again.

I have been privileged to witness, for twenty-five years, the testing of a method—the method of nonviolent resistance, based on inward love, to gain the independence of four hundred million people in India. The movement began in an incident on a railway train in South Africa. Mr. M. K. Gandhi, as he was known then, a lawyer, got on a train with a first class ticket. A white man got into the compartment and objected to riding in the same compartment with a dark-skinned man, called the "guard," and asked that Gandhi be told to get out. Gandhi was put out at midnight at a station. As he walked the platform at midnight in the cold, the idea formed in his mind of fighting injustice with nonviolent resistance. He would not hate, but he would not obey. And he would match his capacity to suffer against the capacity of the oppressor to inflict the suffering—soul force against physical force. He would wear the other down with love. It was a momentous decision, one of the great and far-reaching decisions of human history.

O Father, teach us to face everything with love and only with love. Thou hast melted us by love—help us to melt others by love. For this method of love blesses the one given the love and the giver. Amen.

AFFIRMATION FOR THE DAY: *I shall look with eyes of love on everything and everybody I see today.*

LOVE IN THE GANDHIAN MOVEMENT

We are considering the application in gaining national freedom, of nonviolent goodwill resistance instead of violence and hate.

Gandhi got the idea from a Gujarati hymn, but it was the Sermon on the Mount that fixed it in his mind and determination. He came to India after making South Africa a proving ground for the principle and method—and determined to do something that had never been tried on such a scale before. Would it work? It did work to the degree that it was worked. Violence crept into the movement here and there, and to the degree that it did, it hindered and canceled the power of the movement. For you cannot use alternately the methods of violence and nonviolence with any success. It must be pure nonviolence, and pure nonviolence with goodwill at its center. For outwardly you can be nonviolent and still have suppressed hatred within, in which case you are not nonviolent. The violence shows through the veneer of outward nonviolence and renders it ineffective.

To the degree that the movement of Gandhi was nonviolent, inwardly and outwardly, it was the most powerful movement of this century. The movements of Hitler, Mussolini, Tojo, and Stalin are weak and temporary as compared to the strength and stability of Gandhi's movement. Three of them have passed away; the fourth (Stalinism) is in the process of disintegration. But Gandhism lives on. These four movements were examples of immature power based on physical force; the movement of Gandhi represented mature power based on soul force.

Under the call of Gandhi two hundred thousand of the leading men in India went to jail. Then a strange thing happened—the jails, instead of becoming punishment and a badge of shame, became an honor. You were nobody in India if you hadn't been to jail. The jails became ridiculous—the means, not of punishment, but of promotion. Your weapons were struck out of your hands.

O Father, teach me not merely the goodness of love, but the power of love. All else seems weakness beside it. And teach me to believe in it with an infinite patience that can await results. In Jesus' name. Amen.

"THEY HAVE SOMETHING ON THE INSIDE"

The spirit of the Gandhian movement is seen in this incident. I was in Benares at the height of the noncooperation movement. The government was picking off, not the rank and file, but the leaders, and sending them to jail. Sri Prakasa, a Hindu and one of the leaders, was at a tea party we were having on the opening of an evangelistic series. He laughingly said: "I must eat as many of these sandwiches as possible for I shall soon be on His Majesty's jail fare." He knew he was going to be picked off next. And he remarked: "We can thank our lucky stars that we are fighting people like the British, for they have something on the inside of them to which we can appeal." Then he added this: "We will send the British out as masters, but before the boat has gone out of the harbor we will call them back as friends."

This was a new kind of warfare—a warfare in which you find something good in the one you are fighting and appeal to it. That is mature warfare on a high level. In the old warfare it was the opposite—you made out your enemy to be a devil so you could hate and fight him the more easily. You didn't appeal to any good in him, for there was no good, only evil; therefore he was your enemy.

Under the discipline of having their heads cracked and spending long terms in jail, the leaders of the new India were trained—trained at the expense of the British Government! Sri Prakasa is now the governor of Madras and is loved and respected. The discipline of suffering for a cause prepared him to rule when that cause triumphed. I spoke of "cracked heads"—this literally took place. The police would charge with long bamboo sticks which had metal at the end of them—would charge these unresisting volunteers who had come into some forbidden area, civilly disobeying on a chosen issue. Whack! Whack! would go the sticks, the volunteers falling with cracked heads. Others would march in, unarmed and unresisting, and the same process would be repeated. This was discipline of a high order—mental and spiritual as well as physical.

O Christ, Thou who didst face Thy enemies with no arms save the arms of love and compassion, help me this day to face everything subtle and obvious with Thy love and Thy compassion. I throw away all weapons but Thine. Amen.

AFFIRMATION FOR THE DAY: *I am unarmed, save by the arms of love.*

"THEY ARE BETTER CHRISTIANS THAN I AM"

Through all of this tremendous discipline of the nonviolent, noncooperation movement of Gandhi there runs a Christian note—the note of the cross.

When these Hindu noncooperators stood before British judges to be sentenced, they would often say after the sentence was pronounced: "Father, forgive them; for they know not what they do." One British judge remarked: "They are better Christians than I am." They were not Christians except in spirit. One of those Hindus said to me: "We can now understand the meaning of the cross since we are taking it."

On one occasion some of these noncooperators sent word to the British police superintendent: "Tomorrow is Easter. You will probably want to go to church, so we are not sending any volunteers to be arrested tomorrow." In another place batches of volunteers were being sent to cross a forbidden bridge. The head of the volunteers sent word to the magistrate: "Since it is hot at noontime, we are sending volunteers only in the morning and in the evening, so that you will not have to stand in the heat of noonday." And they named the hour of arrival in order to save the magistrate a long wait, for it was he who had to give the order for their arrest. A war with courtesy in it!

Said a sweating Irish police officer: "If they'd only fight with ordinary weapons, we'd show them something. But this!" and he spread his hands in dismay. While you were suppressing their bodies they were appealing to your soul. You were striking their heads and they were striking your hearts. It was physical force against soul force. And the soul force won! For you cannot go on forever breaking the heads of nonresisting people who show no ill will. It turns your stomach. For your conscience is siding with them and saying: "Maybe they are right." Conscience and compassion is aroused in you and your weapons are struck out of your hands. You are disarmed. You feel the immaturity of physical weapons in the face of the maturity of these spiritual weapons.

Gracious God, we as a race have relied on material weapons, symbols of our immaturity. Help us to take Thy weapons of love and goodwill. For they belong to mature manhood. Help us to take them with our whole hearts. Amen.

AFFIRMATION FOR THE DAY: *The only way to make enemies into friends is to love them.*

THE ATOM OR THE ATMA?

We have been considering the power of soul force as seen in the Gandhian movement. The word for soul in the Hindu language is "atma." At the very time that Gandhi was developing the movement of soul forces, the scientists were making discoveries concerning the power of the atom. So two forces were coming to light—the power of the atma, and the power of the atom.

We know the destructiveness of the power of the atom. I have stood five times on different occasions at the place where the first atomic bomb fell in Hiroshima, Japan. Each time a group of us who were Americans have stood with a group of Japanese pastors and laymen at that spot in a kind of football huddle, really a prayer huddle. We prayed that no Hiroshima should happen to anyone, anywhere, again and dedicated ourselves to peace. On one occasion the traffic stopped reverently while we prayed. The first time I stood there I was so deeply moved that I remarked to the group: "I feel like falling on my knees." The newspaper headlined that statement with a picture of the group. And now since the first atomic bomb was dropped, which destroyed probably 200,000 people and flattened a city, more and more atomic weapons with indescribable destructiveness have come into being.

The question before mankind is this, and it is a real one: Will the future be controlled by the power of the atom or by the power of the atma? Beside that question all other questions pale into insignificance. For the future of the human race is bound up with it. Will the atma control the atom, or will the atom control the atma? Which will be directive? If the atma controls the atom—harnesses the power of the atom for the collective good—we can have a new era for everybody, everywhere. The level of life can be lifted for everybody. But if the atma is controlled by the atom, we enter a dark age of fear and possible universal destruction.

We have seen that deep down in the atma is the basic urge of love. Will that basic urge of love control, or will hate control? The weapon to destroy or to develop is in our hands—the atom.

O Father, we Thy confused and erring children stand at the crossroads. We are afraid to take either way. We are afraid of love and afraid of hate—we are afraid. Teach us to love love and hate hate. We need Thee. Help us. Amen.

AFFIRMATION FOR THE DAY: *Soul force is the final force; all else is weakness.*

AN EXPENSIVE OUSTING

We ended yesterday with the note of being afraid of the way of the atma and afraid of the way of the atom. It reminds me that I, too, was afraid of the way of the atma. When Mahatma Gandhi was about to launch his noncooperation movement I wrote and begged him not to do so. I felt it would cause upset and breakdown of law and order. He wrote me in reply immediately: ·

May I assure you that I will not launch this movement without careful thought, proper precautions and, may I add, not without copious praying. You have perhaps no notion of the wrong that this Government has done and is still doing to the vital part of our being. But I must not argue. I invite you to pray for and with me. Yours sincerely, M. K. Gandhi.

The clarity and courtesy of that letter!

I was afraid of an upset, not realizing that without self-government everything is upside down and cannot be set upright without an initial upset. Gandhi was using the gentlest of upsets to set things up—set them upright. And he accomplished the most astonishing revolution in human history with the least amount of violence.

Note what happened: The white man put Gandhi, a dark-skinned man, out of a railway compartment at midnight. That was an expensive eviction—very. For it meant that Gandhi, in turn, put the white man out of the mastery of the East. Gandhi gained independence for India, and when that happened the keystone of empire fell in the East. Independence came to Burma, Ceylon, Indonesia, India-China, and Malaya. Colonialism in the East is exerting pressure upon the situation in Africa. There, too, it is only a matter of time.

Gandhi, a little man in a loincloth, with no weapons save the weapon of unflinching goodwill, accomplished the greatest political revolution in all human history, barring none, and he did it with the power of the atma.

Will the atom or the atma control the future?

O Father, Thou art opening our eyes that we may see—may see the power of goodwill over ill will. We see it and we see it clearly. Help us to see it until it possesses us completely, so that we will act on it wholly. Amen.

AFFIRMATION FOR THE DAY: *"When a bee steals from a flower it also fertilizes that flower."*

THE SIMPLEST CAN USE LOVE

Some of my readers will probably try to shrug off this whole matter by saying: "Yes, but Gandhi was exceptional. A spiritual genius, but a little queer. In any case the method he took is not for ordinary mortals." But the amazing thing is that his method *is* for ordinary mortals.

I have stood on the road at Vaikom, Travancore, where a historic battle for human rights was fought—and won. When the history of mankind's struggle for freedom is written, then Vaikom will have an honored place. The story is this: The outcastes of Travancore were forbidden to walk on the road to the temple at Vaikom. They would pollute it by their very presence. These outcastes decided to adopt the method of Gandhi—nonviolent passive resistance. They walked along the road and were promptly put in jail. Then a barrier was put up so they couldn't pass the barrier even to be arrested. They decided to sit before the barrier, night and day, in a continuous protest. On one pretext or another they were arrested. They served their sentences, came out, and began to sit again. The sight of these silent, dispossessed people sitting in protest awakened the hearts of even the proud Brahmins, and some Brahmins began to sit with them. That added to the moral pressure. For a year and a half these people sat there in rain and sunshine, in nonviolent but unbending determination not to yield. The Brahmins yielded and the road was thrown open.

Since then the new constitution for India has been drawn up and passed. And the amazing thing is that an outcaste, Bhimrao Ambedkar, wrote most of it and piloted it through the legislatures. He wrote the bill of rights. This is a divine joke on Brahmin India—an outcaste writes the bill of rights under which Brahmin India has to live! Now it is a statutory offense to discriminate against anyone because of caste anywhere! And the offense is punishable by fine and imprisonment. Nonviolent resistance won. And it was won by outcastes!

O Father, I thank Thee for the might, the sheer might of Thy way of love. If we only believe it and have courage to act upon it! Give us that courage! And help me to begin today working the way of love with somebody, somewhere. Amen.

AFFIRMATION FOR THE DAY: *I lack the courage to launch out on the love way. I shall use the courage I have.*

THE BEST RACE RELATIONSHIPS

We have been considering the power of nonviolent love and we have insisted that this method can be carried out by anybody. It is not the method of the spiritual genius—it is the method of anybody, anywhere, with anybody, anywhere. For its power stems from the fact that basically we are made to love and be loved.

The Maoris in New Zealand had no weapons to fight the white imperialists taking possession of their land. One wise leader, upon hearing that the English were marching to attack their village, summoned his people together and told them to prepare a feast, and to meet and welcome the soldiers with songs, dances, and games. The soldiers were baffled by their reception and followed the procession into the village, where they were met by the native chief with friendliness and hospitality. They could do nothing but accept the spirit of their hosts. The soldiers finally withdrew, leaving the tribe in possession of the land, and never made another expedition against them. There is an interesting sequel to this story. If I were to put my finger on the place in all the world where the relationship between the races is the best, I would unhesitatingly say, New Zealand. There the white man and the aboriginal Maori live side by side in mutual respect and love, on the basis of complete equality, both going up together. Maoris have been cabinet members. Each race seems to be proud of the other. There seems to be a complete absence of tension between the races. One of the things that made for this situation is the fact that in the early days a Christian governor and a bishop put through legislation making it unlawful for the Maori to alienate his land to the white man. That kept the Maori from becoming a landless pauper—put an economic base under him.

Goodwill and love laid the foundations of the present relationship between the two races: the Maori met the white man with friendliness and goodwill and a banquet; the white man put goodwill into legislation. Love on both sides laid the foundation for the present relationship. Love never fails.

O Jesus, Thy love never failed. For the moment it may have seemed to fail, but in the end it did not and could not. Help me to believe in and act upon the invincibility of love. For if I fail while loving, I succeed in the very failure. Amen.

AFFIRMATION FOR THE DAY: *Love creates, so all my attitudes shall be attitudes of creative love.*

"CAN SATAN CAST OUT SATAN?"

We have been studying the immaturity of physical violence and force, and the maturity of soul force—the force of love.

Jesus put the matter thus: "Can Satan cast out Satan?" Can you by acting like the devil get the devil out of people? War is an attempt to act like the devil and thus get the devil out of people. It won't work. You cannot get rid of darkness by going out and fighting it with your fist—bring in a light and the darkness is gone. You can only overcome evil with good, hate with love, the world with a cross.

War is the most immature method imaginable of settling international disputes. But, someone asks, are you going to let another nation walk over you? Listen to a parable: Two goats met on a one-plank bridge over a chasm. If one tried to push or butt the other off, both would go overboard. So the more sensible goat lay down on the plank and let the other walk over him—to safety. Then he, too, got up and went on—to safety. Did the goat that lay down and let the other walk over him debase himself? Apparently, for the moment. But he got up with an inner sense of superiority—he was able to live with himself. The other goat wasn't able to live with himself—he was a debate, trying to justify himself. We look on and choose the goat that lay down as the superior goat—superior in intelligence and in spirit. Soul force is maturity; mere physical force is immaturity. Mars would have whispered to each of the goats: "Butt him off!" And both would have gone into the abyss. War is not only a brutal and costly way of settling disputes, it is stupid.

And now we have come to the end of rake's progress: We have discovered atomic energy, the ultimate in physical force, and God is saying: "You wanted force; I let you discover it in the atom. But remember: If you use it again both sides will be ruined—inevitably. So choose." We got the force we were looking for and now we dare not use it. The method is stupid.

Father, Thou art pushing us into a corner. We have wanted force and have depended on force and now that we have it we're frightened. We don't know what to do with it. Save us from ourselves and our stupidities. In Jesus' name. Amen.

AFFIRMATION FOR THE DAY: *Two hates never made a love affair, and two stiff letters never made a friendship.*

"CITIZEN GEORGE WASHINGTON"

We are meditating on the immaturity of physical force and the maturity of soul force. Our fathers sensed this and showed it in an unforgettable scene which needs to be retold to every generation.

I stood in the State House at Annapolis, Maryland, and Governor McKeldin pointed out the spot where George Washington had stood to make his speech when resigning as the commander-in-chief of the Continental armies. He made it to the Continental Congress meeting at that time in Annapolis. A brass tablet marks the spot. The congress had agreed beforehand on a procedure: When General Washington came in they would remain seated with their hats on. And during his speech they would keep their hats on. Only when he had resigned as general would they arise, remove their hats, and salute, Citizen George Washington! The military was subservient to the civil. That was a seed happening. The germs of the future were in it. Intelligence and moral force would take precedence over physical force. That scene should be reenacted before the Pentagon, for the military decides our civil diplomacy again and again. For instance, it decided our arming of Pakistan, thus throwing India open to Russian influences—a stupid blunder. But the military was on top in that issue and the civil was subservient—a costly reversal of our principles. An immature method triumphed over a mature method—a blunder which may cost us not only India but the whole of the East.

Speaking of India, I watched the multitudes worshiping the gods of war, clay images and mustaches upturned. They worshiped them with fervor, and then suddenly the worship stopped, and they took the images down to the pier and unceremoniously dumped them in. When I asked a Hindu what had happened, why that sudden change, he replied: "Oh, as long as we worshiped them there was a spirit in them, but as soon as we ceased to worship them they were just clay." Light dawned: As long as we worship war there is a spirit in it; when we cease it is clay—bloody, muddy clay. I've ceased.

O Father, after looking into Thy face and seeing nothing but love there, how can I worship again the god of war, in whose face I see nothing but hate? The spirit has gone out of it for me. So I bow to love alone. Amen.

AFFIRMATION FOR THE DAY: *War is the vast illusion. I am giving myself to the reality of love.*

CHRISTIANITY AND RACE

Earlier I mentioned the relationship of the aboriginal Maoris and the white New Zealanders as being the best I had ever seen. We must now study maturity in relation to attitudes and practices toward other races. There are many people, otherwise mature, who are quite immature in regard to race. And it is a costly immaturity.

Before we examine it, let us look at our Christian faith to see what its attitudes are, for we are taking our standards on maturity from that faith.

In the time of Christ there was great tension between Jew and Gentile. But it was said by Simeon, in his inspired prophecy, that Jesus would be "a light to lighten the Gentiles" (Luke 2:32 KJV), or it could be translated, "a light for revelation to the Gentiles (RSV). This light would reveal the Gentiles and their worthwhileness and their possibilities. That was the keynote struck in the very beginning: men of other races were not to be problems but possibilities.

This was followed up by Jesus, when he announced His program in the little synagogue at Nazareth: "good news to the poor"—the socially and politically disinherited; "recovering of sight to the blind"—the physically disinherited; "setting at liberty those who are oppressed"—the morally and spiritually disinherited; "proclaiming the acceptable year of the Lord"—a fresh world beginning based on the Jewish year of jubilee, when every fifty years all slaves were freed, all debts canceled, all land redistributed. The people "wondered at the gracious words which proceeded out of his mouth." But Jesus went on and let them know how far He intended to go: Many widows in Israel but the prophet was sent to a Gentile widow; many lepers in Israel but the prophet was sent to a Gentile leper. This program of total redemption was to go to a man as a man apart from race. The atmosphere changed: they were all "filled with wrath." It was too big for their small hearts.

O Jesus, I'm so grateful that Thou didst not bring down Thy standards to our small hearts. For our small hearts can never make Thy new brave world for everybody. Forgive our littleness. Enlarge our hearts with Thy love. Amen.

AFFIRMATION FOR THE DAY: *I belong to a Kingdom which has no frontiers of race or class or color.*

SOME DOOMED TO INFERIORITY?

We are looking at the Christian attitude toward race. Paul, a narrow Pharisee, having inherited all the Jewish racial exclusiveness in an intensified form, comes into contact with Jesus and then writes this amazing sentence: "[In Jesus Christ] there is neither Greek nor Jew"—race distinction; "barbarian nor Scythian"—cultural distinction; "slave nor free"—social and economic distinction; "male nor female"—sexual distinction. (See Col. 3:11; Gal. 3:28.) All these distinctions were wiped out, and a man was looked on apart from race, birth, color, position, and sex. A man was a man, a man "for whom Christ died." No greater leveling-up proposal and power has ever been presented to mankind than this. This is the authentic Christian position. Departures from it are sub-Christian and anti-Christian even though made in the name of the Christian religion. The burning of a cross in the name of race hatred is burning Jesus at the stake.

Some, in their desperation to find Scripture support for their racialisms, turn to passages like the one in Genesis in which Noah cursed Canaan, son of Ham, saying: "A slave of slaves shall he be to his brothers" (9:25). And what had Canaan done to deserve this curse? His father, Ham, saw Noah drunk and uncovered in his tent and went and told his brothers, and they walked backwards and covered Noah with a blanket. Noah awoke from his drunk and uttered this curse. God had nothing to do with it. A drunken man uttered the curse as he came out of his stupor. To get one's racial attitudes from the curse of a drunken man is to get doubtful backing. If God would doom a whole race to slavery because of what Ham did there, then that God would be my devil.

The Christian position in regard to the man of color is this: "Symeon who was called Niger" (literally, "the Black") was a prophet or a teacher in the church at Antioch, and he laid his hands on Paul and Barnabas that they should go and preach the gospel to white Europe (Acts 13:1-3). Paul was ordained by a Negro. That is the position of Christianity—it is color-blind. It sees only a man for whom Christ died.

O Father, as we look into the face of Jesus Christ we see love and only love for everybody, everywhere. May I get my racial attitudes from Him and from Him alone. And then I shall be free—free to live and grow. Amen.

AFFIRMATION FOR THE DAY: *Since God loves all, I will love all with His love.*

". . . THRONES, AND [PEOPLE] SAT UPON THEM"

In the book of Revelation there is a passage which gives the final outcome of the Christian position: "I saw thrones, and [people] sat upon them" (20:4 KJV). That is revolutionary—the people rule!

A little girl speaking to her sister said: "Barbara, I tell you the Bible does not end in Timothy, it ends in Revolutions." It does. And this revolution is one of the biggest of them all—the people sit on thrones!

Heretofore, the people have not sat on thrones—kings and emperors have, but not the people. This is the great transition from privilege to people. Each year in ancient Assyria a common man was chosen to sit on the throne and was given kingly honors for a day, done half in mockery. But one man was chosen, a carpenter, and the day he sat on the throne the real king died. The carpenter stayed on the throne for seventeen years and ruled—faint prophecy of the time when the people should sit on thrones. That idea was very faint in those days. Rather, Aristotle's idea prevailed: "Some people are born naturally as rulers and some are born naturally as slaves, as a dog is naturally a dog and a cat is naturally a cat."

Then came Christianity and with it the rise of man ending in democracy. Democracy is a child of Christianity. Servius, a Roman, said regarding the slave in the markets of Rome: "The stupidest and the ugliest slaves in the market are those from Britain." So the lily-white Caucasian has a slave ancestry too! But a Christian looked at those slaves and said: "Angles, Angles—if they could be Christianized they would be angels." That is the eye of a Christian: man is a possibility, not a problem.

Jerome wrote in the fourth century: "I well remember the Scots in Gaul. They were eaters of human flesh. They had plenty of flocks and herds but they much preferred the ham of the herdsman, or a steak from the female breast as a rarity." The Scotch today are among the finest people of the world and yet they had that cannibal beginning. It was Christianity that started their rise.

O Blessed Lord Jesus, help me to see all men with the eye of faith. Let me see beneath the differences of color and face the image of a man—a man for whom Christ died. And help me to appeal to that man. Amen.

AFFIRMATION FOR THE DAY: *I shall look on all men as possibilities, every person a person "for whom Christ died."*

"THE BELL IS TOLLING, THE TIDE IS ROLLING IN"

We continue this week to meditate upon the text: "I saw thrones, and people sat upon them."

The social revolution is on. The people as people are arising everywhere, tired of being downtrodden and exploited. The Communists did not produce that social revolution. They have betrayed it—betrayed it by turning it into channels of suppression and compulsion. We must rescue it and turn it into channels of freedom and democracy. It cannot be turned back; it can only be directed. Said a Negro minister in regard to the Supreme Court decision and the opposition to integration: "The bell is tolling, the tide is rolling in, and you can't stop it anymore than you can stop the flow of Hampton Roads with your two hands."

I pick up my morning paper and read that the legislature of a certain state votes that "state funds shall be cut off from any integrated school." My guess is that the children, or at most the grandchildren, of the men who so voted will look back with laughter on that voting, as an un-American, undemocratic, and unchristian attempt to set back the clock.

While I was in South Africa, thirty-seven restrictive bills were put through the legislature taking away the last vestige of franchise from the native African. A member made a speech in which he said: "Now that we have clipped the native's wings, we must be kind to him, and we must be an example to the rest of the world of how we treat the native." Willing to be kind, unwilling to be just! Kindness with a denial of justice at its heart is insult added to injury. Two million white South Africans trying to clip the wings of eight million South African Negroes, and, by implication, the wings of hundred and fifty million Africans. An African student came to our Ashram at Sat Tal, India, and said: "I am a Christian and I hate Communism, but I wouldn't mind if it came to Africa if it would wake up the white man to do us justice." That was a bitter and an ominous word, packed with future possibilities.

O God, Thy hand again is writing on the walls of our generation. Give us eyes to see and hearts to heed. For our children's children will reap the harvest of the wrongs we inflict on one another. Give us sense and more sense. Amen.

AFFIRMATION FOR THE DAY: *We cannot keep any man in the gutter except as we stay down with him.*

"WITH LIBERTY AND JUSTICE FOR ALL"

Speaking of South Africa, I recall another African student who came to our Sat Tal Ashram and said: "When the white man came to Africa the white man had the Bible and the African had the land, now the African has the Bible and the white man has the land." And then he added: "But we will take that Bible and the ideas underlying it and we will push the white man out of South Africa unless he is willing to stay on the basis of equality." What did he mean by that? He meant what someone meant when he said: "It is impossible to enslave a Bible-reading people." The ideas of freedom, of the dignity of a child of God, of his equality before God and therefore before man, are bound to make slavery of any kind impossible. Maybe not today, not tomorrow, but the third day, Yes! "I saw thrones, and people sat upon them"—the people will rule and it doesn't say which people, but just people!

I love the pledge of allegiance to the flag. Seldom have greater words than these been put together: "one nation, indivisible, with liberty and justice for all." I have quoted it to India struggling for her independence and I've seen the light go on in the eyes of the people. But once when I heard the pledge repeated my blood ran cold, for it was being repeated by a Negro school. I turned to a teacher and said: "How can your young people say that—'with liberty and justice for all'?" For I knew they were discriminated against and pushed to the wall. "Do you know how they say it?" she replied. "They add two words: 'with liberty and justice for all *but me.*'" A nation that makes a part of its citizenry add those two words is denying the basis upon which its democracy is built. It must do one of two things. Either it must change its pledge and say: "with liberty and justice for some," and in brackets add "white people"—in which case democracy is gone, racialism has been substituted, and Hitler has won; or, it must change its attitudes and say, "with liberty and justice for all," and mean the all, apart from race, color, sex, and religion. Then we are truly democratic.

Divine Spirit, Thy touch is upon the souls of men awakening them to aspiration, to liberty, to justice. We can resist Thee by resisting the rise of man. But if we do we degrade ourselves. Forgive us and save us. Amen.

AFFIRMATION FOR THE DAY: *"With liberty and justice for all"—my motto and my outlook as a citizen and a Christian.*

"EQUALITY CANNOT BE GRANTED"

But someone says: 'We are not all equal, and if we are not, how can we give equal treatment to all?" I know we are not all equal—not in endowment and character. And if democracy is based on equality in character and achievement it is on a shaky foundation. Some white people are superior to some white people. Then upon what is democracy based? It is based on equality of opportunity.

In an address before a Negro mass meeting I quoted the statement of Charles Spaulding, an outstanding Negro businessman of Durham, North Carolina. Interviewed he said: "Equality cannot be demanded, for equality cannot be granted. It must be earned by character and achievement. If the Negro wants equality, except equality of opportunity, he must earn it in the only possible way he can get it—by character and achievement." A silence fell upon that great audience, for what was I saying? "Equality cannot be demanded." But I added: "Note that Mr. Spaulding says, 'If the Negro wants equality, except equality of opportunity . . .'; now that, as I understand it, is the only equality he is asking for. Given equality of opportunity he will, by his own effort, take care of equality in character and achievement. And if he doesn't it is his own fault." That great crowd roared its applause. You cannot give equality to either the white man or the colored man; it has to be earned by character and achievement. But what you can give, and it is in the hands of society to give, is equality of opportunity. I want a society in which everyone born in that society has an equal opportunity with every other person born in that society to climb to the top if his inherent powers and his own efforts allow him to do so. Equality of opportunity is the birthright of everyone born in a society based on "liberty and justice for all." You don't give equality of opportunity; you simply recognize every man's God-given birthright to it. And we must remember that if we deny liberty and equality we lose our own.

O Father of us all, we Thy struggling, sinning children are struggling up toward the light. That light beckons us and calls us. We cannot turn our back on it for if we do we stumble in darkness. Help us. In Jesus' name. Amen.

AFFIRMATION FOR THE DAY: *I am bound in every man's bondage; I am free in every man's freedom.*

"THESE BOYS RIGHT OUT OF THE BUSH"

We must now face a question that lies back of the unwillingness to grant equality of opportunity to all. And the question is this: Isn't it true that there are inherently inferior races and inherently superior races and that these differences are fixed and unalterable? My experience as I have mingled with all races for many years has brought me to a different conclusion. I am convinced that there are no permanently superior races and no permanently inferior races. There are undeveloped races and developed races, but none permanently superior or inferior. Given the same stimulus and the same incentive, the brain of humanity will come out about the same.

Remember the statement of the proud Roman: "The stupidest and ugliest slaves in the market are those from Britain." He believed that, but history has reversed his viewpoint and has rendered another verdict. The British Government, when faced with a delicate local situation in India, would send an Indian Christian official to deal with it, and very often he would be a Christian from among the outcastes. The young man who stood at the top of the University of Calcutta examination with thirty thousand competing, most of them high-caste, was a young man from the headhunters of Assam. And he did it in science. A teacher who had taught in colleges in both Europe and Africa said "These boys right out of the bush in Africa have just as good brain capacity as the students of Europe." In the United States I have asked principals of high schools where there were white and colored children in the same classes whether there was any difference in the examination results and, with one exception, I have had the same reply: "None whatever. You have your very bright white and the very bright Negro students and your very dull white and very dull Negro and all shades between, modified slightly by the cultural background out of which they come." My experience around the world verifies that. And if that be true then it is immensely important. For it means that the teachings of Christianity and the findings of life are converging on the worthwhileness of every man.

O Father, Thy hand is leading us unerringly to brotherhood. For nothing else will work. If we are unbrotherly in attitude we become unbrotherly in fact. We are the payoff. Save us to brotherhood. In Jesus' name. Amen.

AFFIRMATION FOR THE DAY: *"Infinite possibilities in every man"*— *what an attitude and what an outlook!*

"ONE BLOOD ALL NATIONS"

We said yesterday that there are infinite possibilities in every man, of every race, that exposed to the same stimulus and given the same incentives the human brain will come out about the same. There is one blood in humanity: "[God] hath made of one blood all nations" (Acts 17:26 KJV). A friend from India speaking in America quoted that passage and a member of the audience arose and said: "I believe in the whole Bible, all except that verse." But his disbelief could not turn back the facts of science. Under the microscope there is one blood. Four different types of blood, but those four different types are common to all races. You might have a blood transfusion from a man of another race who has the same type of blood as you have, while the blood of your own blood brother might be unsuitable. So you might be nearer in blood to a man of another race than to your own blood brother.

Speaking of blood, there is the basic fear that if schools are integrated there will be intermarriage and a mingling of blood. That doesn't necessarily happen. I have traveled widely in the North where schools are integrated and the only intermarriage I have seen was one I found in Japan—an American couple who had become Bahaists and had gone to Japan to teach. People usually find their mates in their own racial groups. But let it be clearly remembered that blood intermingling is taking place under segregation just as fast, or probably faster, than under integration, and that on a very low level.

As Lincoln said, "This government cannot endure permanently half slave and half free"; so we can take a further step and say: This nation cannot exist half integrated and half disintegrated. There are two groups in our country—the integrationists and the disintegrationists. Our country is disintegrated. And this reaches to the ends of the earth. Our influence in the East is disintegrated to the degree that we discriminate against any man because of his color. It's costly—to us!

O Father, Thou art teaching us brotherhood. And we are learning the hard way. We see that we cannot hurt anyone without hurting ourselves. The results register in us. Help us to learn the intelligent way. Amen.

AFFIRMATION FOR THE DAY: *Not the color of a man's skin but the color of his character is the important thing.*

"WE GO UP TOGETHER"

I was speaking in a women's meeting. A Negro woman had difficulty in hearing because her child was restless. A white woman went over, took up the baby from the Negro woman, and walked the veranda of the church with the child in her arms to allow the Negro woman to listen uninterrupted. I thought I heard Jesus saying: "You have done it unto me." That picture lingers in my memory as a benediction.

A man tells that he had a punctured tire and was about to get out in the rain to fix it when another car ran up alongside, and the driver said: "I'm already wet. You stay in the car. I'll fix it." And he did. And refused any payment. The man who fixed the tire was white and the man in the disabled car was a Negro. And this was in Mississippi. This, too, lingers like a benediction.

A conductor told a Negro woman that she would have to leave the railway car in which she was riding and go into a segregated car as the train passed the dividing line into the South. A white man went to the conductor and said: "If you put her out, you'll have to put me out too." The conductor replied: "But these white people will object to riding in the same car with her." The white man went to every passenger and asked: "do you object?" No one objected. The conductor said: "All right." And nothing more was said. But the courage of the white man spoke loudly and the gratitude of all of us spoke loudly too. That man belongs to the future.

A council of churches luncheon was scheduled to be held in a border city. The hotel man, finding that a great many tickets had been bought by the Negroes, asked if the Negroes could go up by the service elevator. "No," said the council secretary, "we go up together." And they did—by the service elevator. Human beings go up together—or they stay down together. For in degrading any man you degrade yourself. In lifting any man you grow tall in the process. The servant of all becomes the greatest of all. But note the words "the servant of *all*." To be a servant of some—people of my race—does not make you great, except a great snob.

O God, our Savior, we pray Thee to give us the right attitude toward those other races. We cannot have wrong attitudes toward them and have right attitudes toward Thee. For to do it to them is to do it to Thee. Amen.

AFFIRMATION FOR THE DAY: *I stand for man—for his equal opportunity, for his right to rise.*

"THIS PROPERTY NOT FOR SALE"

To be prejudiced against people because of their race and color is as sensible as the attitude of the woman who said she would not vote for a candidate because she didn't like the way he combed his hair.

The people are going to sit on thrones—the future belongs to the people. And you cannot turn back that tide. If you try it you eliminate yourself. The diehards die hard and expensively, but they do die!

The future belongs to the Georgia boy who said: "Of course, let the Negroes attend our schools. Then they will have the same opportunity as we have and we can help to lift them." That boy is in line with the wave of the future. He is mature in his outlook and judgments. Those who stand against equal opportunity for all are immature.

When a respectable Negro moved into a block of all white people in St. Louis, six signs went up on property in that block, "For Sale." Then this sign went up on the largest and finest home on the block: "This property is not for sale. We welcome to our neighborhood any person who is of good character and intends to keep up his property. We do not inquire into a man's politics, race, or religion—only his character." In a few days all the other six signs came down. That man was mature.

In Mississippi a crowd gathered and pulled a Negro out of his church, put a rope around his neck, and was about to hang him, because some young white bloods passing the church had heard stray sentences about "freedom" and had gathered a mob. Before they strung him up someone suggested that the Negro say a word to them. He did. When he ceased the crowd had changed its mind and urged that he be released. The same Negro set up Piney Woods School, appeared on the television program "This Is Your Life," and was voted by the people of Mississippi as its most valued and outstanding citizen. That was maturity. The mob which was about to hang the man was a very immature group. Had they done so they would have hanged themselves and the whole state—to infamy.

O Father God, forgive the narrowness and the prejudices of our hearts. Fill our hearts with Thy overflowing love—Thy love for everybody of every race and color. And help us to help them as Thou hast helped us through grace. Amen.

AFFIRMATION FOR THE DAY: *Since God has no prejudices against me, how can I hold prejudices?*

THREE STAGES TO MATURITY

I have said somewhere in my books that both the individual and the nation go through three stages on the way to maturity: dependence, independence, and interdependence.

The individual goes through those three stages if he ever gets to maturity. First, dependence, or the childhood stage. In the childhood stage the child depends upon the parents, who make all the decisions for the child. If the parents are wise they will prepare and train the child during the stage of dependence to make the transition to independence with the least upset and dislocation. In other words, the parent will help the child during the stage of dependence to come to his or her own decisions—from within. A mother said: "Barbara, hurry up and make up your mind." The little girl replied: "Mother, that's very easy for you, for you have only one mind to make up, but I have half a dozen minds." Blessed is the child who, when he comes to the second stage of independence, has eliminated many minds and has come to one-mindedness.

For the second stage is a very difficult one—the stage of independence, or adolescence. In the adolescent stage the boy or girl wants his or her independence, wants room around the personality to be a person in his or her own right, wants the right to make his or her own mistakes, to become a person and not the echo of someone else. Someone has defined adolescence as "a period of temporary insanity." I quoted that one day to a woman's meeting and a mother came up to me and said: "That was the most hopeful thing you said. For I thought it was permanent." This stage is a stage of great strain between parents and child because some parents want to make all the decisions for the adolescent, and some adolescents want to make all the decisions without relationship to the parents. But whether we like it or not we all have to go through that stage of growing pains when life is chaotic and confused and wistful. Independence comes painfully.

O God, our Father, we come to Thee for guidance and direction, for we are confused and fearful without it. With it we can go through these changes with ease and poise. We have to live through these changes; help us not to muddle through. Amen

AFFIRMATION FOR THE DAY: *I will need insight and understanding sympathy to see what is happening within the adolescent.*

FROM INDEPENDENCE TO INTERDEPENDENCE

On the road to maturity we pass from dependence to independence to interdependence. We have looked at the first two stages.

There are some who have a hesitancy to go from the childhood state to the adolescent stage. They are afraid of being independent—they prefer the securities of dependent childhood. A girl of fifteen, well-developed physically, was mentally and emotionally afraid of assuming the responsibility of growing up. She went around barefoot. I looked down the aisle of a chapel while speaking and I could see her curled up asleep on the floor of the vestibule—curled up like a child in its mother's womb. She was retreating out of responsibility—the responsibility of gowing up. But some are only too eager to assert their independence and be free.

Once they get their independence, however, they find it is not what it is cracked up to be. They find to their astonishment and dismay that they are not free. They marry and then they are not independent. Children come and they are not free. Restrictions of citizenship force them to move along well-defined paths. They are not independent.

Then comes the third stage when having gained freedom we sovereignly take it and surrender it to a higher entity—we lose our lives and find them again. The individual entering marriage loses his or her independence, surrendering it to the union, and finds a deeper fellowship. The individual surrenders his freedom to the life of the country and finds a fellowship in the larger entity. The law of life in the third stage is surrender of independence to interdependence and thus finding maturity. That is one of the most delicate transitions we can make. For just as many refuse or try to refuse to pass from dependence to independence, likewise many refuse to surrender their independence in behalf of interdependence. They are always asserting their independence, refusing to lose their lives in anything higher. They save their lives and they lose them.

O Jesus, Thou hast taught us to lose ourselves to find them again. And Thou hast shown us the way. For Thou didst lose Thy life in loving service and self-sacrifice and has found it again, ruling our hearts. Amen.

AFFIRMATION FOR THE DAY: *My lesser independencies I surrender to higher interdependencies.*

REFUSING TO GROW UP

Yesterday we observed that many refuse the transition from independence to interdependence—refuse to lose their independence in order to find it again in interdependence. They remain adolescent. They may be sixteen or they may be sixty, but they are always asserting their independence: "Nobody will tell me what to do," Meaning "I'm still adolescent."

These are the people who, in a home, a factory, a school, are sore spots. They are on the defensive, about as companionable as a porcupine. They go around looking for slights. And they find them or manufacture them. They go around with a chip on their shoulder—a chip which is probably from the block above! They are unhappy and the center of unhappiness.

These are the people who fill our mental institutions. Everybody is wrong, and if these wrong people would only change everything would be all right, they believe, forgetting or blind to the fact that the cause of all their troubles is within themselves. As Jung says: "Everyone who is self-centered is a greater enemy to himself than all the outer enemies combined can ever be." For instance, here was a very intelligent woman, a college graduate, the head of a library, whose life was a wreck: "Why did my sister leave me and get married? Didn't she know I'd be lonesome without her?" As if sisters didn't and shouldn't get married! If this woman had lost her life in the joy of her sister she would have found it again in a higher fellowship. As it was she isolated herself from her sister and from joy. Ten years later I saw her and her first question was: "How can I win my sister's love?" The answer was simple: she could win her sister's love by being loving to her sister. But she couldn't get it by sitting in the corner and crying for it. She had to lose her life to find it again. But she was an immature crybaby, crying for love and giving none, and full of self-pity and anger because she wasn't getting it. It was a costly immaturity—costly to herself and to everyone else.

O God, Thy patience with Thy immature children is infinite. What a family Thou hast on Thy hands! But having loved us, love us still. And maybe Thy love will kindle ours. And then we shall be free—to live. Amen.

AFFIRMATION FOR THE DAY: *I shall need as much insight into my own immaturities as I have for others.*

NATIONS GO THROUGH THREE STAGES

As the individual who attains maturity goes through the steps of dependence, to independence, to interdependence, so nations do the same.

The first stage in national life is dependence—the stage of imperialism. In that stage one nation decides for the subject nation what is good for it—in its supposed interest. And the imperialist nation can always find reasons for its imperialism—the people are childish, immature, would ruin themselves if we were not here, and we are doing a service to these people by staying.

Said a Japanese to me at the beginning of the opening hostilities between Japan and China: "We are going to do in China what Britain has done in India; we are going to take it over and organize it and develop it, for its own good." It was the mentality and mood of empire. There was a kind of self-righteousness about it, a sense of being commissioned by God to lift the lesser breeds.

And sometimes imperialism gives good government to undeveloped peoples. But soon the mood arises in the subject people that "good government is no substitute for self-government." They come to the stage of independence. They want the right to make their own mistakes, to be a nation in their own right; they want the right of self-determination, of self-expression. As Tilak, the Indian nationalist, said in the early days: "*Swaraj* [self-government] is my birthright." And it is. Imperialism, like parental authority, may be used to get nations on their feet, but beyond a certain point it must step aside and allow the people to develop on their own—to make their own mistakes. The subject people have a birthright to independence. You don't grant independence; you simply recognize the inherent birthright of the people to govern themselves. Britain saw the handwriting on the wall and stepped out of India at the right moment and thereby kept the friendship of India. The Labor Party must be given the credit in large measure. For they could take India no further. Since her independence India now has gone further than our fondest dreams.

Graciuos Lord, in our dealings with people show us how to guide everyone under us to become independent of us. Help us to strive for the maturity of everybody, and in the process we, too, shall become mature. In Thy name. Amen.

AFFIRMATION FOR THE DAY: *When I help others to independence, I make secure my own.*

WE ARE NOT INDEPENDENT

The nations of the earth, for the most part, have found their independence. Some areas are the exception—Africa will be the battleground of human liberties in the next twenty-five years. The so-called "free world" has to dissolve its imperialism and its colonialism. The Communist world has yet to extend freedom to the satellite states—a bondage more secure and inexcusable than the old colonial imperialism. There was some excuse for the old imperialism—subject people were not ready for independence, so it was said. But there is absolutely no such excuse for this new, tougher kind of imperialism in Communism, for the subject peoples under the Communists are highly developed and are capable of their own independence.

But this new imperialism, too, will fail, because it is fighting the deep urges in human nature for freedom. Benes, the great democrat of Czechoslovakia, said that democracy will finally succeed for it is "founded on the necessities of human nature." The stars in their courses and the urges within human nature are both fighting for human freedom.

It is only a question of time when all men, everywhere, will be free—free to determine the course of their own national life. And I want everyone, everywhere, to be free, since I am free only in the freedoms of all people. I am bound in the bondages of all.

But suppose all nations get their freedom, will that be the end? No, for that would bring us only to the second stage of human development—the stage of independence. The stage of interdependence is the stage of maturity for nations as well as individuals. Independence among nations, it is soon seen, is not what it is thought to be. In a world of this kind there is no such thing as independence. We are all bound up in a bundle of life and what effects anyone, anywhere effects everybody, everywhere. Whether we acknowledge it or not we are interdependent—vitally, inexorably, inescapably so.

Father, Thou hast tied us up together in a bundle of life. No man and no nation liveth or dieth to himself or to itself. Thou art pressing us by the very necessities to human brotherhood. Help us to respond with all we have. Amen.

AFFIRMATION FOR THE DAY: *To recognize our interdependence is a budding sign of maturity.*

HALFWAY BETWEEN

We saw yesterday that we cannot stop at independence—we must go on to interdependence. The nations are at the stage of adolescence, asserting their independence. Just as in a home the stage of adolescence creates trouble and strain for the parents and the child, so in the world today we are in an upset period because of the fact that nations are achieving and asserting their independence. Again adolescence among nations is "a period of temporary insanity." It is causing world strain and world fear. The United Nations is the parental authority trying to keep the peace among adolescent nations in their quarrels with one another. And what do they quarrel over? Mostly prestiges, hurt egos, and, very often, over nothing. These quarrels are the growing pains of an adolescent world.

The nations are trying to grow up—to become mature. We are trying to get from independence to interdependence. We are about halfway between independence and interdependence, the stage of an awful vacuum. We cannot go back to independence for we see we cannot. Where is our independence in a world in which one nation can send a fleet of bombers or guided missiles over another nation and can drop atomic bombs on defenseless cities? Our independence is a mere word. Intrinsically we are interdependent. But we are afraid to go on to interdependence— afraid we would be letting go of our independence.

Interdependence would mean world government, a world government in which each nation would be free to carry out its way of life under collective security. We all want that—security and freedom—but we are afraid of the process to it—afraid of this, that, and the other. We are afraid.

In the meantime we are in that vacuum stage where we don't belong to independence and we don't belong to interdependence; we don't belong to anything except fear. And that fear will continue until we arrive at interdependence, at collective security for all under world government.

O God, hold Thy adolescent children steady as we go through this stage of growing up, for we are cocksure and uncertain—we are chaos. Save us from ourselves. We know Thou dost love us; then hold us steady with Thy love. Amen.

AFFIRMATION FOR THE DAY: *I have reached the point of no return—I go on to maturity.*

"HIS STAKE IS A CROSS"

We saw yesterday that we as nations are in that stage between independence and interdependence. We cannot go back to independence, for independence is gone. We can never again be independent, separate entities, for interdependence has asserted itself as a fact—we are interdependent. We are bound up together for better or for worse. Anything that touches anyone, anywhere, touches everyone, everywhere. Though we know independence is gone and interdependence is here, we are afraid of interdependence—afraid to accept it and organize it into world government.

But we will have to have world government if we are to have world peace. There is no peace without government. In what was known as the Wild West, men went around armed. When a dispute arose they would shoot it out, shoot it out personally. For there was no government over them to give everybody collective security. But the moment government was established, those pistols dropped away and men argued their disputes before courts instead of shooting it out. The establishment of government brought peace. The world is in exactly the same position—we have no government over us, so each nation has to go around armed ready to shoot things out at the drop of the hat. The United Nations is a deterrent to war, and we must be grateful for it. But it is not government. The nations have not surrendered their sovereignty to the union. The "veto" is the symbol of that refusal to delegate sovereignty. Each nation is saving its life and losing it in collective insecurity. Will we make world government before collective ruin destroys us? I believe we will. For necessity is going to drive us to world government. God has brought us a long, long way as a race, and I don't believe He will now allow us to destroy ourselves with the atomic bomb. He has invested deeply in humanity—His stake is a cross. He will not fail. But will we fail Him? Possible. Humanity is in the process of becoming mature, trying to grow up. The pangs of humanity are not death pangs, but growing pains. God wills our growing up—we will too.

O Father God, we thank Thee for Thy infinite patience with us, Thy children. In a thousand crises of revolt against Thee, Thou couldst have wiped us out in a moment of anger. But Thy love has held steady and it holds us steady. Amen.

AFFIRMATION FOR THE DAY: *I believe in and shall act upon the faith that God intends to redeem a race.*

· FOUR LEVELS OF HUMAN LIVING

We come now to draw a conclusion and begin a fresh start in our search for maturity.

There are four levels of human living—four possible ways we might try to live. The business of living is to know how to live. Many people know everything about life except how to live it. They fail at the vital place in life—the place of the art of living.

If you are living on the wrong level, with that level's pattern of life in your mind and outlook, it will be impossible ever to become mature. For in that case you are working on the wrong level with the wrong pattern. Carry out that pattern faithfully and zealously and yet it will land you in immaturity. You must be on the right level with the right pattern if you are to become a mature person.

The levels are these: (1) instinct, (2) duty, (3) faith, and (4) "faith working through love."

The level of instinct. Man cannot live on the level of instinct alone. Animals can. If they respond to their physical environment, can take in food and light and air, they will survive. Animals survive by response to environment. But man, who is a moral being, is environed by a moral as well as a physical environment. He must respond to both to survive. He cannot say with the animal: My instincts are sovereign and will determine my conduct. He soon gets tangled with his own moral nature and the moral universe around him. I pick up my morning paper and it tells of a man who steps into a private plane, not his own, flies from New Jersey, lands in a New York street in the early morning, and walks into a tavern for a drink. Asked to explain himself, he says: "I just had an urge to fly." But "the urge to fly" had to be related to the law against larceny and the city's administrative code. So he landed not only on a Manhattan street, but in jail. To live at the impulse of our urges is to live in perpetual trouble and frustration, yet many try it. The cult of self-expression has many devotees.

O Lord, our Maker, Thou hast made us to live with moral law. Help us to remember that while we are made of dust we are also made in Thy image, and we cannot live in the dust while we have this high destiny upon us. Amen.

AFFIRMATION FOR THE DAY: *I am not the creature of instinct, but the creator of purposes.*

"SPITS IN HIS OWN FACE"

We have emphasized that man cannot live by urges alone. He is not a self-sufficient being who can do as he likes—regardless. He cannot break these laws written into the nature of things; he only breaks himself upon them. Our human nature is allergic to evil, so when we sin against the moral universe we sin against ourselves. "He who spits against the wind spits in his own face." You are free to choose, but you are not free to choose the results or consequences of your choices. They are in hands not your own.

And your inner opinions of this moral universe don't matter—the results or consequences register themselves in utter disregard of your opinion.

> The Moving Finger writes; and, having writ,
> Moves on: nor all your Piety nor Wit
>   Shall lure it back to cancel half a Line,
> Nor all your Tears wash out a Word of it.

Two women, widely separated, both married, both churchwomen, said that they had committed adultery with married men and both said exactly the same thing: "But I don't feel any guilt." When I reminded one that the moral law of God says, "Thou shalt not commit adultery," she replied: "I would hardly name it with such an ugly name as 'adultery.' I love him." But in spite of that "love" the moral facts were closing in upon her defenses: the fact that this was driving a wedge between her and her own husband and children; the fact that she was alienating the affections of a husband from his wife and family; the fact that both she and the man were on the defensive, hence uneasy and afraid. On her knees before God her defenses crumbled and she knew she was not an innocent woman wronged by circumstances, but an adulteress. No rationalization could alter that fact. She was living on the level of instinct.

O Father God, give us sensitive moral natures that can feel the slightest conflict with Thy law. Thy law is my liberty and therefore my life. For I am free in obedience and only in obedience. In Jesus' name. Amen.

AFFIRMATION FOR THE DAY: *No refuge in subterfuges, but in His safety.*

THE LEVEL OF DUTY

We saw yesterday that we as moral beings cannot live on the level of instinct without trouble to ourselves and all those around us. When we try it we are trying to live against the grain of the moral universe—it is a losing battle.

So we see this and move up to a higher level, the level of duty. Moral law is introduced and we decide to obey it. So religion is now the doing of our duty. This obviously is a higher level of life. And most Christians try to live on that level. We go to church, pray, give to good causes, and strive to live a good moral life. What else? This is taken for granted as the level on which we should live. But it is a very unsatisfactory level. We are constantly whipping up the will, striving to be good, pushing ourselves to square with the religion of duty. But that leaves a lot of people depleted spiritually and physically. Instead of religion's relieving the strain of human living, it is simply one more area of drive and tension.

A man introduced his wife to me, saying: "My wife is one of your 'wrestling' Christians." And you could see that she was a "wrestling" Christian—wrestling hard to be good, her face tense and anxious and strained. She was so preoccupied with being good that she had little time for leisured good to those around her. Hers was an unattractive piety—noncontagious.

People come up to me after an address and say: "Thank you very much for that address—I'll try harder." I always answer: "Don't." For when you are trying harder, you are on the basis of yourself—you are the center. Your religion is self-centered effort, therefore on the wrong center. God is the center—not you. In a religion of duty God is reference, not resource. We do our duty to God and do not draw our resources for living from God. God is on the margin of our trying—we are the sweating center. We try not only to earn our living by the sweat of our brow but to earn our eternal life by the sweat of our brow.

O Father, help me not to push too hard at the gates of life. For I know that it is not my pushing but Thy offer that is the basis of my finding eternal life. Help me to open my hands and take Thy gift. In Jesus' name. Amen.

AFFIRMATION FOR THE DAY: *Not the lashings of duty, but the longings of love, shall be my spring of action.*

"DEPLETING AND DEFEATING"

The whipping up of the will to do your duty is depleting and defeating. And yet a great deal of preaching is the preaching of a moralism—a striving to whip up fagged wills. As a radiant soul said: "When I hear the word 'sermon,' I know I'm going to get the dickens." Sermons are usually giving the people "the dickens" for not doing their duty.

John the Baptist represented the gospel of a demand: "You can't do this; you must do that." And Jesus said: "He who is least in the kingdom of heaven is greater than [John the Baptist]." Why? Because the kingdom of God did not present the gospel of a demand, but the gospel of an offer. We are to "receive" the Kingdom, not whip up ourselves into it. Those who are in the Kingdom of an offer, though they be the very least, are greater than those who are in the kingdom of a demand. For those who are under a demand end in depletion; those who are under an offer end in repletion. They are replete with all it takes to live, for they are attached to infinite resources. They live by the grace and power of Another.

Then they move up to the next stage—*the stage of faith.* Faith is receptivity—to the Highest. In faith you are not tense and struggling, but open and receptive. On this level you do not whip up the will, you surrender the will. Then you are relaxed and receptive, and faith becomes recuperative. Round our emptiness flows His fullness—and fills us; round our incompleteness flows His perfection—and perfects us; round our restlessness flows His rest—and rests us; round our sin flows His holiness—and invades us; round our selves flows His gracious Self—and displaces us; round our lovelessness flows his love—and loves us into loving. When we know how to take from these infinite resources, we know how to live by fullness not our own. Hence we live fully and overflowingly. Instead of religion being strain, hence drain, it is receptivity, hence release—release from ourselves and release to others.

Dear Father, we do ourselves and others a wrong when we struggle and strain and tie ourselves in knots. We close ourselves to Thy invading resources. Help me to live in the passive voice today—receiving, receiving, receiving. Amen.

AFFIRMATION FOR THE DAY: *The art of living for me is reduced to simplicity: the art of receptivity to grace.*

THE LEVEL OF GRACE

On this level of faith through which we receive grace, infinite possibilities are open before us. We have all the fullness of God to draw upon. That fullness is regenerative, recuperative, reviving. Then your goodness is not artificial—it is artesian. It springs from infinite resources within. So you and your energy are inexhaustible. For the more you give, the more you have to give. Then you live, work, preach, and share out of the overflow.

Many of us are exhausting ourselves against our problems—within and without. Mostly within. For the problems on the outside can be easily handled if the inside is sound and full. But if the Trojan horse of conflict is within, then we easily go down before outer enemies.

The difference between the stages of duty and of grace through faith is seen in John Wesley before and after Aldersgate. Before that experience he was methodical and meticulous in trying to be good. His life was a failure, for it was lived under the lash of duty. Then came the moment when Wesley ceased to struggle; he emptied his hands and took the gift of God—reconciliation and release. He walked out of that meetinghouse, threw his leg over the back of a horse, and went out to save England. He didn't have his own will, whipping it up to do his duty; God had his surrendered will, and through that surrendered will He poured grace and more grace.

Luther, toiling up the stairs on his knees trying to wring merit out of his penances, was one type of man—strained and empty. And Luther, seeing as in a flash that he could receive the grace of God by faith as a gift, was another type. Going up the steps on his knees he shook nothing—but himself; now on his knees receiving the grace of God he shook the world.

The men of action are the men of receptivity. And their acting has upon it, not self-pushing, but self-surrender. Hence people look beyond them to the grace that is working through them.

O grace of God, invade me, pervade me, use me. May grace be written across all I think and will and say and do. Then shall I live by "grace upon grace." And life shall be a song of praise for grace. In Jesus' name. Amen.

AFFIRMATION FOR THE DAY: *"I do not nullify the grace of God," said the world's greatest Christian, Paul.*

"FAITH WORKING THROUGH LOVE"

It would seem that the level of faith receiving grace would be the highest level. I used to think so. But I have been compelled to see that there is another level—the level of "faith working through love" (Gal. 5:6).

Many hold that the method of faith is the method of Christianity—they hold that faith, but their faith does not work by love. It works by fear, by combat, by aggressiveness against others who do not see eye to eye with them about that faith. Hence their faith becomes unfaith. It becomes tension and strain. The Christian faith does not need protection—it needs proclamation. It is its own defense. You don't have to protect the sun because someone throws mud at it. The sun shines and it is its own protection. But these nervous souls are always trying to steady the ark. If they would go out and love everybody, that would be a protection of the Christian faith for it would be a proclamation of that faith.

Our faith must work by love. Love is the applied edge of that faith. It is faith in shoes—faith going out to serve the least, the last, the lost. When our faith works by love, then that shows that we have faith in love. If we perish loving, we perish—we have no other way. It is love or nothing. We will not call in hate and force to fill in where we feel that love will fail. For love never fails. Everything that has no love in it is doomed to failure—love never fails.

Sid Caesar, the television comedian, in an article in *Look*, "What Psychoanalysis Did for Me," concludes with these important words: "This brings me to the most important thing I learned in analysis. I said before that there are no short cuts, but there is one thing that parents can apply to keep their children from becoming delinquents and to keep the disturbed ones from going through the long, arduous and expensive treatment I had to undergo. It's called love." After going through the mazes of psychoanalysis, Caesar came out at the place of love as the supreme necessity of human living. Everything fails except love. Love never fails.

Gracious Father, I see and I see clearly the road I should take—it is the road of love. Help me to make love my motive, my technique, my atmosphere, and my goal. Then if nothing happens I will be the payoff. Amen.

AFFIRMATION FOR THE DAY: *Love, only love, and more love shall be my life strategy and not an occasional attitude.*

"ALTRUISM . . . HAS A BIOLOGICAL FOUNDATION"

To live on the level of faith working by love is not an attempt at an impossible idealism but a basic realism. To live on that level is to live on the level for which we are structurally made.

In his address on Emotional Maturity, Franz Alexander, director of the Chicago Institute for Psychoanalysis, says:

Giving and producing, as Dr. Leon Saul correctly emphasizes in his book on maturity, are not felt by the mature person as an obligation and a duty; he gives, produces and spends his energy with pleasure in the service of aims which lie outside of his own person. Just as for the growing child, receiving love and help are the main sources of pleasure, for the mature person pleasure consists primarily in spending his energies productively for the sake of other persons and for outside aims. This generous outward directed attitude is what in ethics is called altruism. In the light of this view, altruism, the basis of Christian morality, has a biological foundation; it is a natural, healthy expresson of the state of surplus characteristic for maturity.

Here, then, we find both psychiatry and the Christian faith coming out at the same place—the biological necessity of love. To fulfill yourself you must love, for love has a biological foundation. It is not something imposed on us from without by arbitrary divine decree—it is something exposed from within us as the basic thing for which we are made. The biblical commandment says, "Thou shalt love," and the biological constitution says, "Thou shalt love." Life, divine and human, says the same thing: Love!

So when Paul says: "The love of Christ constraineth us" (II Cor. 5:14 KJV), he does not mean that it "constricts us," narrows us. He means that it constrains us to do the very thing for which we are made—to be natural, to be our very selves. When we love we are fulfilled; when we don't love we are frustrated. That's all there is to it. But what a conclusion to come to: Life is love!

O Father, we are coming out to the same conclusion that John came to: "God is love." We are therefore driven to the conclusion "Life is love." Help me then to throw away all my lingering doubts and to throw myself out on love with no reservations. Amen.

AFFIRMATION FOR THE DAY: *Since love is biblical and biological it shall be my choice.*

THE WAY OF CREATIVE LOVE

In our discussion of maturity as maturity in love, we have now reached the point where we can spend the rest of our time together studying the application of the principle of love to human living.

Fortunately the scientific method of testing, proving, verifying, is being applied to love and its results. The famous sociologist Pitirim A. Sorokin has organized a research center at Harvard University to study *creative altruism*, and to study it with the same exhaustive effort that goes into other scientific projects. After exhaustive research Sorokin has come to these conclusions: (1) None of the prevelant prescriptions against international and civil wars and other forms of interhuman bloody strife can eliminate or notably decrease these conflicts. (2) Unselfish creative love, about which we still know little, potentially represents a tremendous power, provided we know how to produce it in abundance, how to accumulate it, and how to use it—in other words, if we could transform individuals and groups into more altruistic and creative beings who would feel, think, and behave as real members of a mankind united into a solitary family.

Sorokin further points out that democracy and freedom are not enough to stop the massive slaughter of human beings, that free people have proved to be no less belligerent and strife-infected than others. Nor can religion as religion decrease hatreds and bring peace, unless that religion is "faith working by love." He points out that unselfish creative love represents tremendous power that may be released into human society. The research in creative altruism finds the inadequacy not in the teaching of Jesus, but in man's willingness and ability to apply those teachings.

In other words, we are finding out by scientific inquiry that all the other ways to peace, save the way of creative love, have proved themselves inadequate and frustrating. Science is beginning to say what the Christian faith has always said: Love!

Father, we are grateful that everything is pressing us toward love—everything is bringing us out at Thy feet. For life will work in Thy way and in no other way. And Thy way is love. Now help us to be all out for love. Amen.

AFFIRMATION FOR THE DAY: *God's pincer movement of biblical and biological pressure finds me in full cooperation.*

"NO FEAR IN LOVE"

We now turn back to I John and look at an important passage: "There is no fear in love, but perfect love casts out fear. For fear has to do with punishment, and he who fears is not perfected in love" (4:18).

Here it is said that love is the remedy for fear. And we need a remedy for fear, since fear is the basic plague of mankind. Someone asked a dean of girls in a woman's college: "What is the basic problem of these girls?" And the dean replied: "Fear. The poor things are afraid of failure, afraid of what others will think of them, afraid of the future—they're afraid." And yet they seldom show it. These lovely things afraid? Impossible. Yet they are afraid deep down. They have pushed their fears into the subconscious and there they fester. These subconscious fears create a climate of anxiety. The girls scarcely know why they are afraid, but they are.

I read of the dismissal of a competent doctor as health officer for a large area because she had lunch with a Negro nurse. This doctor faced the commission which dismissed her. A leading health official pleaded with the commissioners to rescind their action: "If there is one Christian among you, let me hear a motion to rescind this action." He was greeted with silence. No one appeared to advocate the doctor's dismissal and no one on the commission spoke a word either for or against her. As the doctor left she said to them: "Why are you such cowards? You must be afraid you are not doing the right thing." No, that was not their fear. They were afraid of the herd—afraid of public opinion. They were afraid. Probably all of them had a background of Christianity, and most of them a professed allegiance to it. And yet their faith didn't conquer fear. Why? Because their faith did not work by love. Love would have cast out fear. But they had faith without love—hence they had fear. A loveless Christianity is afraid. For the mind believes, but deep down the emotions are held by fear. Therefore, the conduct is determined by the emotions, not by the mind. In any battle between the mind and the emotions, the emotions usually win.

Dear Lord and Father, we need the deep-down emotion of fear to be cleansed from our conscious and subconscious minds. For when we see through the eyes of fear we are a distorted world. Deliver us, really deliver us, from all fear. Amen.

AFFIRMATION FOR THE DAY: *Fear and love cannot coexist—I choose the love way.*

A FALSE IDEA OF GOD

We saw yesterday how fear paralyzes our judgments and distorts our values. A Negro friend of mine, a radiant Christian, was invited to be the guest of a white woman in the Southland who was to take her to the church the next day—a white church. As church time came the hostess began to develop a fever. It ran up to 102°. A doctor was sent for. She could not go to church. The Negro woman went alone. At the church she was accepted and loved. When she returned to the home of her hostess, the fever was gone. What had happened there? The fear of appearing at church with a colored woman had sent her fever up. She was afraid. When the crisis was over her temperature returned to normal. She was a Christian woman, but while she had faith, she did not have a faith that worked by love. Her faith was strong—her love was weak—fear possessed her.

I sat talking with a German pastor who was completing his medical course, preparatory to going to Africa as a medical missionary. He told me of the tragedies which had happened in his home during the war. His father and two of his brothers were killed. The shock to his mother was terrific. Well-meaning friends and even ministers told her that this tragedy had happened to her family as the punishment of God. That sense of guilt, added to the loss of her family, caused a loss of speech. She was dumb for six years—couldn't speak. Then a Christian psychiatrist showed her how false this idea of God was. God was not going around looking for opportunities to punish people; He was love and only love, and the loss of her loved ones was the result of war, which is man-made. God made man free to choose—and man chose this. The wise dealing of the Christian psychiatrist lifted the burden of false guilt from her and she gradually regained her speech. Now she is giving addresses on psychological subjects with a Christian emphasis.

Her faith was not enough to lift her out of that inner paralysis caused by a false sense of guilt, caused by a false idea of God. When God as love was presented and grasped, her love for God was renewed and that love cast out fear. She was free.

Gracious Lord Jesus, give us a touch of Thy fearless love. For Thy love made Thee to walk up to everything and everybody unafraid. Thy love made the cross Thy servant. If I have Thy love I, too, can make everything serve. Amen.

AFFIRMATION FOR THE DAY: *Fear ties me up, love frees me—I belong to love!*

AN ASSURANCE THAT WE ARE LOVED

We are studying that there is no fear in love and that perfect love casts out fear.

Someone puts it this way: "Behind the old vice the forgotten fear will come up (the fear of being excluded from life), and behind the fear (the pain of not being loved), and behind the loneliness and deepest and profoundest of all human desires: the desire to love and give oneself and to be a part of the stream we call brotherhood." Now what is behind the fear? The answer—the pain of not being loved.

Now nothing can cure that fear except a deep-down assurance that we are loved. And here is where the Christian gospel comes with just that assurance, not a verbal assurance of words in a book, but a vital assurance of the Word becoming flesh—God becomes incarnate to reveal His love, His agape. That love was shown in the only possible way, in loving deeds to good and bad alike, and in the most loving of deeds, the deed of giving Himself for good and bad alike at the cross. Now we know that God loves us—loves us not because we are good and worthy, but He loves us—full stop. That cures our central pain, the pain of not being loved. We are loved, not when we are good, not when we are deserving, not if we do this, that, and the other, not because of anything we are, or do, or say—He loves us. He loves us because He *is* love. He cannot do anything other than love us and be God.

When we get hold of that assurance and it gets hold of us, then the fear of not being loved is an impossible fear, for we are loved no matter what we do or become. We cannot drift beyond His love by space, by deeds, or by character. We are loved no matter where we are, what we have done, or the kind of person we are.

But it does something else. When once we grasp this fact that He loves us, regardless, then that love produces love in us in return: "We love, because he first loved us" (I John 4:19). It is not our love for Him that cures us, but His love for us. That love for us awakens a love in us. And then we begin to love in response, begin to love Him and others. Love begets love.

O Divine Lover of my Soul, Thou hast kindled love in me. With such Love loving me, how can I do other than love Thee and everybody? Thou art loving me into love and I must love others into love. I can do it only with Thy love. Amen.

AFFIRMATION FOR THE DAY: *"The pain of not being loved" can never be mine, for I have Him who "is love."*

228

"HIS AGAPE PRODUCES AGAPE IN ME"

We are considering love casting out fear, and perfect love casting out all fear. Now this is an interesting departure from what we would expect. When it says, "There is no fear in love," we would have expected it to say, "There is no fear in trust and faith." We try to match faith against fear, but our fear is the fear of not being loved. Only love can cure that.

When we match our faith against fear, then that throws our attention on ourselves—on our faith. But that makes us self-conscious—I'm exerting my faith. Faith does not come by asserting it. You cannot say: "Come now, I'm going to have faith." Faith is a by-product, a by-product of the invading, persistent love of God. And the moment I begin to love His love, I begin, strangely enough, to love with His love. I love God with the love of God. I love others with the love of God. God has loved me into loving, and into loving with His love.

A friend writes that we can love God only with eros and not with agape. "For," says this friend, "agape is love regardless of the worthiness of the character concerned. But we could not love God if God were not of good character. We love Him because He is such a worthy character. Therefore our love for Him is eros, it cannot be agape." But if I love others with the agape of God, then I love God with the agape of God. His agape produces agape in me and not eros. And then I can love both God and others and myself with agape. For the source of this love is in Him. I am not loving with *my* love, but with *His* love.

On her arrival in China, a missionary was being taken in a ricksha through the crowded streets of the city in which she was to live. A wave of revolt and horror swept over her: "Love these people? O God, I can't. Unless you help me." As she sat in that ricksha a wave of divine love swept across her spirit. She felt her attitude toward the people change to a tender love and concern. For the balance of her days she loved them with God's love.

O God our Father, I am not able to love this way, not able but I'm willing. I'm willing that all my eros shall be transformed by Thy agape into agape. I can love and only love with Thy love. So love me into agape for everybody. Amen.

AFFIRMATION FOR THE DAY: *I am grateful I do not have to love—I have to allow love to love me into loving.*

"I LOVED THE WORLD"

We are looking at the fact that perfect love casts out fear. The psychology of that is sound. For if it had said, "Perfect faith casts out fear," that would have thrown the emphasis and attention on the person who is trusting—I am having faith, therefore I have no fear. I am the center of the faith; I have it. But in love the other is the center of attention: I love God; I love you. That tips the attention to something outside yourself. That casts out the fear "by the expulsive power of a new affection." Anything that leaves you with self-attention—such as the fighting attitude ("I will fight my fears")—leaves you afraid. For you are basically afraid that the universe doesn't back your being the center.

Love delivers from self-attention, give you other-attention; and therefore love, not faith, is the method of getting rid of fear. For love produces faith as a by-product of that love. You are not afraid of people you love; you are afraid of people you dislike or hate.

And "we love, because he first loved us." You don't have to have a developed inherent love. All you need is to expose yourself to His love and let that love operate. We cooperate with the operating love of God. He loves us into loving.

Here is what Commissioner S. L. Brengle, a rare soul, says: "He gave me such a blessing I never dreamed a man could have this side of heaven. Oh, how I loved! In that hour I knew Jesus and I loved till it seemed my heart would break with love. I loved the sparrows, I loved the dogs. I loved the horses, I loved little urchins on the street, I loved the world." Armed with such love there is no fear of anybody, or anything, or any situation. With the key of love in your hands you can unlock any situation. You are not afraid to walk up to anything. For you can always say with a Chinese missionary: "You'll have to love through me today for my love is not sufficient."

Dear Father, in very truth my love is not sufficient. So love through me this day, the unlovable, the indifferent, the enemy, the repulsive. For Thy love in me will make people lovable, will awaken them to response, turn enemies into friends. Amen.

AFFIRMATION FOR THE DAY: *I am not the spring of love— I am the channel of love.*

LOVE MAKES IMMUNE

We said yesterday that love casts out fear and unlocks all doors. An American soldier was captured by a Japanese and was being marched back into the Japanese lines at the point of a bayonet. As the American marched along he began to hum a Christian tune. The Japanese soldier recognized the tune, for he, too, was a Christian. He asked the American if he was a Christian and was told that he was. Then the Japanese handed the American his gun and told him to take him prisoner and march him back into the American lines. He did!

A missionary in China told me that a Communist soldier had come to arrest his family. His little daughter was out in front, and seeing the soldier, she greeted him with a smile and invited him to play mudpies with her. Soon the Communist soldier was absorbed in her prattle and her play and in her outgoing love and trust. After some time the soldier looked at his watch, said it was time for him to go, bade them good-bye, and backed away, bowing. Love diverted him. And love in the heart of the little girl had cast out fear.

I mentioned "Lila of Greece," as she calls herself. She lives on the absolute faith that love is invincible. She is the word of love become flesh in concrete stuations. While I write I know she is a joyous work massaging the sores of lepers with her bare hands. Isn't she afraid of infection? No, perfect love casts out fear. And my conviction is that she will come through this unscathed, that her very love will make her immune. They tell us that ninety percent of the disease germs that fall upon a healthy skin die within ten minutes. Killed by health. Disease germs will be burned up in the gentle flame of her wonderful agape. That's what happened to Jesus. When lepers touched Him, He didn't become unclean as did others; the lepers became clean. Love casts out fear—and leprosy. Love is immune and love sterilizes all it touches.

O Divine Redeemer, touch me into love and may my love sterilize all situations from germs of fear and hate and suspicion. Give me the touch of love upon all I touch today and may my love be a purifying force. In Thy name. Amen.

AFFIRMATION FOR THE DAY: *Love will make me immune to slights, to hurts, to opposition, to everything.*

THE REMEDY FOR RESENTMENTS

We saw last week that "there is no fear in love." Paul adds a number of other things not found in love. There is no impatience, no unkindness, no jealousy, no boastfulness, no arrogance, no rudeness, no insisting on one's own way, no irritability, no resentments (I Cor. 13:4-5). We pause this week to look at the way we get rid of resentments. Many live with resentments against employers, against parents, against in-laws, against life itself. And wherever there is resentment there is discontent. For we cannot live with resentments and be happy. Resentments are poison— poison to happiness, to peace, to usefulness, to those around you.

How do we get rid of resentments? Many try to fight them. But to fight them brings them to the center of one's attention. That is ineffective. For whatever gets your attention gets you!

Others push the resentments down into the subconscious and put the lid on them. That does not get rid of the resentments— they simply work at a deeper level, work as unhappiness, as uneasiness, as fear, as inadequacy. But all this is below the level of consciousness, so the person doesn't know why he is so insecure and inadequate and uneasy. The reason is buried resentments. Here was a man charging a theological professor in South Africa with heresy. The antagonist fought the case on the high level of orthodoxy and a defense of the faith. The professor was condemned and died of a broken spirit. This defender of the faith acknowledged later, in a moment of contrition, that the real reason for the trial was the fact that the professor had flunked him in an exam. The outer reason gave respectability and a religious basis for his hidden resentment. He was attempting to defend the faith for the wrong reasons.

The remedy is not to fight it, or suppress it, but bring it up and look at it, surrender it to God, and then let love, the divine agape, heal the hate and the inner wounds left by it. And this is done effortlessly. You simply open your heart to this divine love and let it in and let it operate—literally operate in taking out the cancer.

O Father, Thy love is so healing. It heals the ulcerous depths and bathes them with the healing ointment of Thy love. And it makes us immune against recurrence, for we are so filled with love and joy that recurrence is unthinkable. Amen.

AFFIRMATION FOR THE DAY: *"My soul is too great and too happy to be the enemy of any man."*

PHYSICAL RESULTS OF RESENTMENTS

We are considering that "there are no resentments in love." Here were two men in a factory who hated each other and sometimes fought. Both got stomach ulcers; both were on the same milk diet. Interesting and important outcome: they wouldn't share their love, so life drove them to share ulcers and a milk diet; they shared the results of their hate. And they produced an ulcerated situation around them which others were compelled to share. The same thing also applies to dumb animals. They, too, share our ulcerous spirit and are affected by it.

It is not enough to say that we have good reason for our resentments. It doesn't matter whether the reason is good or bad—the results are registered within one's self, both spiritually and physically. Here was a woman, deeply religious and faithful in her church life, who had heart attacks. The reason was a son-in-law who got drunk and brought liquor into her house—a house where no liquor had ever been seen. She had a very good reason to be upset. Nevertheless, good reason or no good reason, she suffered heart attacks from it. We are told that there are five million people in America who have perfectly good hearts but with all the symptoms of heart disease—palpitations, pains, and the like. These people are upsetting their hearts with their wrong emotional reactions.

This emotional upset stretches from the very old to the very young. Here was a little boy who started having attacks of asthma as soon as his little sister was born. These attacks came because he was resentful of the little sister and the attention she was getting.

As Smiley Blanton puts it:

The vice-president of a corporation, resentful because the board of directors had failed to vote him an overdue increase in salary, angrily threatened to fire the department supervisor who appeared ten minutes late with a sales report. The supervisor, smarting under the unjustified rebuke, took his wife severely to task when he found the roast slightly overcooked.

All immature reactions.

Father God, save us when we are inwardly eaten by resentments. For they eat like a cancer. Help us to get them up and out and look at them in the light of Thy forgiving love. For in the light of that love no germs of hate can survive. Amen.

AFFIRMATION FOR THE DAY: *"I bear on my body the marks of Jesus"—also the marks of my resentments.*

"DO NOT DISAGREE WITH ME"

We continue to look at the immaturity of resentments whether found in young or old. Judges who judge others for their faults and violations of law can violate the laws of their own beings and violate the peace around them. A notice posted on the wall of the municipal judge's office in Hobbs, New Mexico, says: "While in this office speak in low, soothing terms and do not disagree with me in any manner. Please be informed that when one has reached my age, noise and nonconcurrence cause gastric hyperperistalsis, hypersecretion of hydrochloric acid, and inflammation of the gastric mucosa, and I become unpleasant." The man blamed his condition on two things— his age and what other people did. He missed the point. His immature reactions were responsible; he was responsible for his sensitivity and the consequent bodily results.

A psychiatrist said to me: "The basis of emotional disturbance is anger." The basis of this judge's anger was an unsurrendered, infantile self that had to be agreed with all the time—or else!

Jesus was right when He gave the name Boanerges (sons of thunder) to James and John at their very first meeting. He saw that they each had a touchy, unsurrendered self, ready to fly into a thunderstorm when that self was crossed.

He set his face to go to Jerusalem. And he sent messengers ahead of him, who went and entered a village of the Samaritans, to make ready for him; but the people would not receive him, because his face was set toward Jerusalem. And when his disciples James and John saw it, they said, "Lord, do you want us to bid fire come down from heaven and consume them?" But he turned and rebuked them. And they went on to another village (Luke 9:51-56).

Of course, the Samaritans were wrong in their race prejudices, but James and John were equally wrong in their reactions— "fire from heaven." And they tried to associate Jesus with their reaction of anger—"Lord, do you want us to bid fire. . . ?" We try to Christianize our wrong reactions. It won't work.

O Jesus, Lord, we are so grateful for Thy reaction in that situation. Thou didst meet it with dignity and strength. Help me in similar situations to meet all childishness with maturity, all anger with love, all disturbance with peace. Amen.

AFFIRMATION FOR THE DAY: *Had the fire-from-heaven attitude continued we would never have heard of the disciples again.*

"HE NEEDED CONVERSION"

A crisis will often bring out a basic immaturity. Here is the instance in baseball history of a towering giant in pitching skill. He stood right at the top. But in a crucial game he had to be taken out of the box, for he had slumped badly and had left the score heavily against his team. Instead of taking it in his stride as a mature person would, he stamps angrily out, gets into a wrangle on the way out, and goes home before the game is finished, like a sulking child. What was the matter there? The secret of this childish reaction was revealed a few days before, when in another important game he had to be relieved toward the close of the game. The relief pitcher won the game for him. Instead of showing his gratitude, the star had this reaction: "What made me weaken and throw that ball? If I hadn't done it, I could have been carried off the field on the shoulders of the players." He wasn't rejoicing that his team had won, in spite of his lapses; he was miffed that he didn't get the acclaim of being carried on the shoulders of his teammates. Highly skilled as a pitcher, immature as a person. The anger was not the disease—it was a symptom of a self-centered self. He needed conversion!

We are now in a position to ask the question, What is the remedy for resentments and anger? The answer is simple. Don't deal with the anger and the resentments. They are symptoms—the disease is deeper: a self-centered, unsurrendered self. As long as that self is unsurrendered to God these outbursts will come. For the self is still there watchful of its own position and power. Therefore it is a touchy, ready-to-explode self when it is crossed. That self must be surrendered to God, and I mean surrendered. The basis of your life must be shifted from self to God. When that is done a basic orientation of the whole life takes place. You are not holding yourself together in self-conscious watchfulness. God has you. Your attention is now centered in God, not in you. He is your vindicator. If He approves of you, what does it matter if every other person in the world disapproves of you? You are secure—in God. The losing of your life in surrender produces the finding of your life in security.

O Jesus, how blessedly Thou dost put Thy finger on our problems when thou dost say: "He who finds his life will lose it, and he who loses his life for my sake will find it." I would lose my life in Thy blessed will and find it again in freedom—from anger and resentments. Amen.

AFFIRMATION FOR THE DAY: *Any resentments I have are the outcroppings of an unsurrendered self.*

A NOBLE LETTER

We are meditating on this statement, "There are no resentments in love." In a prayer group someone said: "I have a resentment I can't get rid of." The leader said: "The way to get rid of resentments is to love the Lord so much and be so happy and so secure in that love that someone could come up and hit us in the face and we would only react in feeling sorry." This friend in the prayer group jumped up and said, "It's gone. The resentment is gone. What a burden is lifted!" She was so happy she put her arms around the woman next to her and laughed and cried a little.

This letter written by one of the noblest missionaries I know illustrates how the divine agape can and does deliver from resentment and fear. The letter is written to a seminary classmate, now a minister:

Dear A.: Since the publication in _____ of December 16, 1954, of the attack upon me, I have had a divided mind as to how to proceed. I am not, never have been, and have no intention of becoming a Communist, card-carrying or otherwise. . . . My first reaction to the item in the _____ was one of indignation and anger. I felt a desire for revenge. I became burdened with self-pity and self-righteousness. At the same time I was afraid. For we live in times when false charges of the sort you have made can be damaging beyond all chance of repair regardless of the facts. And it is not only the victim who must suffer, but his family as well.

It so happened that my father's copy of _____, dated December 16, 1954, arrived in the mail on December 24, Christmas Eve. My wife and I had planned to attend a midnight Communion service that night. I must confess that I went to that service most reluctantly. There was fear and hate in my heart. As I sat in the pew during the early part of the service listening to the Christmas carols I wondered whether I would be able to go forward to the Communion rail when the invitation came. Then the thought came to me: "How do you stand on loving your enemies? These two men are your enemies. They have attacked you falsely and said all manner of evil against you. Do you love them?"

O Father, when hate and fear invade me and take possession of me, where can I turn save to Thee? I cannot cast them out. They will not go at my command. Only by the expulsive power of Thy love will they go. I surrender to that love. Amen.

AFFIRMATION FOR THE DAY: *I shall come out on the love side of every situation.*

THIS NOBLE LETTER CONTINUED

We continue the letter begun in the preceding meditation:

I was stumped. I didn't know what to do. I prayed: "Oh, Lord, how can I love them? I can't pretend. You know I don't love them. I'm in trouble. I want to take Communion, but I am not at peace with my neighbor. Please help me."

Suddenly I had a great and thrilling sense of the Spirit. It may seem difficult to believe but all of a sudden, and in a complete and final way, I quit hating you. I was freed of all that. I felt whole and restored. I cannot say that I loved you in the way that I loved my blood brother. In that I still fall far short. But I loved you in this way: I loved you because Christ had first loved me. I suddenly realized that if He holds nothing against me, despite all the things that I have done, how can I possibly hold anything against you? He died for you as well as for me. How then can I possibly lay a finger on you? If I hate you, I hate one whom He loves. I was disarmed. I had no more hate. I had no more desire to strike back.

Now this is the wonderful thing that I discovered about the love of Christ. Once I accepted it and all that it meant so far as my attitude toward you was concerned, once I let go of the hate and the desire to strike back, I wasn't afraid any more. It was hard even to remember what it had felt like to be afraid, even though just a moment before I had been an agonized bundle of fear and hate. I was not only free of hate, I was also free of fear.

Just thinking about it one would assume that if you were assailed by enemies who were trying to destroy you, and suddenly you were stripped of your capacity and will to hit back, the result would be panic and ultimate disaster. What can be worse than to be under attack and suddenly find yourself disarmed? But it is a mystery of the Spirit that if God in Christ Jesus disarms you, instead of fear you have peace, tranquility, and a sense of the most wonderful security that can possibly be imagined. And that is what happened to me last Christmas Eve waiting for Communion. I went forward to the Communion rail with joy.

O Father, this deliverance from fear and hate is beyond us. We cannot understand it. But we can accept it and rejoice in it and give it lavishly to others. Pour it into us that we may pour it into others—into everybody. In Jesus' name. Amen.

AFFIRMATION FOR THE DAY: *Love and joy are Siamese twins; resentment and gloom are also Siamese twins.*

"THAT LETTER IS PURE AGAPE"

We conclude this amazing letter:

I went forward to the rail with joy. The one who had claimed me had claimed you. He had paid the price. You were His. I could not lay a hand on you. I was well. I haven't hated you since. I am free from every bit of fear. It is all gone.

I know about your meeting with the representatives of the mission and with the people of your presbytery. I know you have no letter from me and you cannot name the chaplain who you say discussed me with you. I have been told that I have a sound libel suit against you. Well-meaning friends have said: "Character assassins should be silenced." All these things I know. But I also know that if I got into a libel suit against you I would probably end up hating you and trying to destroy you. In a selfish way I want to keep what came to me by God's grace last Christmas. I wish to go on looking at other men, even my enemies, and seeing, not monsters, but living souls for whom Christ died. So I shall not sue you, nor make any demands upon you save the demands which we all inevitably make upon each other in Christ.

May His blessing be upon you and His grace abide with you, and give you peace. I have written this because of Him. Your Brother, S.M.

That letter is pure agape. It is a miracle of attitude—one moment hating and fearful, the next moment loving and without fear. And the initative was with God—"We love, because he first loved us." That is Christianity in action.

A devoted missionary nurse had been divorced by her husband, who took another woman. She has driven herself in achievement to show that she is as good as and better than the other woman, to make her children and grandchildren proud of her. She has given herself to lepers. But she has been under great stress and strain, because deep down there was unforgiveness of the husband and the other woman. Then she saw she must surrender this unforgiveness to God. She did. Something was released within her. She was freed from tension and fear, and agape replaced eros. Now there is no resentment in her love.

Gracious God and Father, if there is any eros lingering in me, any loving of people to make others love me for the loving, then cleanse away this eros and replace it with Thy pure agape. For I do not want to love for the wrong reasons. Amen.

AFFIRMATION FOR THE DAY: *Love is food; hate is poison.*

"GOOD BOY—BARRING WHAT HE DOES"

There are one or two loose ends we must pick up before we go on. Does loving with this divine agape mean that we can shut our eyes to the wrong in the person whom we love with agape? No, it means that we love the sinner and hate the sin—as God does.

This letter from an intelligent woman makes the point clear:

The sentimental love comes without rhyme or reason. You meet some people and love them instantly. Others you are forced to know a long time to understand, and others you are plain allergic to. Now I understand that we are to love all men with the love of Christ—that alone is required: the love of doing a person good, seeing not the man that is, but the man you can help him to be; the love that makes us willing even while he is a sinner to lay down our life for him. I am sure that is what is meant. When I saw that, the burden lifted from my soul. For I had that kind of love in my heart—a love that suffers long and is kind.

This kind of love is illustrated in the mother who said to the judge before whom her boy was being tried for an offense: "Johnny is a good boy, barring what he does."

"Mary," of whom I have written, picked up a drunk and took him to his home in her car, and said of him: "He is such a nice, lovable man, but he has just missed his way." That is loving with agape—loving in spite of the sin.

On the other hand, there are those who are outwardly righteous, but who lack the loving attitude. Of one woman it was said: "She doesn't swear, but she makes everybody else around her swear." Outwardly correct and inwardly curdled. It is harder to have agape toward these than toward the blatant sinners. Jesus knew that. But after He had spoken stinging words about this outwardism in the Pharisees, He ended His woes with weeping over the city. So both in His woes and in His weeping, agape was seen. He loved the publican and the sinners and He loved the Pharisees enough to wound them that He might really heal them.

O Christ, do not withhold Thy lancet if Thou seest that I need a spiritual surgical operation. For Thy wounds are healing and only healing. I cannot hold any hidden resentment without disaster. So cut, Kindly Surgeon. Amen.

AFFIRMATION FOR THE DAY: *In my agreements and in my disagreements love shall be my motive.*

"THERE IS NO TENSION IN LOVE"

We take another step in agape: "There is no tension in love." There is tension in eros, for eros is acquisitive love and when it cannot get the object of its love it is full of tensions and frustrations. But agape is not a possessive love; it loves calmly and without frustration, for since it does not want the object of its love it can love even if there is no response. Agape suffers long and is kind even while suffering long. But eros is nervous and strained and fearful, afraid that the object of the love will slip away and be lost. So eros religion does not release from strain, but it often adds to it. If our love for God is eros instead of agape it may increase our tensions.

Many things may produce tensions. A fear of life and responsibility may produce tensions. A little boy on his way home from school said: "I wish I was home, with all my homework and all my chores finished, that I was married and had children and was dead." He was afraid of life and responsibility, with the same fear that the Hindu has of going through eighty-two million rebirths before he can obtain moksha, or salvation.

Some episode may set up a buried tension. A young man saw his father fall over and die on a handball court. He became frightened. Later on he fell on the floor and became purple. The doctor found nothing wrong with his heart, and his blood pressure was normal. When this was explained to him he got over his tension.

A wrong idea may produce a tension—and a pain. A woman complained of a pain in her torso. The doctor could find nothing wrong. Then the doctor said: "I've found your trouble: your ribs are too close to one another. Take breathing exercises each morning." She did. In a few days she was well!

We are fast producing what one book describes in the title: *The Neurotic Personality of Our Time.* Our nerves which can carry beneficence are carrying the opposite; hence we become nerve conscious, hence neurotic.

Dear Lord and Father of mankind, forgive our feverish way; reclothe us in our rightful minds and help us to know the beauty of Thy peace and calm. Help us to know how to live on Thy peace, to take it by handfuls from Thee. Amen.

AFFIRMATION FOR THE DAY: *My nerves are not responsible, they are only responsive to me.*

BASIS OF LIFE COMPETITION

What are some of the things that produce tensions in our modern life? These tensions invade the very young. A little girl said to her mother: "I feel very nervous." And the astonished mother said: "Why, what do you mean by being nervous?" And the little girl replied: "I feel in a hurry all over." A lot of people "feel in a hurry all over." What has produced this inner restlessness and tension?

First, at the basis of our Western life is competition, a fierce competition. Success is looked on as the basic good. What that success is doesn't matter much; we want to succeed, to come out beyond the rest.

This desire to succeed takes many forms. We want to succeed in business—that is, economically. We want to succeed socially. Many become social climbers. And if they can't make it they are tense and anxious and frustrated. And if they do succeed they are tense and anxious about holding their position against newcomers.

Two well-born and blue-blooded dogs were walking daintily along the street with noses in the air when they met a big alley dog. Embarrassed at being in such company one of the lady dogs said, "We must go. My name if Miji, spelled M-i-j-i." The other said, "My name is Miki, spelled M-i-k-i." The alley dog put up his nose and said: "My name is Fido, spelled, P-h-y-d-e-a-u-x."

A mother said to her minister: "I wish something would change my daughter's disposition. Whenever she goes to a party and someone has a dress prettier than hers, she is very unhappy and miserable."

This "keeping up with the Joneses" keeps everyone on a tension. A cartoon shows a sweating father piling thing on thing in a vain struggle to keep up. At the bottom is a modern ranch house, on top of it is a new car, then a television set, then a refrigerator, then bureau drawers with pearl necklaces hanging out, and so on up to the toppling top. He's keeping up with the Joneses, and tense and anxious in the process. Our modern life is shot through with competition, hence tensions.

O God, our Father, we are fevered and anxious and tense. Save us from this self-destruction. For we wear ourselves ragged and are in spiritual tatters. Give us the joyous calm of Thy blessed presence, the holy calm pervading us fully. Amen.

AFFIRMATION FOR THE DAY: *I do not have to keep up with the Joneses; I have to keep up with Jesus.*

"IN FOUR MINUTES"

We ended yesterday with emphasis on the tensions of modern life based on inner and outer competitiveness.

I give a good many talks on radio and television and those in charge seldom compliment me on what I say, but they almost invariably say: "Why, you hit it on the nose," meaning you stopped at the exact second. "And you did it without a manuscript—wonderful." Not the content, but the timing of the conclusion was the important thing. Tension.

Front-page headlines of a large newspaper said: "Communion Distributed to 10,000 in Four Minutes," a description of a large religious convention which partook of Holy Communion in exactly four minutes. The description in the article was a compliment to the organizing genius of the man back of this communion precision. The fact that ten thousand partook of the Communion was not the big thing—it was the timing. We did it faster than anybody else. Tension.

Ellen Y. was a child prodigy. Her parents were excessively proud of her and expected her to lead the honor roll. But the child, under this competitive expectancy, began to come down with an infection every time an examination was announced. That saved her from the competition, an escape out of it. Tension.

A schoolteacher writes:

When I was a child my parents were too exacting, often using the phrase: "What will people think?" I took it to heart more seriously than they intended. I thought everybody looked at me and thought: "What an awful thing she is!" I feared people and, as I grew older, feared that I would fail in all my examinations. Then later I was always afraid I would lose my job at the end of the year. None of these things happened, of course. At the Ashram I was born into an entirely new person. Now I am thankful for these awful experiences because I feel I understand people's difficulties more than most people do, and am understood better also.

All of these represent the competitive pressures.

O Father, when we get our eyes on others and what they think we are under false pressure. We are bowing at the shrine of herd pressure. The herd is God. Forgive us if we see them instead of Thee. For Thou dost have the last word, not they. Amen.

AFFIRMATION FOR THE DAY: *I am emancipated from herd pressure, because I've surrendered to His pressure.*

CAUSES OF STRESS

We have been looking at the tensions that arise from the competitive nature of modern life. One more illustration before we turn to another source of tensions.

Here was a man who broke out in boils periodically. At the basis of such outbreaks was his fear that a man where he worked was trying to take his job: "As I thought about it I would boil inside." The inner boiling produced the outer boils, cause and effect.

Many of our tensions, however, come not from without but from within. Our wrong attitudes toward life produce tensions from within. In my book entitled *Mastery* I mentioned a Montreal doctor who has propounded the thesis that stress is the cause of all diseases. He says that the pituitary and the adrenal glands keep the body in balance when stress comes upon one. They can succeed if the stress is not too great, but if it becomes too great then the defenses break down, the body is thrown out of balance, and one may develop any kind of disease to which he is prone. That statement, if it turns out to be true, is important. That plays straight into the hands of religion, which is supposed to give inner stability, poise, security, and peace.

But not all religion does that. Paul has something to say on this subject and it is very much to the point:

But understand this, that in the last days there will come times of stress. For men will be lovers of self, lovers of money, proud, arrogant, abusive, disobedient to their parents, ungrateful, unholy, inhuman, implacable, slanderers, profligates, fierce, haters of good, treacherous, reckless, swollen with conceit, lovers of pleasure rather than lovers of God, holding the form of religion but denying the power of it (II Tim. 3:1-5).

Here are nineteen things that produce stress—"times of stress." We would have expected the things that produce stress to be from without—wars, famines, earthquakes, tornadoes, but they are not mentioned; all these nineteen things are from within, every one of them. So things that produce stress may be from without and they may be from within. And the ones from within are the most decisive.

O God, our heavenly Father, we come now to the crux of our problem in dealing with stress. Help us to have courage to face the fact, and to face it fearlessly, that most of our stresses come from within. Help us to try not to dodge that fact. Amen.

AFFIRMATION FOR THE DAY: *Calm and joy are inside jobs.*

"AN EXCUSE FOR MY BAD DISPOSITION"

We saw yesterday that all of these nineteen causes of stress are from within and not one from without. That is important for we often, very often, try to blame our stresses upon this, that, and the other in our environment. A man came to a psychiatrist and said: "I want you to give me an excuse for my very bad disposition." Many go to psychiatrists and others to find the basis of their upsets in childhood treatment, in home and office influences, and so on, to get away from the fact that they themselves are responsible.

But Paul puts his finger on the first cause of stress: "For men will be lovers of self." Self-centered love is the primary cause of stress. When you are a self-centered and self-preoccupied person you are off-center, for the universe does not back your being God. You feel that nothing is backing you except yourself; hence you are uneasy. Then the second cause of stress is "love of money." Men who put their whole weight down on loving money are uneasy and at stress because they are afraid that money might slip away from them and leave them with nothing but emptiness. Money-loving people are uneasy people. And rightly, for they can take nothing with them. And yet while everyone knows that, so few act upon that knowledge.

The third "love" among the nineteen mentioned yesterday is "love of pleasure." A person who loves pleasure is always uneasy and at stress if nothing is taking place in the form of entertainment. For the "pleasure" distracts them from their own inner emptiness. And when they are having no distracting pleasures they are bored—with themselves.

These three—love of self, love of money, love of pleasure—are important causes of stress. These loves have gone astray and have fastened on the wrong things. These loves need to be redeemed and until they are they are causes of "stress," hence of personality disruption and disease. And these are found in religious people: "holding the form of religion."

O Jesus Master, teach us how to let our faith in Thee get into our tensions and release them and make us free. Teach us the power of Thy Spirit to untie our knots, loose us from inner conflicts, and make us free—free indeed. Amen.

AFFIRMATION FOR THE DAY: *I am free from this trinity of loves because I love the Trinity.*

"HAPPY PILLS"

We have seen the two great sources of stress—one from without and one from within. Now what is the remedy for stress?

Some try shortcuts. This fact is revealing: Enough sleeping pills are sold in the United States each year to put every man, woman, and child to sleep for twenty-three days. That is a pathetic reminder as to how people turn to shortcuts that lead into wilderness.

Also proposed and used as a remedy are the so-called "happy pills." These pills were unknown four years ago, yet this year 35,000,000 prescriptions for them will be filled, at a cost to the public of perhaps $150,000,000, and tranquilizers will rank as the fifth-largest-selling prescription drug.

A good many side effects of "happy pills" have been found in patients. Among them are liver damage, lowering of the blood pressure, drowsiness, and excessive sweating.

Depressed people often become even more depressed following drug therapy. After the effects wear off they are "down." Some have been known to attempt suicide under the influence of happiness pills.

Moreover, psychologists feel that many people who are taking these pills are dodging their problems. To have to face up to their problems may bring initial anxiety, but if they do so, such people tend to become mature persons. Failure to face problems makes such persons immature.

The most significant fact of all is this: Happiness pills do not cure any disorder of the mind. They do not cure manic-depression, nor schizophrenia, nor any other disorder. The neurosis is still there.

To sum up: It is a safe wager that people in the future, as in the past, will find their happiness within themselves and their relationships with God and man, not in a bottle.

The immaturities of our civilization were never more conspicuously pointed out than by the avidity with which people turn to immature methods of getting rid of their problems. "Happy pills" are a sign of a basic unhappiness.

O Father, we need Thy grace and Thy power to help us not to get hung up on the snags of these shallow remedies for our basic strains and stresses. Help us not to treat symptoms but diseases. Help us to take Thy way. Amen.

AFFIRMATION FOR THE DAY: *I have a "Happy Pill"—surrender to Christ, infallible remedy.*

WHAT HE HAS HE SAVES

We have been looking at several attempted shortcuts out of inner stress and tension. Eventually they lead into a wilderness.

And eros religion, which is egocentric religion, just does that. For eros religion depends upon the self to get rid of the problems of self. It is the attempt to lift oneself by one's own bootstraps: by the use of slogans, by techniques. While helping momentarily, like happy pills, none of these methods gets to the basis of the problem, the problem of self-centered preoccupation. They may even increase it by calling attention to the self and its problems.

Only agape religion is the answer. For agape has at its center Divine Self-giving. This agape love sacrifices itself for us and our redemption. This agape love then creates us in its own likeness. Self-giving creates self-surrender in us. When that takes place then we get ourselves off our own hands into the hands of God. Until that self-surrender takes place you are at tension, for you belong in God's hands and in no other place. Outside of God's hands you are at tension; inside of God's hands you can let go, relax, and know that you are at home. Listen to this: "From this Ashram experience I carry in my heart today a peace and composure that is a surprise to me. I did not realize that I could surrender the burdens, most of which I had created for myself, to Jesus. It is wonderful how much easier things have become this way. I like it." And this is the woman who, when her husband left her for another woman, tried to show herself, her children, and her grandchildren, that she was just as good as and better than the other woman—she tried to show it by devoted service as a nurse to lepers.

One woman put it this way: "It is so comfortable to get yourself off your own hands into the hands of God." It is! There you are released and relaxed and can rejoice. It *is* comfortable—very!

There is no real remedy for tension and stress this side of, or outside of, self-surrender—a complete self-surrender. What He has He saves—from tension and stress.

Gracious Father, I'm so grateful that there is an open door out of my tensions. It is at Thy feet where I lay myself down completely with no strings attached. My tensions are the result of running away from Thee. Save me. Amen.

AFFIRMATION FOR THE DAY: *Tension and stress are sin—sin against the grace of God which is always at hand.*

ONE STEP FORWARD, TWO STEPS BACKWARD

We said yesterday that self-surrender is the remedy for tension. The absence of that self-surrender brings this from a woman:

I've been going one step forward and two steps backward for fifteen years—sweating, swearing, giving up and then starting again. Think I'm over the hump now. But still can't see why I had to fight so hard, and so many people, jobs, when all the time there was something there for the asking and the receiving. Something like the illustration you used of the Brahman bull eating out of the garbage can, when there were green fields nearby open and inviting.

On the contrary, this comes from a full surrender. A doctor writes:

Following our conference I had a wonderful release from the tension I'd been under, knowing so long as I committed myself to Christ, whatever came would be all right, even if it was not what I had wished. The amazing thing is that having been completely willing to accept even what seemed adverse, everything has come out right. My urticaria has completely disappeared, not at once but after a few weeks. As to my working relations, a committee met to discuss the future plans for my work, both what I should be doing and where. I prayed that every member of the committee would be enabled to face the problems we should discuss honestly and frankly and that the decisions would be those that would advance the work most, regardless of what it would mean to me personally. I believe I was thoroughly honest in this. The result of the committee meeting? Just as I had hoped! Now I don't look on this in the least as a slick way of getting your own wishes. I feel one has to be willing, if it is God's will, for the apparently adverse decision. And, after all, if this is God's will there will be good in it!

Here was a medical doctor cured of his urticaria—rosebud blotches over the body—and cured of his tensions by surrender of himself and his tensions to God. But there was the further step: he made the initial surrender, but he also cooperated with God in carrying out that surrender into his life plans. He let God have him and his life plans. So initial surrender and continual cooperation with God are the two secrets.

O Father, we often give ourselves and then withhold our life plans. Help us to give both. For Thou cannot control us unless Thou dost control us wholly. So my person and my plans are both Thine and Thine forever. Amen.

AFFIRMATION FOR THE DAY: *No eating out of garbage cans—the green fields of God are at hand!*

"WHAT YOU NEED IS CHRIST"

We quoted yesterday a doctor who got rid of his tensions and his urticaria at the same time by surrender. Here is another: a doctor was called to see a man who had been shooting craps on a riverbank, gambling, drinking, dissolute, and with an ulcer that hemorrhaged badly. The doctor looked him over and said, "What you need is Christ," and walked out. The man was so angry that he could have shot the doctor. But this blunt statement of the doctor's convicted him; he was converted and is now a preacher in that same riverbank district—his church has a Sunday school of over two hundred.

The interesting thing is that the doctor was himself unconverted when he said this and he himself was suffering from a stomach ulcer. He blamed his condition on his father's domineering. But one day the Inner Voice said: "You are revolting against your heavenly Father." He was converted as he lay in a Roman Catholic hospital looking at a crucifix. When he surrendered his revolt and his consequent tensions to God, his ulcers cleared up. Today the walls of his clinic are filled with Christian mottoes; he prays over his patients and has a radio period everyday giving the Christian message. He does all this without strain and without tension, for he is fully surrendered to God and draws on the resources of God for surgery and soul-saving.

A wife was tense and nagging toward her husband. He went away and his wife had a new chandelier put in during his absence. On his return he brought home a big ham and when he took it off his shoulders it struck the chandelier and smashed it. He waited for the storm to break. But the wife came down and said: "It's all right, dear. We can get another one." The husband looked at her and asked: "What's happened?" And she replied: "I've been converted since you were gone." The husband was intrigued and said: "Sit down and tell me about it." She did and he, too, was converted. A tense, nagging wife was transformed into a channel of love and grace by surrender.

Slogans telling you to be peaceful and calm may do good, but surrender of the tense self to God is decisive. It hits the spot. For the tensions are symptoms of an unsurrendered self.

Gracious Father, I cannot exorcise the demon of worry and tension. It is beyond my control. But I can surrender the tense, worrying self, and Thou canst cast it out with a word. I do. And I accept Thy deliverance, accept it now. Amen.

AFFIRMATION FOR THE DAY: *I rest in the quietness of God so nothing can disturb my calm.*

"CAUGHT MY POISE AND I'M WELL"

We are looking at the way surrender to God reduces tensions and produces healing. A woman had a very bad eye condition. She was upset and distracted and full of tension. She made a full surrender of herself to God. The eye went back to normal. The doctors gave up the study of her case, for they said they couldn't fit it into any category of law. Surrender of herself, not merely the eye, was the answer! The soul tension produced the tension in the eye.

Then this letter:

Three and a half years ago I had come to the place where past years of great guilts, resentments, anxieties, hates had seethed and eaten on me until I had an eczema condition on my hands that made them look like raw hamburger. The family doctor said there was nothing wrong physically except nerves. A skin specialist said the same. I saw a minister and he introduced me to Christ and I surrendered myself to Him. Went to bed that night and slept the first decent night's sleep for years. Next morning all the knots, butterflies, and cement slabs I'd carried were gone. I didn't use any medicine on my hands and in a few days they began to heal and became well. Then came a period of rebellion and my hands broke out again. I straightened that out, surrendered it to God, and now I've caught my poise and I'm well.

A minister was in the hospital with a bad heart attack. He was resentful of everything and everybody—bawled everybody out, including nurses, doctors, and the chaplain. The basis of his condition was a conflict with the church secretary, who had been at the church for many years. She bossed everybody and everything. He couldn't move without her approval. This tension had brought on his heart attack. He will never be a well man until he surrenders that tense, anxious self to God. Only God can lift him out of that descending spiral. His religion did not include surrender so it had to include an upset heart and an unhappy person. Either we surrender to God, or we surrender to unhappiness and disease.

Dear Father God, myself in my hands is a problem and a pain, but myself in Thy hands is a possibility and a power. So I turn over to Thee all my problems—and the self, which is the greatest problem of all. Amen.

AFFIRMATION FOR THE DAY: *In the quietness of God all my abnormalities become normal.*

TENSIONS CAUSE ILLNESS

We have been looking at the fact that inner tensions cause illness of soul and body.

A mother dedicated her son to God from birth. He became a minister. But when it came to giving him up in marriage she said she couldn't. She could give him to God, but not to another woman. Her love was eros—possessive love. She became bedridden with arthritis. Then her son talked with her and got her to see that she must surrender him completely, not only to God but to marriage. The mother did so. She became a changed woman and got up from her bed, free from tension and hence free from arthritis.

Here is a letter:

Several doctors diagnosed my physical condition as a serious illness and confined me to my bed for a long time. I was placed in the hospital with what the doctors called "nervous exhaustion" and a few other things. For several weeks the nurses would bring me sleeping pills and sedatives which had no effect. I don't think I would have ever recovered if I hadn't read and absorbed your book *Abundant Living*. By reading this book I saw that my real illness was fear and the tension that came from it. After reading portions of the book I would take the sedatives and the sleeping pills that the nurse would bring and hide them under the pillow or throw them under the bed. For after reading a portion I would have no trouble in falling off to sleep. The nurse found several of these pills and gave me a good bawling out, but I told her that I had found something much more powerful for the rest and peace of mind which I needed.

Sometimes the tension comes from a buried guilt. A German girl married a major of the United States army. She felt inferior as she knew little of the English language. But deeper down was a guilt—a buried guilt. She had had a baby at the age of eighteen under the Nazi regime when the Nazis wanted babies. She was afraid to tell her husband and, consequently, had a nervous breakdown. But when she brought it all up and told a chaplain and buried it in the love of God, she was free and well and whole. The tension was gone.

Dear Jesus, my Lord, I know there is no place where my tensions can be dissolved save in Thy love. Let that love absolve my guilts and take away my tensions as I expose everything to Thee. Amen.

AFFIRMATION FOR THE DAY: *I will have no home-grown illnesses, the result of my tensions.*

DAY-BY-DAY THINGS WHICH CAUSE TENSIONS

We have been noting the tensions that come from a deep-buried fact—a kind of life tension. We have seen that they can be released by self-surrender—not merely the surrender of the tension, but of the person who is behind the tension and probably causing it.

But what about the things that arise day by day and cause tensions? What about the daily problems and situations and people we meet and the pressures upon us? How do we meet them? Same way: Surrender them to God as they come up. And ask for and listen for guidance about that particular thing. Jesus said that a man who has bathed does not need to bathe again, except for his feet. The daily and hourly contact with the dust upon sandaled feet made continuous washing of the feet necessary. Some of us have been washed clean of basic tensions. There are no fundamental and deep-seated conflicts within us. We are washed clean of all that by self-surrender. But the daily conflicts with problems and persons make a daily surrender necessary—the feet have to be continuously cleansed.

Jesus was fundamentally at peace with God—there were no areas of conflict between Him and the Father. Hence no daily self-surrender was necessary. It was a life fact. But He got into situations that had to be surrendered to God before He emerged in full peace. At three places he was "troubled." One was the coming of the Greeks, apparently to invite Him to come to Athens and be their honored teacher, and thus he would bypass the approaching tragedy at Jerusalem; it was Athens without a cross, or Jerusalem with a cross. He said: "Now is my soul troubled. And what shall I say, 'Father, save me from this hour?' No, for this purpose I have come to this hour. Father, glorify thy name. . . . And I, when I am lifted up from the earth, will draw all men to myself" (John 12:27-28, 32). He surrendered His will on that issue, decided to go to Jerusalem, not Athens. The tension let down. He was at peace. Within a few moments he regained His poise. Surrender was the answer.

O Father, day by day as I face issue after issue, problem after problem, give me the grace to surrender everything to Thee without question and without reservation. For Thy will is our highest interest, always and everywhere. In Jesus' name. Amen.

AFFIRMATION FOR THE DAY: *My technique: Surrender of each problem into the hands of God as it arises.*

SURRENDER IS A CATHARSIS

We looked yesterday at one of the three crises in which Jesus was at tension. The second one was in Gethsemane, where having surrendered to the cross at the coming of the Greeks, He found the issue arising again: If He should go on to the cross, wouldn't He cause the Jewish leaders and people to take sides and thus arouse them to greater evil? He who came to save men from sin was apparently arousing men to greater sin by going on. Should He do it? "Not my will, but thine, be done," was the decision. The issue was surrendered. The tension of the bloody drops of sweat let down. He was at peace: "Rise, let us be going"—be going to meet the cross.

At the cross the final surrender came. "My God, my God, why hast thou forsaken me?"—the cry of dereliction. But again surrender brought Him through: "Father, forgive them," and "Into thy hands I commit my spirit." He died with that peaceful prayer upon His lips.

At each crisis there was one strategy and only one—surrender. Is that the strategy for us? Yes, surrender and obedience. I was awake at night with a heavy burden upon me. I have learned to turn the wakeful period at night into a listening post. I ask the Father if He has anything to say to me? And in this instance He said, "Yes, I automatically take upon Myself everything that falls on you. My love does that. So I've got your burden. There is no reason for both of us to carry it. I can do it better than you. So you release it to Me." I did, and fell asleep. And when daylight came He and I solved it together—I supplied willingness and He supplied power.

Surrender is a catharsis. Instead of "blowing your top" to get rid of the tension, as is sometimes advised by people who don't have any other remedy, you surrender it to God. The blowing-the-top method is only a temporary release of tension. Resentments pile up again and another blowup is necessary. The unsurrendered self is still there—the cause of the tension.

Blessed, Blessed Jesus, Thou hast shown us The Way. Help us to take the way of surrender in every situation, big and little. And then help us to cooperate with Thee after the surrender. For in cooperating with Thee, I'm working out my highest interests—always.

AFFIRMATION FOR THE DAY: *No dodging of problems, no suppressing into the subconsious, but surrendering them.*

"AN HOUR IS PAR"

Before we leave the discussion of freedom from tensions, let it be said that it is a mark of maturity to gain quick release from tension. The immature person recovers slowly from shocks and griefs that cause tension. In a really mature person an hour should be par. Within an hour we should be able to get it off our hands into the hands of God by surrender. Play the game of "An Hour Is Par" and see if you can foreshorten the hands of God. "Father, into Thy hands I commend my problem," should be the immediate reaction of a mature person.

A story is told of a woman who caught the train just as it was about to pull out. She was standing in the aisle with her suitcase in her hand, all excited and breathless. The conductor came along and said: "Madam, put down your suitcase. We can carry that too." If God has us He has all our burdens too. Then release them to Him as fast as they come up. Paul says: "Do not let the sun go down on your anger"—don't take resentments and burdens to bed with you.

On a college campus in the South there is a fresh-made grave open near the path where students and professors can throw in their idle gossip as they go by. On another college campus is a little black-painted monument to an "Octopus Club," which voluntarily voted to die because it had degenerated. As we stood around a grave made for the purpose of throwing in our tensions and fears and resentments, one woman said: "If I threw in all I need to throw in, I'd have to have a truck."

Get into the habit of burying your tensions in the love of God—at once! Roy L. Smith was lying awake struggling with a problem that had become a tension when God said to him: "You and I are in partnership. You take the day shift and I'll take the night shift. I'm taking over; you go to sleep."

Within an hour we should be able to turn over to God all our tensions, all our frustrations and blockings, and find a way out through Him.

O Father, help me to surrender to Thy timing. May I say: "My times are in thy hand." For Thy timing is always perfect. Thou dost not only work out my problems for me but Thou dost do it in perfect timing. I thank Thee. Amen.

AFFIRMATION FOR THE DAY: *Not lagging behind God, nor running ahead of God, but walking with Him.*

253

"NO GLOOM IN LOVE"

We have seen that "there is no fear in love," and now we note: "There is no gloom in love."

In the list of the fruit of the Spirit in Gal. 5:22, it is no mere chance that the order is: "Love, joy." Joy comes after love. When there is love there is joy and where there is no love there is no joy.

But this is true provided the love is agape and not eros. You can have a joyless eros, for eros is acquisitive love, and if you love with eros love and do not get the object of your desire you may be quite unhappy. Said a young woman: "I love that man and if I can't get him I will be very unhappy." She did not get him and landed in a mental institution. She loved with the wrong kind of love. Had she loved him with agape love she would have surrendered him to God and said: "If it is the best for him to have me, or if it is the best for him not to have me, in either case I love him so much that I want his highest interest." Then she would have been at peace. And she would probably have got the man! For a woman like that is worth having!

Agape love is always joyous, for agape love is a self-giving love. And it is always "more blessed to give than to receive." Alfred Adler, the famous psychiatrist, said: "I suppose that all the ills of human personality can be traced back to not understanding the meaning of the phrase: 'It is more blessed to give than to receive.' " Not only do personalities become disrupted by not understanding the meaning of that phrase, but homes are unhappy for the same reason. It is a fact that ninety percent of unhappy marriages are due to the fact that one or the other of the partners is immature, sometimes both. They want to receive rather than give. One man went into debt to get his wife this, that, and the other thing. The marriage went on the rocks. He tried to buy her love and she had a love that depended on what she got. In contrast, "Mary" writes: "I don't care what kind of letters I get, but I want to send only letters that lift and inspire." No wonder she is radiant with joy!

O Father, help me to love Thee one hundred percent for nothing. I love Thee because Thou hast first loved me and Thou hast created agape within me. And let me think agape, live agape, and pour out agape to everybody regardless.

AFFIRMATION FOR THE DAY: *I am a "son of joy"—my chief characteristic shall be joy.*

"LETTERS THAT LIFT AND INSPIRE"

We ended yesterday with the words of "Mary," who said: "I don't care what kind of letters I get, but I want to send only letters that lift and inspire." That same "Mary" was treated very shabbily by another person, and she writes: "I wrote him a Jesus letter and I am so happy." A "Jesus letter" and happiness are the same!

"Mary" had a manuscript sent back from a publishing house and she wrote: "Weren't they lovely to read it and spend so much time over it? Whether it is published or not really doesn't matter. The fact that I've lived through these things really does matter."

"Mary" sat in an airport in the early morning hours and looked at two sleepy little girls. She began throwing kisses at the little girls, and they began to throw them back in reply. Soon they had forgotten all about loss of sleep. They were awake and laughing and gay—awakened by agape.

In contrast to this was the cartoon of a woman standing in a doctor's office and saying to the doctor: "Doctor, this is terrible—you going off on your vacation and leaving me all alone with my ingrown toenail." She had not only an ingrown toenail, she had an ingrown love. And she was a very unhappy person as a result.

For fifteen years or more I tried to persuade an intelligent woman to get interested in something other than her own inner conflicts and consequent unhappiness. Each time when she was about to become outgoing she would say that there was one more layer that must be brought up and dealt with. She put in fifteen years of self-centered misery. Then finally her money gave out and she was forced to work—became a receptionist in an institution. Had to be interested in other people and their troubles. The change! She was happy! Because creative.

A woman said to me: "People are interested in happiness. Tell them how to be happy." The only recipe I have for happiness is this: "Forget your own happiness. Go out to make someone else happy, and happiness will see you out." In that case you'll have joy which is deeper than happiness.

O Jesus, it was said of Thee that Thou wast "anointed . . . with the oil of gladness beyond thy comrades." And we know why. Thou didst give Thyself with utter abandon to making other people glad. Teach me Thy secret. Amen.

AFFIRMATION FOR THE DAY: *My face shall be a ten-minutes-to-two face, not a twenty-minutes-to-four.*

"JOY IS THE CHRISTIAN WORD"

Yesterday we said that there is something deeper than happiness, and that is joy. Happiness comes from happenings, but joy may be within in spite of happenings. "Happiness" is the world's word; "joy" is the Christian's word. The New Testament does not use the word "happiness" or promise it—it uses the word "joy." And for a reason.

Many people are expecting happiness from following the Christian faith—God will arrange the things that happen to me so they will all add up to happiness. When the things that happen to them do not mean happiness, such people are dismayed and feel God has let them down. Why should this happen to me? They expect to be protected from happenings that make them unhappy. This is a false view and leads to a lot of disillusionment. For the Christian is not necessarily protected from things that make people unhappy. Was Jesus protected from happenings that make people unhappy? Was Paul? Their Christian faith got them into opposition, into persecution, into death. How could a faith that has a cross at its center promise exemption from happenings that ordinarily bring unhappiness? Then what is the answer? The Christian faith offers joy in the midst of happenings which make people without that faith unhappy. When the Christian doesn't find joy on account of his happenings, he can always find joy in spite of them.

The Christian is taught not merely to accept limitations, but to use them. Take what you have and make something out of it. You must learn to live in spite of. Carlyle once said: "You may hear it said of me that I am cross-grained and disagreeable. Dinna believe it. Only let me have my own way exactly in everything with all about me precisely as I wish, and a sunnier or pleasanter creature does not exist." But Carlyle was being satirical here. We must make our happiness not dependent upon happenings. We can make everything into something else—can *use* everything.

O Jesus, who for the joy that was set before Thee endured the cross—yes and more, used the cross for redemption—teach me the secret of Thy joy. For Thy joy is a joy won out of the heart of pain. Give me that rugged joy. Amen.

AFFIRMATION FOR THE DAY: *I always have an open door, no matter what happens: Joy in spite of!*

EVERYTHING FURTHERED HIM

Christian joy, we have said, is an incorrigible joy, not dependent upon happenings but upon relationships with God which persist unchanged amid the change of our happenings. For instance, in writing this portion on joy, I was struck by a happening that for the moment knocked the breath out of me. And the Father said as I surrendered it to Him: "I cannot approve of what has happened, but if you'll cooperate with me, we will rescue some good out of it." Peace and joy settled into the jostled depths—in spite of! The King James Version says: "All things work together for good to them that love God," but not necessarily. The Revised Standard Version puts it: "We know that in everything God works for good with those who love him" (Rom. 8:28). All things do not of themselves automatically work for good—they may work for evil. But "in everything God works for good with those who love him"—He rescues out of everything something good. Note it is "*with* those who love him"—if you cooperate *with* Him, then He and you together can rescue out of the heart of every evil happening some good. That gives you a solid basis for joy—the joy of victory in every happening *in spite of*.

Paul's whole life was an illustration of rescuing some good out of every evil happening:

I want you to know, brethren, that what has happened to me has really served to advance the gospel, so that it has become known throughout the whole Praetorian guard and to all the rest that my imprisonment is for Christ; and most of the brethren have been made confident in the Lord because of my imprisonment, and are much more bold to speak the word of God without fear (Phil. 1:12-14).

This imprisonment in itself was evil—an injustice. Of itself it would not have worked together for good. It worked for good only when God and Paul rescued good out of it. The good was that the gospel was being furthered. Paul's being in jail or out of it was irrelevant—the furtherance of the gospel was his central purpose.

O Jesus, Thou hast the secret of transforming everything. In Thee everything is opportunity. Help me to find opportunity in opposition—an opportunity to show Thy Spirit. For Thy Spirit is the key that opens everything, everywhere. Help me to show it. Amen.

AFFIRMATION FOR THE DAY: *God and I will rescue out of every happening something good—it is there.*

"MATTER OF CHARACTER
RATHER THAN CIRCUMSTANCE"

A man has invented a house with what he calls a "push-button happiness" in it. You push a button, and the humidity changes, the smells are abolished, and every unpleasant thing is counteracted. So you'll be happy with your wife, for your environment is perfect! Will you? I saw a palace of a home where the environment was perfect. But the husband lived in one end of the house and the wife in the other, and they seldom spoke. The unhappiness was within.

India's "River of Sorrow," Damodar River, has been the source of floods and devastation. Now dams have been put in. It is the source of flood control, electrification, and canals for irrigation. The "River of Sorrow" has become a "River of Joy."

A lady writes: "Six months ago my husband passed away and I felt lost and afraid to face life. After hearing you on the radio yesterday morning, I awakened with power in my soul this morning to face life—or 'walk up to it,' as you put it."

Mary Riding, wife of a pastor, is perfectly helpless from arthritis; she is blind and can only use two fingers to turn on the radio. If she has joy it is no push-button joy. Her room is the confessional of the city. People can tell things to her they can't tell anyone else, for she can't see who they are! She collects bells and gives a talk on bells, getting someone to ring them as she talks. She is radiantly happy and her life rings the bell with everyone with whom she comes in contact. Her husband's most effective sermon is entitled "Singing in the Rain."

Buddha said to the herdsman Dhaniya: "I am free from anger, free from stubbornness. My house has no cover, but the fire of passion is extinguished—then rain if thou wilt, O Sky." That phrase, "then rain if thou wilt, O Sky," is beautiful, but it is the statement of resignation. But the Christian doesn't resign himself to things—he rejoices in everything. He sings in the rain!

O Father, teach me to sing in the rain. Teach me to sing when there is nothing to sing about save the joy of having Thee. And that is enough to make my heart sing forever. For Thou, and Thou alone, art the fountain of my joy. And Thy joy is joy. I thank Thee. Amen.

AFFIRMATION FOR THE DAY: *My heart is at peace, and my all belongs to Him, so rain if thou wilt, O Sky!*

"HALLELUJAH CHORUS" AT A FUNERAL

Henry Ward Beecher once said: "Blessed are the happy-hearted, for they bless everybody." And the happy-hearted can be the unhappily circumstanced. A man without legs was preaching from a wheelchair in India and was joyous. When someone asked him about his handicap he replied: "A little thing like my handicap has nothing to do with my joy—it's within."

A Welsh miner was badly mutilated in a mine cave-in. He had to have his leg amputated hurriedly when he was taken to the surface. No anesthetic was available. The pain was excruciating. In the midst of it he began to hum a Welsh tune. The miners gathered around him, caught up the tune, and the operation was performed to the music of singing miners. That is a sturdy joy—the joy of in-spite-of!

An electric lamp, unlighted, fell off my table. In falling the lamp was lighted and there it lay amid the wreckage—alight! If catastrophes make wreckage they can also set us alight within. Beethoven was stone deaf and yet wrote his most wonderful music unable to hear a note of it! The fall set him alight! Paul, shut up in prison, couldn't preach, and it was a good thing, for if he had been free to preach, his sermons would have been lost. But bound in prison he wrote his immortal letters upon which the ages have lived and will live. Shut up he walks the earth free—free to bless and guide and save. When Mrs. Underwood, a devoted missionary, was shot by a Korean Communist, I attended the funeral in Seoul, and at the funeral the "Hallelujah Chorus" was sung. That's that place to sing the "Hallelujah Chorus"—at a funeral! I heard it sung in the cement basement of a burned-out school in Japan. Everything was gone except that cement basement. It might have been a Wailing Wall—it was the place of exquisite music.

"Some people complain that roses have thorns; I'm grateful that thorns have roses." The Christian sees the roses and rejoices, and some see the thorns and complain. The Christian transforms everything because agape love has transformed him.

O Christ my Lord, I thank Thee that Thou didst see the saint in the harlot and the publican and Thou didst call out the saint by Thy creative love. Give me the power to see and to create what I see. But only as I am possessed with agape can I do it. In Thy name. Amen.

AFFIRMATION FOR THE DAY: *I belong to "the happy-hearted," so I shall bless everyone I touch today.*

"NO NEGATIVISM IN LOVE"

A real sign of maturity is freedom from negativism and an accentuation of the positive attitudes. "There is no negativism in love." Love is at the basis of creation. God created free beings, for it is the very nature of love to create. Parents create through love. They want children upon whom they can lavish their love. Where there is no love, or little love, there creative attitudes and impulses are absent. And negative attitudes and impulses take their place. The person himself becomes negative.

Prejudice has been defined in this way: "You are down on whatever you are not up on." Yesterday a food expert said of a certain Government board: "They seem to have a motto on their walls: 'Everything that is new is wicked, and everything that is old is sacred.'" They live in a state of *no!*

When Sir Francis Drake discovered the potato in Peru and brought it to Scotland, the people wouldn't use it since it was not mentioned in the Bible! When streetlamps were introduced in Boston, ministers preached against them, saying: "If God had intended this He would have made the sun brighter and the moon more brilliant." Anesthetics were opposed by ministers who said that pain is the result of sin and ordained by God and should not be interfered with. Negativism would have blocked all progress if possible.

One of the most beautiful passages in the New Testament is this: "The divine 'yes' has at last sounded in him" (II Cor. 1:20 Moffatt). "For all the promises of God find their Yes in him" (RSV). Jesus is the Divine Yes—He affirms life, affirms personality, affirms joy, affirms progress, affirms everything that is good and God-created. When you are in Him you are positive, hopeful, creative—you are a yes. You believe belief out of the beliefless, faith faith out of the faithless, and love love out of the loveless. You are the divine positive with an impact upon the human negative. Sin is negative—it is "missing the mark"; goodness is positive with all Reality behind it.

O Father, I would be linked to Thee so that Thy creation can continue in me. I would be a walking expression of Thy creative activity. May the divine yes sound in me continually. May I be creative in all I think and do and say, for I'm surrendered to the creative God. Amen.

AFFIRMATION FOR THE DAY: *The divine yes will work in me today, so I shall belong to the divine positive.*

"DO NOT LOOK DISMAL"

We are meditating on this statement: "There is no negativism in love." Recently a woman consulted me as to why she couldn't hold a job. She was an efficient stenographer and typist, but she lost job after job. It was soon apparent that in spite of her efficiency she was basically critical and negative. For this reason she was not wanted. Had she taken the attitude of love and appreciation, people would have been changed by her positive spirit.

On a door in Canada was this sign:

> Smile and the world smiles with you,
> Kick and you kick alone;
> For a pleasant smile will let you in,
> Where the kicker is never known.

A smile is a universal language, easily understood and universally loved. Jesus said: "Do not look dismal" (Matt. 6:16). And that is as much a command as "Thou shalt love," for a smiling face is love's frontage. Dr. Walter C. Alvarez said: "I would turn down all candidates for a medical training who obviously did not like people." I would certainly make the same recommendation for the ministry—no one should enter the ministry who does not obviously like people. For you cannot change people unless you believe in people—believe in them in spite of what they are. You see in them what they become.

Will Rogers, beloved by his countrymen, said: "I've never seen a man I didn't like." He set himself to like, and under that attitude people became likable. He produced what he saw. I said to a Japanese college president as I pointed to a twisted root hanging on the wall: "You Japanese are wonderful. You see beauty in an ugly root like that." And he replied: "Is that root ugly?" His eye for beauty had produced beauty out of ugliness.

Jesus saw the writer of a Gospel in a tax collector and produced it; a saint in a Magdalene and produced it.

O Jesus, my Lord, Thou hast accepted me when I couldn't accept myself, loved me when I couldn't love myself. And when I cannot depend on my own faith I can depend on Thy faith in me. Thy love puts back my shoulders and makes me walk with sure tread. Amen.

AFFIRMATION FOR THE DAY: *"In the mud and scum of things, there's something that always, always sings."*

"THE TRUE LIGHT IS ALREADY SHINING"

John, in this Epistle, was full of love, and hence full of faith and full of the positive, "because the darkness is passing away and the true light is already shining" (I John 2:8). And in saying this he helped the passing of that darkness. His whole Epistle, throbbing with love and hope, has pushed back the darkness by its very love and hope. The calamity howlers help to produce the calamity they howl. The critical help to produce the things they criticize.

John tells of his faith in children, in young men, in fathers: "I write to you, children, because you know the Father. I write to you, fathers, because you know him who is from the beginning. I write to you, young men, because you are strong, and the word of God abides in you, and you have overcome the evil one" (2:13-14). This was a sign of real maturity—a positive and constructive interest in and faith in all ages—children, young men, fathers. John was probably past ninety when he wrote that. His love was so mature that it embraced all ages. Very often we show our immaturity by being interested only in our own age group. He was suffering neither from hardening of the arteries nor hardening of the categories. He believed in youth: "You are strong, and the word of God abides in you"—and produced what he believed in.

If we take negative attitudes we produce the negative. A schoolteacher said to her class of small children: "I'm leaving the room. Now don't put beans in your ears while I am gone." Of course, they all had beans in their ears when she returned. Hugo Münsterberg used to tell his students at Harvard, according to R. M. Veh, that anyone could turn dishwater into molten gold if he would just stir it for fifteen minutes while taking care that the word "hippopotamus" never came into his mind. The more you try to forget it the more you remember it! Negativism of thought and love defeats itself. As you think negative you become negative—the payoff is the person.

When you think and act positively you become positive—again the payoff is in the person. You become what you think and do.

O Jesus, help me to live in a state of yesness—yesness to Thee and yesness to life. Help me to embrace everything today as opportunity. In Thee everything is opportunity. Help me then to look not for opposition, but for opportunity. In Thy name. Amen.

AFFIRMATION FOR THE DAY: *All things belong to me—all teachers, all facts, all time—for I belong to Christ.*

CHANGE THE CLIMATE!

The results of negative thinking and of active thinking are obvious. A girl had a suppressed hatred for her father-in-law, for he was domineering. The hatred produced a complex. The pagan psychiatrist to whom she went told her to go out and "tell everybody to go to h_____." She did, beginning with her father-in-law. Result? A momentary letting off of steam and permanent consequences in human relations. She disrupted everything she touched. Two hates never made a love affair. Your blowing off steam results in the other person's doing likewise. Like produces like. If that psychiatrist had known the Christian answer—unquenchable love—the girl would have been healed, and she would probably have healed the relation with her father-in-law.

There was an ice jam above the Niagara Falls. Workmen tried dynamiting it. But it was of no use. Then the climate changed, a thaw came, and the jam was melted away effortlessly. Change a climate with a changed spirit, and problems are not so much solved as they are dissolved. They melt away.

Shortly after the invention of fluorescent light, the new lighting system was introduced in a certain office in Kansas City. The light left a ghostly color on everyone's face. Soon the employees began to tell one another how unwell and sickly the other one looked. And soon there was an epidemic of illnesses among the employees. The management suspected the cause and had the lighting system changed. The illnesses stopped.

A nurse had tuberculosis and was in a sanatorium. Her mother had written to her: "Whom the Lord loveth he chasteneth." But the nurse did not feel that her illness was punishment. She kept repeating to herself "that the works of God might be made manifest in him"—a verse from the statement of Jesus concerning the man born blind: "It was not that this man sinned, or his parents, but that the works of God might be made manifest in him." She took the illness not as punishment but as opportunity and became well. She is now married and happy and useful. She lived on the positive.

O Strong Christ, give me Thy positive strength. For if I look at my weakness I shall become weak. But if I see Thy strength I'll become strong. For I become what I look at. Help me to look at Thy loving strength that I may be lovingly strong. Amen.

AFFIRMATION FOR THE DAY: *I am strong in the strength of Christ, loving in the love of Christ.*

A FOOD TEST

We are meditating on the statement "There is no negativism in love." Not that love never says no! It does. But it doesn't stop at no! It says no to the little in order to say yes to the big. Negativism ends with the negative; positive love begins with the negative and ends with the glorious, positive creative. It is finally a yes!

The person who is negative narrows his interests, his likes, his outlook, his spirit. A chart has been devised to test whether one is a food neurotic. David Harold Fink, psychiatrist, has prepared a food test: watermelon, mushroom soup, fried eggs, lima beans, tomato juice, rice pudding, sour cream, turkey, sausage, currants, rhubarb, asparagus, cabbage, oatmeal, milk, veal, cheese, lamb, coffee, plums. You score five points for each food you dislike. If you score only five, you are a well-adjusted person; if ten or fifteen, average. If twenty-five, then hypercritical; and if forty or more, lacking in emotional stability. Fink says: "Professor Wallen's discovery actually amounts to a sound and ingenious application of a well-established psychological principle: With the development of neurosis the individual's viewpoint becomes exceedingly narrow; as the condition progresses, more and more things are viewed with active distaste—including the food he eats."

Here the Christian principle of agape love comes into its own. For agape love is expansive. It takes in more and more people and more and more things. Earlier I mentioned my own case: When I arose from my knees after seeing forgiveness in His eye and knew I was reconciled to God through grace, I felt as though I could put my arms around the world and share this with everybody. Five minutes before, I was wrapped up in myself and my own problems; five minutes later I was released from my problems and wanted to love everybody into what I had found. The process of Christianizing a personality is the process of enlarging his interest and his loves. In the really mature Christian personality there is concern for and even love for enemies. And this love knows no boundaries of race, or class, or color, or creed.

O Father God, my heart is bowed in deepest gratitude for Thy amazing agape. It humbles me and raises me to the highest heaven of glory—now. And gives me the impulse to share this with the least, the last, and the lost. I thank Thee. Amen.

AFFIRMATION FOR THE DAY: *I shall find something in every person and every situation which I shall like today.*

"LOVE—MY REASON FOR LIVING"

We are looking at the fact that God's agape love in Christ creates an ever-expanding love and interest in us. Makes us affirmative on wider and wider scales.

Here is the experience of "Mary"—the most radiant Christian I've ever known: "Since August 13th I take advantage of every opportunity that comes. [On that date she made her full surrender and received an infilling with the Spirit.] Can't say no anymore. Only yes to everything. In return life says yes to me in everything. You don't get paid in Christ, you get repaid." I mentioned Sister Lila, the Greek, who said the same thing. She is filled with the purest agape for strangers, for lepers, for people of all classes and races. She said: "Be careful what you ask me to do, for I'll say, yes. I am living in a state of yesness to God." And you *were* careful about what you suggested to her to do, for you knew she was ready to go anywhere, try anything that was right. You might think that such a person is open to suggestions of evil. Oh no, you simply couldn't suggest any evil to her. The agape within her carried a negative quality in the very positiveness of her love. "Perfect love casts out fear," and it casts out all other evils as well.

"Mary" gave this as her philosophy of life: "To make love my reason for living." Say that to yourself again and again and see what happens to you. No deeper reason for living is possible.

This is the statement of a simple, radiant soul. Listen to what the profound scholar Bishop Westcott says: "The whole aim of the Gospel is the creation and strengthening of love. To this Christ's life of sacrifice pointed from first to last." The whole end of the Christian discipline is to create a positive, loving person.

The antithesis of love is not always hate—it may be just indifference. The priest and the Levite didn't do anything positively evil in the story of the Good Samaritan—they just passed by on the other side.

In India a missionary said of her gardener: "He's good at digging but not at growing." A good many people are good at getting rid of weeds, but not good in producing worth.

Dear God and Father, make me skillful in bringing out the good in everybody and everything. Give me eyes to see the good, and love to produce the good. And help me to nurture it in everything I touch today. In Jesus' name. Amen.

AFFIRMATION FOR THE DAY: *I belong to growth and construction, not to grouch and destruction.*

"A SAINT HAS QUIT WORRYING ABOUT HIMSELF"

We continue to emphasize that love is free from negativism. Jesus had to say to Peter: "Get behind me, Satan! You are a hindrance to me; for you are not on the side of God, but of men." Yet the following chapter in Mark tells of His taking Peter to the mount of transfiguration to let him see His glory. Ended in positive!

A plain-featured young woman made up her mind to be the kindliest and most loving person in her group. And she was. And was greatly loved. She centered on positive love and kindness to others and grew beautiful in her plainness.

At a time when negative criticism of the Bible was rife among liberal university professors, some of that type at the University of Chicago wrote to Daniel Kirkwood, famous astronomer of Indiana, often called "The Kepler of the West," hoping to get a statement from such a famous source so they could hang his statement to their belts: "What do you think of Christ and the Bible?" and the famous astronomer replied: "I believe that Jesus Christ is my Savior and the Bible is the book that tells me of Him." Long after their skepticism has died, his simple but profoundly positive statement will live on.

Henry Fawcett, brilliant student at Cambridge, lost his eyesight in a hunting accident. He bitterly resented his blindness. A former instructor wrote him a letter: "It must be our own fault if such things are without alleviation. Give up your mind to meet the evil in the worst form it can assume. It will lose half its terrors if regarded steadfastly in the face." Fawcett turned from the negative to the positive. He became a professor of economics at Cambridge University, then postmaster general of England, and a member of the British Cabinet. The negative creates nothing; the positive creates everything. And the agape of God says: "Behold, I make all things new." And it does!

O God of the Loving Heart, help me to make all things new—all things that I touch today. Help me to make the ugly beautiful, the ignoble noble, and the disheartened courageous. Love me into loving, and may I love others into loving. Amen.

AFFIRMATION FOR THE DAY: *I will make my impediments into instruments, my calvaries into Easter mornings.*

"THERE IS NO SELF-SEEKING IN LOVE"

We turn this week to consider: "There is no self-seeking in love." This seems to be the most difficult of all Christian demands upon human nature. This was expressed by a leading businessman in a group after I had talked on what the Christian gospel demands of us: "Then there is no place in Christianity for the successful man of affairs? He must turn his back on himself, his business, on life itself, and be a canceled nonentity."

The question of what happens to the self—the essential person in a religious system—is of the greatest importance. For it is the one thing, and the only thing, we own. Does Christianity cancel the self? Must the man who follows it turn his back on himself, his business, life itself? And does he become a nonentity?

That is the greatest twist ever given to the Christian demand. And if it were true we couldn't take it. For the Christian answer would be a no! And you cannot live on a no; you have to live on a yes.

The Christian demand seems to be a central no, to the self. "I am crucified . . . ," says Paul (Gal. 2:20 KJV). The essential self is crucified. What could be more decisive? But note he added two words: "I am crucified with Christ." Those two words make all the difference. If you make yourself the center of yourself, if you seek your own, if you look after Number One, as society bids you to do, if you are, in short, a self-centered person, then do you escape crucifixion? Not at all. You run straight into it. You will be crucified upon the cross of your own frustrations, conflicts, and unhappiness. Every self-centered person is unhappy and frustrated, even though he is outwardly successful. Why? Because he has made himself God. And the commandment is: "You shall have no other gods before me." He breaks that commandment and is broken by it—inwardly.

The Christian answer is in the two words: "I am crucified *with Christ.*" How was Christ crucified? Deliberately and by His own choice: "I lay down my life." The Divine Agape loved men enough to die for them. Lost His life—and found it!

O Divine Redeemer, we thank Thee for showing us the way—the way of agape that gives its all and then finds its all. If we miss the way of agape we miss the way to live. We would live and live abundantly. Show us. Amen.

AFFIRMATION FOR THE DAY: *The biggest question in life: Who shall own my life?*

SELF-REALIZATION THROUGH SELF-RENUNCIATION

We saw yesterday that the crucifixion we undergo in obeying the Christian way is "with Christ." His crucifixion was not a negation of Himself, but a consecration of Himself to death for the sake of others. "He . . . became obedient unto death, even death on a cross." There He hit bottom in self-giving. Then the upturn: "Therefore God has highly exalted him and bestowed on him the name which is above every name." His self was renounced and realized through love.

The Christian way, then, is self-realization through self-renunciation, and then self-dedication to others in agape. It is in the agape that the self is realized. If the love is eros the self is not realized, for eros is acquisitive love. This makes the self the center. Such love has to be redeemed. Eros is unconverted agape.

Not what you do, but why you do it, is important. Two persons may do the same thing—the action of one may be good, and the other bad, for the motive behind each deed is different. Two people may love God, but for entirely different motives. Meister Eckhart long ago condemned those who love God "as they love their cow—for the milk and cheese and profit it brings them."

"I love my Daddy; he gives me pennies everyday," said a little boy, revealing his eros love. We smile at the little fellow's basis of love and yet a great deal of our love for God is of the same order. We love God because He gives us health, success, pleasant surroundings here, and heaven hereafter. No wonder a Muslim saint was seen going along with a lighted torch in one hand and a pitcher of water in the other, and when she was asked why, she replied: "I want to burn up heaven and I want to put out the fires of hell so people will love God for God." The self is not lost in this loving of God for this, that, and the other. Therefore it is never found. Eros wants something in return and gets nothing—nothing but frustration. Agape wants nothing and gets everything.

O Jesus, when we lose ourselves in love to others we are doing the thing for which we are made. So in fulfilling Thy purpose we are fulfilling that for which we are made. Then help us to give way to agape and give out agape with no reservations. Amen.

AFFIRMATION FOR THE DAY: *Center yourself on yourself and you won't like yourself, nor will anyone else.*

"LOVE SEEKETH NOT ITS OWN"

Paul says: "Love . . . seeketh not its own." Love there is agape. Eros love does seek "its own" and therefore cannot be fitted into the Christian system. Agape, by its very nature, is Christian.

When the Scripture says: "And do you seek great things for yourself? Seek them not." The emphasis is "for yourself." It is legitimate and right and our privilege to seek great things for others. But an interesting and important thing happens: When you seek great things for others, great things come back to you. You lose your life and find it again.

Jesus said: "Do not lay up for yourself treasures on earth." Many quote that: "Do not lay up treasures on earth." But the emphasis is "for yourselves." Money consecrated to human need is money creative.

In Korea a big bell was to be cast which, the Koreans thought, would offer prayer for the people. The people gave money, gold, silver, and bronze to make the bell. But when they cast the bell it would not hold together—it fell apart. It lacked inner cohesion. It was revealed that only a human sacrifice would hold it together. A beautiful girl offered herself. She threw herself into the molten metal and then the bell held together and now tolls for the people. Our work, our very selves, will not hold together unless there is a self-surrender at the basis of all. When the self is thrown in, then everything coheres. And the music of our lives has a tone that is missing otherwise. Without the cross Jesus would have been a great and honored teacher, but the cross turns good views into Good News. And it rings through the ages.

Peter said: "Lo, we have left everything and followed you. What then shall we have?" (Matt. 19:27). In Luke: "Lo, we have left our homes and followed you" (18:28). The second statement is nearer the facts: They had left their "homes," but not "everything." They hadn't left themselves! They disputed on the way as to which of them should be greatest. The self was still there and seeking "its own." Their love was eros: "What shall we get?" Jesus was not followed for Jesus, but for what they got out of following Jesus.

O Jesus, let me follow Thee out of pure agape. Thou art my heaven—I want no other. Any other heaven would be thrown in—an extra. In Thy presence is fullness of joy and fullness of everything. Thou art my everything. I thank Thee. Amen.

AFFIRMATION FOR THE DAY: *Psychiatrist: It is a million chances to one that the self-centered will be unpopular.*

"A MUTUAL SELF-SURRENDER"

A psychiatrist was discussing psychiatry and religion. He said some interesting and important things: "The basis of emotional disturbance is anger. The anger may show itself in pains and in throwing things around, but the basis is anger." "Most women resent their sex." "Most women have a neurotic need when they begin to smoke." "To want something is normal; to need something is neurotic." "The necessity of being independent of each other in real love." In regard to the last statement I raised this question: Can you be independent of each other in real love unless there has been a basic self-surrender to each other? Would not independence of each other result in a struggle for independence on the part of each, in other words, in a pulling apart? But if there is a mutual and basic self-surrender, then independence is freely and gladly given to each other, for at the basis of that independence is self-surrender.

Psychiatry, without the Christian insight of self-surrender, was proclaiming a dangerous half-truth in suggesting that independence is necessary in true love. Self-surrender to each other is necessary in true love, and a mutual giving of independence is a by-product.

The same thing can be said of psychiatry's insistence that we accept ourselves. There is a truth there. Self-rejection and self-hate are as bad as other-rejection and other-hate. We must accept ourselves. But we cannot accept ourselves if we are self-centered selves. That would mean accepting a false, festering self. You can only accept a self that is surrendered to God. Then you are on the right basis. Then you can accept yourself—in God. And you can love yourself—in God.

Anders Nygren seems to teach that there can be no self-love. But if you love God and others with agape, can you not love yourself with agape? You are to love your neighbor as yourself—both with agape. God accepts us in agape love and we should accept ourselves with agape love.

O Jesus Master, Thou hast loved me into loving and into loving myself. I couldn't love myself with any self-respect until Thy touch of love upon me made it possible to love myself. Now I have a self I can live with. I'm grateful. Amen.

AFFIRMATION FOR THE DAY: *I cannot love or accept an unsurrendered self, for it is not lovable.*

"TAKE MORE—I LOVE HIM SO"

We are considering that "there is no self-seeking in love." Note that I do not say, "There is no self-love in love." There is. But it must be agape love for ourselves, for ourselves *in* God. While there is self-love in God, there is no self-seeking. That would pervert agape into eros—a self-seeking love.

Here was a mother worrying over the possibility that some girl might come and take away her darling son, and worrying over the possibility that some young man might not come and take away her daughter. In both cases she was worrying over herself. She was primarily thinking of herself, secondarily of her children. She was loving them with the wrong love, eros love.

On the other hand, here was agape love. A boy gave his blood for his buddy. He gave the required amount. Then the doctor said: "It is finished. You may go." "No," said the boy, "take more, take more. I love him so." He was thinking of this friend, not himself—agape love.

A mother stood up in one of our Ashrams and said: "Pray for me. I have difficulty in managing my husband and my children. "Managing"—a revealing word. We did pray for her—prayed that she would cease to try to manage her husband and her children and love them for their own sakes. Then there would be no need to try to manage.

Erich Fromm, the psychiatrist, defines love: "Love is union with somebody or something outside of oneself under the condition of retaining the separateness and integrity of one's own self." And we may add, "retaining the separateness and integrity of the other self." The mother mentioned above did not fulfill the latter—she wanted to make herself dominant, to "manage" her husband and her children. She was quite immature, trying to appear mature.

When we are fully surrendered to God then we can and should love ourselves—love ourselves in God. And the self that we love is a lovable self, for it is on the right center with the right motives.

O Jesus, Thy love never wears thin. For it is agape, and always agape. Therefore we grow in the wonder of it, glory in the beauty of it, surrender to the call of it, and long to be the channel of it. At the touch of Thy agape we are at Thy feet. Amen.

AFFIRMATION FOR THE DAY: *When I surrender myself I am obeying the very law of my being, hence I'm fulfilled.*

"I AM HIS AND FOREVER"

We continue our meditation: "There is no self-seeking in love." Karen Horney, the psychiatrist, says: "The feeling of being loved, and even more of being lovable, is perhaps one of the greatest values in life." It is. But there is one emphasis left out there: "the feeling of loving." For without loving, you will not be loved and you will not be lovable. But it must not be an eros love, for eros love blocks being loved and blocks being lovable. However, agape love makes you loved and makes you lovable. But psychiatry, knowing little of agape love and viewing love as almost entirely eros love, is hesitant to put in "loving." The Christian has no such hesitation. For he sees love as agape love, therefore a safe and saving love.

"A sincere man," says the psychiatrist Jung, "knows that even his bitterest opponents, or any number of them, does not equal his worst adversary, that is, his other self, who hides within his breast." But the sincere Christian need not look on his "other" self as an adversary. For in fact he has no other self. He has surrendered his self—his one self—to God, has been unified by that surrender, and now is "controlled by the love of Christ," that is, by agape. Not that the self, surrendered to God, may not try now and then to revert to its old autonomy; but if the self is really surrendered it bounces back to its proper alignment to God.

For this surrender of the self is a once-and-for-all business, even when a daily surrender is involved. The daily surrender is not really a surrender of the self, but an unfolding of the once-and-for-all surrender. It is an application to a specific thing of a surrender once made. A friend writes of her victory: "When I said: 'I am His and forever,' it was the 'and forever' that did it." No surrender is really surrender unless it is "and forever." That takes our hands off the gift. We don't give a book to another person, at the same time holding on to one corner. We give it and we let it go—hands off. Eros still has its hand on the other corner—agape lets go of it completely.

O Jesus, I want to give, and give with agape love that is one hundred percent for nothing. No strings attached, no canceling "riders," no "ifs" or "buts"—a clear-cut and all-out surrender, given gladly and willingly, for the agape I have for Thee. Amen.

AFFIRMATION FOR THE DAY: *I do not give unless I give up; so I give up, all out, for nothing.*

"HE TOOK IT!"

Why is it that "love seeketh not her own"? The answer is simple: Love, being love, has surrendered itself and does not seek its own, because basically the self is not its own. Self-surrender is inherent in love.

A Burmese government official, who gave up his official position to become a teacher in a Christian school at a much lower salary, gave up a good deal, but not himself. In an Ashram he told of his death—death to himself. He had the black coffin made and wanted me to bury him! But he had to bury himself! He did. He said: "Now I know the difference between surrender and struggle. Now I say to everybody: 'I love you. I love you.' I used to use M—MUST, now I use W—WANT. I felt I *must* do this, I *must* do that; now I feel I *want* to do this, I *want* to do that. The M has been turned upside down—W—and that is the meaning of surrender; it turns myself upside down. And with it my world."

A wife said to her husband after her Quiet Hour in which she got guidance: "Did you ever buy something and pay for it and still not get it?" and he answered, "No, did you?" And she quickly replied, "No, but the Lord did; He bought you but He has never got you." And the husband replied very sincerely: "Well, He can have me, guts, feathers, and all." And he meant it. A new man.

An Episcopalian young woman told our Ashram group: "I heard about surrender and I began surrendering all over the place. But nothing happened. God didn't seem to take the gift of myself. But at four o'clock this morning I said to Him: 'There it is. You can take it or leave it. But I'm tired of giving it. You can do what you like.' And by jingo, He took it! If it hadn't been at such an unearthly hour and if I had been properly dressed I would have gone up and down the halls of this dormitory shouting: 'He took it! He took it!' " That would have been a sight: A shouting Episcopalian at four o'clock in the morning! But it would have been a beautiful sight of a soul released from self-preoccupation and bondage.

O Jesus, I know that in love there is no self-seeking—it is all a seeking of Thee. And then to our glad surprise we find ourselves—in Thee. Bound to Thee, I'm free—free indeed. Amen.

AFFIRMATION FOR THE DAY: *Like the seed that loses itself in the soil and finds itself in flower and fruit, so lost in God, I'm found—fruitfully found.*

"THERE IS NO PRIDE IN LOVE"

We come now to consider another phase of maturity: "There is no pride in love." That is, there is no pride in agape love. There is pride in eros love. For eros is acquisitive. Applied to the gaining of salvation it climbs the ladder, rung by rung, by its own efforts. When it reaches the topmost rung of self-effort, it is then ready for union with God. Salvation is my attainment. At the heart of that striving and of that salvation there is pride, subtle spiritual pride, the worst of all prides. In India I have seen men sitting on beds of spikes, have seen them beating their backs with chains that had knives attached to them, have seen men hang head-down over a fire swinging through the flames, have seen men sitting in a vow of silence—speechless. But all of these were where men could see them and admire them and, in many instances, give them divine honors. And they received these honors as their due. They had attained this spiritual eminence. Pride was eating at the heart of this piety. Therefore it was immature piety.

But in agape love there can be no pride. For by its very nature it produces humility, as eros by its very nature produces pride. For agape love gives without reference to the worth of the object of that love. If we take agape love it is with no sense of having a right to it, or of being worthy of it. We take it as recipients of grace. We become little children and "receive the kingdom of God." We empty our hands of all our striving, all our goodness, all our works—we receive the gift of God. And when that grace of God enters our hearts it is so unmerited, so overwhelmingly gracious, that it sends us to our knees in the deepest gratitude. By its very nature it pushes out all pride, for there is just no room for pride. The inner climate is now humility.

And you don't try to be humble in agape—you just are. For when you try to be humble you are not humble. Humility is such a delicate virtue that if you speak of it, it is gone. So you don't speak of it. It speaks itself, for in agape love you are always pointing to Another. Pardon has melted pride.

O God, our Father, how can I thank Thee enough for grace. It humbles me to the dust and puts me into the highest heaven at the same moment. Tears of sorrow for my past and tears of joy for Thy grace mingle, and the tears of joy are the last tears. Amen.

AFFIRMATION FOR THE DAY: *How can I be proud looking into the face of Humility?*

"I AM SORRY"

We are meditating on this fact: "There is no pride in love." Here was a mother who was full of resentments when she saw her daughter walk down the aisle with a Negro girl in a high school commencement procession. "Why did that have to happen to me?" It hurt her pride. The daughter said: "But, Mother, there are only four types of blood, and Negroes have all four types just as we have. She is the most popular girl in the class. I was a lucky girl to draw her." The mother talked to a very wise friend about it. And the friend suggested to the mother that she say to her daughter: "I am sorry." She hesitated, for it meant surrendering all her pride, but finally she did it. When she did it, he daughter replied: "Oh, Mother, that is wonderful." And the girl, who had always hesitated and even refused to join the church, did so—did so because the breaking down of her mother's pride broke down her opposition.

I saw in a Chinese rubber association club in Malaya a revolving colored light in the center of the club with an inscription on it: "RESENTED BY MR. SOON SHAMA"—the P had dropped out. My inner comment was: "It was presented by this man, but resented by the rest of us." For one could see that he was trying to do what Jesus spoke of when He asked: "Which of you by taking thought can add one cubit unto his stature?" (Matt. 6:27 KJV). He was trying to add a cubit to his stature, trying to be bigger by a revolving lamp, his name imposed on everybody at every revolution.

> Pride goes before destruction,
>   and a haughty spirit before a fall (Prov. 16:18).

But the fall is not necessarily outward—it may be a fall in the estimation of people, and the destruction may be the destruction of influence. "Whoever exalts himself will be humbled"—humbled in his loss of influence, in the inner deterioration of character.

When you love Him with agape love you are not concerned as to what happens to you, but concerned as to what happens to Him.

O Jesus Lord, where my treasure is there is my heart also. My treasure is in Thee. Thou art my treasure. I have no treasure beyond Thee. Therefore I am released from my pride. I have no pride, for I haven't myself. Thou hast me. Amen.

AFFIRMATION FOR THE DAY: *If my pride is crucified, my person lives.*

"I WANT TO BE SAVED!"

We are meditating upon the fact that the cure for pride is not to fight it, nor to suppress it, but to surrender it to Christ and receive agape love, and that new affection which springs up within casts out pride. Birth, race, learning, ability, achievement, good looks, clothes, money, class—all these produce pride. Agape love cancels them all—effortlessly. Receive it as a little child and they are all gone!

A Ph.D. said to a friend: "Do you mean to say that I with all my learning have to repent and receive grace like anyone else?" We have quoted " 'Knowledge' puffs up, but love builds up." That is the essential characteristic among all systems of self-salvation based on self-discovery, self-realization, self-redemption—they puff up. Only love, agape love, builds up!

In contrast to the above, another Ph.D., a psychologist, came to see me and, without preliminaries, said: "I want to be saved!" A few minutes of instruction in how to surrender, then prayer on bended knees, and the light had broken in. As we arose he was a completely released man—"saved"! He received the Kingdom "as a little child," and the Kingdom invaded him through the open door of receptive faith. "God opposes the proud, but gives grace to the humble" (Jas. 4:6).

In any friendship—human or Divine—pride can shut out the Father and our brother—and it shuts in ourselves, locks us in. Only love—agape love—can tear down the walls. And we receive that love—receive it as a child.

Over the radio comes the story of a pastor who gave to one of his parishioners a puzzle: Find the cow. The parishioner was open and receptive and instead of trying by concentration to force herself to see that cow, she sat receptive and waited for the cow to show herself. She did—quickly. The pastor said in astonishment: "But no one ever found the cow so quickly. How did you do it?" The woman replied: "I sat receptive and open and the cow showed herself."

O Jesus, in our pride we try to take the Kingdom of heaven by force—try to force it open at our insistent demand, instead of receiving it as a little child. Forgive me that I do not empty my hands and take the gift—the gift of grace. Amen.

AFFIRMATION FOR THE DAY: *In a kneeling position, I can see furtherest—into the very heart of God.*

276

"YOU DO NOT NEED ANY FACTS"

We continue our meditation on the surrender of pride and becoming as a little child.

Thomas Huxley once wrote to Charles Kingsley: "Science seems to me to teach in unmistakable terms the Christian conception of entire surrender to the will of God. Science says: Sit down before the facts as a little child, be prepared to give up every preconceived notion, be willing to be led wherever nature will lead you, or you will know nothing." The scientist has to be humble, or he will never be a scientist. If he comes to nature proud, ready to force his views on nature and bend her to his assumptions, then nature will close up.

A minister was notorious for his censoriousness, criticizing everybody and everything. He criticized the Revised Standard Version of the Bible. His son brought the Revised Standard Version to him and said: "Dad, you're wrong; here are the facts." The father replied: "Son, when you know you are right you do not need any facts." The facts bumped into his pride of opinion and he took the pride of opinion, and mental and spiritual emptiness! Had he sat down before the facts as a little child, had he been prepared to give up every preconceived notion, and had he been willing to follow wherever the facts led him, he would have received the kingdom of God and the kingdom of facts, and their powers would have been behind him and would have furthered him and sustained him. Now he has pride of opinion.

Cesare Cremonini (1550-1631), Italian astronomer, in order to avoid admitting his error in challenging the discovery of Jupiter's moons, refused to look through a telescope throughout the last twenty-one years of his life. Pride closed the heavens to him and shut him off from accomplishing his life work. He would not receive the Kingdom of Fact as a little child and so he could not enter it. The science of astronomy swept on without him and left him, isolated by pride.

So Jesus and science both demand the same thing—they both demand self-surrender, one to the Person who is the truth, the other to the facts. Pride blocks access to both.

O Father God, I know that until I lay my senseless pride at Thy feet, I am blocked from Thee and from myself, from my usefulness. I am blocked. Help me to bend the knee to Thee and to the facts; then I shall stand straight before everything. Amen.

AFFIRMATION FOR THE DAY: *In the presence of the vast humility of God, my pride is silly and senseless.*

"RIGOR OF DEVOTION"

Eros is self-salvation, egocentric; agape is God-salvation, God-centric. So all eros systems are popular, for they leave the self intact—at the center of things. This passage gives a picture of the eros approach: "These have indeed an appearance of wisdom in promoting rigor of devotion and self-abasement and severity to the body, but they are of no value in checking the indulgence of the flesh" (Col. 2:23). This system of Gnosticism against which Paul was writing had an appearance of "wisdom"— it seemed to produce rigor of devotion and self-abasement. But it left the self at the center—I am producing rigor of devotion, I am abasing my body. The "I" was on parade, very subtly, but still there, dressed in rigor of devotion to God and apparently specializing in self-abasement.

The Christian faith does not demand rigor of devotion, as if God were a spiritual taskmaster, whipping His slaves to bend lower and to be more ardent in self-abasement before Him. He does not want our worship. He wants our love. And if we love Him we will worship Him—commune with Him—for worship is communion. And the Christian faith does not demand self-abasement. For you can abase yourself and all the while be saying deep down, "Look how wonderful I am to abase myself in this way." You can be proud of your humility.

Attempts to gain salvation through lopping off here and lopping off there, giving up here and giving up there, humiliating yourself here and humiliating yourself there, are vain attempts at getting rid of yourself through self-abasement. But Christianity does not teach self-abasement. But self-surrender does not leave the self intact. Self-surrender is self moving out of the center and letting God take the center, with the self on the margin, with God in control and the self in obedience. That puts God and you where both ought to be.

Father, I thank Thee that I can get rid of my pride in Thy way—just take Thy agape love by self-surrender and my pride is gone, dissolved in Thy overwhelming love. There is simply no place for pride when with empty hands I take Thy gift. Amen.

AFFIRMATION FOR THE DAY: *I do not whip up my will into worship; my grateful heart can do nothing else.*

"SELF-ABASEMENT"

We have been meditating on this idea: "These have indeed an appearance of wisdom in promoting rigor of devotion and self-abasement and severity to the body, but they are of no value in checking the indulgence of the flesh." All this "rigor of devotion," "self-abasement," and "severity to the body" are rooted in egocentric attempts at salvation. And it gets you nowhere. It got Luther nowhere as he climbed the stairs on his hands and knees. It got Wesley nowhere as he practiced the rigors of devotion in his Holy Club. And it gets the Hindus nowhere as they practice austerities to find salvation. And it gets the modern man nowhere as he is told to discover himself—his potentialities within. All of it leaves you self-preoccupied, going around in circles. I saw a white swan with its long neck curved, preening the feathers in its side and swimming at the same time. But the swan was going around in circles, getting nowhere; for it had no purpose of direction, except self-preoccupation. A lot of religious activity is just that—going around in circles because it is preoccupied with itself.

Paul pronounced a final verdict of doom on all such efforts: "But they are of no value in checking the indulgence of the flesh." Or as the marginal reading put it even stronger: ". . . are of no value, serving only to indulge the flesh." For the attempt to put down the flesh only calls attention to the flesh. A holy man of India met me at the door of his Ashram and the first thing he said to me was this: "I haven't seen a woman for forty years." But it was the first thing he said to me! Evidently, "women" were on his mind and had been for forty years! His method of shutting off women from his eyesight resulted in transferring them to the inside, transferring them to his imagination where they stuck like burrs. It served "to indulge the flesh"—from within. And it left him proud of his attainment.

There is only one way to get rid of egocentricity, and that is self-surrender. "Where your treasure is, there will your heart be also"—if your treasure, your self, is in God, then you'll love God and yourself, in God.

O Lord Christ, Thy way seems so simple and it is. But we have complicated things because we just don't want to surrender the one thing we must surrender, to get anywhere—ourselves. And now I reduce it all to Thy simplicity—take me over entirely. Amen.

AFFIRMATION FOR THE DAY: *I do not put myself down in self-abasement; when I look at Jesus on the cross, I am down.*

"WAS A LAKE, NOW A MILLPOND"

Yesterday we noted the difference between self-abasement and self-surrender.

As we walked out of a Corporate Quiet Time at the Ashram, a lady said: "I took it. I took it. To think all my life I have been waiting to be worthy. I took it as I was. Why did I have to wait sixty-two years? Why didn't somebody tell me sooner? I am weak with glory. I feel like a me that has walked off and left a shell." A lifetime of self-preoccupation, attempting to make herself worthy. A few moments of self-surrender and taking the gift, and she walks out of her confining shell of egocentric preoccupation—free! It was an effortless getting rid of self and its pride of worthiness. No pummeling, no preening—just surrender. And it was done. And done permanently if she keeps to that basis of self-surrender. For the self-surrender opens the door to grace and more grace.

A lady who belonged to the aristocracy, so-called, of the Southland, telling of her surrender to God and the consequent transformation, said: "The body of water before our house, I always called, before I was changed, a lake; now I call it a millpond." Pride had turned all her millponds into lakes, and the surrender of self and pride turned all her so-called lakes into millponds. When she reduced her lakes to millponds she grew in stature, became real, living in a world of reality, became mature.

A little baby brother got an earache and a lot of attention on account of it. His sister of four, wanting attention too, announced that she had a "pretense earache." When the baby's earache was better the next morning, the little girl was asked how her earache was getting on. She said: "My pretense earache is gone too." A lot of us are living in worlds of pretense, trying to get attention by being this, that, and the other. But real self-surrender wipes out all this world of pretense—pretense of birth, of learning, of age, of connections, of ability, of accomplishments, of happiness—wipes them all out. We live in a world of mature reality.

Father, wipe out the last vestige of pretending pride and make me real—real to the very core of my being. So I face Thee honest, face the world honest, face myself honest. Now I know reality and only reality—before Thee, others, and myself. Amen.

AFFIRMATION FOR THE DAY: *"From the unreal lead me to the Real; from darkness lead me to the Light."*

"NO CONTINUING SELF-CONDEMNATION IN LOVE"

We come now to a further step in maturity; "There is no continuing self-condemnation in love." There is no maturity possible if there is a continuous sense of self-condemnation. For the self-condemnation will tie up all the inner life in knots and will keep the personality from functioning naturally and normally.

The Epistle of I John, which we are making the basis of our study of maturity, is very clear on this point:

By this we shall know that we are of the truth, and reassure our hearts before him whenever our hearts condemn us; for God is greater than our hearts, and he knows everything. Beloved, if our hearts do not condemn us, we have confidence before God; and we receive from him whatever we ask, because we keep his commandments and do what pleases him (3:19-22).

This is a remarkable passage, for it seems to say that God is less hard on us than we are on ourselves: ". . . reassure our hearts before him whenever our hearts condemn us; for God is greater than our hearts." We would have expected the opposite. God accusing us when our hearts were excusing us. In putting it as it is above, there is a manifestation of pure agape—love taking our side against inner accusation of guilt.

Does this mean, on the other hand, that God has turned from being fatherly to being grandfatherly? Does He excuse us, even when our hearts accuse us? Or is there something deeper?

There are two kinds of guilt—a false guilt and a real guilt. Our hearts may condemn us of both kinds. Many suffer from self-condemnation through false guilt. A nurse felt miserable and condemned because she had gone to sleep while on a case. She said she had even lain down on a nearby bed and slept when the patient slept. Should she confess this to the superintendent? There was no doubt about her inner turmoil. But it was a morbid guilt, false and useless, and I could assure her it was so.

O Father, we know that our guilt is real. Thou wilt not let us off lightly. Thy love will hold us to the highest. But when we nag ourselves with useless, unreal guilt, open our eyes that we may see Thy loving compassion cleansing us from it. Amen.

AFFIRMATION FOR THE DAY: *No nagging of myself over little things, no excusing myself in the big.*

FALSE CONDEMNATION

We ended yesterday with the case of the morbid conscientiousness of a nurse who was in a tailspin of self-condemnation because she had gone to sleep on duty. I told her that Jesus did not cast off His disciples who had gone to sleep when He was going through His Gethsémane. At the close He said: "Arise, let us be going." He would say the same thing to her: "Arise, let us be going to the next duty. Forget the past." I told her that I was a representative of society; she had confessed it to me; that was enough. We are all imperfect people doing an imperfect service.

Here was a very conscientious Christian woman in charge of a girls' hostel. A maidservant got into trouble with a manservant and had to be dismissed. The Christian woman carried a sense of guilt because she felt she should have saved this maidservant from this ruin. But when I asked her if she knew anything about it, or suspected anything, she said she knew nothing and suspected nothing. Then I told her that her conscience was clear and the weight of guilt she was bearing was a false sense of guilt. She knew nothing and was therefore not responsible for something she did not know.

Both of these women had immature consciences, fastening on marginal things and passing by the central. For while they were morbidly fastening on marginal things which they could not change, they were forgetting the central thing, namely, that they were hurting their own personalities, making themselves half-persons, and spreading gloom around them.

Our consciences are a capacity to judge between right and wrong. But we put the content into what is right and wrong by our training. Therefore we must have well-trained consciences, mature consciences. Paul had the highest type of conscience in these words: "My conscience bears me witness in the Holy Spirit" (Rom. 9:1). His conscience was under the tutelage of the Holy Spirit.

O Holy Spirit, train my conscience, after Thou hast cleansed it, from the morbid, the trivial, and the marginal. I would have a conscience which will approve what Thou dost approve and condemn what Thou dost condemn. In Jesus' name. Amen.

AFFIRMATION FOR THE DAY: *My conscience trained by the Spirit will be an illuminated, mature conscience.*

Ps. 130:3-6   **Week 41—TUESDAY**
"WHAT WOULD JESUS APPROVE?"

Our consciences must be mature consciences, well trained
under the Holy Spirit. Some people's consciences are trained
under the customs of their group. I once asked a Hindu: "Suppose
you were to break caste and no one knew about it, what would
happen?" He replied: "My conscience would trouble me." His
conscience had been trained to keep caste and would trouble him
if he broke it. My conscience had been trained not to keep caste
and would trouble me if I kept it. Our consciences were trained to
approve directly opposite things. It is important, very important,
that our consciences be trained under the highest. The highest is
Jesus. The Holy Spirit trains our consciences under the standard
of Jesus. Our consciences are trained under one question, "What
would Jesus approve?"

There was nothing picayunish about Jesus. He broke taboos and
customs and went straight to one objective—human need. He
condemned those whose consciences tithed mint and anise and
cumin and passed over the weightier matters of justice and mercy
and love. So if our consciences are trained by the Holy Spirit
according to the pattern of Jesus, they will not be troubled over the
marginal issues, but untroubled over the central issues. They will be
balanced and healthy. If our consciences are trained under the
customs of our group, they will approve and condemn what the
group approves and condemns. A wealthy woman said to a friend:
"My son is well adjusted." And when the friend asked, "To what?"
she replied: "To being rich." But suppose circumstances changed
and riches were no longer a sustaining fact, then what? A
maladjusted person with a confused conscience. So young people
who are brought up in groups where lipstick and neckties are taboo
are filled with conflict when they adopt either one. But the real
Christian, with his conscience trained under Jesus, knows that
neither lipstick nor "unlipstick" availeth anything, but only a new
creature. The new creature can wear it or not wear it, and be
unaffected. The God who painted the lilies and made leaden skies
understands.

O Father, we thank Thee that Thou art not a mote-picking,
fussy policeman of the universe. Thou art our Father and we
know that Thou dost desire fundamental loyalty to Thee. The
rest is marginal. We give Thee that central loyalty—fully. Amen.

AFFIRMATION FOR THE DAY: *I bear no self-condemnation within
because I bear Jesus-commendation within.*

A FALSE CONSCIENCE

We have seen that we build up false guilt over false issues. I asked a Hindu: "What is sin?" And he reached up and broke the twig of a tree and said: "That is sin. I have hurt life." And according to his standards he was right. But it landed him in impossible situations. A cobra ran out of our bathroom into the compound toward a Hindu gardener, and when he was about to let it go by, my wife called to him: "Kill it! Kill it!" He did, but then he was very sad. He had taken life. My wife assured him that she was responsible and not he, for she had ordered him to kill it. His face brightened. That false standard of sin leads India to allow monkeys to eat up twenty percent of the crops in one state amid a people who are semistarved. The conscience trained under Jesus leads us to revalue our values.

On the other hand, in our civilization the mores, the customs of society, determine conscience. The Kinsey report tells of widespread sexual looseness among married and unmarried, and this low standard of sex morality begins to determine conduct: "Others do it. Why cannot I?" A low-level conscience is produced. And this invades church circles where consciences are supposed to be trained under the Holy Spirit after the pattern of Jesus. On page 219 I mentioned two women, both of them religious, who had confessed they had had sex relations with married men and both had said: "But I feel no sense of guilt." When I quoted, "You shall not commit adultery," one replied: "But I wouldn't call it by such an ugly name as adultery." And then she added that she went into this relationship to try to win the man to Christ. And she was serious! Another woman said that she and the man with whom she was having an adulterous relationship would have a Quiet Time together at nine o'clock wherever they happened to be, together or separated by miles. A false conscience had been produced.

But in all three cases the false world and the false consciences collapsed and left these people in moral ruins. The only open door was repentance leading them to the feet of Jesus—the Savior.

O Jesus, one look at Thee and Thy complete honesty and purity and all our false worlds and false standards and false consciences collapse. But out of that collapse we can rise by Thy power into conversion and into a new, cleansed conscience. Amen.

AFFIRMATION FOR THE DAY: *A cleansed conscience is the surest guarantee of a cleansed character and life.*

A CLEANSED CONSCIENCE
The Christian faith undertakes to cleanse our consciences as well as to cleanse us as persons. Note: "How much more shall the blood of Christ, who through the eternal Spirit offered himself without blemish to God, purify your conscience from dead works to serve the living God" (Heb. 9:14). The conscience is cleansed from dead issues—"dead works"—and made alive to living issues and made sensitive to the moral values in Jesus. A new conscience is produced to guide the new man into new relationships with a new set of values.

The mature Christian conscience is a conscience that has been cleansed once and for all from all we have done and have been. When Christ authoritatively says, "Your sins are forgiven," the conscience accepts it and ceases to trouble us about those sins any longer. If conscience is the voice of God in the soul, then what God accepts conscience accepts, what God forgives is forgiven by conscience, what God buries conscience buries, and what God wipes out of the book of His remembrance conscience wipes out of remembrance too.

Paul puts it forcefully: "There is therefore now no condemnation for those who are in Christ Jesus" (Rom. 8:1). If you are in Christ you are not in condemnation. To keep on condemning yourself for something that God has forgiven and buried is disloyalty to God. I inwardly object to a part of the communion service in one of the denominational rituals—my own—when, after having accepted forgiveness and after having partaken of the communion, we then begin all over again and say: "O Lord . . . that takest away the sins of the world, have mercy upon us. Thou that takest away the sins of the world, receive our prayer. Thou that sittest at the right hand of God the Father, have mercy upon us." It seems to cancel all that has happened and we are begging God to forgive what He has already forgiven. And we go out with a guilt-laden conscience instead of an Easter morning within us. The whole thing tends to become a guilt-ridden piety which drags its ball and chain of guilt into everyday living.

O Jesus, my Lord, what Thou hast cleansed help me not to call uncleansed. For at Thy word sins are forgiven, and what Thou dost forgive, help me to forgive and to forget. And help me to go on my way rejoicing in that blessed, blessed forgiveness. Amen.

AFFIRMATION FOR THE DAY: *I shall not bring up what God has buried, nor remember what God forgets.*

WHEN GOD FORGIVES, WE SHOULD ALSO FORGIVE

When forgiveness comes it comes and there is no mistaking of it. A woman writes:

Today after despairing of ever attaining to it, it finally happened. The best part of it was not as a storm or a quiet stealing into the heart—it came like this: dark curtains around me are lifting; cleansing winds of heaven are blowing over and round me; cool, sweet water is flowing in. Now there is neither pain nor great joy. Just a solid calm, and Him—He is here!

And where He is there is forgiveness—and peace.

An air force officer writes: "Have just finished reading *How to Be a Transformed Person*, for the second time. You see, I was so mixed up in my mind, soul, and body, that I needed a book like yours to explain and more or less lead me into the light. I'm in. What a wonderful, joyous, indescribable feeling. To think I took so long, trying to have my cake and eat it too."

These two have the authentic ring of Christian forgiveness about them. No continuous beating of the breasts at the self-condemnation within, but an opening of the inner heart to let the forgiving grace of God steal in. It is immaturity to be wearing hair shirts of self-condemnation as if that would atone for sin. This is maturity: "That you may stand mature and fully assured in all the will of God" (Col. 4:12).

How are we "fully assured"? John gives four lines of assurance in his first Epistle: (1) "By this we may be sure that we know him, if we keep his commandments" (2:3)—assurance through the will; (2) "He who loves his brother abides in the light" (2:10)—assurance through the emotions; (3) "Whoever confesses that Jesus is the Son of God, God abides in him, and he in God" (4:15)—assurance through the mind; (4) "And by this we know that he abides in us, by the Spirit which he has given us" (3:24; see also, 4:13)—assurance through the Holy Spirit to the total person. Here is assurance to the will, to the emotions, to the mind, and to the total person—it is total assurance.

O Father, what Thou hast buried help me not to dig up again. On the grave of my past sins help me to write, "No Resurrection," and mean it. Let me go on my way assured that I am accepted, not through my goodness, but through Thy grace. In Jesus' name. Amen.

AFFIRMATION FOR THE DAY: *Deeply assured before God, I shall face all my responsibilities with deep assurance.*

"REASSURE OUR HEARTS BEFORE HIM"

In this Epistle of I John the words "sure" and "confidence" are used twenty-nine times. So the note of assurance, of confidence, throbs through the Epistle as a heartbeat.

But being "sure" is different from being cocksure. This certainty is shot through and through with a deep humility. For the certainty is the result not of reaching but of receiving—it is the result of grace. That brings a deep humility. It sends you to the dust and raises you to the highest heaven at one and the same time. Grace is written across everything you do and say and are: "I am by the grace of God what I am."

This passage is to the point: "We . . . know that we are of the truth, and reassure our hearts before him" (3:19). You cannot reassure your heart before Him if you are not of the Truth—unless the Truth backs you, sustains you, furthers you. To try to get God to reassure you personally, apart from the reassurance of the Truth, is a snare and a delusion. This passage: "Demetrius has testimony from every one, and from the truth itself" (III John 12). Suppose everyone, even God Himself, personally testifies to you, but the Truth itself doesn't? Are you secure? No, God and the Truth itself must testify to you. Then you are secure. If "everyone" also testifies to you, then you are trebly secure. But if God and the Truth testify to you, then you have cosmic backing—you are sufficiently sure. If "everyone" says the same thing, then that is an extra thrown in! But you can do without it if you have the first two.

Note: "reassure our hearts *before him.*" We do not reassure our hearts before the herd—that would mean a herd-righteousness; nor before ourselves—that would mean a self-righteousness; but we reassure our hearts before Him—a real righteousness. And the amazing thing is that He is more just and more loving than our own standards—"God is greater than our hearts" and corrects our false guilts. "Love covers a multitude of sins," and this Divine agape covers not only a multitude of sins, but also covers a multitude of false guilts as well. It covers us and covers us—past, present, and future!

O Blessed Love, I am at Thy feet, humbled and hallowed, bound and free, all Thine and wholly myself. Thou dost untie all my false knots and then Thou dost bind me with unbreakable cords of love. Blessed bondage, blessed freedom. Amen.

AFFIRMATION FOR THE DAY: *My past buried in the love of God, my present held by the love of God—I'm safe.*

"THERE IS NO EMPTINESS IN LOVE"

We have been considering: "There is no self-condemnation in love." You cannot be mature if self-condemnation is eating within. It ties up the personality. And the glory of the Christian is that Christ specializes in wiping out self-condemnation: "Neither do I condemn thee: go, and sin no more" (John 8:11 KJV). "For God sent the Son into the world, not to condemn the world, but that the world might be saved through him"—saved from God-condemnation and self-condemnation.

A schoolteacher in India had a sense of guilt over an affair with a man who had betrayed her. She tried to excuse the guilt by saying to herself that she had been under a semi-intoxication with a drug. But the conscience refused to be stilled. She writes: "To think, I was five years in hell, but five minutes of talk and prayer with you, and I was in heaven. I went away on wings." Grace did it.

> Waste no tears
> Upon the blotted record of lost years,
> But turn the leaf and smile, oh smile to see
> The fair white pages that remain for thee.

This is good, but you cannot smile about the fair white pages that remain unless something is done about "the blotted record." That blotted record is canceled—and better, wiped out by the forgiving grace of Christ. And what He forgives we must not dig up again. It is gone—forever.

But that leads to another step: It is not enough to know that the past is blotted out; we must know that we have inner power to face the future with adequate resources at our disposal. We must be reassured not only as to the past, but as to the present and the future.

Our next step in maturity then is this: "There is no emptiness in love." Love—agape love—provides us with adequate resources to meet the present and the future—adequate resources and to spare. Agape love is by its very nature adequacy—plus.

O God, our Father, fountain of agape love, take my emptiness and turn it into fullness, my halfwayness and make it all-the-wayness, my incompleteness and make it into Thy completeness—at least as much as I can hold. In Jesus' name. Amen.

AFFIRMATION FOR THE DAY: *Not my responsibility but my response to His ability.*

SADDEST WORD: "VACUUM"

We have been looking at the fact that immaturity may come from inner blocks, but that it can also come from inner inadequacy, emptiness.

A missionary once said to me: "A lot of us missionaries should be shipped home, labeled 'emptied missionaries.'" They had good intentions, good desires, good opportunities, but they lacked what it takes to meet adequately and overflowingly those opportunities.

We have mentioned the replies of outstanding men when they considered the saddest word in the English language. The replies were: Oscar Hammerstein II: "The saddest word is 'But.'" Karl Menninger; "Unloved." Bernard Baruch: "Hopeless." George Balanchine: "The saddest word in the English language or in any language is 'Vacuum.'" Alex Tolstoi: "The saddest word in all the world, the word that has brought the world to its present state is 'Atheism.'"

The last two named are important: "vacuum" and "atheism." They both speak of emptiness. And the word "atheism" is to be applied not only to those who reject the idea of God, but also to those who live without vital contact with Him. They, too, are a-theist, without God. To all practical purposes, those who reject God, as well as those who exist without realizing God's resources for living, are a-theists, without God. Or if God is without and not within, to that extent too, it is a-theism. Only as God is possessed within, or better still, only as God possesses us within is there real theism.

This Epistle puts it thus: "And by this we know that he abides in us, by the Spirit which he has given us" (I John 3:24). It is the Spirit within which gives us the adequate knowledge that God "abides in us." We cannot live adequately on a God outside of us, calling Him in at intervals to help us out of our difficult situations. To have a God outside of us is to have an immature relationship with God, producing immature Christian personalities. The relationship must deepen from "with" to "within" before the person can be made mature. God without us is pre-Christian and sub-Christian. God within is Christianity.

O God the Spirit, we would know Thee as the most intimate fact of our lives—know Thee as the deepest fact within, available, adequate, and always there. For we would love love in inward intimacy. We thank Thee for this possibility. Amen.

AFFIRMATION FOR THE DAY: *God is my fullness, His absence my emptiness.*

THE SPIRIT WITHIN

Justice Holmes speaks of having "a feeling of intimacy with the inside of the cosmos." That is good. For it is wonderful to have a feeling of at-homeness in the cosmos. The orphanage, the estrangement, is gone and we are reconciled with reality. Recently a professor of mathematics in a college said that before he began attending our mission meetings he had high blood pressure and was on a diet. In less than a week he was eating everything and his blood pressure was down fifteen points. What had happened? The sense of estrangement had gone—he was reconciled to God by self-surrender, therefore reconciled with himself and with this body. His digestion returned to normal and his blood pressure came down. He had a "feeling of intimacy with the inside of the cosmos."

But even that, while it is good, is not enough. For the "inside of the cosmos" is impersonal. We as personal beings cannot be satisfied with the impersonal. The personal seeks the Personal, and the inner personal seeks the Inner Personal. And the glorious thing is that the Inner Personal seeks the inner personal. Being love He seeks the object of His love—seeks us. In that mutual seeking and finding and finding within, we come to mature relationships, and hence to maturity.

William Ernest Hocking once said:

Of all animals it is man to whom heredity counts for least, and conscious building forces for most. Consider that his infancy is longest, his instincts least fixed, his brain most unfinished at birth, his powers of habit-changing most marked, his susceptibility to social impressions keenest—and it becomes clear in every way that nature, as a prescriptive power, has provided in him for her own displacement. . . . Other creatures nature could largely finish: the human creature must finish himself.

And in finishing himself he can decide what influences can help shape him. Of all the choices given to man the highest choice is the possibility that God, the Creator of heaven and earth, should come and abide within him, in the Spirit, and help man finish the work of His own creation.

O Father, I am awed at the possibility of having Thee within me recreating me into Thine own image. Love could conceive of nothing higher, plan nothing greater, and carry out nothing more wonderful than just this. Amen.

AFFIRMATION FOR THE DAY: *I choose to be "a habitation of God in the Spirit."*

THE SPIRIT COMES TO ABIDE

We saw yesterday that the greatest choice man has is to choose to let God, the Spirit, help re-create him from within the citadel of his being. That opens infinite possibilities. And there is a further step to be noted: This coming within is not a fleeting, momentary coming for special purposes, on special occasions. He comes to "abide."

In the Epistle of I John the phrase "abides in" is found twenty-four times. Seventeen times it refers to our abiding in God, and seven times to His abiding in us. The stress seems to be on our abiding in Him. There is no question about His abiding in us if we will to abide in Him. For it is His settled purpose to abide in us: "And I will pray the Father, and he will give you another Counselor, to be with you for ever, even the Spirit of truth, whom the world cannot receive, because it neither sees him nor knows him; you know him, for he dwells with you, and will be in you" (John 14:16-17). That is the Divine Purpose, clearly expressed, to pass from the "with" to the "in"—and to abide in us forever. That takes Christian experience out of the hide-and-seek, transitory glimpses of reality conception and puts it in the conception of a permanent, continuous abiding of the Spirit within.

Three psychologists emphasize three different interpretations of the end of man. Freud says the main driving urge in man is the quest for pleasure—the sex urge; Adler says the main driving urge is the quest for power—the self-urge; Vikor Frankl says the main driving urge is the quest for meaning. All three of these statements have a truth in them, but not one of them has the whole truth. Only the whole truth comes when the Spirit of Truth, the Holy Spirit, comes within us and fulfills our total being by making the sex urge creative on the physical and the spiritual levels; by making the quest for power the power of love; by making the quest for meaning the quest for total meaning—God's meaning. He brings us to maturity by bringing us to maturity of quest.

O Blessed God, our Father, Thou dost take the scattered and often contradictory urges up into the perfect purpose of Thy love and blend them into a perfect whole. As I am caught up into a perfect purpose, so I shall be a perfect person. Amen.

AFFIRMATION FOR THE DAY: *My aims have become an aim; my loves have become a love—I'm single-pointed.*

"ALIVE AS LONG AS HE LIVES"

We saw yesterday that God, the Spirit of Truth within, brings life into total meaning and fulfills the end of our being, makes us mature. He gives us Goal and gives us power to move on to that Goal.

The Hindus believe that the sight of an empty pitcher, or an empty bucket, is inauspicious. In a deeper way the sight of an empty person is really inauspicious. For he is missing the end of his being. The end of his being is to be filled with God, the Spirit, and to be alive with God, the Spirit.

Harry and Bonaro Overstreet say that the end of man's being is "to be alive as long as he lives." Some people are not alive while they are living. A G.I. came back to his home town and inquired: "Is so-and-so alive yet?" And the reply: "No, not yet."

Plotinus, the sage, said: "I spent the whole day trying to make a corpse stand up. I decided it needed something on the inside." Unless we get something on the inside we are just that—a corpse! And unless that "something" is a Someone we are still not "alive." Religion as rite, or ceremony, or creed, or custom, is on the outside. It leaves you a corpse or half-alive. Only religion as experience—the experience of the Holy Spirit within—will make you alive—alive to your finger tips, alive to life, alive to the needs of the world, alive to maturity.

This trying to gain maturity by outward observances recalls the experience of the Arabians whom Lawrence brought to England during World War I. Water was everything to these men of the desert. So when they saw there was running water in their rooms in the hotel they were delighted. When Lawrence came back he found they had unfastened the faucets from the pipes and had put them in their suitcases so they could have running water in Arabia! Many are like that—they think they can get maturity by a gadget, a slogan, an idea, without getting in touch with the Source of Maturity, the Spirit of Truth within. The Holy Spirit is a mature Spirit, and our maturity comes from response to and receptivity of the Source of Maturity.

O Spirit of Truth, guide me into all truth. Not only truth as a concept, but truth as a living experience. May there be such a transformation; may I be so truthful that I shall become truth. I can surrender and receive. I do. Amen.

AFFIRMATION FOR THE DAY: *I am alive with life; I am alive to my fingertips with God.*

SPRINGS OF THE EMOTIONS IN THE SUBCONSCIOUS

We were meditating yesterday on the impossibility of becoming mature through the daily repeating of verses of Scripure, through slogans and outward observances. Such methods may help, but we remain immature unless and until we get into vital contact with the Spirit of Truth—the Holy Spirit within.

Nor will knowledge, psychological and scientific, as such, make you mature. For our immaturities are largely in our emotions. Therefore it is possible to be mentally mature and emotionally immature. The emotions remain immature unless there is an emotional pressure of the Divine upon our emotions, cleansing, redeeming, and inspiring our emotions. Only the Spirit of Truth, who is also the Spirit of Love, working in direct and immediate contact with the within, can make us emotionally mature. A marriage counselor and his wife, experts on marriage relations, seek a divorce. A psychiatrist bangs down the telephone in a fit of temper when interrupted during a conversation with a patient who is emotionally upset. In both cases knowledge was there—mature knowledge—but the springs of the emotions were not touched. These springs of the emotions are in the subconscious mind. The area of the work of the Holy Spirit is largely, if not entirely, in the subconscious. If we surrender to the Holy Spirit all we know—the conscious—and all we don't know—the subconscious—He will enter into the subconscious and cleanse and control and coordinate the driving urges and consecrate them to Kingdom ends. Then the conscious mind and the subconscious mind will not be at cross-purposes, but under a single control they will beat out music vaster than before—and more harmonious music. Mind and emotion and will are no longer pulling in different directions, but held by the charioteer, the Holy Spirit, they are driven toward the goal of maturity.

This unifying of purpose and goal is seen in the disciples of Jesus. After three years of intensive training under Jesus, they were mature in knowledge of spiritual things, but immature in emotions—wanting to call down fire, arguing over first places.

O Jesus Master, Thy blessed Maturity kept patient under the immaturities of Thy disciples and made them at last stand out as marvelously mature. Have patience with my immaturity. And maybe I, too, shall stand at last mature and whole. Amen.

AFFIRMATION FOR THE DAY: *My subconscious held by the Spirit is my reservoir of power to live by.*

"PSYCHOTHERAPY DOES NOT CREATE SAINTS"

Prior to the coming of the Holy Spirit on the day of Pentecost the disciples were very immature disciples of a very mature Master. But when the Holy Spirit entered into them, took them over and made them over, they suddenly became mature in their reactions and their relationships. They loved enemies, walked out of councils with joy when beaten, went into prisons with no more jolt than when one passes from one room to another. They embraced death singing and praying—for their tormentors. How could such advanced maturity come out of such advanced immaturity, and how could it come out suddenly? The only answer: the Holy Spirit within!

Ancient history? Then listen to the same thing brought up to date: A well-dressed woman said to Charles Morgan: "Dr. Morgan, on a Sunday evening, a very wet evening, years ago I slipped into the back pew in Hope Church, Springfield. There were very few present. I was a sinner and came in out of the rain. You gave as your text: 'She only touched the hem of His garment.' I do not recall your sermon, but in the midst of it I saw myself, as I was, and as I could be. It burst on me like a flood. I heard a voice saying: 'Arise to better things.' I went to my lonely room and fell on my knees and prayed to that which talked to me. I asked for strength and forgiveness and I received it. I left Springfield for Chicago where I founded a home for wayward girls. Since then I have such homes in other cities." One moment she was an immature bundle of sex impulses and another moment she was a creative being, dedicated to the rescuing and nurturing of people with tangled-up lives and emotions.

Someone puts it thus: "Psychotherapy does not create saints. True Christian conversion has a deeper content then psychological change. Psychological treatment can bring about a rearrangement of the mental and emotional pattern but it does not bring new power into life." The Holy Spirit brings new power into life—power to change thought and emotion—power to change the total life.

O Holy Spirit, I am powerless to change basic emotions. But I can consent for Thee to change me. I do. My whole being is open to Thy operations. Depths which I cannot control are open to Thy control. Take over the total me. Amen.

AFFIRMATION FOR THE DAY: *The total me helped totally by the Spirit is totally safe for total living.*

EMPTINESS IN EROS LOVE

We considered last week that "there is no emptiness in love." There is emptiness in eros love. For eros love is acquisitive. But agape love is, first of all, receptivity—"we love, because He first loved us." The first law of life for creatures is receptivity. Striving without receptivity ends in exhaustion—and frustration. For striving without receptivity is based on pride: "I can do it myself"—"I have enough resources of my own." When this self-striving exhausts itself, there is a sense of frustration.

Agape love is based on self-surrender to God's agape love. Then God's love is "poured into our hearts through the Holy Spirit which has been given to us" (Rom. 5:5). This pouring into our hearts of love is a *Gift* "given to us." A child can receive a gift and only the child-like can receive this Gift. Pride and self-sufficiency are swept away and we become pure receptivity. Therefore, we become pure activity with such abundance that we cannot help but give it away. We would burst if we didn't. John puts it: "And from his fullness have we all received, grace upon grace" (John 1:16). You haven't been able to give away one grace before another grace floods in—grace upon grace. So you are hopelessly and gloriously behind in giving away what is given to you. Eros is poor; agape is divinely rich.

I used to think of myself as a reservoir with a given quantity of resources and that whenever I drew off anything from the reservoir I had that much less left to draw upon. So one's resources had to be watched and guarded against exhaustion. Now I see myself, not as a reservoir, but as a channel attached to infinite resources. The more I draw, the more I have and the more I can give. So my supply need never be exhausted, since my sources are inexhaustible. You can always love with His love, trust with His trust, be adequate with His adequacy. Without this you exhaust yourself against the problems of the day. Eros love is an exhausted love; agape love is an inexhaustible love. It has enough and to spare. It preaches, lives, and rejoices out of the overflow. There is always the overflow, for there is always the inflow. Love is never empty.

O Gracious Father, this "grace upon grace" sends me to my knees in humble gratitude. There is no place for pride to lift its head in this. I am bowed down with this "weight of glory." And yet I soar on wings of victory—Thy victory. Amen.

AFFIRMATION FOR THE DAY: *Today every grace that comes will have written upon it: "More to follow."*

ANOINTING—SYMBOL OF DEDICATION

We must look at another phase of this, "There is no emptiness in love." This passage is important: "The anointing which you received from him abides in you, and you have no need that any one should teach you; as his anointing teaches you about everything, and is true, and is no lie, just as it has taught you, abide in him" (I John 2:27). Here it is said that "the anointing . . . abides in you," and ends with the exhortation to "abide in him." The "anointing" then is a "him"—Him, the Holy Spirit. So this is the anointing with the Holy Spirit which is to teach them "about everything."

Why is "anointing" used instead of the "filling of the Holy Spirit"? Perhaps the reason is that anointing was used in those days to set aside a person to a special office of priest, or prophet, or king. It was a symbol of dedication. To have used "filling" would have been to use a term with less specific content. The Holy Spirit comes to cleanse and also to consecrate the cleansed person. Our powers are taken over by the Holy Spirit and they are all heightened—a plus added to them—making us adequate to do anything we are called to do.

And we are made adequate not only in act but in knowledge: "His anointing teaches you about everything." Gnosticism, the background of this Epistle, against which John was writing, taught that the Gnostics, the Knowers, knew by superior inner intuition which made them superior. John said in answer that those fully in Christ had an anointing which taught them about everything— that anointing was the Holy Spirit within.

Jesus emphasized this: "But the Counselor, the Holy Spirit, whom the Father will send in my name, he will teach you all things, and bring to your remembrance all that I have said to you" (John 14:26). "When the Spirit of truth comes, he will guide you into all the truth. . . . He will glorify me, for he will take what is mine and declare it to you" (John 16:13-14). Here is to be given nothing less than a school of the Spirit, set up within the receptive heart where the learner will be guided into nothing less than "all truth."

O Divine Teacher, teach me. But I know that I cannot be taught unless I am wholly responsive to Thy teaching. Give me then the listening ear and the willing will that, not Thy thunder, but Thy whisper will be sufficient. In Jesus' name. Amen.

AFFIRMATION FOR THE DAY: *I may be only a beginner in the school of the Spirit, but I am an eager, open beginner.*

THE SCHOOL OF THE SPIRIT

Yesterday we emphasized the fact that Jesus had said that the Spirit of Truth, the Holy Spirit, would set up within a private school of the Spirit where He would "teach" us "all things" and "guide" us "into all truth." And John adds in his first Epistle: "The anointing which you received from him abides in you, and . . . teaches you about everything."

There are three things here: (1) the Spirit of Truth will teach us all things—the intellectual conception; (2) He will guide us into all truth—the emotional acceptance; (3) the anointing of the Holy Spirit teaches us about everything—the volitional dedication. The stages are important: first, the concept must be grasped by the mind—"teach you all things": second, the concept must be emotionally accepted and made our own—"He will guide you into all the truth." A teacher can teach you truth but fail to guide you into possession of it as your own life choice. Here He teaches and guides into possession of truth; or better, the truth takes possession of you. Third, the anointing teaches you about everything—the anointing, which involves dedication to, means that we learn the truth by being dedicated to the truth. In other words we learn the truth by doing the truth. This is the modern emphasis of "learning by doing." So here is a school of the Spirit in which the mind grasps, the emotion accepts, the will acts upon. The total person is informed of, transformed by, and dedicated to—truth.

And all this is done by Him who not only teaches truth, but is Himself the Spirit of Truth. What you get from Him is not only truth, the bare facts, but the spirit of truth—the facts plus the very spirit of truth, or reality. It is possible to have the truth and not the spirit of truth.

This school of the Spirit set up within the depths of our personality trains the mind to grasp truth, the emotion to accept truth, and the will to act upon truth, thus making the total person truth, hence mature. This means that we are under the intimate, twenty-four hour-a-day tutelage of the maturest fact of the universe, the Holy Spirit. If we respond our maturity is guaranteed.

O Spirit of Truth, I enroll in the school of the Spirit—a life enrollment. I would be an eager, responsive student in the school of living. For if I do not learn how to live I miss the central thing. So I am all out for this. In Jesus' name. Amen.

AFFIRMATION FOR THE DAY: *I am a trainee of the Spirit.*

THE WHOLE PERSON MUST GO TO SCHOOL

In this school of the Spirit the first requirement is full surrender to the Teacher—the Holy Spirit. For this is not a school in which we can send our mind to school to be informed and leave the emotion and the will free to roam where they will. The whole person must go to school. And the whole person must be surrendered to the mind of the Spirit. For this is teaching in the art of living. And you cannot live in the mind alone, the emotion alone, or the will alone. The whole person must be responsive to the whole person of the Spirit.

Without this total surrender of the total being we could never become mature. For the mind might be under the Spirit and the emotion under the flesh, and consequently the will under conflict. The person is a blur—or worse, a civil war. Absolute surrender is absolutely necessary. "He who wills to do the will of God shall know of the teaching." If we do not will to do, we shall never know. Moral response is the price of knowledge in a moral universe.

A teacher in a public school said: "It's none of the business of the school board as to what I do outside school hours. If I teach my classes satisfactorily, in my private life I can do as I like." She said this to justify drinking, gambling, and wild parties outside of school hours. But she brought a divided person to the teaching, and these two sides of her canceled each other. In the school of the Spirit the Holy Spirit, the Teacher, is the Spirit of Truth, and hence we cannot bring to this school anything less than total response to the Spirit of Truth.

This does not mean that we cannot enter this school unless we are mature. It means the opposite. It means that you know that you are immature in mind, in emotion, and in will—that you are an immature person. But it also means that you are willing to be different—in mind, emotion, and will. The will to be different is the only requirement for entrance and for continuance. Given that, anything can happen. Without that, nothing can happen, except frustration.

O Spirit of Truth, I would be so responsive to Thee that I shall become truth, so loving that I shall become love, so real that I shall become reality. I'm in Thy school to be and not merely to hear. So I'm in with all I have and am. Amen.

AFFIRMATION FOR THE DAY: *I'm in the school of the Spirit, to think His thoughts, feel His feelings, will His purposes.*

ROUND-THE-CLOCK TUTELAGE OF THE SPIRIT

This school of the Spirit set up and operating within, in the depths of the personality, where the total person is under the round-the-clock tutelage of the Spirit, makes other methods of producing maturity seem outward, mechanical, and amateurish.

Take Gnosticism. Salvation was to be gained by climbing the ladder of thirty-six steps to God by inward knowledge. But that knowledge, or gnosis, did not include the body. This high knowledge was consistent with low morals. Gnosticism collapsed from that dualism—a house divided against itself that could not stand. A pillar of the church committed adultery. Brought before the judge, he was asked: "How could you, a pillar of the church, do this?" And the man replied: "Oh, the old Adam did that." And the judge replied: "Then I sentence the old Adam to nine months." That happened on a wide scale in regard to Gnosticism. Life said to it: "I sentence you to extinction because of your dualism."

Take modern psychiatry. It, too, undertakes to cure maladies of the personality through knowledge. Jung says psychiatry has four steps: confession, explanation, education, transformation. The two middle steps—explanation and education—are scarcely able to produce the last—transformation. It can produce alleviation, reformation, realignment, but hardly transformation.

In the school of the Spirit there are four steps: (1) confession, (2) self- and sin-surrender to God, the Spirit, (3) acceptance by faith of forgiveness and reconciliation to God, the Spirit, (4) transformation. For in confession everything is brought up and out—complete honesty; in self- and sin-surrender there is a transfer of the central allegiance from self and sin to God—complete recentering; in acceptance by faith of forgiveness and reconciliation there is a wiping out of all barriers between the soul and God. Hence there is transformation. For God's power, now free to operate, transforms the honest, the surrendered, the receptive soul.

O Gracious Teacher and Transformer, I bring to Thee confession, surrender, and acceptance and I find from Thee transformation. And since the transformation is from Thee through grace alone, then humility is of the very essence of this transformation. I thank Thee. Amen.

AFFIRMATION FOR THE DAY: *I am under the Great Transformation. I belong to It and am becoming It.*

WILLINGNESS, ONLY REQUIREMENT

If it seems to some that complete honesty, complete surrender, complete acceptance, are too high an entrance requirement for the school of the Spirit, let me remind you again that the Spirit requires but one thing and one thing only: willingness—a willingness to be completely honest, a willingness to complete surrender, a willingness to complete acceptance. When we supply willingness—He supplies power. He cannot supply the willingness, for we are free agents, but when once we supply the willingness, the way is open for everything.

But perhaps you are not even able to supply the willingness, for the will is bound up with emotions and habits. Are you then permanently blocked from entering His school? No. If you can say, "I am willing to be made willing," that is sufficient. For the Scripture says: "The Spirit also helpeth our infirmities" (Rom. 8:26 KJV), or, "The Spirit helps us in our weakness" (RSV). That "weakness" may include, and include particularly, the weakness of the will. There is a section in the school of the Spirit for retarded pupils.

I know a public school where the principal refused to accept the idea of children with permanent low IQs, fixed and grooved in inferiority. She got each teacher to pledge herself to find something to commend in each pupil. In some pupils it was difficult to find anything to commend. But the teachers found it, or created it; and soon when commendation, instead of condemnation, became the atmosphere, that whole block of pupils who had been doomed to inferiority were registering normal IQs. The same thing happens in the school of the Spirit. There the atmosphere is agape love—creative love. That love wipes out all self-condemnation and all feelings of inferiority and gives the sense that we belong—belong to the Highest—that we are on the Way—the Way to everything. The Creative Spirit makes us creative. The Divine Person makes us persons. In the school of the Spirit there are no impossibles. Anything can happen—under Him.

O Spirit of my spirit, Soul of my soul, Life of my life, I am so grateful that Thou dost not take one glance at me and consign me to the dustheap. Thou dost see what I do not see and Thou dost produce what Thou dost see. I thank Thee. Amen.

AFFIRMATION FOR THE DAY: *Under Thy appreciation of me, I am appreciating myself, and others, and life itself.*

AN IMPOSSIBLE STANDARD?

In this inner school of the Spirit a new kind of teaching takes place—the Teacher and the pupil become one in knowledge, in love, in action. This is according to the capacity of the pupil to respond and receive.

A missionary couple, married late in life, were deeply in love. One morning at the breakfast table he told of a dream he had had the night before. The wife said, "Why, Frank, did you dream that dream, or did I?" They were so in love that they couldn't tell which one dreamed the dream—they were one! It is so in the school of the Spirit. Life flows into life, thought into thought. And you can't tell where you end and He begins.

An impossible standard? No, the Acts of the Apostles has the same standard: "It has seemed good to the Holy Spirit and to us." The Holy Spirit and they did what Jesus suggested: "If two of you agree on earth about anything they ask, it will be done for them by my Father in heaven" (Matt. 18:19). The word "agree" is a word that expresses the harmony of two perfectly attuned musical instruments—the word "orchestrate" would express it. If two of you shall orchestrate—be attuned in perfect harmony—anything is possible. When the Holy Spirit and we orchestrate—think, feel, and act together—then identified in purpose we are also identified in power. This is a school where not only information is imparted, but transformation as well. What He transfuses, He transforms. His resources become our reserves. We can call on them for everything we need to do. We then find ourselves literally doing things we can't do. Everything we do and think and say has a plus—a Divine Plus added to it. You can't tell where your energy ends and His begins, and where His energy ends and yours begins. You are a very ordinary person linked with extraordinary power and you leave results all out of proportion to your powers.

O Teacher and Inspirer, Thy teaching becomes enablement, Thy light becomes life. What Thou dost tell me to do becomes easy to do, for I know I'm not doing it—I'm only consenting to Thy doing. What a partnership! Amen.

AFFIRMATION FOR THE DAY: *God and I are partners—I share all I have and He shares all He has.*

301

MATURITY IN THE LIFE OF PRAYER

We have been thinking about a school of the Spirit set up in the depths of the personality in which we are trained in maturity of character and life. Compared to this, all other methods of attempting to be mature seem amateurish, marginal, and fitful. This is the only mature attempt at producing maturity—and producing maturity by an inner, immediate, continuous impact of the maturest fact in the universe, the Holy Spirit.

One of the things the Spirit within helps us to find is maturity in the prayer life: "Likewise the Spirit helps us in our weakness; for we do not know how to pray as we ought, but the Spirit himself intercedes for us with sighs too deep for words. And he who searches the hearts of men knows what is the mind of the Spirit, because the Spirit intercedes for the saints according to the will of God" (Rom. 8:26-27). Here we find Paul putting his finger on the central point of our "weakness"—weakness in prayer life. And because we are weak in our prayer life we are weak in maturity. If the prayer life is immature the whole life is immature. For prayer is the central resource for maturity in any person's life. And there is no exception. If we are weak in prayer, we are weak—full stop. If we are strong in prayer, we are strong—full stop.

As I travel through the world and get in contact with men and women of all races, I find that the greatest source of weakness in character and influence is to be found in the prayer life. Most of the casualties in the spiritual life are found at the place of a weakened prayer life. When the prayer life is toned up the whole of the rest of the life is toned up with it. Prayer is pivotal. I find I am better or worse as I pray more or less. If prayer fades, power fades. When I pray I'm like an electric bulb put into the socket, full of light and power. When I don't pray I'm like that same bulb pulled out of the socket—no light, no power. And it is as simple as that. And it works with a mathematical precision. In prayer our weakness is linked to Almightiness, our ignorance linked to Infinite Wisdom, our finite self to the Infinite Self.

O Gracious Father, how grateful I am that I am not left alone to flounder in my weakness—I can be attached to Thy strength. I am not left alone in my sin—I can be attached savingly to Thy holiness. I am not left alone—I can be attached to Thee. Amen.

AFFIRMATION FOR THE DAY: *When every other way is closed, the way of prayer is open.*

PRAYER IS SELF-SURRENDER

We are meditating on the place of prayer in maturity. John, toward the end of the Epistle, mentions prayer as the crowning fact: "And this is the confidence which we have in him, that if we ask anything according to his will he hears us. And if we know that he hears us in whatever we ask, we know that we have obtained the requests made of him" (I John 5:14-15). Here is a sweeping statement regarding the scope of prayer: "If we ask anything . . . he hears us." And further: "And if we know that he hears us in whatever we ask, we know that we have obtained the requests made of him"—He hears anything we ask and we obtain whatever we ask. This is sweeping and all-embracing. But note I have left out one qualifying phrase: "according to his will." "Anything" and "whatever" are qualified by "if we ask . . . according to his will." That phrase is all-important, for without it prayer can become illusion. I can ask anything and if I only have faith enough I will get it. My faith is the qualifying factor. That has caused an enormous amount of confusion and disillusionment. It has turned prayer into magic—the wand is faith. Wave that wand of faith over situations, and miracles happen! When we believe that faith is the only condition we have missed the point. "According to his will" is the basic condition. Exercise faith within that condition and anything can and does happen.

But that condition defines prayer, *Prayer is self-surrender.* Not merely the surrender to the will of God of the thing for which we are praying, but deeper still—it means the surrender of the person who is praying to the will of God. And not a surrender of the person in reference to the particular thing at issue—it means a permanent surrender as a life attitude. When that is done we are free to ask "anything" and God pledges "whatever" we ask! A freedom in prayer comes as a result of this losing of one's life into the will of God. Surrendered wholly to Him, then faith is not worked up; it is the atmosphere in which we live and move and have our being. There the surrendered become the masterful—they lay hold on and command infinite powers and apply them to human need.

O Father God, I thank Thee that when I am prepared to do Thy will, Thou art prepared to do my will. We are one in will and hence one in power—according to my capacity to receive. I thank Thee. Amen.

AFFIRMATION FOR THE DAY: *My will aligned to His will, I can ask "anything" and get it, or something better!*

"EVERYTHING SEEMS ORDINARY—EXCEPT"

We finished yesterday saying that when we surrendered to the will of God, God undertakes to surrender to our wills; when we do what He says He will do what we say! We share His power because we submit to His will. The book of Revelation puts it: "He who conquers, I will grant him to sit with me on my throne, as I myself conquered and sat down with my Father on his throne" (3:21). And how did Jesus conquer? He conquered when in the hour of Gethsemane He said: "Not my will, but thine be done." He accepted the cross and found a throne. We accept the will of God in complete surrender and we, too, find a throne. We rule because we don't want to rule—we want to serve. And the servant of all becomes greatest.

A minister was introducing a speaker and he said: "Everything about this man seems ordinary—his appearance, his training, his name. Everything seems ordinary except the achievements of the man—they are extraordinary. The only way to account for what he accomplishes is that he doesn't accomplish it, but that he lets God accomplish it through him. He is wholly surrendered to God." He was right. Here was an ordinary man doing extraordinary things, because he was surrendered to God beyond the ordinary. He was free to command the forces of God because he was free to obey them. "The meek inherit the earth," for they have learned to submit, to surrender, to receive.

Prayer is surrender and, consequently, receptivity. The unsurrendered cannot receive. They withhold the inmost self and hence block the receptivity. They do not give; hence they cannot receive. When Jesus touched the dumb man who could not speak, He did not touch his tongue first—He touched his ears first. For the hearing was the basis of his trouble. He could not receive with his ears; therefore he could not give with his tongue. When the receptivity became normal the activity became normal. Prayer as self-surrender clears the way for receptivity and hence for an amazing activity. The first law of life is receptivity; the second law of life is activity. Prayer is both.

O Father, help me to align my will to Thy will for life direction. And then I will align my will to Thy will as power for life direction. I thank Thee for this blessed working partnership. I supply willingness, You supply power. Amen.

AFFIRMATION FOR THE DAY: *I may be an ordinary man, but I shall do extraordinary things through God.*

ALIGN OUR WILLS TO THE WILL OF GOD

Prayer aligns our wills to the will of God. As a friend and I were motoring along, we saw that the car ahead of us had a wheel out of alignment. My friend observed: "That tire is doomed to half a life unless it is realigned." I look at lives doomed to half a life, because they are out of alignment to the will of God. Recently I went to see an old man who is radiant and happy and keen at ninety-one. On the table lay a bookmark which read: "He that doeth the will of God abideth forever." The man was ageless and deathless and was looked on as Christian No. 1 in that city. On the same day I saw a woman of eighty-one who had lived a base life, and who kept saying, "I'm damned. I know I'm damned. And God doesn't hear my prayers. Everyday for six months I've prayed that God would send me a letter from my son. But no letter. God has deserted me." She was expecting a miracle without aligning her life to the will of God. You pray with your life and not merely with your lips. God hears *you*, instead of what you say.

Prayer organizes thought and life around the will of God. A man said to Whistler: "I don't seem to be able to fit this picture of yours into this room." And the painter replied: "You have begun at the wrong end. You must fit the room into the picture." Prayer organizes life around the Picture of God—Jesus. In prayer.

> That one Face, far from vanish, rather grows,
> Or decomposes but to recompose,
> Become my universe that feels and knows.

We see everything from a standpoint—that Standpoint, Jesus. When Jesus touched the blind man's eyes and asked him if he saw, he replied: "I see men; . . . like trees, walking." His sight was out of focus. Jesus touched him again, and the man saw all things and all men plainly. Unless we learn to surrender in prayer, all things are out of focus—the big seems little and the little seems big. Prayer puts everything in focus. And the Supreme Value stands out—Jesus only!

O Jesus, Thou art the value of all my values. Without Thee there is nothing valuable. Everything turns to dust and ashes without Thee. With Thee everything takes on significance. Everything becomes big with meaning and destiny. I thank Thee. Amen.

AFFIRMATION FOR THE DAY: *In prayer I do not overcome God's reluctance but lay hold on His highest willingness.*

"THE PULL HAS GONE"

We know prayer does something for the pray-er—aligns him to the will of God, brings everything into focus, and adds a plus to all he does and says and is. But does prayer really influence things outside oneself?

We know that telepathy is a fact. One mind can influence another mind and the distance doesn't seem to matter. If one person can influence another person across distances—can throw a thought into his mind, give his will a gentle push, and change his emotions—then why couldn't God and we, working together, influence a people and situations for good? For instance, at one of our Ashrams a woman said that for twenty years she had been praying for her husband to become a Christian, but no response. We went into the chapel together and knelt and prayed for him to become a Christian. When she got home a week later this was the first thing he said to her: "While you have been away I've decided to become a Christian. I'm joining the church next Sunday." Coincidence? Perhaps, but perhaps not!

For instance, I have a snapshot of three women taken at one of our Ashrams. One, the wife of a dean in a state university, had her neck so twisted that she could not see in front without moving her whole body sideways. It had been in a cast and she was going to have an operation for it after the Ashram. The first day she asked me if I would pray for her. We went to the chapel and I prayed for her, laying my hands on her. I knew I had no healing in my hands, but I put them at His healing disposal. The next morning she stood up at the early morning Quiet Time and said, "The pull has gone." In a few days the face straightened out and now she is normal. She sent me the cost of the operation for my work in India and then added: "Now that I cannot talk about my operation, what can I talk about?" She could talk about her healing—and has!

Prayer is receptivity and she opened her mind and soul and body to the healing power of God. Faith does not produce the healing—faith is the cleared channel through which the healing of God flows.

O Father God, we know our faith does not heal; it only opens the channels for Thy healing. My eyelids do not see; they only open to let the light in. So my faith opens the doors to let Thee in. Come in and heal me every whit. In Jesus' name. Amen.

AFFIRMATION FOR THE DAY: *Prayer gives a new dimension to life—when the outlook isn't good, the uplook is.*

"LATER" NEVER CAME

We wrote yesterday of the first woman of three who appeared together in a snapshot. The second was a woman whose weight was down to about a hundred pounds; her liver was diseased and she was in wretched health generally. She came to that same chapel mentioned yesterday; we had prayer together and hands were laid on her. When she went to her room she reached for a cigarette, as she was a heavy smoker and had been smoking three packs a day for twenty years. As she reached for a cigarette this time, she pulled her hand back: "Why, I don't want that now. I will later." But the "later" never came. She has not touched them for three years and the desire has never returned. She gained nearly fifty pounds in a few months, which was too much! Now she is down to normal. And the liver disease cleared up immediately.

Here God did not touch the disease directly; He touched the cause of the disease—the cigarette habit—and the disease disappeared.

The third person in the group had a cyst, and an operation was to have been performed after the Ashram. She had been prayed for and had had hands laid on her. But no apparent results. Then she became interested in finding the fullness of the Holy Spirit. The thought of healing was pushed to the edges; her desire for the Holy Spirit became dominant. And on communion morning she was filled with the Holy Spirit as she bowed in prayer. That afternoon as she sat with a group talking about the wonderful thing that had happened to her she announced: "The cyst has broken." It had. When the doctor examined her after her return home from the Ashram he announced that there would be no operation for there was no cyst.

This was healing indirectly, fulfilling the verse: ". . . will give life to your mortal bodies also through his Spirit which dwells in you" (Rom. 8:11). This is perhaps the highest kind of healing—a healing through the Spirit dwelling within and giving life to our bodies: In three ways—direct touch, removal of cause, and by Spirit within—God healed.

O Spirit Divine, Thou art the source of my constant healing, quickening my mortal body by Thy indwelling. May I never block that healing by blocking Thy operating power within me. May I keep the channels clear so that Thy life can flow in every part of me. Amen. AFFIRMATION FOR THE DAY: *Prayer breaks old habits, pulls us out of old ruts, and makes us free to live!*

WHAT IS MORTAL SIN?

The passage we are looking at in I John regarding prayer says: "If anyone sees his brother committing what is not a mortal sin, he will ask, and God will give him life for those whose sin is not mortal" (5:16).

What is this "mortal sin"? In the New Testament there is a sin which is "mortal"—a sin for which there is no forgiveness—and that is the blasphemy against the Holy Spirit. And what is the blasphemy against the Holy Spirit? The scribes had said that Jesus cast out evil spirits by Beelzebul (literally, "the lord of filth"). That is, the Spirit by which Jesus cast out evil spirits, the Holy Spirit, was a filthy spirit. The saying that the Holy Spirit is a filthy spirit is the blasphemy against the Holy Spirit. This is plain from the passage. "'Whoever blasphemes against the Holy Spirit never has forgiveness, but is guilty of an eternal sin'—for they had said, 'He has an unclean spirit'" (Mark 3:29-30).

Apart from that "mortal sin" we are invited to pray for our brother and "God will give him life for those whose sin is not mortal." This invites us to intercessory prayer for others and God has promised to give "life" to the one prayed for. This is a wide-open invitation and gives us infinite possibilities in influencing others. This is the highest kind of prayer for it is the most unselfish. You are praying not for this thing, that thing, or the other thing for a particular person—you are praying for "life" for that person. And you can always pray with faith for "life" for people, since that is what Jesus came to give: "I came that they may have life, and have it abundantly." So to pray for "life" for people is to pray in line with the purpose of His coming.

We are mature to the degree that we are mature in prayer, and we are mature in prayer to the degree that our prayer becomes intercessory prayer, and our intercessory prayer is mature to the degree that it asks for "life" for the one prayed for. When we stand before God, like the High Priest, with the name of our brother written on our heart, then we are really praying.

O God, I stand before Thee and lift my brothers to Thee for Thee to give them life. I can ask nothing higher and I can be content with nothing less. For life is what we need and life is what I get in asking for life for others. I thank Thee. Amen.

AFFIRMATION FOR THE DAY: *Prayer for "life" for others is my highest prayer— I shall pray it often today.*

MATURITY IN SPIRITUAL CONTAGION

We now turn to another phase of maturity, a very important phase—maturity in spiritual contagion. Unless our maturity results in spiritual contagion it stops this side of maturity—it is immature maturity. For the end objective of life seems to be the production of life.

Franz Alexander, a psychiatrist, says:

All energy which is not needed to maintain life can be considered as surplus energy. This is the source of all sexual activity; it is also the source of all productive, creative work. This surplus of energy shows itself in the mature person in generosity, the result of the strength and overflow which the individual can no longer use for further growth and which therefore can be spent productively and creatively. The mature person is no longer primarily a receiver. He receives but he also gives. His giving is not primarily subordinated to his expectation of return. It is giving for its own sake. . . . In the light of this view, altruism, the basis of Christian morality, has a biological foundation; it is a natural, healthy expression of the state of surplus characteristic for maturity.

The mature person is a sharer of his surplus by his very maturity as a mature person. If he is not a sharer he shows his basic immaturity. And this works back upon itself—the more he shares the more mature he becomes.

We can share our spiritual life in many ways: In helping to relieve poverty and in removing the cause of poverty: in various forms of church and community work; in cleaning up civic situations; in youth organizations; and in just being helpful and kind. But these are marginal ways of sharing—the central method of sharing is the sharing of the highest, Christ. The central method of sharing is winning others to Him. Evangelism is the central expression of the Evangel.

To be able and willing to share Christ with others is the highest and most mature sign of maturity. It shows that we are mature enough to have a surplus—an exportable surplus.

O God, may I not hold my surpluses in selfish harboring, but may I pour them out to human need. In doing so I know I'll not be impoverished, but replenished. For as I give I'll receive, pressed down and running over. In Jesus' name. Amen.

AFFIRMATION FOR THE DAY: *The one thing I have worth exporting is Jesus—I shall export Him today.*

THREE CARDINAL URGES

We are studying a sign of maturity—a spiritual surplus—a surplus which we can share in evangelism.

There are three cardinal signs of the new life in Christ: (1) the desire to pray, (2) the urge to join with others in worship, (3) the desire to bring others to Christ. Without the last-named there is no new life. For Christianity is a contagion as well as a conception. And if there is no contagion there will soon be no conception. If a church or individual Christian loses its power to convert it has lost its right to be called Christian. If we cease to be evangelistic we will soon cease to be evangelical, for it is a law of the mind that that which is not expressed dies.

Bishop Stephen Neill, of the World Council of Churches, says:

It is not for any minister to say, "I am not an evangelist." The minister has been ordained for the purpose of winning men and women to Christ and if he is not doing it, it is to be questioned whether he ought to be in the ministry at all. So with a layman; if he is not willing to be a witness it is time he gave up calling himself a Christian.

Why is this so? Simply because if we fail to win others to Christ and to the Church, there will be no Church in the future. When we of the Church today die, the Church dies with us—unless the Church of tomorrow has been won in the meantime. If you, as a member of the church, fail to win someone else, you have a part in the death of the church. If others fail with you there will be no Christian church one hundred years from now. Every year your church loses many from its membership through unconcern, change of address, or death. If you do not win at least that many new Christians, your church is dying. Moreover, unless the congregation to which you belong increases at least 17 percent each year, it is already dying, for that is the rate of increase of the population of the United States.

If you think you can live as a Christian in a private world of your own, you are an idiot. For that is what the word "idiot" literally means—one who lives in a private world. There are no private worlds.

O Father, Thou hast bound us up in a bundle of life. We are responsible for one another. And especially responsible for one another in the deepest things in life—our spiritual life. Help me this day to introduce someone to Thee. Amen.

AFFIRMATION FOR THE DAY: *Give me today: an open door, an open heart, and open lips.*

ALL OF US—EVANGELISTS OF SOMETHING

There are no private worlds—we belong to one another for good or ill. And we are all propagating something. "Out of the abundance of our hearts" our mouths speak—speak something. Some propagate a grouch—they spill over on those whom they meet and douse them with their grouches. That is their evangelism. Others propagate their sex. They play up their sex appeal—the low-cut dress, the silent yet clamorous invitations to look. Sex is their evangelism. Others propagate themselves. They introduce the self into every conversation and into every situation. In my Quiet Time I read recently Peter's saying: "Lo, we have left everything and followed you" (Mark 10:28)—everything except themselves. "And James and John . . . said to Him: . . . 'Grant us to sit, one at your right hand and one at your left, in your glory.' . . . And when the ten heard it, they began to be indignant at James and John" (Mark 10:35-41). With the gospel in the person of Jesus standing right with them, they were preaching the gospel of their own selves.

All of us are evangelists of something. Then I choose Jesus! You are as mature as the thing you propagate. The only way to be really mature is to propagate the highest Maturity—Jesus; then you become what you give out. You as a person are born of the qualities you habitually give out.

You don't have to be a saint to make Jesus your evangelism. You are not proclaiming a perfect proclaimer, but a perfect Savior. You are pointing to Him, not to you. And the Savior is presented as the Savior of the proclaimer—Savior from pride and pharisaism, as well as the Savior of those to whom you proclaim the Savior. The Evangel evangelizes the evangelists in the process of evangelization. Inwardly you go to people on your knees.

You don't have to be a saint to share Jesus, but you do have to be sincere. We are all imperfect proclaimers of a perfect Savior. But in proclaiming the Perfect we tend to become more perfect.

O Perfect Savior, I point to everything with hesitation, except to Thee. There my hesitations drop away and I point without hesitation: "Behold, the Lamb of God, who takes away the sin of the world." And in the pointing I too am perfected. Amen.

AFFIRMATION FOR THE DAY: *I shall lean heavily upon the verse "The Holy Spirit will teach you in that very hour what you ought to say."*

"HE KEPT LOOKING DOWN"

This impulse to share is inherent, because, as we said before, the deepest urge in human nature is the urge to love and be loved. And this urge is found in animals too.

Rags, an airedale, missing three days, was found when a faint barking was heard from a fifty-foot dry well on abandoned property. A man was lowered into the well and Rags was found uninjured but weak from hunger. The man put Rags into a sack and in doing so he felt something hit his leg. He found that a large rabbit had fallen into the well too. The rabbit was put into the sack, but in coming up the sack hit a crosspiece and the rabbit fell back into the well. With frantic eagerness Rags consumed the food and water brought to him, but when the owners wanted Rags to go home with them he would not budge from the mouth of the well. He kept looking down. So someone went down again and brought up the rabbit, the friend who had shared a truce of comradeship with him in their mutual disaster. When the rabbit was brought up safely, Rags sniffed him eagerly and then willingly headed for home.

That same impulse is in the heart of every person who has really tasted Christ—he cannot be content to be rescued alone: he can be content only when those who have shared his pit have been rescued.

And a divine persistence takes possession of us. Rags would not budge until his companion was rescued. Two young men went out in visitation evangelism to call on a couple; when the woman met them at the door she said, "Not interested," and shut the door. Again they went and the man met them this time and said, "Not interested," and shut the door. The third time they went and the couple invited them in. The woman was converted then and there, the man later.

In one visitation evangelism campaign, a young couple, who had been Christians for only six months, won twenty-six people in one week. One man was visited seven times. On the seventh visit he caved in saying: "Well, if it means so much to you I'll try it."

O Jesus my Lord, how can I be silent about Thee. If I did the stones would cry out. Save me from guilty silences when so much is at stake—the destiny of human souls. And help me to do it with naturalness and joy and conviction. Amen.

AFFIRMATION FOR THE DAY: *Silent about Him, vocal about other things, all my values would be twisted.*

"TWO COKES AND A DECISION"

We ended yesterday on the note that to be silent regarding the Highest is to be guilty of a guilty silence. John S. Bonnell tells of a man who was introduced to Rotary and to other clubs and institutions when he came into a new community to live. But when he stood before the church to be received into membership he was surprised that the man who was sponsoring him was the same man who had introduced him to everything in the community, yet had not said a word about his church or his Christ. Vocal on the marginal and silent on the Central.

Youth is often more direct and to the point. Two teen-agers going out on a visitation evangelism campaign went to the soda fountain and said to the girl behind the fountain: "We want two Cokes and a decision for Christ." And they got the decision for Christ!

If youth can do it old age can do it too. In Japan a mother had reared five sons, all of whom turned out to be doctors. She could have felt lonely with all her children gone and could have developed self-pity. Instead she said to herself: "Now that my physical family is gone I'll arise a spiritual family." She and a twelve-year-old boy linked up in visitation evangelism. He would carry her on the back of his bicycle to call on people. She won nine people to Christ, including the leading drunkard of the city—also including the boy who took her around. And she did this after seventy. She had raised two families, physical and spiritual.

In Korea one would have expected the tides of war to leave the church in ruins. Instead, the Korean church doubled its membership during the war, from five hundred thousand to one million. Why? Because when the members were scattered they witnessed, set up little groups, for evangelism is an integral part of their Christianity. Before one is baptized he has to show someone he has won to Christ, as a sign that he is a real Christian. That is mature immaturity.

O Lord and Master, I have one request: Put the impulse and the will to share Thee at the very center of my love and loyalty to Thee. For Thou didst share Thyself with me—unworthy as I am. Help me to catch the fire of Thy sharing and the blaze of Thy love. Amen.

AFFIRMATION FOR THE DAY: *"Freely have I received so freely do I give"* shall be my motive and my motto.

"GET DRUNK AND GO TO HELL"

We have said that anybody can do this work of winning others. And you can do it under all circumstances. A pastor was dying of cancer and he asked his whole congregation to visit him, one by one. And he told each one what a wonderful thing it is to be a Christian and what a wonderful thing death is when you are a Christian.

A man without legs or arms made everyone who came to him read John 3:16: "God so loved the world that he gave his only Son, that whoever believes in him should not perish but have eternal life." He helped transform many people by the reading and he himself was transformed in the process.

One man who was confronted with the challenge to do visitation evangelism said: "Why I couldn't do that. I'd be tongue-tied." He tried it, found he could do it. When he died two years later a space was reserved in the church for those who had been led to Christ by him. There were 231 people.

A man read in the paper about this visitation evangelism and he said to himself: "They'll be calling on me. For I'm not a Christian, or a member of the church." So on Monday night he shaved and waited for them to come. They didn't come. Tuesday night he did the same and they didn't come. He said to himself: "I'll give them one more night." Back of the scenes this happened: when the workers got their assignments this man's card turned up on top. Embarrassed they stuck it down underneath—he was considered too tough. The second day that card turned up on top and was stuck down underneath. When it turned up the third time they said they had better call on him. And did. The man met them at the door and said: "Well, you've come at last. Come in." And then he told them what had happened, how he had shaved and waited for them two nights and how he had said to himself: "I'll give them one more night and if they don't come, I'll get drunk and go to hell. It's a good thing you came tonight." Dramatic? Yes. But deep down in every man is that wanting for somebody to give the inner gentle push that will lead to Christ.

O Christ, my Lord, help me this day to give someone that gentle inner push that will lead people to Thy feet. For we all belong there—at Thy feet. That is our homeland. And help me not to look at my weakness, but at Thy wonder. In Thy name. Amen.

AFFIRMATION FOR THE DAY: *Perhaps I shall have to awaken the desire for Christ and then appeal to it.*

THE GOD URGE NATIVE TO US

This need of Christ is central in every human life. Viktor Frankl, a Vienna psychiatrist, says that the God urge is native to man, as native as the self urge or the sex urge or the herd urge; that if you suppress God in your lives you will get a complex exactly as you do when you suppress any of the other urges; that about 50 percent of his patients are suffering from the suppression of God in their lives. If that be true, nothing else is of like importance. It means that in every human heart is an ally when we approach people for Christ.

This finding of God is the central problem in every life. A woman was talking to "Mary" about her problems. In the midst of it "Mary" said: "Now before we go into your problems, may I ask whether you have surrendered yourself to Christ." And the woman replied: "No, I don't suppose I have." Then let's attend to that first," said "Mary." They went to their knees, and the woman arose a changed and happy person. "Now," said "Mary," "tell me about your problems." And the woman laughed and said, "But now I have no problems; that was it." And "Mary" remarked, "Now I've found out how to save time."

A doctor, after weeks of deep conviction of sin and failure, came to a crisis and felt he could not go on. One night he prepared for himself a fatal dose and sat up all night in an agony of mind, determined to end his life if peace did not come before morning. At 5:00 A.M. he remembered the prodigal son and realized how the Father went out to meet him. The doctor identified himself with that prodigal son and as he sat there the love and forgiveness of God came to him. He fell on his knees and with tears surrendered himself to God. He spent the balance of his days helping others find that release.

Every human soul needs just that in one form or other. The Roman Catholic bishop of Indiana said: "Forgive us, but we are going to ring every doorbell in Indiana." He will do it for the Church—and Christ. We will do it for Christ—and the Church. And in doing so we will become mature.

O Master of my heart, I have looked into Thy face and I can never be satisfied until others look into that "one dear face." For this side of that vision, life stumbles in darkness from event to event. With that vision we are on the Way. Amen.

AFFIRMATION FOR THE DAY: *Since the God urge is native to everyone, I have an ally in every human soul.*

MATURITY IN LISTENING AND RECEPTIVITY

We now turn to something closely akin to what we have been discussing; namely, maturity in listening and receptivity.

The first law of life is receptivity. The first act of a child is to receive. Instinct provides that the child turn to its mother's breast—to receive. That first law of life—receptivity—begins there and goes through life. We can expend only what we receive and no more.

In a radio or a television set, if the reception is bad, then the outcome—the voice or the vision—is bad.

Jesus said, "Consider the lilies of the field, how they grow." How do they grow? By striving, getting into an agony of desire to grow, by working hard? No, the lilies grow by receptivity. They take in from soil and sun and atmosphere and they give back in beauty. They grow effortlessly without strain and without drain. So Jesus points us to the lilies and asks us to grow by receptivity.

The nervous, pushing, active type of modern living has lost the art of receptivity, of being quiet, of listening. It pushes itself against the problems of living and exhausts itself upon those problems. Hence our mental institutions are filled with disrupted, exhausted persons. One out of ten Americans is a mental patient. And think of those who never get to institutions or psychiatric offices, but who are a problem to themselves and to others in the ordinary relationships of life. They bring themselves to this state by pushing, by pulling, by tense striving—all outgo and no income. When they get to the stage of being neurotics they continue this meaningless outgo. They talk interminably and write long and exhausting letters, going round and round on the same things and getting nowhere. They have acquired the habit of outgo and they can't stop it. They lack receptivity. If they should learn how to listen, to receive, they would be well.

And many semiexhausted souls would be well and whole and adequate for living if they should learn the art of receptivity, of lowly listening, of the Great Intake.

O Spirit Divine, teach me how to receive, to take. My hands are so full of problems that I have no room to receive. Help me to empty them, turn them up to Thee, and then receive, receive, receive—to overflowing. In Jesus' name. Amen.

AFFIRMATION FOR THE DAY: *If the first law of life is receptivity, it shall be my first emphasis.*

RECEIVING AT FIRSTHAND
We are looking at the necessity of receptivity, of listening, of taking. We are as mature as we are mature in receptivity. Without receptivity there can be no maturity. When expenditure is greater than intake, decay sets in. And if such expenditure is kept up, then death results. Receptivity is a maturity *must*.

In the parable of the sower Jesus gave four stages to maturity: "And other seeds fell into good soil [receptivity] and brought forth grain [response], growing up and increasing [renewal] and yeilding thirtyfold and sixtyfold and a hundredfold [reproduction]" (Mark 4:8). These then are the stages: (1) receptivity, (2) response, (3) renewal, (4) reproduction. Everything depends upon the first stage: receptivity. Without it nothing else happens. So all efforts at maturity are a striving after wind unless we begin with receptivity, continue with receptivity, and end with receptivity. We are as mature as we are receptive. And receptive of agape love.

In the Christian faith we have the open invitation to receive firsthand. Jesus is a mediator only in the sense that He mediates God to us. He who takes hold of Jesus takes hold of the very self of God. No church in real Christianity intrudes itself between you and God, saying, "You can get to God only through me." Jesus is God come to us. And when you find Him you find God.

A bookshop carried a sign: "Secondhand theology for sale." A lot of theology is secondhand theology. But in real Christianity everything is firsthand. Someone asked Rufus Moseley if he was a mystic, and his reply was, "No, I'm just a firsthander." And because his religion was firsthand, it was vital, fresh, spontaneous, and bubbling.

Our power of spiritual reproduction is dependent on our power of spiritual receptivity. And the receptivity must be firsthand if it is to be real receptivity. Books, sermons, services are good if they take you beyond themselves to the living Christ and get you to set up a living relationship with Him and in Him and through Him with God. In Him secondhandedness drops away and we receive directly.

O Christ, how can I thank Thee enough for the blessed face-to-faceness, for this blessed immediacy—nothing between. Then I take with both hands and open heart. I take Thy blessed All into my little all. And am full—to overflowing. Amen.

AFFIRMATION FOR THE DAY: *When the firsthand is open, why should I live on the secondhand?*

WAYS IN WHICH GOD MAY SPEAK

How do we receive firsthand from Christ? I would outline the steps as follows:

1. *Expect Him to speak to you.* The God who could not speak to you would be a dumb God, less than the creatures He has made. The psalmist says:

He who planted the ear, does he not hear?
He who formed the eye, does he not see? (94:9).

And we may add: He that made the tongue, shall He not speak? We can communicate with one another. Can He not communicate with us?

2. *Expect yourself to hear and receive what He speaks.* You are made to receive His communications as definitely as a radio or a television set is made to receive the broadcasts. You and God are affinities.

3. *Tune into Him by complete surrender to Him.* Without complete surrender to Him you are off the beam. Until you are surrendered you are listening to yourself and its clamorings. Surrender is turning the dial until it clicks with His will.

4. *He may speak to you through His word.* I find it well to begin my Quiet Time by reading from the Word, preferably from the New Testament. These words of the New Testament have had fresh, firsthand contact with the Word—the Word made flesh. Hence in a peculiar way God speaks in these words. They are inspired because they are inspiring. God has gone into them, for God comes out of them. By beginning with the words of the New Testament you get a brainwashing in the mind of Christ. You voluntarily wash your thinking in His mind and thought. Your values become Values. Your thought becomes Thought. Your mind becomes Mind. Your being becomes Being.

5. *He may speak to you through His guiding someone to speak His message to you.* As someone speaks to you there is a warmth about certain sentences. They place their hands in yours, as if intended for you. They are a direct message of God to you carried by another.

O Father, Thou art the God who speaks. And Thy speaking is always love speaking. And when Thou art speaking, love is speaking the most loving thing possible to me in my situation. Help me to take it just as lovingly. In Jesus' name. Amen.

AFFIRMATION FOR THE DAY: *"I'll be somewhere listening—listening for my name."*

318

MORE WAYS IN WHICH GOD MAY SPEAK

We are continuing our consideration of how Christ speaks to us and how to receive from Him:

6. *He may speak to us through some opening providences, through some opening need.* Here is a need. I can meet that need; therefore that need is a call to me from God. Don't wait for specific guidance when there is specific need at hand. Here is a passage to the point: "Do whatever your hands find to do, for God is with you" (I Sam. 10:7). When God is with you, then everything is an open opportunity. You can do everything in His name and for His love.

But there may be a specific need which you can specifically meet—a need at home or abroad. Then that need may be your call. God fits the man and matches him against that need. After working for some years with the outcastes of India, I saw a need to work among the high-caste intelligentsia. It grew upon me. And God gradually prepared me to meet that need. I cannot remember any single moment when He called me. But I knew that He had matched me against that need.

7. *He may speak to you through your heightened moral intelligence.* When you are surrendered to Him, He can think His thoughts through you. Your thinking and His thinking are intertwined like the words and music of a song. Jesus said to His disciples, "And why do you not judge for yourselves what is right?" (Luke 12:57). He expected them to be so attuned to Him that they would judge for themselves what was right. "The meek will he guide in judgment" (Ps. 25:9 KJV). The meek—the surrendered—will be guided to right conclusions.

8. *He may speak to you through the Inner Voice:* When these other ways are not available for guidance, then He speaks directly through what I would call the Inner Voice. It is not an outer voice—a voice that can be heard by the ear. The words frame themselves within the mind. You can speak to yourself without an audible voice; in like manner God can speak to us. But it is real speaking.

O Christ, my Lord, Thou hast promised that Thy sheep shall know Thy voice. I want the trained inner ear to hear the Inner Voice. For everything depends on my right recognition of Thee speaking. "Speak, Lord, for thy servant hears." Amen.

AFFIRMATION FOR THE DAY: *My trained ear shall hear His voice and my disciplined will shall act upon it.*

SPEAKING THROUGH THE INNER VOICE

We ended yesterday with an emphasis on receiving through the Inner Voice. How can we distinguish between the Inner Voice and the voice of the subconscious?

There is a general test: Does this voice that speaks within me fit in with the general guidance which I have through the life and teaching of Jesus? Is it contrary to what I see in His spirit and teaching? If so, then I must suspect it; nay, I must reject it. For God cannot speak out of two sides of His mouth in contradictory ways—one in Jesus and the other to you directly within. God speaks in the same accents and with the same emphasis in Jesus and in you.

There is another way by which we can distinguish the voice of God from the voice of the subconscious: the subconscious tends to argue, to try to convince you, but the voice of God simply tells you. It is self-authenticating. When you hear your mother's voice over the telephone you need no corroboration. You simply say: "It is you."

Today I received a letter from a very spiritual friend and that friend said: "Today the Father told me that I must go beyond merely saying, 'I am sorry.' He told me that I must say: 'You were right in the matter.' " That was real guidance, not only because the friend said I was right, but his action fitted in with the spirit of Jesus. That friend came clear with no loose ends left.

In recent years I have found myself waking in the early morning hours. Instead of fretting about not being able to sleep, I decided I would turn that wakeful period into what I call my Listening Post. When I awaken I say to the Father, "Have you anything to say to me?" I then relax and become perfectly passive and I listen with all my being. For what He tells me may have life importance. Sometimes it is a small thing: "Write that letter." Sometimes it is big, involving a real change in life and attitude. And sometimes He draws me into wordless communion with Himself. Thus a possibly fretful period has become a very fruitful period.

O Father, Thy voice is always redemptive, for whether it speaks in correction or in commendation it is always for my good. Love speaks when Thou dost speak, whether Thy voice is approval or disapproval—Love always speaks. I thank Thee. Amen.

AFFIRMATION FOR THE DAY: *If I am to be a Spirit-guided man, I must be a Spirit-possessed man.*

DESTINY IN THREE FORMS

We are emphasizing the art of receiving. A very able pastor, laid low with a heart attack for eight months in a hospital, received a booklet from the hospital entitled "Prepare to Meet Thy Good." He thought at first that the last word was misspelled. But it wasn't. The pamphlet said that the setup in the hospital was all for one thing and for one thing alone—the patient's good. So prepare to meet that "good"! Don't fight it, feel it is bondage, or something to be tolerated—prepare to meet your "good." His whole attitude changed, and when he came back to his pulpit he preached as his first sermon, "Why I Thank God for My Heart Attack." Before, he had been struggling and tense and anxious. Now he became surrendered and receptive and relaxed. Now he knew how to take.

Some time ago I went to a college and found that my subject had been announced as "How to Stand and Take It"—their choice of a subject! This subject pointed to the attitude of being able to take what comes, to stand anything that happens. But sometimes, rather than "stand up and take it," we have to lie down and receive it. And make something out of it! We inwardly prepare to meet our good! For when we are in Him everything that happens can be for our good, for our healing, for our education, for our maturing.

Viktor Frankl, the psychiatrist, says: "Destiny appears to a man in three principal forms: (1) as his natural *disposition*, or endowment, what Tandler call man's 'somatic fate'; (2) as his *situation*, the total of his external environments; (3) disposition and situation together make up man's *position*. Toward this he 'takes a position'—that is, he forms an attitude." The attitude he takes is the most important. For he can take the attitude of learning, receiving, of making something out of his disposition and his situation and making them further him. He can take his physical handicaps and make them spiritual assets—he can take his adverse environment and make it burnishing powder to burnish and brighten his soul.

O God, my eternal Teacher, help me to be taught by everything that happens and by every person I meet. May I be receptive from everything and everybody, so that life becomes my schoolroom—all set for my good. Amen.

AFFIRMATION FOR THE DAY: *Since the Father is conspiring to make all things work for good, I shall "prepare to meet my good."*

CONVERSION IS CONVERSION TO RECEPTIVITY

Jesus said that conversion means a conversion to receptivity: "Except ye be converted, and become as little children, ye shall not enter into the kingdom of heaven" (Matt. 18:3 KJV). The child is open, receptive, eager, responsive. Two Indian children were offered a mango by a Catholic priest as our bus stopped. One girl became self-conscious and wouldn't take it. The younger child, with no self-consciousness, came up with a smile and took it. She entered the kingdom of fruit by receptivity. When we become self-conscious, the kingdom of God is closed to us. When we look at Him and take what He offers, the kingdom of God and its powers belong to us.

Conversion is conversion to receptivity. Prayer is receptivity. Its attitude is this: "Speak, Lord, for thy servant hears" (I Sam. 3:9). Many think of prayer as: "Listen, Lord, for thy servant speaks." This attitude is like that of the man who sees the President, with ten minutes for the interview. The man talks glibly for nine minutes and then says: "Mr. President, if you have anything to say to me, please say it." We do that with God. Our first attitude should be to listen, then request.

A group of 120 people listened to God for ten days in an Upper Room. Those ten days were "the ten days that changed a world." These people listened and received—received the Holy Spirit and went out to do the impossible. They changed the values, the outlook, the spirit of humanity. And did it effortlessly.

A group of people at Antioch listened and heard God saying: "Set apart for me Barnabas and Saul for the work to which I have called them," and out of that listening came a missionary movement that went from Asia, to Europe, to us, to the world, and transformed everything it touched.

Just as the kingdom of sound and scene floating through the air belong to the radio and television receiving sets, so the kingdom of God and all its powers belong to those humble enough to receive.

O God, my Father, I humble my heart; I open my upturned hands; I am open to receive Thy bounties, Thy blessings, Thy being. I belong to the renounced in spirit and as such the Kingdom belongs to me. I take it, take it, take it. Amen.

AFFIRMATION FOR THE DAY: *I am a person of the bent knee, the upturned hand, and the full heart.*

BODILY HEALTH AND HEALING

We come to study this week the art of receiving bodily health and healing. Many are mature at the place of receiving spiritual life for their souls but don't know how to receive physical life for their bodies. They have compartmentalized the power of their faith, confining it to the spiritual, but allowing it to function but faintly in the material. Our faith should function in the total person. Jesus said to a sick man: "Wilt thou be made whole?" (John 5:6 KJV). One would have expected Him to say: "Wilt thou be healed of thy sickness?" But Jesus was interested in something more than healing disease—He wanted people to be "whole," of which the healing of sickness was a part. The fact is that sickness cannot be cured unless the total person is cured. For if there is sickness in any portion of the person—in his spirit, in his mind, in his emotion, in his body—it will pass over to the other portions and infect them.

Sometimes the body gets sick and passes on its sickness to the mind and the spirit. And sometimes the mind and spirit get sick and pass on their sickness to the body. Some doctors estimate that 75 percent of illnesses are rooted in mind and spirit. One doctor told me that every disease, either in its inception or in its development, is affected by mind and emotion.

The old adage "He who physics the mind will have no need of physics" has a truth in it—a real truth. Someone has defined the Christian Ashram (place of spiritual retreat, of which we have six throughout the United States) in this way: "The Ashram is a positive healing of Christian love to mind, spirit, and body." Is that the right order? Is the mind first, the spirit second, and the body third? Yes. For if you put the body first, as some do, then you make Christianity a healing cult. That puts us at the center—God our servant. The first thing in Christianity is reconciliation with God—God is the center. When you are reconciled to God you become reconciled to yourself and hence reconciled to your body. The healing of that reconciliation with God is passed on to the body.

O Father, when I am reconciled to Thee, I can live with myself, I can live with my body, I can live with my brothers, I can live with nature—I can live! Help me to be alive on all fronts—alive with Thy vitality—alive! In Jesus' name. Amen.

AFFIRMATION FOR THE DAY: *My impact upon myself and upon others shall be a positive healing to mind, spirit, and body.*

HEALING TO MIND, SPIRIT, AND BODY

We said that the Ashram is "a positive healing of Christian love to mind, spirit, and body." We begin with the mind—is that right? Yes, for that is where Jesus began. He went out saying: "Repent, for the kingdom of God is at hand." Repentance was His first emphasis. In the Greek, repentance is *metanoia*—literally, "a change of mind," a change of viewpoint, a change of conception. For that which is in the mind as thought will pass into the emotions as feeling, then into the will as action, then into the body as result.

A doctor said to a minister: "I've taken out a part of this man's stomach, but unless you do something for him he'll be back and I can't take out any more of his stomach." Wrong thinking, producing wrong emotions, had produced stomach ulcers which no operation could cure. It could relieve temporarily, but the cure awaited the cure of the mind and emotion.

A girl of thirteen in our Ashram had a flair for bandages. She came to the table with her hand bandaged and was eating with her left hand. When I asked her to show me the hurt portion she uncovered a perfectly well hand. She gained attention by the bandaging. Now that avenue is closed to her and she is becoming ill in general—for the same reason—to gain attention. The sickness is emotional.

In Guayaquil, Ecuador, a boa constrictor slithered through the open window of a hospital in which there were paralysis cases. All but three of the patients jumped from their beds and ran. They thought they were paralyzed—and were. When stronger thought took possession of them they were not paralyzed—they ran.

In the hospital at Vrindaban, India, a nurse told me of a Hindu woman who had all the symptoms of advanced pregnancy. The doctors were puzzled about certain factors and put her under an anesthetic. The moment she got under the anesthetic her abdomen flattened out. Her strong wish to have a child and her suggestions to herself that she was to have a child produced all the symptoms of pregnancy.

O Christ, my Savior, save me from any lingering wrong viewpoint or thought. Correct and cleanse me at the source and then the stream will run clear. May my inmost thought be Thy thought; then I shall be Thine in all I do and am. Amen.

AFFIRMATION FOR THE DAY: *I have a right to health; therefore I shall meet the conditions of health.*

EFFECT OF MIND ON BODY

We are studying the necessity to change our thinking—to repent. In America ten million people—one in every sixteen—are suffering from some form of mental disorder. According to the National Association for Mental Health there are more people in mental hospitals than in all other hospitals combined. In large measure we have succeeded in conquering contagious diseases, only to find that the contagion of wrong thinking and emotions is more dangerous than germs.

In an Indian hospital a woman was operated on; the next day she began to have convulsions and her temperature rose to 105 degrees. The doctors could find nothing in the blood to account for it. They were puzzled. Then the nurse said: "This patient told me that she went into those convulsions to see if her husband really loved her and how much the relatives really cared." By her very thinking, she could send her temperature up.

Here was a young couple who suffered from various allergies. They moved to another section of the country to get rid of them, but the allergies were due to the fact that the mother-in-law, who lived nearby, had never accepted the wife and wanted her son to marry someone else. The young people were allergic to the mother-in-law, not to this, that, or the other!

If our thinking is the first thing to change, then what are some of the ideas we must change if we are to be basically healthy? First, *we must give up the wrong notion that the world owes us happiness.* That idea sends a lot of people on the wrong tangent and is at the basis of much marital unhappiness. Give happiness and you won't have to demand it; you'll have it—in abundance. Second, *we must give up the notion that we can harbor fears, resentments, self-centeredness, and guilts and that nothing will happen to us physically.* Maybe not today, or tomorrow, but on the third day it will affect you. "Nothing is covered that will not be revealed," and it may be revealed in bodily infirmity.

O Jesus, my Lord, put Thy finger on any hidden thinking or attitude which may be deep within me. And help me to expose it to Thy healing light. For when I bring it to Thy light I know Thou dost not punish but purify me.

AFFIRMATION FOR THE DAY: *The world doesn't owe me happiness—it simply gives me opportunity to make myself happy.*

SOME IDEAS WE MUST GIVE UP

We are continuing the enumeration of wrong mental attitudes we must change if we are to be healthy. Third, *we must give up the notion that God will pass a miracle over us and heal us without our cooperating with Him in giving up thinking and emotions which produce disease.* The promising of healing to people regardless of whether they give up wrong thinking and emotions has left behind a lot of disillusionment and wreckage of faith. Fourth, *we must give up the notion that healing can only be sudden, on-the-spot healing.* It does sometimes work that way, but more often it works gradually as we cooperate with God in eliminating the causes of disease. Fifth, *we must renounce the attitude that we can skip the healing of spirit and take the healing of the body.* In the definition of the Ashram, the order was "a positive healing of Christian love to mind, spirit and body." The healing starts from the mind in letting go of wrong thinking, passes on to the spirit where wrong attitudes and emotions are changed with the change of the mind, and finally it gets to the body. Sixth, *we must give up the idea of trying to deal with symptoms and go down to the disease.* For instance, we are told that enough sleeping pills were sold last year in the United States to put every man, woman, and child to sleep for twenty-three days. And all those sleeping pills did not do a bit of permanent good. For down underneath this sleeplessness, except in the case of the physically ill, was a conflict within which caused the inability to sleep.

If these are some examples of the wrong thinking which we must let go, what are some right mental attitudes which we must take if we are to be well? Someone asked me: "What is the secret of your amazing health?" It has been amazing, for I've been speaking from two to five times a day for forty years, with no vacations except to work on a book, and yet I seem to be in perfect health. I replied: "Well, I suppose it is because I have learned the art of receptivity. I take grace not only for my spirit, but for my mind and body as well."

O Jesus, my Lord, Thy grace is available for the total me: grace for my spirit to cleanse me from deep, inner conflicts; grace for my mind to convert it and quicken it; grace for my body to heal it and vitalize it. I thank Thee for grace. Amen.

AFFIRMATION FOR THE DAY: *All my thoughts and attitudes shall be health-producing.*

RIGHT THINKING AND RIGHT EMOTIONS

We have emphasized that the secret of physical health is receptivity. God is life and love and if I have learned how to breathe in life and love, just as I breathe air into my lungs, then every cell of my body is bathed in that healing life and love. His life absorbs all my tiredness, and His love all my conflicts which produce the tiredness. I am fresh—in Him.

When I replied to the lady mentioned yesterday that I thought the secret of my health was receptivity, she replied: "Yes, but isn't it also right thinking and right emotions?" And I replied: "yes, because if I have wrong thinking and wrong emotions, that will block the receptivity automatically." Right thinking and right emotions keep the channels clear for grace to operate. I would define right thinking as thinking that keeps within the general sphere of the mind of Jesus. That would mean that my thinking would have to be positive not negative, appreciative not critical, creative not destructive, loving not hating, moving within law not asking for exceptions.

And right emotions? There is only one criterion for our emotions: love! Love God and man—with no exceptions! This means that all that cannot fit into love must go—envy, jealousy, resentments, fear, tensions, self-centeredness, and guilt feelings. And when you let these go, then grace automatically comes in and takes over.

In addition to these, what other suggestions have I to offer those who would be healthy and vital? Well, I take exercises that last ten minutes before going to bed. That time is my own. So I take three exercises, each one thirty times. This takes the congested blood out of my brain, distributes it through my body, and I go off to sleep relaxed. No crutches like sleeping pills needed. When an inwardly battered person arose from her knees after surrendering her conflicts and herself to Christ, she opened her handbag, took out a flask of liquor, a gold cigarette case, and a bottle of sleeping pills, with the quiet remark: "I won't need those things now." And she didn't. Grace had taken over.

O grace of God, take full possession of me—mind, spirit, and body. And let me live, move, and have my being within the sphere of grace. For when I'm in grace I am in health and life and peace. Amen.

AFFIRMATION FOR THE DAY: *I think thoughts of health, feel feelings of health, and will the purposes of health.*

"CRUTCHES"

Yesterday we ended on the note of letting go crutches of various kinds: narcotics, sedatives, "happiness pills." It is startling to see how many depend on crutches to hobble down through life. One third of doctors' prescriptions, we are told, are now for various types of "happiness pills." These are for sick and lamed humanity, treating symptoms rather than diseases.

At a service club luncheon, where ladies were present, it was announced that the club members were supporting an Anticancer Drive, and all members were urged to get behind the drive. In front of the speaker's table was a row of intelligent women, all of whom were smoking blithely away, apparently oblivious to the fact that they were a part of the disease rather than the cure.

The next thing I would suggest in order to maintain health is right habits of rest. In a National Preaching Mission a prominent member of the team, after two weeks, came down to breakfast and announced that he was "across the ropes" and would have to quit and go home. Why? He would stay up until midnight talking over problems with ministers and others. At ten o'clock I would excuse myself and go to bed. For I've found that "he who talks and runs away may live to talk another day." Right habits of rest and recuperation are necessary. Prolonged periods of rest and recuperation are not necessary if you have right thinking, right emotions, right habits, that enable you to receive grace continuously. Those who know say that if you give nature twenty-four hours of complete rest and relaxation she will balance the accounts, throwing off all fatigue toxins within that period. If after twenty-four hours you are still tired it is a tiredness of the mind and spirit, not of the body. Of course, if there is a structural disease the case is different.

Fulfill these suggestions and grace will invade you with healing. The words of Angelus Silesius, "Bloom, frozen Christian, bloom. May stands before your door," could be, "Bloom, broken-down Christian, bloom. Grace stands before your door."

Oh Healing Christ, lay Thy hands of healing upon my mind, my spirit, my body. For I turn them over to Thee. What Thou hast, Thou dost heal. Thou hast the whole me; then heal me wholly. Amen.

AFFIRMATION FOR THE DAY: *I do not need crutches when I have the Everlasting Arms.*

"STRONGEST WHERE I WAS WEAKEST"

We have been studying how grace can come in and take us over and make us over if we clear away obstructions of wrong thinking, wrong emotions, wrong habits, and wrong attitudes toward life. Two tablets are very precious to me for they represent two types of healing—one for the spirit and mind and one for the body. One is in Memorial Methodist Church in Baltimore. When the congregation moved from the little church where I was converted to a larger church, they cut the altar rail where I had knelt and had given myself to Christ and made a prayer desk out of it, with this inscription: "At this place Stanley Jones knelt and gave himself to Christ," and invited others to do the same. Just as Zacchaeus is said to have watered periodically the tree in which he climbed and met Christ and a new life, so I, too, go back and kneel at that prayer desk periodically in the deepest thanksgiving a human heart can know.

The other tablet is in the Central Methodist Church in Lucknow, India. Located toward the back of the church it reads: "Near this spot Stanley Jones knelt a physically broken man and arose completely whole." That was forty years ago. And the infirmity from which I was healed has never returned.

If I could put up another tablet it would be not for some crisis in healing as these two tablets represent, but for that continuous healing which grace gives day by day, year in and year out. This continuous healing is what Paul means when he says: "He who raised Christ Jesus from the dead will give life to your mortal bodies also through his Spirit which dwells in you" (Rom. 8:11). The indwelling Spirit giving life, day by day, to our bodies is the most glorious healing of all.

Since He has my health I now pay little attention to it. Other people's problems absorb my attention. As I was about to visit the pyramids in Egypt, a man who paid a lot of attention to his health, giving himself "attention pains," asked me: "Will your nerves and arteries stand it?" I replied: "I haven't asked them and don't intend to."

O Father, give me mature attitudes toward my body. Help me not to be interfering by my anxiety with Thy healing processes always at work within me. Help me to turn my health over to Thee while I get interested in others. Amen.

AFFIRMATION FOR THE DAY: *I shall not worry about my health—I shall think in terms of others.*

MATURITY REGARDING MATERIAL POSSESSIONS

We turn now to another area which can show either maturity or immaturity—the area of material possessions.

There are two John 3:16s. We think of only one: "For God so loved the world that he gave his only Son, that whoever believes in him should not perish but have eternal life." It is no wonder that Christians of all ages have fastened on this verse as the greatest in all literature. For into these twenty-four words has been packed more of truth than in any other twenty-four words in our language.

But there is another John 3:16: "By this we know love, that he laid down his life for us; and we ought to lay down our lives for the brethren" (I John 3:16). Both of these have the same theme—He gave His life for us; and both have the same number of words—twenty-four. And yet we have taken to one and not to the other. The latter is seldom quoted. Why? Perhaps for the reason that in the first passage God does everything and we have only to *believe*. In the second, God does His part—"he laid down his life for us"; and then it says that we are to do our part—"we ought to lay down our lives for the brethren." That last part isn't quite so popular. So we have made popular the one and soft-pedaled the other.

The same thing happened in regard to two breakings of bread in the early Church—one the bread of the Love Feast, the koinonia, and the other the bread of the Holy Communion. Both were in the Acts—the breaking of bread in the koinonia was the more prominent. Then gradually the bread of the Holy Communion took its place. Why? The latter commemorated what He did for us in laying down His life for us. The bread of the fellowship pointed to a common daily bread—we share our bread with one another. And the early Church did just that; they shared what they had with one another—they were of "one bread." Gradually that idea was lost and we took "the One Bread." We took what He did for us and gradually let drop what we should do for others. So in these two John 3:16s we took what He did for us and passed by what we are to do for others.

O Jesus, Thy patience and love are astounding. How dost Thou put up with us and bear with us? The wonder of Thy love sends us to our knees. Bear with us more and maybe we shall yet take Thy whole way in all our ways. Amen.

AFFIRMATION FOR THE DAY: *I shall possess my material possessions—they shall not possess me.*

MATURITY IN DOING THE LITTLE THINGS

John insisted that since "He laid down his life for us," we should "lay down our lives for the brethren." This is true to the Christian ethic: What God does in Christ, we should carry out through Christ. We do what God does. Our ethics are founded in the character and example of God. He laid down His life; we should lay down ours. Nothing is sounder than that.

But when we look at the next verse we find no dramatic application of this principle. We would expect it to point to some dramatic martyrdom, telling us how we can lay down our lives for the brethren. Instead it says: "But if any one has the world's goods and sees his brother in need, yet closes his heart against him, how does God's love abide in him? Little children, let us not love in word or speech but in deed and in truth" (I John 3:17-18). One commentator says that this sounds like an anticlimax—from martyrdom to material goods. But this is true to the Incarnation. In the Incarnation, ideas and principles take flesh, take shoes and walk. The Word becomes flesh. And that becoming flesh was very undramatic—a babe in a manger, a carpenter at a bench, an itinerant preacher sleeping on hillsides, dying on a roughhewn cross, and laid in a rock tomb. The outer shell of this Incarnation was ordinary. But He put into that outer shell an extraordinary spirit. Every little thing became big, for He did it in a big way.

So here John says, "Don't look for a big demonstration of your love by a dramatic martyrdom, but demonstrate your love by little acts of meeting your brother's need, by sharing your material goods." Nothing could be sounder and more mature than that. For many show their immaturity by refusing to do anything because they can't do everything. Because they can't set the world on fire they won't light a candle. Because they can't save a world they refuse to save a brother in his need. Jesus said, "He who is faithful in a very little is faithful also in much." Maturity is doing the little at hand, thus opening the way for the bigger in the future.

O Jesus, Thou didst show the way to the big. It lay through the little. Thou didst redeem the world in the big, because Thou didst redeem every little thing that came Thy way. Teach me this day to do every little thing in a big way. Amen.

AFFIRMATION FOR THE DAY: *My goods are possible good or possible evil.*

"A STRAIGHT WAY FOR . . . ALL OUR GOODS"

On the first Thanksgiving Day, Governor Brewster, of the Massachusetts Colony, preached a sermon on this text: "Then I proclaimed a fast there, at the river Ahava, that we might humble ourselves before God, to seek from him a straight way for ourselves, our children, and all our goods" (Ezra 8:21). The first Thanksgiving was a fast—we have made it into a feast. The first was to humble ourselves before God—we congratulate God and ourselves for our prosperity. The first was "to seek from him a straight way for ourselves, our children"—to find out God's destiny for us; we take it for granted we know our destiny and that it is being fulfilled in us. The first Thanksgiving sought "a straight way for . . . all our goods"; we seldom seek guidance for all our goods but consume our goods, as much as we can, in celebration.

The seeking "a straight way for . . . all our goods" is important. For what we do with the material registers and decides the spiritual. Our material acts become our spiritual attitudes. We become in spirit what we do in the flesh. When James spoke of those whose "riches have rotted," it was really more serious than "rotted riches"—it was the outer manifestation of rotted spirits. When material wealth does nothing more than accumulate, it is "rotted riches." For wealth is like manure: put in one pile it is a stinking mass, but distributed across the fields it produces golden grain. Wealth concentrated in the hands of the few decays, but distributed it brings a harvest of opportunity.

So the person in quest for maturity says to himself: "Am I mature or infantile at the place of my material possessions?" Concerning his toys the child is always saying: "It's mine." The immature person takes the same attitude toward his possessions: "It's mine." Is it? When a wealthy farmer said to a minister: "If these broad acres aren't mine, then just whose are they?" The minister replied: "Ask me that question a hundred years from now." Only what you have within is yours and will go out with you. And what you do with the material will determine how much you possess within.

O God, my father, help me to hold my possessions in my hand and not let them get into my heart. Help me to possess my possessions and not let them possess me. Then teach me the principles upon which I must handle the material. Amen.

AFFIRMATION FOR THE DAY: *When I seek guidance for all my goods, then all my guidance will be good.*

PRINCIPLES AND PROCEDURES
IN HANDLING OUR GOODS

Yesterday we raised the question, On what principles and procedures should we handle "all our goods"?

First, *we should not offer to God our goods in lieu of surrendering ourselves to Him.* Every time he took up with a different woman a certain married man would give his wife a new car, a fur coat, a refrigerator. He gave these in lieu of giving her his loyalty and his love. The gifts became loathsome. After he had surrendered himself to God, a candy manufacturer said: "I've been giving my money to God, but I've never given myself." Now the self and the money both belong to God. He grew up to maturity overnight.

I watched a bird which was making the cross on the top of our chapel in Sat Tal, India, a center of operation for catching insects. He would make sudden flights this way and that way, always returning to the cross. We often use the cross for our own purposes, making it the place from which we forage for ourselves. Our religion gives respectability and standing for our greeds. Often men will join the church which offers the greatest opportunity to sell their goods among the members. The cross is used as a basis for foraging for themselves.

Second, *we should give back to God one tenth of our income.* That isn't really giving—it is paying rental to God for the use of His air, water, light, earth. That paying of rental acknowledges God's ownership of all. Just as you pay rental to a landlord as a symbol that he is owner, so we pay to God a tenth as acknowledgment that He is owner of the nine tenths—owner of all.

Third, *we have a right to as much of the nine tenths for our use as will make us more fit—mentally, spiritually, and physically—for the purposes of the kingdom of God.* We have a right to have our needs met. The rest of our income belongs to those whose needs are not met. We then hold the rest, after our needs are met, at the disposal of God so that he may meet the needs of others through us. Ourselves and our possessions belong to God.

O blessed, blessed Father, let me not be afraid of Thee and Thy will at this point, for Thy will is my highest interest—always. When Thou art asking us to give something outward, we know that it is only to give us something inward. In Jesus' name. Amen.

AFFIRMATION FOR THE DAY: *Jesus is Lord—Lord of my inner possessions and my outer possessions—Lord.*

MORE PRINCIPLES AND PROCEDURES

We are looking at the steps in maturity in regard to material possessions. Fourth, *included in our needs is the need for reasonable security for ourselves in old age and for those dependent on us*. "For those dependent on us," but they should not be too dependent, so dependent that we weaken them. A chance for a good education is the best heritage we can leave our children. The rest is up to them. It leaves the initiative with them. "Reasonable security for ourselves" would mean that we are provided with sufficient security in old age so as not to become a public charge, nor a charge on relatives.

Fifth, *after these needs are met the rest belongs to the needs of others*. To meet the needs of others means we hold our surplus, beyond need, for the guidance of God for its distribution. For instance, "Mary," who is very sensitive to the voice of God, heard Him say: "Take a fifty-dollar note and put it into an envelope." She obeyed. As she walked past a coat on a coatrack she heard Him say: "Drop the letter into that pocket." She obeyed. The coat happened to belong to a theological student who that day had had necessary dental work done and had no money to pay for it. The amount of the bill was fifty dollars. When he put his hand into his pocket and found an envelope marked "From the Lord," with the fifty dollars inside, he went to his knees in gratitude. And since he didn't know who gave it, he had to be nice to everybody in repayment! That fifty dollars was alive and creative because it was meeting a need.

A street sweeper found six thousand dollars in New York City and when asked why he had not kept it he replied quite simply: "Because it wasn't mine." Concerning that which is in our possession but doesn't belong to our need, we can simply say: "It's isn't mine." It belongs to other people's need. So our giving after our needs are met is not really giving—it is being a steward of what belongs to others. That takes away the element of pride in giving; we are not *giving*—we are simply being faithful to a trust as stewards.

O God, our Father, help us to live as those who must give an accounting. And help us so to use our accounting that we shall hear Thee say: "Well done, good and faithful servant." For we succeed in life as we succeed in that hour. Amen.

AFFIRMATION FOR THE DAY: *Nothing belongs to me—I have been entrusted with much.*

PRINCIPLES, NOT PRESSURES

We take the next step in getting to maturity in regard to material possessions. Sixth, *let principles, fixed in habit, and not pressures, decide your giving, and fix those principled habits early before wealth accumulates*. If you wait till wealth accumulates, then it will be difficult to fix principled habits, for the process of accumulating wealth will itself fix its own habit—that of accumulating more.

When a wealthy man gave six million dollars to each of six different hospitals in Houston it made him feel so good that he set up a foundation of 160 millions. When a bishop of the Methodist Church went to thank him for giving six millions to the Methodist Hospital, he said: "But I wouldn't be giving these millions now if I hadn't learned the habit when I had nothing. I gave my last one hundred dollars to a little church; that laid the foundation for my giving now. Many millionaires don't give now because they have never laid the habits of giving."

"Mary" would not have given the fifty dollars to that theological student if she hadn't learned the habit of giving in the very beginning of her Christian life. A few days after she was converted she heard God say: "Give that one hundred dollars for missions." That one hundred dollars represented the only security she had ever had and it was all the money she possessed. She obeyed. She laid the foundation of her sacrificial, guided giving.

I have just been listening to a government official who has been an open witness to Christ amid Hindu surroundings. He gave, and gave generously, to a Christian cause. And then came the command: "Give all." He did. It was a leap in the dark. But he received a promotion—an unexpected one. And that promotion gave him in a year, in extra pay, the exact amount he had given when he gave his "all." He didn't give it with expectation or desire for return in kind. He gave out of love; and love returned, pressed down and running over.

O God, help me to have no meaningless money—money without a meaningful purpose. Put the soul of purpose in all I possess. I consent. And I will obey Thy guidance. For I cannot be mature in character and immature in charity. Amen.

AFFIRMATION FOR THE DAY: *My person and my purse shall have the motto "Seek first his kingdom."*

INVEST IN PEOPLE

Someone has said that "the extent of the elevation of an animal in the scale of existence, and of course any rational being, can be infallibly measured by the degree to which sacrificial love controls that being." If little sacrificial love, the life is low; more sacrificial love, the life is higher; complete sacrificial love, the life is highest.

Our attitudes toward material possessions are mature or immature according to whether sacrificial love is present or absent from those possessions. A woman was afraid she was about to have a cerebral hemorrhage, since she was dizzy and had a terrible pain in her head. A friend suggested she remove her hat. When she did the dizziness and the headache disappeared. One of those new-fangled clasps which keep women's hats on was pressing on a nerve. Some people are dizzy and have a spiritual headache because something is pressing on the nerve that leads to the pocketbook. And the thing that is usually pressing on the nerve is unsurrendered wealth—wealth in our hands instead of God's, wealth with no meaning in it.

Invest in people, for the bank of human character is the one bank that will never break. Dr. Santi, of Italy, brought in two orphans and said to his wife: "We must give them a home." Out of that experience came a home for five hundred children. He and his wife are rich, for they have invested in persons.

A boy heard that one thousand dollars would put up a church in shattered Korea. He wanted to have a church in that land, so he went from door to door selling Jello and raised the money for the church. He is rich, for he invested in people.

A servant was sent to the railway station to meet Sir Bartle Creer. The servant had never seen him and didn't know how to recognize him, but the one directing him said: "Look for someone who is helping someone else." The servant saw a man helping an old lady, went up to him, and said: "Are you Sir Bartle Creer?" And he was. If you want to recognize a mature person, look for someone who is helping someone else. We are as mature as we are mature in sacrificial love.

O Jesus Master, it was said of Thee that Thou didst go about doing good. Some of us just go about. Help us to have a divine purpose in all our doing, in all our possessions. May nothing about us be at loose ends. In Thy name. Amen.

AFFIRMATION FOR THE DAY: *My wealth, great or small, shall be big with the purposes of God within it.*

MATURITY IN LOVE REEMPHASIZED

As we near the end of our study of maturity from the Christian viewpoint, we must turn back for a final emphasis on the central thing in Christian maturity—maturity in love.

Sometimes we love with the wrong kind of love. Therefore, that love is an immature love. It must be love of a certain quality if it is to be mature love. My conviction is that most marriages go to pieces because the partners haven't grown up, except physically. They are immature and most often immature in love. This immaturity in love is usually evident in two ways: the love is preponderantly physical and the love is preponderantly self-centered. When love is weighted at the place of the physical with a minor emphasis on the mental and spiritual, it is an immature love and is bound to be fitful and will eventually fade out. "That's all you think of," said a disappointed mate as she felt the marriage going on the rocks of an immature love. It did.

Or the love may be immature in that it is a demanding love. It is weighted at the place of wanting to be loved. It is possessive: "I want him [or her] for me." The emphasis, consciously or unconsciously, is on what I get out of it.

When the emphasis is self-forgetful love for the total person—spirit, mind, and body, in that order—then it is mature love.

A person can have an immature love while in Christian work. He may love causes instead of people. He may love his work for the wrong reasons. He may love it for what he gets out of it—self-display, approval, success. He must love his Christian work because He loves Christ; and if that were all he would get out of it—the privilege of showing his love for Christ—he would still do it gladly and without regrets.

Fritz Kunkel says: "The abnormality of the child's environment may be described generally as the absence of the right kind of love." The abnormality in any environment—home, business, church—is the absence of the right kind of love—mature love.

O God, our Loving Father, take my loves and purify them from all immaturities—from jealousy, from self-seeking, from centering on the marginal. Make me mature in my love, and then I shall be mature indeed. In Jesus' name. Amen.

AFFIRMATION FOR THE DAY: *I need not merely to love but to love with the right kind of love—agape love.*

"LOVE IN SHOES"

To see whether our love is mature love, agape love, put "I" in the place of "love" in a portion of Paul's description of love in I Cor. 13:4-7: "I am patient and kind; I am not jealous or boastful; I am not arrogant or rude. I do not insist on my own way; I am not irritable or resentful; I do not rejoice at wrong, but rejoice in the right. I bear all things, believe all things, hope all things, endure all things." How do I come out? Am "I" and "love" identical? Our growth in maturity is a growth in that very identification.

And the love must be "love in shoes." Love must be first, last, and always my method. Note: my method, not my meditation. To sit and "broadcast love" to everybody may be beautiful and helpful, provided it doesn't stop at broadcasting mentally. That can be easy and cheap and sentimental. But if the meditation becomes a method—the habitual way of meeting every situation with everybody, everywhere—then it can be beautiful. But if it remains a meditation, then it is a word become word and not the word become flesh. A musical breadbox will play its music only as it is passed to someone at the table. Standing unpassed it is without music. Love without being shared is love without music. A steam iron is without steam unless it is actually being used. And love that is not expressed is not love.

Without this expressed love we are sick. In a sanatorium I announced that the patients would have an opportunity to sew for China relief during the Sino-Japanese War. We provided the garments and the patients had only to sew them up. I thought there would be a rush to get the garments at the close of the chapel service. Not a person took a garment. They were not interested in anything except themselves. That's why they were there. Their love had become ingrown and self-centered, and hence they were sick personalities. I quoted Menninger as saying: "The greatest problem in any well-conducted sanatorium is how to get the patients to do anything"—anything outside their own interests. For the moment they would begin to love, unselfishly, outside themselves, they would be well.

Dear Lord and Father, Thou hast made us for Thyself and since Thou art love Thou hast made us for love. When I give myself to loving everybody, then I find myself in that love. Help me today to give out love and only love. Amen.

AFFIRMATION FOR THE DAY: *Love unexpressed is love faintly existent, or nonexistent.*

WE LIVE WHEN WE LOVE

In his book *Love Against Hate*, Karl Menninger says: "The psychologist, speaking for science, is like a voice crying in the wilderness: 'The disease of the world is the disease of the individual personality,' he says. No one listens. 'The World War of today is a reflection of multiple miniature wars in the hearts of individuals,' he persists." If the sickness of the world is the sickness of the individual, and if the sickness of the individual is a lack of love, then the sickness of the world is the lack of love. Therefore, out of sheer necessity we are being driven to the feet of Christ to learn love. And love is not an elective course in the school of living—take it or leave it and nothing happens—it is a *must*. Smiley Blanton, a psychiatrist, sums it up in the title of his book *Love or Perish*. Alfred Adler, another psychiatrist, puts it this way: "All the ills of personality can be traced back to the fact that people do not understand the meaning of the phrase: 'It is more blessed to give than to receive.' " Jesus made that statement two thousand years ago; and the science of the mind, after experimentation with this business of living, comes along and says: "If you don't understand that, you don't understand how to live." So if you approach life either through the way of Christ or through the way of science, you come out at one place—love. As someone puts it: "Only to the extent that we love do we live." Or in other words: Only to the extent that we are mature in love are we mature.

"Mary," of whom I have written elsewhere, specializes in love. She says: "It is the easiest thing that I do." No wonder the wife of an Episcopal clergyman said of her: "The New Testament will never be finished as long as 'Mary' is alive." For she is the perpetuation of the agape love of the New Testament—the real apostolic succession and the only succession that matters. Emil Brunner, the theologian, said: "Find and join the church that has the most love in it and that will be the truest church."

O Gracious Father, purify my loves from all self-seeking. Give me Thy agape love and only Thy agape love. For if I fall down here I fall down. Nothing, absolutely nothing, can atone for the lack of this. In Jesus' name. Amen.

AFFIRMATION FOR THE DAY: *Where love is, there is the truest church; and where love is, there is the truest Christian.*

"THE VINEGAR BIBLE"

Yesterday we said that the church which has the most love is nearest to being the true church.

There is a Bible called the "Vinegar Bible," a copy of which is in the restored Williamsburg buildings in Virginia. It is called the Vinegar Bible because the word "vineyard" was misprinted "vinegar." A lot of people seem to be still using a Vinegar Bible—their religion makes them bitter and prejudiced and sour. A church sign says in regard to the Bible: "Take it in, live it out, and pass it on." But some people make the motto thus: "Take it in, fight it out, impose it on others." And yet the center of the Bible message is love! Paul could say: "Though I speak with the tongues of correct doctrine, and have a faultless ritual, and an ornate service, and yet have no love, I am nothing."

This letter shows we are maturing into a religion of love:

In the Year of our Lord, 1682

To ye aged and beloved, Mr. John Higginson:

There is now at sea a ship called Welcome, which has on board 100 or more heretics and malignants called Quakers, with W. Penn, who is the chief scamp, at the head of them. The General Court has accordingly given sacred orders to Master Malachi Huscott, of the brig Porpoise, to way lay the said Welcome slyly as near the Cape of Cod as may be, and make captive the said Penn and his ungodly crew, so that the Lord may be glorifed and not mocked on the soil of this new country with the heathen worship and these people. Much spoil can be made of selling the whole lot to Barbados, where slaves fetch good prices in rum and sugar, and we shall not only do the Lord great good by punishing the wicked, but we shall make great good for His Minister and people.

Yours in the bowels of Christ
Cotton Mather

Today the Quakers are one of the most respected and loved religious groups in the world. Why? They have made love central. Cotton Mather is mentioned in our histories; the Quakers are enshrined in our hearts.

O God, take all vinegar out of our thoughts and out of our systems and out of our religions. Make us the people of love. For love cures all diseases. We grow sick without love and we grow well with love. Give us love and more love. Amen.

AFFIRMATION FOR THE DAY: *My reading of the Bible shall not put "Vinegar" in my system, but the love of Christ.*

"TO BE LOVED, BE LOVABLE"

We mentioned "Mary" as saying, "It is the easiest thing I do—to love." And the interesting and important thing is this—that everybody can love. If what I have said in this book is true, namely, that the basic urge in human nature is to love and be loved, then when you love you are not going against the grain of your nature. When you love, you are going with it. For you are made to love. A woman in Greek history, when pressed to hate, cried dramatically before all: "I was born to love and not to hate." We are all born to love and not to hate. Not merely by a decree of God, but by the very decree of our own natures. When we hate we violate the law of our being; when we love we fulfill the law of our being.

Donald A. Laird tested his class at Colgate University. He asked his students to write as rapidly as they could the initials of the persons whom they disliked. After thirty seconds, some listed as many as fourteen sets of initials, while others could think of only one. Laird makes this interesting commentary: The men who wrote the longest lists were themselves among the most unpopular on the campus.

Benjamin Franklin once said: "If you wish to be loved, be lovable." And we may add, "And love." For if you love you will be lovable and whoever is lovable is loved.

We mentioned the girl who decided that she was very plain-faced and that therefore she could not depend on her face to get on. So she decided that she would be the most loving girl in her group. She became just that and, at the same time, became the most popular girl in her group. The motive wasn't too high in the beginning—to love in order to be popular—but soon the love method carried her beyond her original motives. Soon she loved because she loved to love and was loved in return. When you make love your method it will soon be your motive. So put this before you as your life motto: "Love shall be first, last, and always my method." And that method will become motive and the motive will become me.

O Jesus, my Lord, make me so loving that I will become love. But I can't do this. You love me into loving. I can only consent and cooperate. Help me to do everything through love and for love and by love. In Thy name. Amen.

AFFIRMATION FOR THE DAY: *I shall not love to gain love—that would be eros. I shall love to give love—that is agape.*

"DO NOT SHOW THEIR LOVE"

"They do not love who do not show their love." When activated by love every little thing you do for another says, "I love you." A wife used to tuck into many places, such as a pocket of her husband's laundered shirt, a note saying: "I love you." So the husband was constantly running across those heartwarming words—a lovely surprise party around every turn.

But too often we are like the Vermont farmer, described by Kenneth Hildebrand in *Achieving Real Happiness*. The farmer was sitting with his wife one evening, looking at the beautiful valley below them. The descending sun laid long, friendly fingers of shadow across the fields, and the scene was filled with peace. At last the farmer spoke quietly, as if reluctant to break the spell: "Sarah, we've had a lot of ups and downs together during these forty years, and when I have thought of all you've meant to me, sometimes it's been more than I could do to keep from telling you." Reticence dammed up the expressing of love.

From the same source comes this lovely last letter of a dying woman to her blind husband. It is an example of love expressing itself naturally:

My dear, dear husband, I am sorry that I can leave so little to you in material things, but some sweet memories I hope you will always cherish. Our lovely evening chats, our Ninety-first Psalm, our hope of God's healing those dear eyes, and all the blessed simple things that have made life so sweet with you. May those experiences of our lives together warm your heart as you dream on. Be sure to have faith and trust His loving care. You are so brave! . . . I have tried to make you my example. Your great patience, your love for everybody, your meekness, your allegiance to your Master and your lack of knowledge of your own greatness! You have done much to make me feel that life was worth living. Your noble soul makes me feel that God will bring us together again . . . perhaps to work together in His Kingdom. Loving you always, my darling. Your wife.

O Father, this agape love never fails and it never dies. For it is a spark of Thy agape love and therefore eternal. Help me to cherish it, feed it, live it, and rest in it. And make it my attitude to everyone, everywhere. Amen.

AFFIRMATION FOR THE DAY: *"Nothing is covered that will not be revealed".—I shall reveal my agape today.*

LOVE IS POWER

We are looking at the fact that "love never fails." Gandhi was beaten by a Muslim in South Africa. A police officer came to make an inquiry. Gandhi replied that he did not want to prosecute the man: "I expect to win him by love and patience." "Where did you get this?" inquired the police officer. "From the Sermon on the Mount," replied Gandhi. The police officer became Gandhi's devoted follower.

A friend loaned my book *Mahatma Gandhi: An Interpretation* to a leader of the Karen Rebellion in Burma. The leaders of this six-year-old rebellion sat in the jungle underground night after night around a campfire reading it. Men who were using violence and hate were drawn to nonviolence and love as a method.

I went to a school for the blind and deaf in Korea which is run by a man and wife who are radiant with the love of God. This pastor was captured by the Communists and was bound and taken out to be shot. One of the leaders among the Communists said, half scornfully: "You're a Christian preacher; then preach us a sermon on Christianity before we shoot you." The man did. He forgot himself and his impending death and for forty-five minutes he expounded God's love in Christ, and especially God's love in the cross. He preached as he had never preached before. And the communists saw that he meant it. At the close the Communist leader turned silently away and motioned to his followers to free the pastor. They did. Love never fails.

Government officials in India are supposed never to be wrong. It is always the subordinates who have to take the blame for mistakes. But a very high-up government official, a sincere Christian, said to a subordinate: "I'm sorry. I made that mistake. It was my fault. I take the blame." The clerk burst into tears. Love never fails.

O Christ, whether we be policeman, or rebel, or Communist, or just person, we are all beaten to our knees by the might of Thy gentle love. For everything else is weakness. This alone is strength. Help us to make it our motive and our method. Amen.

AFFIRMATION FOR THE DAY: *There is no power save the power of love—I shall use that power and only that power today.*

THE GOLDEN TEXT OF MATURITY

We come now in the closing weeks of our quest for maturity to consider the question "How?" A lawyer came up to me at the close of a meeting and in an almost belligerent mood demanded: "Man, how?" That he needed change, that he wanted change, was obvious, but he was puzzled at the place of "How?" He represents many.

Paul was perhaps one of the most mature men who ever lived. While he lived, and since, he has been battered by arguments pro and con, criticized, rejected, loved, and yet he stands as one of the soundest and greatest of men. He incarnates Christian maturity. What was his answer to "How?" He gives it in this luminous passage: "And we all, with unveiled face, beholding the glory of the Lord, are being changed into his likeness from one degree of glory to another; for this comes from the Lord who is the Spirit" (II Cor. 3:18).

The steps are these: First, *we must get straight, and get it straight once and for all, the pattern of our maturity: "into his likeness."* The pattern of maturity is unique. It is not the pattern of maturity worked out by philosophy, or by psychology, though it may coincide with these patterns here and there. It stands in its own right—unique and alone. Unique and alone, because it is not pieced together by man, but placed before us by God—Jesus is God's self-revelation. We are to be made in the likeness of God—the likeness of God as seen in Jesus. Of Him someone says:

Jesus was not a philosopher searching for truth—He was the Truth. He was not a reformer—He was a Re-creator. He was not a mystic—He was Reality. He was not a visionary—He was the Light of the World. He never reasoned—He knew. He was never in a hurry, never afraid; He never showed weakness; He never hesitated; He was always ready. He was always sure. He had no sense of sin, no need of forgiveness. He never sought or needed advice. He knew why He came and where He was going. He knew the Father. He had no sense of lack or limitation.

He is God simplified.

O Jesus, Thou hast answered us the question "Show us the Father, and we shall be satisfied," for in Thee we see the authentic likeness of the Father. And what we see makes our hearts deeply satisfied and makes them atingle with anticipation. Amen.

AFFIRMATION FOR THE DAY: *"Into his likeness"—that is my destiny and that shall be my direction.*

GETTING THE PATTERN OF MATURITY CLEAR

The first step in maturity is to get the pattern of that maturity clear. Until we get that clear we will be like the man who "mounted his horse and rode off in all directions." Going everywhere and nowhere. Until we get the pattern fixed we are at the mercy of every suggestion.

The two greatest interpreters of the Christian Way, and the two best illustrations of it, were Paul and John and they both agreed on the goal. John says: "Beloved, we are God's children now; it does not yet appear what we shall be, but we know that when he appears we shall be like him, for we shall see him as he is" (I John 3:2). "We shall be like him"—nothing less than, and nothing other than, *that*. Paul's goal coincides: "changed into his likeness." We are certain now as to where we are to head in—"into his likeness." Is there anything higher, or better, in heaven or on earth, than to be "changed into his likeness"? I have scanned the horizons of the earth and the horizons of thought—and have scanned them for over half a century—to see if there is any other comparable pattern. It's a life conclusion: There is none. To paraphrase the words of Coleridge: Beyond that which is found in Jesus of Nazareth the human race has not, and never will, progress. He is the absolute Ultimate in character for God and man. And that is not my judgement—it is the verdict of history.

And there are no alternatives in maturity—it is maturity according to Christ, or immaturity. For all departures from His character are departures from goodness. All deviations from His maturity are deviations into immaturity.

A blind man asked a piano tuner, tuning a piano, how he did it and was told that the middle C wire was used as standard. Middle C was put in perfect tune through a tuning fork, and then all the wires on each side of it were tuned to it. Jesus is that Middle C note. He is Standard. Everything in heaven and earth is attuned to Him when it is in tune. Everything is heaven and on earth not attuned to Him is out of tune. And there are no exceptions.

O Jesus Master, Thou are our Standard Note. Every time I think thy thoughts; feel Thy feelings, do Thy will, I am in tune—in tune with Thee, with God, with myself, and with the music of the spheres—I'm in tune. Amen.

AFFIRMATION FOR THE DAY: *My destiny is now clear—it is up to me to make my steps clear to that destiny.*

MATURITY OPEN TO "ALL"

We have seen that the first step in maturity is to get the pattern clear. To take the pattern of society in which one lives as the standard and adjust to that, as is often suggested by psychiatry, is to adjust to maladjustment, to adjust to immaturity. That would result in the condition a man said he was in after psychiatric treatment: "Before I was treated I was abnormally maladjusted; now I'm normally maladjusted." And he wasn't joking.

We are to be adjusted to nothing this side of the highest—the Highest in heaven and earth—Jesus Christ. In Christianity sin is *amartia* (literally, "missing the mark"). Applied, it means that sin is missing the Mark—Jesus Christ. All departure from His mind and spirit is sin. That is not a legal definition of sin but a life definition. It is an unfolding Standard and therefore never outgrown. Our code is a Character. That is fixed and yet unfolding—fixed in history and yet unfolding as the Spirit unfolds Him more and more.

As I write this I can hear the reader saying to himself: "Isn't that impossible for the ordinary person? Are you not paralyzed instead of inspired, paralyzed by the very loftiness of the Standard?"

That leads us to the next step: Second, *this pattern of maturity as "in his likeness," is open to all—open to a person as a person, and the ordinary person especially*. The passage says: "And we all . . . are being changed." Note the word "all," and in his "all" Paul included the Corinthians to whom he was writing:

Do not be deceived; neither the immoral, nor idolaters, nor adulterers, nor homosexuals, nor thieves, nor the greedy, nor drunkards, nor revilers, nor robbers will inherit the kingdom of God. And such were some of you. But you were washed, you were sanctified, you were justified in the name of the Lord Jesus Christ and in the Spirit of our God (I Cor. 6:9-11).

To these people he says: "And we all . . . are being changed into his likeness."

O blessed, blessed Jesus, my heart beats faster in anticipation at the possibility that the latchstring is low enough for all of us—even for me—to reach and walk into this amazing possibility to be made into Thy likeness. I thank Thee. Amen.

AFFIRMATION FOR THE DAY: *That word "all" takes me in just as blessedly as the "whoever" of John 3:16.*

DOESN'T ASK ABOUT ORIGINS, ONLY DESTINATIONS

This open-to-all possibility regarding maturity is the most breath-taking and nerve-tingling fact about Christianity. It doesn't ask anything about origins, only about destinations: "Where do you want to go?" And it provides for both the gradual and the sudden maturing of character. This sudden maturing of character can take place because the person is suddenly adjusted to the most mature fact of the universe—Christ.

Jim Berwick, a railway brakeman, drunk as he brought his freight train into Chicago, was converted in the Pacific Garden Mission. He said: "I've never had a desire for drink from that day. And then I took out my plug of tobacco and placed it before God and said: 'O God, if you have taken away desire for liquor, will you take away the desire for tobacco?' He did. From that day I've never wanted it." Seventeen years later he was carrying around that plug of tobacco, now as hard as a rock, as a symbol of change. He walked out of the world of degradation, of desire, of drink, into a world of mastery, of ministering, of maturity. And he did it suddenly. By grace.

Here was a down-and-out and here was an up-and-out, a young minister, discouraged and beaten and empty. He saw on the signboard of a great church where a great minister ministered: "Jesus Christ is in this church; anything can happen here."He went inside, knelt, and surrendered to this Living Christ who was in that church. And something did happen there. He went out, with defeat and discouragement and emptiness gone. He became the pastor of a great church. He was just as suddenly made mature as that brakeman—mature in attitude, in goal, direction, and resources.

If these two illustrations are too low or too high, then here is one halfway between: A woman was about to leave the Ashram as hopelessly upset and neurotic. She surrendered herself and her nerves to Christ, is adjusted and happy, and is joyously giving her life to retarded children. No wonder Paul said: "We all"—it was just that.

O my Lord, I thank Thee. Wherever human nature opens its depths to Thy healing grace, there the miracle of change takes place. Then help me to open everything, literally everything, to Thy healing. Amen.

AFFIRMATION FOR THE DAY: *My motto today: "Wherever Jesus Christ is, there anything can happen"—and He is with me.*

MATURITY AMONG ALL AGES

We now turn to another phase of "And we all." We have seen the possibility of maturity, sudden and gradual, that is open to all levels of moral life. We now look at that possibility in all ages of life.

John showed an amazing maturity in being interested, and affectionately interested, in all ages when he wrote this passage: "I write to you, children, because you know the Father. I write to you fathers, because you know him who is from the beginning. I write to you, young men, because you are strong, and the word of God abides in you, and you have overcome the evil one" (I John 2:13-14). John, the aged, now above ninety, was interested in children, in young men, and in "fathers"—the advanced in years. And his interest was one of commendation and of faith and of approval.

It is a sign of maturity when you can be at home with all ages, a sign of immaturity when you can be at home with only one age group—your age.

Some outcaste Christians were being picketed by Arya Samajists. The Christians were not allowed to go out of their houses for a month to get work or food. The pressure was intended to make them sign a statement that they were no longer Christians. They refused. Boys and girls from a Christian boarding school nearby gave up a third of their food at each meal for a month to help these Christians. Here was real maturity in outcastes and in boys and girls.

At a public high school in Lubbock, Texas, is a permanent sign on the lawn: "Morning Devotions, eight to eight-thirty each morning." It is run by the young people themselves and attended by an average of 350. Maturity? Yes, very real maturity. "There's nothing wrong with this young generation, except the older," I said to an audience one day, and a boy of twelve piped up and said: "Say, you've said something." Two girls came to the dean of a junior high school and said: "We don't think our parents are fit to bring us up." This younger generation is a fine generation badly led.

O Father, we thank Thee that this blessed maturity is open to a little child, that a child's spirit of open receptivity is the very essence of maturity. Give to me, I pray Thee, and to all of us the open receptivity of the childlike. The Kingdom of maturity will then be ours. Amen.

AFFIRMATION FOR THE DAY: *My maturity will depend not upon my years, but upon my yearnings.*

MATURITY AMONG CHILDREN AND YOUTH

We have seen John's positive faith in all ages. His agape love broke down the barriers between ages and made him feel a sense of solidarity with people as people of all ages.

A little girl, after seeing a movie on armies going to war, turned to her mother and said: "Someday those who make war are going to call the people to war and they won't go." That little girl is worth knowing. The future belongs to her.

A boy said to his mother: "Mother, what's the sense of these young people taking up habits like smoking and drinking when they'll have to give them up when they become Christians?" That lad, too, is worth knowing. The future belongs to him and his kind.

Said the little daughter of a missionary who was captured by the Chinese Communists and then released: "They're hungry; that's why they have captured my Daddy. So I'm sending them a dollar I saved." When the Communists got the note and the dollar, they were deeply touched by it and said: "That's human nature before it is spoiled by capitalism." We prefer to think of the little girl and her attitude as human nature touched by Christ. But that little girl is worth knowing. The future belongs to her and her kind.

A modern young woman wrote to me: "A mature person uses his emotions instead of letting his emotions use him." That represents emotional youth at its finest. That girl is worth knowing too. The future belongs to her and her kind.

Another modern young woman said an illuminating thing: "Christianity is like a kiss. Don't analyze it—enjoy it." That young woman, too, is worth knowing. She sees into the meaning of the gospel as something to be enjoyed and not discussed and dissected.

An American airman shot down a Japanese plane which was above him, and as the Japanese plane hurtled toward the sea, past the plane of the American, the Japanese pilot raised his hand in salute. It so moved the American pilot that he became a Christian and is now the dynamic pastor of a large church. Both of these young men were worth knowing. The future belongs to such as these.

O Master of my heart, I thank Thee that Thou didst set the child in the midst and didst call young men to Thy fellowship and didst entrust them with Thy Kingdom. Help me to look with creative eyes on all ages. Help me to see and appeal to the good. Amen.

AFFIRMATION FOR THE DAY: *The child-heart of open receptivity shall persist through the passing of the years.*

MATURITY CAN BEGIN LATE

We have looked at childhood and youth and noted that they are worth knowing. We must look at old age and see the glory of old age linked with God.

Victor Hugo when facing death said: "I feel that I haven't expressed half that is within me." Creative still at the end!

When some young people in the home saw Grandma always reading her Bible, one of them remarked: "Grandma must be cramming for her finals." Perhaps, but perhaps to her case might be applied the remark of a woman as she went past me while I was reading my Bible in the Pullman: "You must love the Author." Grandma loved the Author!

Spellman, the great scientist, did not begin to study until he was between fifty and sixty. Handel was fifty when he published his first great work. Fabre, poet of science, was eighty when France discovered him.

Santa Monica, California, has observed since 1936 what is known as "Mother Stephens Day." When she and her husband came to Santa Monica, Mrs. Stephens was just recovering from a severe illness at the age of sixty-seven and she promised her husband she would take no further part in public life. But for the next thirty-one years, until she died at the age of ninety-eight, she was one of the most vital factors in the social and spiritual development of Santa Monica. She organized the Santa Monica Woman's Club, the Red Cross chapter, the Council of Social Charities, Community Service in Santa Monica, Community Chest, Santa Monica Welfare and Industrial Thrift Shop, and Santa Monica Mental Hygiene Society, was president of the board of education, and was a member of the advisory board of the Bank of America. When she was ninety-six she sent word to the ministerial association: "My family say I should give up my work. Should I live to be an old lady perhaps I will stop, not when I'm only ninety-six."

Father, Thou canst put within me the deathless spirit of creativity. Live within me, create through me, help me to be alive to my fingertips with Thee. And may death be beaten back by creative life within me. In Jesus' name. Amen.

AFFIRMATION FOR THE DAY: *I am as old, not as my arteries, but as my attitudes.*

"BEHOLDING THE GLORY OF THE LORD"

We have looked at "we all" in Christian maturity. Since Christian maturity is not found at the top rung of the ladder of human striving, but at the bottom rung where God descends and offers grace to the least, the last, the lost, as the method and means of maturity, then it is open to "all"—and to all equally. There is none disqualified, except the person who disqualifies himself. Then what are the next steps?

Third, *you are made into the image of that on which you habitually concentrate your attention*—"*beholding the glory of the Lord.*" If you concentrate your attention on the faults of people around you, you become a faulty person. If you look with eyes of creation upon people, you become a creative person. If you look at yourself, you will become a self-conscious person. The "living creatures" in the book of Revelation were "full of eyes in front and behind . . . full of eyes all round and within" (4:6-8). Note: the last-mentioned eyes were "within" and the first-mentioned eyes were "in front." We must look primarily "in front," and only secondarily "behind," thirdly "around," and last "within." If we reverse that order and keep our eyes "within" (on ourselves), then "around" (at others), then "behind" (at the past), and last, "in front" (looking at Him), we will be a person in reverse. We must gaze at Jesus and only glance at what is "behind," "around," and "within."

In industry there are courses in "Imagineering"—a course that stimulates creative imagination and hence creates creation. The process of Christian maturity is the process of the redemption of the imagination—redeeming it from self-concentration, sex concentration, herd concentration, money concentration, past-failure concentration, sin concentration—and concentrating it on "the Lord." You become Christ-conscious instead of self-conscious; you become future-conscious instead of past-conscious; you become creative-conscious, since your attention is concentrated on the Creator and the Re-Creator. The imagination is redeemed, and with it the whole person.

O Jesus, my Lord, when I look at myself I feel collapsed and inadequate, but when I look at Thee I feel that anything is possible. For Thy eyes hold creation within them, and when I look into them creation begins in me. Help me to look long and longingly. Amen.

AFFIRMATION FOR THE DAY: *If I look in I'll be discouraged; if I look around I'll be distracted; if I look at Jesus I shall have peace.*

"LIKE THAT AT WHICH WE HABITUALLY GAZE"

We have been considering the fact that the method of being made in His likeness is simple and very profound. "Behold the glory of the Lord." We become like that at which we habitually gaze. A woman who habitually looks in the looking glass and makes it the center of her attention becomes a looking glass. And a looking glass has nothing behind it; it is a series of reflections. A man who looks at life with sex-filled eyes becomes sordid and lustful in appearance.

But the person who gazes and keeps on gazing at Jesus becomes like Him in appearance. "Oh, you with heaven in your face, give me a penny," said a beggar to Pennyfather, the saint. I look over audiences and I look for the face that looks redeemed. Nietzsche says: "If the Christians want us to believe in Christianity they must look redeemed." Few have the redeemed look. And they are the ones who are looking at Jesus.

But it is not enough to look at Jesus—you must see "the glory of the Lord." The King James Version says: "Beholding as in a glass the glory of the Lord." The Revised Standard Version omits "as in a glass," and puts it "beholding the glory of the Lord." "As in a glass" makes it secondhand; it is a reflection of reality, not reality itself. But "beholding the glory of the Lord" is firsthand—you see Him direct. Much of our looking at Jesus is secondhand, "as in a mirror," reflected through the church, through books, through nature, through people. Hence much of our Christianity wears a secondhand look. It is moonlight (reflected) instead of sunlight (firsthand). One young minister said to another: "You speak with authority; I quote authorities." One was firsthand and the other secondhand.

Why is every painted picture of Jesus unsatisfactory, however fine? Because we have looked into His face at firsthand in the Gospels and everything else is secondhand. "Mary" was listening to a sermon from a man who spoke out of firsthand contact with Jesus, and she said to herself: "Listen, ears, this is not preaching, this is revelation."

O Jesus, the firsthand image of the Father, help me to see "the glory" of everything Thou didst say and think and do. For in Thee is "the glory"—the glory of the firsthand revelation of Reality. I gaze at that glory and become luminous. Amen.

AFFIRMATION FOR THE DAY: *I shall look at the humiliation of Jesus, but I shall look longer and steadier at His glory.*

"WITH UNVEILED FACE"

If at the center of our Christianity is an emaciated, sorrowful Christ, then we will be made in the image of that Christ—we will be spiritually emaciated and sorrowful and gloomy. The religion of a crucifix—a dead Christ hanging on a cross—creates dead-faced followers of a dead Christ. We must behold "the glory of the Lord" if our lives are to be glorified likenesses of a more glorified Lord. Jesus is now the glorified Lord, and when we plug in to Him we plug into glory. The glory side of the gospel was what Paul was bursting to express—"who is the Glory."

But if we are to see that "glory" in the face of Jesus Christ we have to take the next step: Fourth, *we must look at Him "with unveiled face."* Many look at Him with veiled faces and wonder that the likeness of His image is so faint upon them. They hesitate or refuse to look with "unveiled face."

Just what does "with unveiled face" mean? If it means anything it means that we must be completely honest with God, with ourselves, with others, with life. We must come clear—absolutely clear. We must have unveiled faces—no masks, no putting on of fronts, no make-believe. We have mentioned the steps of psychiatry toward transformation, as given by Jung. He names them: confession, explanation, education, transformation. Christianity begins at the same place: confession, sin- and self-surrender, acceptance of the grace of God, transformation. Both begin with "confession"—the "unveiled face." The Moral Rearmament Movement has four steps: absolute honesty, absolute purity, absolute unselfishness, absolute love. Here, too, the first step is absolute honesty—the "unveiled face."

What are some of the veils that we have to let down? We would name them as follows: (1) *Acceptance of responsibility for what we are.* We must cease the attitude of blaming this, that, and the other for our present condition. To try to lay blame on environment or on people gets you nowhere. Only when you accept the final responsibility for what you are does the door into release begin to open.

O Father God, help me to accept responsibility for what I am. For had I decided differently, I would have been different. Deep down I know that. Then I bring up all the old buried alibis and excuses. I am open to Thee—fully open. Amen.

AFFIRMATION FOR THE DAY: *I hide behind no masks; I stand before Him, myself, and the world, clear.*

"LETTING DOWN THE VEILS"

We are looking at the veils which we must let down if we are to see "the glory of the Lord." We noted the first: acceptance of responsibility for what we are. A motto on a college wall ways: "There is no power in earth or heaven that can make a man do wrong without his consent." Only that part of our environment to which we respond can affect us. If we decide it will not affect us it will not. So I'm responsible for what affects me.

(2) *Be specific and let down the veils of fear, of resentments, of pride, of envy and jealousy, of self-centeredness, of bad temper, of inferiority, of guilts.* And anything else not included in this list—things of which you may be conscious or unconscious. Say to God: "I surrender all I know and all I don't know." If anything comes up later, that, too, is surrendered beforehand. Some things may be buried deep in the subconscious, but as you let the conscious things go, the layers to the buried subconscious will be lifted, allowing the rise of the subconscious into the conscious. And when once you surrender all the conscious, the Holy Spirit, given access to the subconscious by consent, will bring things up. But don't worry as to whether there is something you haven't brought up from the subsconscious. Such worry will tie you up with needless question marks. If you honestly surrender all you know and all you don't know, then you can take it for granted there is nothing more. If there is, then it's the Holy Spirit's business to bring it up.

(3) *Let down the last veil—the veil of doubt of acceptance.* It is not enough to give up; you must take. Faith is the leap in the dark and then finding yourself on the other bank that separates you from the old. Weighted down by two suitcases, I once tried to leap across a stream in the dark. I landed a little over halfway! But now you are no longer weighted by the things you have surrendered in step two. Faith is free to land you on the bank of forgiveness, of acceptance—it will land you in His arms. Or to change the figure: You will see with cleared vision the most beautiful sight this world holds—the sight of His reconciled face.

O Christ, my Lord, Thy face is the object of my life quest—Thy face reconciled. I see it! Not through my goodness, but through Thy grace. I've only taken down the veils. Thou art always there. It is I who have been away. Now I'm back. Amen.

AFFIRMATION FOR THE DAY: *There are no veils now, hence no vagueness—all's clear.*

"CHANGED INTO HIS LIKENESS"

We come now to the next step: Fifth: *the change begins: "are beings changed to his likeness."* Sometimes the change is gradual, sometimes sudden. But whether gradual or sudden, it is "change." And that is the important thing: not where you are but the direction in which you are headed. You are under the blessed law of change. The old dead ends are gone—you're on the Way! And on it with both feet! When someone asked a boy where he was from he answered: "I came from Elkhart—you can get anywhere from Elkhart." Your starting point may be insignificant—your destination is significant and gives you significance. I belong to what I'm after and not to what I've left.

This is effortless change. You don't change by tugging and pulling at your bootstraps. That doesn't change you; it only exhausts you. The flower is changed effortlessly by gazing at the sun. It keeps the channels open and the sun does the rest. Christianity is maturity by gazing. "Look to him, and be radiant." Moses looked into the face of God and his face shone. He had to put a veil over it. But we look into the face of God—veiled in human flesh—and that is accommodated glory, glory tempered so we can look at it without being blinded. Electricity of high voltage is run through transformers so we can use it for ordinary purposes. Jesus is the Transformer that makes the power and grace of God available for ordinary mortals to live by.

Note the passive voice: "are being changed." That makes all our goodness rooted in goodness; all our maturities gifts of grace. That puts humility and gratitude at the heart of our maturity. All other efforts at maturity result in pride of attainment; this ends in humility of obtainment. Hence it is real maturity. Maturity with pride at its center is basic immaturity. Hence there can be no real maturity except the maturity which comes through grace.

Maturity by consent and cooperation is a sound maturity, open to all, and with no strain and stress in it—it is relaxed, receptive maturity. Hence fun. There is life and more life for a gaze.

O Jesus, My Lord, I thank Thee that my responsibility is to look at Thee with unveiled face and to cooperate with what I see there. It is Thy responsibility to change me. That keeps my eyes on Thee instead of me. And how I grow—amazingly! Amen.

AFFIRMATION FOR THE DAY: *I do not have to construct and complete, only to cooperate.*

"FROM ONE DEGREE OF GLORY TO ANOTHER"

Here is the next step: Sixth, *we are under the process of an endless change: "from one degree of glory to another."* This distinguishes Christian maturity from all other maturity. Christian maturity can never say: "Now I am mature"—full stop. Since it is related to the Absolute Maturity of God, the Infinite, it will always be a relative maturity. This puts humility and progress at the heart of this maturity: humility, in that it is all of grace, and further because you can never say that you have arrived; and then progress, for there is always something beyond.

A psychological-philosophical writer on maturity says that the end of maturity is to be able "to enjoy your maturity." This conclusion suffers from the fatal defect that it leaves you centered on yourself—you "enjoy your maturity." Anything that leaves you centered on yourself is an immature maturity.

Christian maturity centers you on God—He will be the eternal Object of that maturity. It is a God-centered maturity and not a self-centered maturity. It is therefore mature maturity.

But it is a maturity that keeps us on the stretch for more receptivity. For we are always seeing more things in God to receive. The finite will infinitely approach the Infinite, but will never arrive. In that eternal growth will be our eternal happiness.

This growth will be from one degree of glory to another. The soul gets on by a series of crises. Its growth isn't always regular and even. More often it is irregular and uneven. For instance, there is the rapid climb of the soul in conversion. Then we are on a higher tableland. But on that tableland there are ups and downs. Then we discover the possibility of deeper surrender of deeper areas which makes possible a deeper appropriation of grace. That leads to another rapid climb, and life is on a still higher level. And the process is continued eternally. Satisfied, deeply and fundamentally, but forever unsatisfied. Not dissatisfied, but forever unsatisfied. Rejoicing in what we have and reaching for more.

O God, my Father, I'm eternally at the Goal and forever on the Way. I have and I long to have. I see, and I see there is more to be seen. I sigh with a deep satisfaction and I sigh for a greater capacity to receive more. I thank Thee. Amen.

AFFIRMATION FOR THE DAY: *I go from one degree of glory to another by grace and more grace.*

356

"THIS COMES FROM THE LORD"

We come now to the last step: Seventh, *at the center of this maturity is an eternal obedience: "for this comes from the Lord who is the Spirit."* At the center of all this is "the Lord." Here Jesus is called "the Lord." This fits in with the earliest Christian creed: "Jesus is Lord." "If you confess with your lips that Jesus is Lord . . . you will be saved" (Rom. 10:9). "No one can say 'Jesus is Lord' except by the Holy Spirit" (I Cor. 12:3). These words "Jesus is Lord" are in quotation marks showing they were used as an early Christian confession. In fact they were the earliest Christian creed—"Jesus is Lord." All of religion reduced to three words—"Jesus is Lord." And early Christians were profoundly right in fastening on that statement as summing up the Christian faith. For the primary need of human nature is to find something to obey, something which bends the knee and says: "My Lord."

To this, psychology would agree. For psychology says there are three basic needs in human nature: (1) to belong, (2) to have significance, (3) to have reasonable security. The first need is "to belong." This cuts diagonally across the modern notion that the first thing is personal freedom. The first thing is not personal freedom, but personal bondage. If you make the first thing personal freedom it will be a freedom to tie yourself up in knots and be a problem to yourself and others. The first thing is personal bondage. To what shall I give my supreme allegiance, my ultimate loyalty? We are free to choose, but free only to choose what we shall obey. I choose Jesus! I will say, "Jesus is Lord!" and say it with my life.

"But this comes from the Lord who is the Spirit." The Spirit lives within. Therefore the authority is not an external, on-the-throne authority. The authority is within. And as we obey that Authority we soon find we are obeying the very laws of our being. We find our freedom in His will. For when we do His will we do our own deepest will. The Authority then wills our own deepest interests. When we bend the knee we stand straight. When we are bound we are loosed for creation. We lose and find ourselves.

O Jesus, Thou art Lord! I bend the knee in obedience and then I bend the knee in gratitude. For that obedience opens the door to Thy power. Thy perfect will is my perfect freedom. Now I'm free to develop in maturity forever. Amen.

AFFIRMATION FOR THE DAY: *The Lord, the Spirit within, is the source of everything when He is the Lord of everything.*

"KEEP YOURSELVES FROM IDOLS"

We come now to our last week in our quest for maturity, for Christian maturity.

John ends perhaps the greatest exposition of maturity ever penned with these strange words: "Little children, keep yourselves from idols" (I John 5:21). It seems a letdown, an anticlimax. Here he had been talking in the loftiest terms of walking "in the same way in which he walked"; of being "like him, for we shall see him as he is. And every one who thus hopes in him purifies himself as he is pure"; of laying "down our lives for the brethren"; "God is love, and he who abides in love abides in God, and God abides in him"; and then he ends with the apparently innocuous exhortation: "Little children, keep yourselves from idols." And that stark statement is the end. On what we have called "the capstone of revelation," the last inscription is this: "Keep yourselves from idols." Did John end this mature exposition of maturity with a very immature ending? Or was this the very climax?

I am persuaded that John was never more guided of God than when he put in that statement. With profound insight he put his finger on the greatest single hindrance to maturity—"idols." We usually associate idols with a low-level expression of religion—the idols of pagan faiths. But idols are an expression of a universal tendency—the tendency to substitute—to substitue something in the place of God. Anything that becomes a center of love and attention—a love and attention greater than the love and attention we give to God—is an idol. Anything that pushes God to the margin of our lives and takes His place at the center is an idol. Idolatry is substitution—substitution of the unreal for the Real. Anything or anyone whom you substitute in the place of God as the object of your absolute loyalty and love is an idol.

You can readily see that the greatest hindrance to Christian maturity is just this tendency to idolatry—this tendency to a divided loyalty. We don't reject God; we simply substitute something or someone else at the center, and God is pushed to the edges. There He can but faintly influence the life, and immaturity results. Idols are the enemy.

O God, our Father, we come now to face our real problem in maturity—the problem of divided loyalty. Help me to see clearly, to act decisively, and to love Thee with an undivided love. For if I don't, I cancel everything. In Jesus' name. Amen.

AFFIRMATION FOR THE DAY: No *"just as good" substitute for me; I'm out for the Real.*

"IS JESUS AN IDOL?"

Does Jesus come under this demand that there be no "idols"? Is Jesus an idol, coming between us and God? No. An idol misrepresents God—Jesus represents God. Ask one question about an idol—Is God like this in character and life? If not, it is a misrepresentation of God. Is God like Jesus in character and life? Yes! For He is "the express image of his person" (Heb. 1:2 KJV).

He fulfills the desire back of idols—namely, the desire to have God near and understandable. He takes the place of idols by bringing God near and by making Him understandable. He cures us of idolatry by fulfilling the necessity lying back of idolatry. A mother said to her little boy who wanted her to stay in the room with him because he was afraid: "Don't be afraid, son; God will be with you in the dark." "Yes," the boy said, "but I want somebody with a face." Jesus gives God a face—and what a face! A little fellow was afraid and his father took him in bed with him, and the boy asked before he would drop off to sleep: "Is your face toward me, Daddy?" Jesus gives God a face, and that face is toward us—always.

And that face speaks: "You shall love the Lord your God with all your heart, and with all your soul, and with all your mind, and with all your strength." The demand is *all* the heart, *all* the soul, *all* the mind, *all* the strength. The whole person, wholly His.

When a subject of the kings of Britain took the oath of allegiance, he stood before the king with some earth between his hands and, folding them, said: "I, Phillip, Duke of Edinburgh, do become your liegeman of life and limb and of earthly worship, and in faith and truth will I bear arms unto you to live and die against all manner of folks, so help me God."

A purified version of that is what happens when we surrender to Christ. "Jesus is *Lord!*" When Jesus said to the devil in the third temptation, "Him only shall you serve," the account adds, "Then the devil left him." The devil could not stand the "Him only" attitude and decision.

Dear Lord, I am Thy spiritual liegeman with a single loyalty and devotion. And it is of life and limb and property—all. No trucking with idols—substitutes. There can be no substitute for Thee. Amen.

AFFIRMATION FOR THE DAY: *No god-shelf with Jesus as one of the many; for me it is "Him only."*

THE "IDOL" OF THE SELF

The first idol we are looking at is the idol of the self. Unless we get the idol of the unsurrendered self off its throne, we will be perpetually immature.

Here was a successful executive and churchman afflicted with asthma. The doctors gave him all the "shots" there were for all the allergies conceivable. No result. His last attack left him purple and near death. Then the doctor tried a different approach: "Are you in inner tension about anything?" And the man answered: "I don't know anything that is bothering me." But the next day he sent for the doctor and said:

I haven't been able to dismiss from my mind what you said about tensions. In fact I haven't closed my eyes all night, for I've talked to the Chief all night. As I prayed it seemed that letters of fire appeared on the ceiling: "Seek ye first the kingdom of God." Then the same thing was on the darkened walls and the floor too—it was everywhere. I began to realize that I had been a selfish, egocentric individual. I had been fighting my way up in the business world for years to the place where I am now making $25,000 a year. But the struggle has been so all-consuming that I have pushed God's kingdom into a secondary place. But I promised the Chief this morning that I am going to quit worrying about the kingdom of Frank Derfer and think about the kingdom of God. I shall ask for a position of lesser importance in the company so I can spend more time working for God. I don't know whether it will cure my asthma or not; I'm not doing it for that reason; but I do know that God had to allow me to come to a bed of affliction where I nearly died to make me realize I had been essentially selfish.

Until that idol of a central selfishness was dethroned he was, and would have continued to be, emotionally, physically, and spiritually an immature personality.

The tension of an unsurrendered self is the most basic of all tensions, for when you are on the basis of your self you have the feeling that there is nothing cosmic backing you—you alone are backing you; you feel insecure and become full of tension.

Dear God, Thou art trying to relieve us of this burden of the unsurrendered self—a burden which we cannot bear without disaster. Help me to take that inmost idol and smash it by surrender to Thee. In Jesus' name. Amen.

AFFIRMATION FOR THE DAY: *If I seek first the kingdom of God, then all things are added, including myself.*

"IDOLS" LET US DOWN

Another idol is the herd. To fit into the herd mentality and attitudes—this constitutes the moral code of many people, even religious people. I recently spoke in a denominational college where hypocrisy was in reverse—the people talked as though they were worse than they actually were. One professor said to the dean on arrival: "Now don't ask me to pray or to take part in religious activities. I'll be a sheep in wolf's clothing. I'm with you inwardly, but I cannot afford to be with you outwardly." He was in bondage to the herd. For the herd attitude was not to appear religious. It was "smart." The result was a moral blur. The persons who adopted that attitude became immature actors of a part, wearing masks, leaving no impression except in the impression of unreality.

Another idol akin to the herd, but based on a smaller unit, is the idol of a group, religious or otherwise. Many go from group to group looking for the perfect one. They often think they have it—in the beginning. They think: This is it! Then they begin to find that the feet of the idol is made of clay—the group has its imperfections, because it is made up of imperfect people, especially imperfect since they joined it! Disillusionment sets in—sometimes embitterment. So these lost souls wander from group to group looking for the perfect idol. And they never find it. God has willed it so. For if we fasten our loyalty upon anything less than the Divine, it will let us down, and was intended to let us down. So disillusionment tosses us to His breast.

Some make an idol of their denomination. A Presbyterian woman was told: "In an exchange of territory fifty congregations of Methodists in Korea became Presbyterians." "Wonderful," said the woman, "that is the real Christian spirit." "Yes, and fifty congregations of Presbyterians became Methodists." Her face fell: "Why how could they?" Another; "Our order is not the largest order in the Roman Catholic Church—the Dominicans are; or the richest—the Franciscans are; but our order is at the top in humility." Proud of their humility! An idol!

O Father, we sometimes consciously, sometimes unconsciously, interpose between Thee and ourselves some idol which absorbs our loyalty and our love—a loyalty and love belonging to Thee alone. Forgive us and help us to tear it from its throne. Amen.

AFFIRMATION FOR THE DAY: *I lean lightly on my "group," but I put my full weight down on Jesus.*

VARIOUS "IDOLS"

A teacher of a Bible class was teaching the lesson concerning the Pharisee and the publican, and depicting the Pharisee in pretty black colors, when at the end he said: "Now let us pray and thank God that we are not like that old Pharisee." Unconscious pharasaism!

Others make money an idol. Perhaps the most widespread and popular idolatry is the worship of "the golden calf." The "Cult of the Golden Calf" has more devotees than any other cult, perhaps more than all the other cults put together. And probably it leaves more disillusionment behind than all the other cults put together. For it can give you everything, everything except what you really want and need—inner peace, security, God. We say: "I feel like a million," and yet millionaires are probably as unhappy a group as may be found in our civilization. When Paul said that the love of "money is the root of all evils." he could have said, "especially the root of the evil of unhappiness." For those who lean upon the rod of wealth to sustain them find that it breaks and pierces their hands, and their hearts.

Then there are those who make an idol of a loved one, living or dead. I have seen two people, apparently happily married, so absorb each other's attention and love in public and in private that they had little or no room for others, for the needs of the world, for God. The idol of the "other" had gathered everything to itself. The consequence was that both were immature persons. Their persons had shrunk with the narrowness of their interest. A mother can be "wrapped up" in a son, and the "wrapped up" expresses it. Sometimes people become "wrapped up" in memories of a departed loved one, and their souls are embalmed in that interest. The loved ones are idols pushing out God.

Some put a virtue, of which they are proud, in place of God. The good pushes out the Best. "I am honest in business," can be an idol. I have mentioned a big businessman who said: "I have given my money to God, but not myself." He tore the idol down and enthroned God— and was free!

O Father God, Thou art pressing, pressing, ever pressing to get possession of the inmost shrine of our loyalty and love. For we know we are in bondage till we surrender the center. When we bend the knee there, we are free everywhere. Help us to do it. Amen.

AFFIRMATION FOR THE DAY: *If I make anything an idol, it will let me down when the storms break.*

SUBSTITUTING EROS FOR AGAPE

We have defined an idol as something put in place of God, a substitute. Sometimes we substitute a half-performance in place of an all-out performance, a whole promise compromised in execution.

King Zedekiah had made a covenant with all the people in Jerusalem to make a proclamation of liberty to them, that every one should set free his Hebrew slaves, male and female, so that no one should enslave a Jew, his brother. And they obeyed . . . and set them free. But afterward they turned around and took back the male and female slaves they had set free, and brought them into subjection as slaves (Jer. 34:8-11).

Two things brought a blur instead of a blessing—they proclaimed "liberty," not to slaves, but to Hebrew slaves, a blurred principle of liberty; and then the blurred principle became a blurred performance—they set them free and then took them back into bondage, and inwardly enslaved themselves in doing so. They became slaves to inner conflict. "The slaves enslaved the enslavers"—they always do.

Our substitutions of half-performances for whole promises bring whole inner bondage. We become an inner battleground, strewn with the wreckage of broken promises, half-fulfilled pledges, and taken-back consecrations. We promised much, did little, and became less.

We now come to the last idol we will consider—the idol of the substiution of eros for agape. If agape love is the highest manifestation of the character of God, then any twisting of that manifestation into something less is the most serious idolatry of all. For it turns the very nature of God into something other than it is—it misrepresents God. Eros does that. It uses the word "love" but puts into it the content of possessive love—"I love for what I get out of it." And it says in effect: "God is like that—He loves for what He gets out of it." "God is misrepresented by our representation. But agape love says in effect: "I don't want to get, I want to give: I love for nothing, because I can't help it, for I am Agape." Anything less than, or other than, that is a substitution.

O Gracious Father, help me at this point, for if I get this wrong everything goes wrong with it. Purify all my eros loves into agape love. I must come out in life at agape, or else forever remain immature. Help me here. Amen.

AFFIRMATION FOR THE DAY: *If my "love" can mean either eros or agape, I have settled for something this side of the Best.*

MATURITY OPEN FROM ALCOHOLIC
TO APATHETIC

We come to our last day together and the last emphasis must be upon the highest maturity in the most mature of faiths—agape love. And when I think of one of its supreme illustrations I need not turn to the early days of martyrdom, but fresh out of the heart of Communist China comes this one: Three Christian preachers were hailed before a Communist court and when the "judge" heard they were Christian preachers he said: "It seems to me I remember that their Founder was crucified. So crucify them." They were crucified, but their tormentors didn't know enough about the story to lift them up, so they dragged them into the public street where they lay amid the dust and flies and gaping crowds. And lying there, what did they do? With swollen tongues they preached the gospel to the onlookers—preached it till their dying gasps on the third day.

Few of us are given the privilege of being nailed to outer crosses to show our agape. But we may be nailed to unseen crosses of opposition in the home or business or shop or school; nailed to the cross of the lifelong denial of a life partner; nailed to the cross of a bitter destiny to life with an affliction, perhaps incurable; nailed to the cross of the humdrum; nailed to the cross of a denied life ambition—in all of these circumstances, and others, we can react in agape love and witness with life and lips to our love and loyalty to Him who is agape. In doing so we show our maturity—and grow into maturity.

As I was writing this page a basket of fruit was brought to my room in the hotel, telegraphed from a distant city by an ex-alcoholic, a woman. She wrote: "When my father whom I loved deeply died, I was lonely and lost. A void was left within. I put a bottle there—became an alcoholic." The bottle let her down of course, as all idols do. Then she met the Real in Jesus. And suddenly her immaturities dropped away and she now stands basically mature and radiantly happy and useful. So maturity is open to everybody, from the alcoholic to the apathetic, to the degree of surrender and obedience to Jesus—the Maturest Fact of the Manifested Universe.

O Jesus, we began with Thee and we end with Thee. For Thou art the alpha of our maturity and the omega of our maturity. In Thee our maturity is guaranteed. For if we remain in Thee we shall be like Thee—and that is Maturity. Amen.

AFFIRMATION FOR THE DAY: *Jesus—the source of my maturity, the means of my maturity, the end of my maturity.*